DATING, MATING, AND MARRIAGE

SOCIAL INSTITUTIONS AND SOCIAL CHANGE
An Aldine de Gruyter Series of Texts and Monographs

EDITED BY

Peter H. Rossi • Michael Useem • James D. Wright

Dating, Mating, and Marriage

Martin King Whyte

Aldine de Gruyter
New York

ABOUT THE AUTHOR

Martin King Whyte is Professor of Sociology at the University of Michigan. He received his undergraduate education at Cornell University and MA and Ph.D. at Harvard University. His primary research interests are the sociology of the family and social change in the People's Republic of China. He is the author of *Small Groups and Political Rituals in China* (1974); *The Status of Women in Preindustrial Societies* (1978); *Village and Family in Contemporary China* (co-authored, 1978); and *Urban Life in Contemporary China* (co-authored, 1984).

ALDINE DE GRUYTER
A Division of Walter de Gruyter, Inc.
200 Saw Mill River Road
Hawthorne, New York 10532

Library of Congress Cataloging-in-Publication Data

Whyte, Martin King
    Dating, mating, and marriage / Martin King Whyte.
        p. cm. — (Social institutions and social change)
    Includes bibliographical references.
    ISBN 0-202-30415-9. — ISBN 0-202-30416-7 (pbk.)
    1. Marriage—United States. 2. Dating (Social customs)—United
States. 3. Mate selection—United States. I. Title. II. Series.
HQ728.W526 1990
306.81'0973—dc20   89–17996
                                                                          CIP

Manufactured in the United States of America

10 9 8 7 6 5 4 3 2 1

CONTENTS

ACKNOWLEDGMENTS

Many individuals and organizations deserve thanks, but of course no blame, for assisting this study from its inception to its completion. Initially a Rackham Faculty Fellowship from the University of Michigan provided me with support while I developed the plan for the research reported here. I received advice, criticism, and assistance from a large number of individuals, including Arland Thornton, Karen Mason, Al Simkus, Erna-Lynne Bogue, Eloise Elliott, Pat Preston, Chen Jieming and Xu Xiaohe. Ronnie Whyte provided invaluable support at each stage of the research, from serving as a "guinea pig" respondent for several of the earliest draft versions of the questionnaire to listening patiently as draft chapters were read to her. I would also like to thank participants in the Faculty Family Studies Seminar and the Center for Research on Social Organization brownbag talk series at the University of Michigan, who were subjected to earlier versions of portions of this study and responded in helpful ways. A subsequent, companion research project devoted to replicating the current survey in Chengdu, China, has been generously supported by the US-China Cooperative Science Program of the National Science Foundation. Even though few of the results of this companion project are directly visible in the pages that follow, the support and encouragement received have enriched this study in many ways. Alice Hogan wielded a sharp editorial pencil, helping me to clear up problems in the final manuscript.

My greatest thanks go to the staff and students who participated in the project that forms the primary basis for this study, the 1984 Detroit Area Study (DAS) survey. The skilled expertise provided by the DAS directors, secretarial staff, students, and professional interviewers, makes it possible for faculty investigators with minimal or rusty survey research skills to translate their ideas into substantial and high quality research. In the case of this particular rusty investigator, the Directors for the 1984 DAS Survey, Jean Converse and Stanley Presser, provided instruction, guidance, patience, and good humor that made the laborious and lengthy survey process both enjoyable and enlightening. Stanley also proved a delightful and helpful teaching companion for the final DAS seminar, devoted to guiding our graduate students in writing data analyses based upon the survey. Together Jean and Stanley made conducting the survey seem more like summer camp than boot camp, and I will always look back fondly on our shared experience. Other participants in the DAS "team" also deserve sub-stantial credit for guiding this study through to its conclusion. In particular, Carol Crawford prepared countless versions of revised questionnaires and managed the DAS office with charm and competence. Several talented teaching assistants— Lynette Kono, Jason Lee, Paula Rust, and David Williams—played key roles in guiding the students and advising the investigator. And the two dozen students enrolled in the 1984 DAS training course and the like number of professional interviewers from the Survey Research Center at the University of Michigan provided the manpower and skill at every step of the way, and particularly for the interviewing field season, which were essential for the success of this project. Last, but not least, the 459 respondents who willingly let us probe into their private lives and marital histories provided the basic fabric from which I attempt to answer a wide range of questions about dating, mating, and marriage in the pages ahead. This was truly a team effort, and I take pride in, but not full credit for, the results.

Martin King Whyte
Ann Arbor, Michigan

Chapter 1

THE WHY AND HOW OF RESEARCH ON MATE CHOICE

One can hardly open a newspaper or turn on the television these days without being plunged into an ongoing debate about whether the American marriage is "in trouble." Since marriage is the central building block of family organization, sometimes the debate is escalated to a higher level. Perhaps the family itself is "on the way out." It should be noted, of course, that such debates are hardly new in American society. Indeed, a penchant for nostalgia and a stubborn conviction that things are now "going to the dogs" seem to be ingrained parts of the American temperament, and repeatedly since colonial times doomsayers have been predicting the demise of marriage as an institution.[1] Earlier in this century some of the leading social scientists joined the chorus of pessimism. For example, John B. Watson, one of the founding figures of American psychology, opined in 1927:

> Family standards have broken down and parents contribute little to the behavior of their children. The automobile and other things have taken the child out of control. The mystery and beauty of marriage and the rearing of children has pretty well broken down. In fifty years [i.e., in 1977], unless there is some change, the tribal custom of marriage will no longer exist (Watson 1927, p. 1).

A decade later Pitirim Sorokin, a Russian emigré who occupied a similar position of eminence within American sociology, chimed in with a similarly bleak view:

> The family as a sacred union of husband and wife, of parents and children, will continue to disintegrate. Divorces and separations will increase until any profound difference between socially sanctioned marriages and illicit sex-relationships will disappear. . . . The main sociocultural functions of the family will further decrease until the family becomes a mere incidental cohabitation of male and female, while the home will become a mere overnight parking place mainly for sex relationship (Sorokin 1937, p. 776).[2]

Clearly these dire predictions have not been fulfilled in American society, and perhaps this fact should warn us to be skeptical of such prophecies in general. Still, recent trends in American society have convinced some critics that doomsayers such as Watson and Sorokin were not wrong, but simply a trifle hasty. Perhaps phenomena such as the sexual revolution, growing acceptance of co-

1

habitation and even unwed motherhood, renegotiation of gender roles, the increasing brittleness of marriages, and the rise of a service economy to supply
needs that used to be met within the household, are finally bringing about the
often and prematurely predicted doom of marriage as an institution. But, then
again, perhaps not. Perhaps marriage is simply evolving, rather than declining.
The "critics of the critics" in this debate, or in other words those who argue that
American marriage is not in any general sense "in trouble," contend that the
doomsayers mistakenly equate any signs of change in family life with deterioration. They point out that marriage is still an extraordinarily popular institution in
America, entered into at earlier ages and by higher percentages of the population
than is the case in many other Western societies, and that marriages are in many
ways healthier and happier today than in the past.[3] We cannot be sure who to side
with in this debate unless we examine the evidence about the state of marriage in
American society.

At the most general level, the present study was motivated by this debate about
the state of American marriage, and by a desire to collect and examine some
concrete evidence that would throw light on the issue. However, as might be
expected, in pursuing the topic I was forced to define what I was doing in a more
narrow and concrete way, and I was also led to consider other kinds of questions
that do not bear directly on the state of American marriage. So while at the end of
this study I will offer some thoughts on the "big question" of what is happening
to American marriage, I hope the reader will find the concrete detours and
discussions of other topics interesting, even if it may not always be clear how
these relate to that big question.

My first step in defining the present study was to observe that when people talk
about marriage as an institution being "in trouble," they are actually talking
about two somewhat different things. These two different things arise because the
term marriage refers both to the act of getting married, as well as to the state one
is in after one weds. So the code phrase "marriage in trouble" can refer either to
a claim that people are increasingly reluctant to marry in the first place, or that
those who do take "the big step" are increasingly unlikely to "live happily ever
after." Most research to date, however, has focused overwhelmingly on marriage
in the second sense and not the first—in other words, on the nature of relations
within existing marriages, and on such matters as separation, divorce, and remarriage. The process by which people do (or do not) get married, however, has
received surprisingly little scrutiny. When I began reading up on such matters as
dating, mate choice, and weddings in America, I was surprised to find how little
was systematically known on these topics.

To be sure, we have lots of research on trends in marriage ages, and there have
been a number of studies over the years on dating behavior, but these tell us only
part of the story. Even many of the existing studies of dating behavior tend to be
conducted among small and unrepresentative samples (e.g., students on one
college campus) or concern things that have dubious relevance for how marriage

partners are actually chosen (e.g., asking interview subjects to rank various criteria for selecting a mate).[4] In reading this literature I was unable to find answers to what seemed to be fairly basic questions about the process of mate choice in America. For example, at what age do young people typically start dating? How many people end up marrying their "first sweetheart?" What is the average length of time that newly marrying couples were acquainted or dated prior to marriage? What percentage of couples get formally engaged? How many people are still virgins when they marry? What percentage of couples live together before they marry?[5] How many people marry someone from the same religious background as themselves? What proportion of couples have a religious as opposed to a civil wedding?

As soon as these sorts of basic factual questions are raised, one immediately thinks of another set of questions concerning changes over time in the process of mate choice in America. Most of those questions find no ready answers in past research. Do people start dating earlier now than in the past? Do they date more people than their parents or grandparents did prior to marriage, or do they date fewer? How much has virginity at marriage actually declined? (In this case there is no reason to doubt the direction of the trend, only its magnitude.) Do people have more marital prospects that they can select from nowadays? Has parental influence on dating and mate choice declined in America? Do more people marry outside of their ethnic group, religion, or class level than in the past? Are weddings becoming simpler and more unconventional, or on the other hand are they becoming increasingly elaborate and costly? If we are going to examine the state of marriage in the first sense—i.e., entry into the wedded state—answers to questions such as these should be important.

As the reader can probably surmise, after pondering the matter to this point I decided to initiate a study to relieve our common ignorance about American mate choice by finding answers to questions such as these. As I began to formulate my research plan, however, my thoughts turned back to the other side of the term marriage, and I began to consider the question of how these two aspects were related. One might say that I was forced to face up to the "so what" question: So what if I discover all sorts of hidden secrets about the nature of mate choice and how this process has changed over time in America? Does how the couple got to the altar really tell us anything about what will happen after they get married? In other words, does premarital history and the nature of one's experiences in mate choice have any impact on how durable or satisfying the resulting marriage will be?

As I considered this general question I was again left with a series of questions for which there were no answers in the existing literature. In this case there are lots of what social science jargon calls "hypotheses" floating around in the form of old wives' tales and friendly advice from relatives, but very little systematic treatment in our academic journals. Is it good (in terms of having a lasting or happy marriage) to have had many dating partners or only a few? How important is it (in the same terms) to marry someone from the same class, religious, and ethnic background as oneself? Do people who "marry up" (in social class or other terms) tend to be happier with their marriages than people who "marry down?" Is it better to remain a virgin until marriage? Does premarital cohabitation serve as a valuable preparation for marriage? How important is it to have a big and formal wedding? My grandmothers might have had firm answers to most of these questions, but I do not think my professional colleagues would be satisfied with them. Gradually, my general concern about the state of American marriage evolved into a decision to carry out research to fill large gaps in our knowledge about the nature of the mate choice process in American society, how that process has evolved, and whether it has any effect on the marital history and conjugal relationships that are produced by marriage.

Because of the way my thinking developed on these topics, the research to be reported here is less tightly focused than might otherwise be the case. I did not set out to test a particular pet theory, or to examine a narrow range of hypotheses or topics. Instead, my approach has been eclectic from the beginning. I wanted to discover as much as I could, within the constraints posed by time, energy, and financial resources, about the evolving nature of American mate choice, and its effect on marital relationships. As the reader will see as he/she proceeds onward, this approach gives the text a bit of an "everything you ever wanted to know about mate choice and marriage in America and a number of other things you wouldn't have thought to ask" quality. However, in terms of trying eventually to speak to the debates about the nature of marriage in America, I think that my eclectic approach has clear advantages.

The Detroit Survey

Once I had selected the range of questions I was interested in, I had to decide how to go about studying them, and that decision in turn required me to narrow my sights further. It would have been nice, for example, to conduct interviews about mate choice and marriage all over the United States, but limited funds and the availability of an important survey research training facility in my own department, the Detroit Area Study (DAS), led me to design a survey that could be carried out in the greater Detroit metropolitan area.[6] My proposal for a study of mate choice and marriage relations was selected and became the basis for the survey to be discussed here, which was carried out in 1984.[7]

Detroit is obviously not typical of all of America, or even of all of urban America. There are a number of distinctive features of Detroit as a city, and of the population of which it is composed. It will be obvious, for example, that Detroit's development has been shaped in major ways by the dominance of the automobile industry. It is known as a "blue collar" town, with more people employed in heavy industry and fewer in light industry and services than in many other cities. And due to the recent problems of the automobile industry, Detroit has experienced more unemployment and economic distress than other cities in the last few years. The ethnic composition of the city is somewhat different from other large American cities. As an urban area it has both more "old ethnics," many of them Catholics, than some other cities, and unusually large concentrations of Arab-Americans. However, Hispanics and Asian-Americans are relatively under-represented compared to cities in America's "sun belt." The pattern of settlement in Detroit is somewhat distinctive, with the highest proportion of single family homes of any large American city, and a correspondingly smaller proportion of high rise apartment dwellings. These are only a few of the features that make Detroit somewhat different from other urban locales in America.

Since circumstances dictated that I conduct my research in Detroit, I obviously cannot claim that my results can be generalized to all of American society. However, I would argue that Detroit is not so atypical that my results say nothing about the experiences of other Americans. Instead, I will argue throughout (without, in some instances, firm evidence to support this argument) that developments in mate choice and marriage in the Detroit area, as revealed in the 1984 survey, probably differ in details, but not in general patterns, from what would be found in many other large urban areas in America.[8] Several features of both Detroit and the survey provide the basis for this claim.

First, I stress that the sample was drawn not from Detroit city per se, but from the greater Detroit metropolitan area, defined as the area covered by Wayne, Macomb, and Oakland counties, and containing more than 4 million residents. People living in the city of Detroit proper constitute less than 30% of the total population of the tri-county area, according to the 1980 census (U.S. Census Bureau 1982, p. 90). Since the city and its suburbs are included, there is considerable variety within the sample—multiple ethnic groups, blacks and whites, a variety of religions, both the country club set and welfare mothers, and so forth. While I usually use the terms "Detroit" and the "Detroit area" in discussing the population studied, the reader should keep in mind that this is only for convenience, and that it is this larger and more diverse population that was actually surveyed.

Another thing to keep in mind is that Detroit shares with the rest of America a footloose quality. Many of the people who now live in the area did not grow up there, and they or their children may well move out after a few years. For example, about one-third of our survey respondents were living someplace else at the time that they first got married and moved to the Detroit area subsequently. In this sense respondents can be seen as a slice of a larger American society (in this case including rural as well as urban areas), rather than some sort of self-enclosed and unique urban community. Even if there are distinctive traits about the kinds of people who live in the Detroit area, by including questions in the survey about a wide variety of background characteristics it will be possible to take the influence of this distinctiveness into account—for example, by comparing the marriage patterns of blacks and whites, of new ethnics and old ethnics, and of blue and white collar workers. Although on repeated occasions in the pages that follow I will point out such differences to the reader, still on balance I am impressed by the general patterns that emerge in the results, patterns that seem to occur across various subgroups.

Finally, the issue of "typicality" can be addressed by comparing the results of this study with earlier research carried out in other locales or nationally. One of the major contributions of the current study, as previously noted, is that it presents systematic information on many aspects of mate choice that have not been studied before. Yet this is not always the case, and in a number of instances the Detroit results can be compared with the findings of prior studies. Where possible, the reader will be presented with comparisons in the following pages. Where the current findings about general patterns and trends can be compared with such earlier studies, the agreement is usually quite close.[9] This general agreement with earlier studies provides additional confidence that the findings reported here do not simply reflect peculiar features of the Detroit area. For these reasons, then, even though this is a study of the marriage behavior of people living in the Detroit area, I think that it has much to say about trends in urban America generally.[10]

There were other constraints on this study besides the limitation to the Detroit area. To study changes in mate choice patterns over time, one would ideally like to have a time machine readily available. With such a machine one could, for instance, go back in time to the Detroit area of the 1920s and 1930s and interview people about their dating and mate choice practices. Since this is obviously not practicable outside of Hollywood, I was forced to adopt a less desirable alternative. I could use people's memories as my time machine, and ask interviewees of a variety of ages how they had experienced dating and how they had met and married their eventual spouses. Then, assuming that their memories were relatively accurate (an important assumption that will be discussed in subsequent chapters and in Appendix 1), by comparing people who married long ago with others who married more recently, I could derive some kind of measure of changes over time. I would thus use retrospective questions about premarital experiences to substitute for the unavailable time machine.[11]

However, this is not a perfect substitute, even if we ignore the problem of fallible memories. The main problem is the very fluidity of population mentioned earlier. Since many of the people who presently live in the Detroit area and are part of our sample did not live there when they were dating and planning to be married, and since many of those who did live in the area in earlier decades have since died or left, the results of these recollections cannot be taken to represent changes over time in Detroit dating and mate choice behavior. Instead of a "pure" picture of changes over time in that city, what we have is an examination of the contrasting experiences in dating and mate choice of present residents of the area who were born and who first married over a 60 year span of time (from

1925–84). So while at times I refer to changes in mate choice practices, the reader should keep in mind that what is involved is contrasting premarital experiences of younger and older respondents (or, even more indirectly, contrasting recollections about premarital experiences).

My interest in how dating and mate choice experiences affect the nature and fate of the subsequent marriage cannot be examined in the ideal way with the Detroit interview data. To properly deal with this question, one should conduct what in the jargon of the trade is called a *longitudinal* study. This means that one should interview young people prior to marriage about their dating experiences. Then one should follow them over the years, reinterviewing them periodically to find out about their mate choice process, their marital relationships, and their subsequent marital history. Longitudinal studies of that kind are infrequently carried out, and for obvious reasons. Such studies are very expensive and difficult to conduct, since you have to keep tracking down members of the original sample who don't oblige the researcher by staying in one place. But the main drawback of longitudinal research is that you have to wait a long time to get your final results, and the nature of both human curiosity and professional careers is such that few of us have the required patience.[12] So in this study I follow the well-worn but less desirable path of using a "cross-sectional" design. What this means is that in the summer of 1984 we interviewed a cross-section of the population, but only at that one point in time, rather than following them over the years.[13]

Why is this less desirable? For one thing, it means that there may be many things that differ between older and younger respondents other than when they were born or first married. If we find differences between newly married women and women who have been married longer, we can't be certain with a cross-sectional design whether these differences indicate a regular pattern in stages within marriage. We could only be certain of this if we switched to a longitudinal design and reinterviewed the younger women when they reached the later stage in life (or used the imaginary time machine again to go back to an earlier point in the lives of the older women). Therefore, we want to know things about changes over time, but we can only do this by comparing different women, and such comparisons may be misleading.

Another problem with cross-sectional surveys is the possibility that more recent events and experiences may bias the recollections people have about their earlier experiences, making it difficult or impossible to be certain about trends and causation. For example, one of the most basic questions we could ask concerning the influence of premarital history on the fate of the subsequent marriage is whether people who are more deeply in love when they marry are more likely to have happy marriages, as our culture says that they should. We can (and, in fact, in our questionnaire we did) ask people to recall how much in love they were when they married (see the discussion in Chapter 3). But how do we know that what they tell us now is what they would have told us back when they

were first preparing to marry? And isn't it likely that women whose first marriages ended in divorce will tell us now that they were not really deeply in love
prior to their marriage? If this is the case might we not be led by such results to
assume erroneously that being very much in love "causes" happy marriages,
whereas in fact it might be the case that having an unhappy marriage leads one to
understate now the degree of love one felt back then? In any case, throughout this
study I will have to wrestle with the problems of trying to infer changes over time
and causation from data that are not ideally designed for such purposes.

A third and final less than ideal feature of the Detroit study is that we ended up
interviewing only women and not men. To be specific, our sampling target was
defined as "ever-married" women between the ages of 18 and 75 living in the
greater Detroit area. (In other words, respondents did not have to be married
currently, but they had to have been married at least once in order to be interviewed.) I was unable to secure additional funds to augment the DAS budget in
order to either interview the husbands of these women (if any) or a separate male
sample. Therefore I am limited throughout this study in only being able to report
how mate choice and marriage experiences looked to the women involved. Of
course, it "takes two to tango," and female respondents provided us with a
wealth of information about their spouses, so I can investigate some features of
the husbands and how these relate to the nature and fate of the marriage. But I do
not have direct reports from the husbands on such things as when they started
dating, whether they were virgins at marriage, how they see the division of
chores in the household, or how satisfied they are with their marriages. Therefore, strictly speaking, I can only present here an account of trends in mate
choice and marriage relations as these are perceived by wives or former wives.

The strategic choice involved here was a difficult one. I was informed that the
DAS budget was sufficient to interview 450–500 respondents under normal
circumstances. To interview only couples might have resulted in only 200 couples being studied, since to interview both partners is complex and expensive.[14]
But ending up with only 200 couples would have placed very severe limits on
what variations within the population I could examine in my research regarding
race, religion, and social class. So it was decided that we should interview only
one partner. At that juncture there was still the matter of deciding whether to
interview wives or husbands. This was close to being a "coin toss," but with
regard to some of the questions I intended to ask, such as those about the nature
and scale of the wedding celebrations, I felt that wives would have clearer
recollections than husbands. Therefore, on this basis I decided to make our target
ever-married women.[15] In the end we succeeded in interviewing 459 women.

After wading through this list of qualifications and caveats, the reader may
well ask whether this study of mate choice and marriage will be able to produce
results of general interest. Although the final answer to such a question must rest
on the reader's own judgment, I would argue that in spite of such limitations, the
study reported on here is both the most comprehensive and most definitive

examination of evolving mate choice and marriage relations in America yet attempted. Even though there are a variety of limitations in the design of this study that prevent me from being as conclusive on certain points as I would wish, still I have had a very rich and high quality set of data to work with, and these data have been able to provide answers to some basic questions about the American way of marriage answers I had found lacking when I started. Therefore, the limitations just described are cautionary notes that have to be taken into account in interpreting this study's findings, rather than indicators that the entire study is fatally flawed.

Outline of the Study

This volume represents a report on the results of a survey of mate choice and marriage experiences of women in the greater Detroit area. As previously noted, it is based on face-to-face interviews that were conducted with 459 ever-married women in the summer of 1984. Although in the pages that follow I will draw on my general reading of materials on social trends in American society, the core of this study, and the basis for any claims to novelty, are these interviews. The questionnaire asked each respondent to supply information on a wide range of topics—regarding her social background and the backgrounds of her parents, her early dating experiences, the background of the man who became her eventual (first) husband, the background of another male she had considered marrying (if any), the nature of the wedding celebrations held, her subsequent marital history (including characteristics of a subsequent or most recent husband, if relevant), and about a wide variety of aspects of her relationship with her first or most recent husband—marital communication, pattern of leisure activities, chore division, conjugal decision-making, marital conflict, spouse abuse, and so forth.[16] The range of these topics allows me to reconstruct the dating and mate choice experiences of our respondents and also to examine whether these have been related to the outcomes of their marriages.

The wide variety of predictions and hypotheses about mate choice and marriage relations that were examined in this project will not be discussed at this time. Instead, specific predictions are introduced and discussed in each substantive chapter, as they are about to be tested using the Detroit area survey data. The chapters follow the major topical areas covered in the questionnaire. Chapters 2 and 3 are linked and provide evidence on the extent to which changes in dating and mate choice customs are occurring. Chapter 2 covers a variety of aspects of dating experiences, including when each respondent first began dating, how many males she recalls dating, when she began to "go steady," how many such steady boyfriends she had, attempts by parents to influence her dating pattern, and the timing of her first sexual experience.[17] In examining such questions respondents are grouped not in terms of such customary divisions as age cohorts (defined in terms of years of birth), but according to what I call "marriage generations," i.e., by the years in which they first got married. The major question here is whether women who entered their (first) marriages in different periods had similar or contrasting experiences in the dating stage.

Chapter 3 follows up this inquiry with an examination of the actual mate choice experiences of respondents. In this case I am interested in such things as the age of each respondent when she first married, her personal situation at that time (e.g., whether she was living at home, was employed, was already pregnant), how certain she recalls being of her marital decision, and where the wedding was celebrated, and how elaborately. Again I am interested in whether women in different marriage generations had similar or contrasting experiences in the nature of their entry into marriage. Together these two chapters provide the primary evidence on the degree of constancy or change in dating and mating in urban America.

Chapter 4 looks at many of these same dating and mate choice experiences in a different way. In this case the issue is what kinds of women tended to start dating early vs. late, who was most likely to remain a virgin until marriage, what sorts of people experienced the largest and most elaborate weddings, and so forth. In other words, I want to know whether there are any underlying common principles that explain why some women had different sorts of premarital experiences from others—something other than simply the matter of what year they first got married (which is the focus of Chapters 2 and 3). Understanding the social origins of variations in dating and mate choice experiences will be an important first step before taking up the question of how variations in the subsequent marital history and marital relationships of respondents can be explained.[18]

Chapter 5 takes up one important remaining issue about the process of mate choice and how that process has changed over time: an examination of who married whom, in terms of things such as class origin, educational levels, race, religion, and national origin. In addition to simply documenting the extent to which Detroit women married within or outside of their own group or level, this chapter will address the same sort of social trend issue examined in Chapters 2 and 3. Has the degree of "status matching" of partners in marriage declined, remained much the same, or increased over time? Since similarity of backgrounds is often considered an important prerequisite for a successful marriage, the material introduced in Chapter 5 will again form the background for consideration, in the remaining chapters, of the outcome of the mate choice decisions of Detroit area respondents.

Chapter 6 begins to introduce material on the actual marriage experiences and marriage relationships of the women we interviewed. Much of the focus of this chapter is simply descriptive. Basic factual information about the marital histories of respondents is introduced there. How many women are still married to their first husbands? How many have been widowed or have divorced and have not remarried? How many have been married two, three, or even more times?

Chapter 6 also discusses the general patterning of intact marriages, as revealed by the items in the survey. For example, what are the general patterns of chore division between spouses? How often do couples spend their leisure time together or separately? What role does each partner play in managing income they or their spouse earns? How frequently have respondents experienced various forms of spouse abuse? How many of the women interviewed perceive that they share the same basic values as their husbands? In general how satisfied are respondents with their marriages, and with various specific aspects of their conjugal relationships?

While the major aim of Chapter 6 is descriptive, it will also focus on the general issues of variation considered in earlier chapters. In particular, is the patterning of marital relations of women who married at an earlier point in time different from those who have married more recently, and if so are the differences ones that can be interpreted as hopeful or pessimistic in terms of the prospects for marital relations now and in the future? And what are the social features that are associated with variations in the patterning of marriages? Are the marriage patterns of the poor, blacks, Catholics, or of other groups different in major ways from those of other groups? The answers to these and other questions should produce a fairly comprehensive picture of the pattern of marriages among women in the Detroit area.

Chapter 7 confronts the central issue toward which all of the preceding analysis has been building, in order to answer the "so what" question. That chapter examines the fates of all of the first marriages of women in the Detroit study. The analysis presented is concerned with whether those marriages lasted "till death us do part," or ended in divorce or separation. For those first marriages that are still intact, I will be concerned with how successful or satisfying they are, or on the other hand with how conflict-prone and unsatisfying they are. I will be particularly concerned, given the origins of my interest in this research, with whether any of the variety of premarital experiences discussed in the first half of this book have an influence one way or the other on what could be called "marital success." But in order to consider such premarital influences in context, it is also necessary to examine a wide range of other features that might also have an influence on the outcome of the marriage—income, race, religion, wife employment, social networks, and so forth. Thus in some sense even though my initial interest was in the impact of premarital experiences, what will be presented in Chapter 7 is more in the nature of a general survey of what sorts of things do or do not make a difference in marital success. As the reader will see, the findings of this research raise serious questions about much received wisdom on what makes for good versus bad marriages.

The final substantive chapter of this study considers the nature of remarriages, as opposed to first marriages. The majority of all respondents have been married only once, but for those who have been to the altar at least twice, we collected information on various aspects of their "second time around": the background of the subsequent husband, how the wedding was celebrated, and the nature of the patterning of relations in their new marriages. The underlying general question addressed in Chapter 8 is how similar or different are remarriages in comparison with first marriages, and insofar as there are differences visible, to what extent do these indicate more or less problems in remarriages, in comparison with first marriages.

Chapter 9 reports overall conclusions. In the final chapter, I will draw together what has been learned from this project about the nature and evolution of mate choice and marriage relations, and how my findings differ from both conventional wisdom and previous research findings. With those general statements as a background, I will proceed to offer my thoughts on the "big question" which inspired this research in the first place—is American marriage as an institution "in trouble," or are the doomsayers exaggerating and misreading the evidence? I do not propose to offer specific advice to individuals contemplating trips to the altar, although some of the specific findings of this project could be read as providing helpful clues about what makes for marital success. Rather, I will be concerned in general with the state of health of American marriage.

The nine substantive chapters are followed by two appendixes. Appendix 1 is devoted to a general discussion of the methods used in collecting and analyzing the Detroit Area Study survey data. How various problems and potential biases were examined and treated is discussed in some detail. Finally, Appendix 2 describes all of the questions from the survey that ended up being used in the current volume. That appendix also discusses how the responses to these questions were reorganized and collapsed into scales prior to analysis.

Conclusions

My aim, then, in the pages that follow, is to present a systematic analysis both of the ways in which the process of dating and mate choice has or has not changed in urban America, and of what makes for a successful or unsuccessful marriage in the contemporary era. The number of specific issues investigated along the road to dealing with these two major topics is too diverse to make a preview of the main findings here possible. However, one underlying theme that emerged from many of the separate analyses reported in this study deserves to be highlighted in advance. It is by no means an easy manner to preview this theme, since the available terminology fails to capture its essence fully. Words such as "tolerance" and "options" suggest themselves, or perhaps in a more negative vein, "normlessness" or "anomie." But the phrase that seems to me to capture this underlying theme most accurately is the "decline in conventions." Oversimplifying a great deal, the reader will see evidence in the pages that follow that suggests we have gone from a situation in which there was a "right way" and a "wrong way" to conduct premarital relations, or to pattern one's marital relationship to a situation in which alternative ways of behavior lack such clear moral meanings. Whether the issue concerns retaining virginity until marriage, marrying someone of the same faith, or dividing the chores within a marriage, there is declining consensus about what is acceptable and what is unacceptable. Perhaps because of this decline in conventions and reduced clarity about moral standards, behaving in conventionally proper versus improper ways no longer makes the difference it once did for marital success.

Another implication of this trend is that social background traits such as class, educational attainment, ethnic background, and religion, which used to distinguish fairly clearly between those who followed the conventionally proper modes of premarital and marital relations and improper ones, no longer seem to have so much predictive power.[19] The "bread and butter" social background measures that have been used by most social scientists in the past in explaining mate choice and marital variations are not much help in interpreting the results of the present study. Therefore, it is not simply the case that conventional norms about premarital and marital relations have weakened. In addition, a picture of America as a social hierarchy composed at the top by a prosperous, white, largely Protestant upper and middle class that conforms to "proper" ways of acting prior to, and after marriage, and at the bottom by lower status ethnic groups and classes who are more likely to engage in "deviant" practices, no longer seems very accurate.

What the implications of this decline in conventions is for marriage as an institution can be debated. Should we interpret these changes as indicating the traumatic impact of rapid social change in the twentieth century, growing moral decay and decadence, or simply general confusion about how to behave? And does this trend therefore provide support for the view that marriage is in trouble, since the moral underpinnings regarding what kinds of behavior are acceptable and unacceptable in marriage have weakened? Or should this trend be interpreted more positively? Perhaps what this change provides evidence for is the breakdown of rigid moral preconceptions about how people should live and the emergence of an increased ability of individuals to suit their premarital and marital lives to their own needs and preferences, without much regard for social conventions. Perhaps by being able to break away from the grasp of traditional conventions and the social status concerns these reflect, individuals may be able to construct more satisfying marriages. Rather than being part and parcel of a decay of marriage in America, the trend toward greater tolerance and options represented by the decline in conventions may indicate escape from rigid and stultifying marriages. If the latter speculation is correct, then a more upbeat conclusion about the meaning of this trend for American marriage as an institution would be warranted.

These are large and amorphous issues, and it is unlikely that I will be able to fully resolve them using data from the Detroit area survey. My purpose in introducing this theme is simply to alert the reader to its importance. In the specific chapters that follow I will point to the various pieces of evidence that lead me to stress this underlying theme of a decline in conventions. At the end of the study further thoughts will be offered about what this general trend means for the future of American marriage.

Notes

1. It could be argued that this tendency of Americans toward self-criticism is rooted in the belief among the original colonists that they were establishing a new and more perfect society, the "new Jerusalem," and perhaps even preparing for the second coming of Christ. Given such a lofty aspiration, the mundane facts of human behavior and social arrangements at any particular point in time are bound to be considered disappointing, and perhaps indicative of moral decay and social decline. These same impulses have fueled the long-standing American penchant for erecting separate, utopian communities where, since colonial times, some Americans have tried to establish better and more satisfying marriage and family forms. See, for example, the examples discussed in Kephart 1982.

2. For related predictions by other eminent thinkers, see Russell (1929) Moore (1958).

3. The argument about evolution rather than deterioration in American marriage is perhaps most closely identified with the work of sociologist Talcott Parsons, but his views have been echoed by many others. For recent examples, see Bane (1976); Levitan and Belous (1981); Berger and Berger (1983). For a caustic review of this debate in earlier decades of this century, see Lasch (1977). For an examination of trends from a demographic point of view, see Davis (1985).

4. Literally dozens of studies have been conducted in which respondents are asked to rank the importance of a variety of criteria—e.g., honesty, good looks, good income, sense of humor, etc.— in selecting someone to marry. For one review of this research, see Powers (1971). However, in such research there is almost never an attempt to examine whether such criteria have anything to do with the actual selection of a mate, and the few studies that do examine this question generally come up with a negative response (see, Udry 1965).

5. These questions illustrate issues on which there is a fair amount of research, but unfortunately not research that provides direct answers to such basic questions. For example, there have been many studies over the years of premarital sexuality, but few since the Kinsey surveys that provide answers to what percentage of newly marrying couples in different eras were still virgins when they married. Similarly, the U.S. Census bureau has provided estimates on the growing number of cohabiting couples in American in recent years, but since such couples can arise through a variety of circumstances—from couples who do not later marry, among divorced individuals, among the widowed elderly, and so forth—such figures do not allow me to estimate what percentage of couples cohabited before they married.

6. The Detroit Area Study (DAS) is designed to provided intensive, "hands on," training in all stages of survey research for students at the University of Michigan, and particularly for graduate students in sociology. As part of that training, the students participate in preparation and interviewing for a metropolitan area survey, and these surveys have been conducted annually since 1951. The topic for the survey changes each year, and individual faculty members compete by submitting proposals, with the proposal and faculty member selected determining the topic for the ensuing year. Well known studies carried out through the DAS include Blood and Wolfe (1960) and Lenski (1961) (see also Duncan, Schuman, and Duncan 1973). For an overview and bibliography of the more than 400 publications that have resulted from this unique resource, see Converse and Meyer (1988).

7. Details on how the study was organized and carried out will be found in Appendix 1.

8. In other words, the frame of reference is urban or metropolitan America, and I have less confidence that my findings can be generalized to the America of small towns and rural areas.

9.   A distinction must be made here between reports about average tendencies and time trends, on the one hand, and about the interrelationship between presumed causes and predicted outcomes. While the average tendencies and time trends reported in the pages that follow generally correspond closely to the findings of earlier studies, in a fair number of instances the observed patterns of association among variables stand in contrast to earlier reports. The contrasts in findings of the latter type do not necessarily indicate that Detroit area marriages are unusual, and they may provide clues to important new developments in marriage relations.

10.   On a related note, readers may be surprised to find relatively few sections of this work that refer to distinctive customs and histories of Detroit and its various neighborhoods. While in part this absence of local color is due to my conviction that what I am illuminating in this study is American mate choice and marriage generally, and not the peculiar versions practiced in Detroit, it is even more due to the fact that the kinds of statistical data that are produced by a questionnaire study such as this one do not readily yield local anecdotes and color.

11.   One implication of this approach, however, is that the project ended up interviewing only individuals who had been married at least once. Therefore the data we collected are not an ideal means to examine attitudes toward marriage of single persons who have never made the trip to the altar. As a consequence, this survey cannot tell us what is distinctive about those who never marry, whether the reasons for never marrying have changed, and whether there is a growing group of confirmed non-marriers in American society.

12.   In fact, many important longitudinal studies have involved new researchers going back, often after a generation or more, to restudy the original communities or respondents that were surveyed by earlier investigators. For example, see Elder (1974); Thornton, Freedman, and Camburn (1982) Caplow et al. (1982). A major exception to this pattern is the ongoing "5000 families" or "panel study on income dynamics" research being conducted by colleagues at the University of Michigan (see Morgan et al. 1974).

13.   It may be possible to reinterview the 1984 respondents again in the future to see what has happened to them and their marriages, but no such research is presently contemplated.

14.   The main concern is that one partner not influence the answers of the other, such as by suggesting how certain questions should be answered. The solution to this problem of "contamination" is to arrange to interview the husband and wife separately and simultaneously, but this is often difficult to arrange and expensive, in terms of interviewing costs. Thus the same budget will result in fewer total interviews, in comparison with a design that calls for interviewing only a single partner.

15.   The age limitations of 18 and 75 evolved out of a desire to avoid highly atypical early teenage brides on the one hand, and severe problems of memory loss among older women on the other. We also restricted our sampling to noninstitutionalized women—those residing in ordinary residential households. The selection of married women has some benefits. In particular, some earlier DAS studies, and particularly the Blood and Wolfe study (1960), involved interviews with wives only, so I can make some comparisons that would have been impossible had we interviewed only husbands. However, a number of cogent criticisms have been made of the tendency of family sociologists to interview wives but not husbands (see, in particular, Safilios-Rothschild 1969). For more details on the sample and methods used here, see Appendix 1.

16.   The wording of those survey questions used in this report is given in Appendix 2.

17.   Some question may be raised about use of the term "dating," here and throughout this study. Some would argue that the term is out of date and bears an antiquated ring, just as the term "courting" came to be in earlier years, and that terms such as "going out with" or simply "seeing" are in more common use among today's young. Others would argue that the very act of dating, in the sense of a young male and female pairing off to engage in a particular recreational or romantic activity, is going out of style, and is being replaced by more informal and group-based forms of youth activity (see Murstein 1980). However, there is no single alternative term that is suitable for replacing the term dating here. And our respondents had no trouble in responding to the term where it was used in our questionnaire (see the specific wording of the relevant questions in Appendix 2). None of them

seemed puzzled by the term or claimed that it did not apply to the activities they were describing. Thus for want of a better term, and because I am skeptical of the argument that dating has gone out of style (even if the term is less often used by young people, or by particular segments of the young, such as high school students), I will stick with this term in the current study.

18.   The reason this understanding is important is somewhat technical. If in later chapters we find that marital success or failure is related to some of the premarital experiences described in Chapters 2 and 3, it will still be necessary to ask whether those premarital experiences "really" have that effect, or whether the effect is attributable to the underlying social sources of variations in those premarital experiences. To disentangle the issue it will be necessary to control for the underlying social background factors involved to see whether the premarital experiences in question still have some influence on marital outcomes even after this control is imposed, and in order to do that we need to discover what the underlying social background factors are. To give a concrete example that will come up later, if we discover that having an elaborate wedding is related to having an enduring and satisfying marriage, and if we have learned from Chapter 4 that more prosperous families tend to have more elaborate weddings than poorer families, one may wonder whether the true explanation of the former finding is not that large weddings produce successful marriages, but that higher class standing and prosperity make it easier to have a successful marriage (or produce more pressure on couples to do so). By controlling for social class origin and related factors statistically, we can examine whether elaborate weddings have an independent influence, net of such class factors, on the outcome of the marriage. See Chapter 7 for the results of this examination.

19.   However, race still appears to make a substantial difference in most of the realms that will be investigated in the current study. The impact of race will be addressed systematically throughout the chapters that follow.

Chapter 2

DATING

One of the most intriguing questions about mate choice in America is how the nature of dating has changed over time. We know surprisingly little about this question. Our American "dating culture" gives popular approval to young people pairing off with various romantic partners, without adult supervision and without defining those partners necessarily as potential mates. We think this dating culture evolved gradually during the latter part of the 19th century and early in the 20th century. Prior to that time, pairing off was more subject to direct adult supervision and was interpreted more in terms of the immediate goal of choosing a mate. The venues available for such pairing off were relatively limited compared to present times, and for middle-class couples, at least, the dominant practice was for the male to visit the female in her home. Terms such as "courting" and "keeping company" were used for such activity, and the archaic tone of such terms today conveys how much change has occurred in premarital relations.

The exact reasons for the emergence of a dating culture are still being debated. Some scholars place major emphasis on factors such as growing affluence and a proliferation of recreational venues aimed at the young, longer periods of schooling in predominantly coeducational schools, and the growth of forms of employment which took adults away from the home and therefore made it more difficult for parents to supervise the leisure time activities of their adolescent children. Others stress the rise of individualistic and consumption- and market-oriented philosophies, which provided subtle underpinnings for new modes of recreational romance and "playing the field." Some writers have even placed major stress on technological innovations—on the development of the automobile in the 20th century (and of the bicycle in the 19th), and of accompanying innovations such as drive-in movies, which helped to free young daters from the scrutiny of their parents. But so little research has been done on the topic of the emergence of the dating culture in America that it is difficult to be specific about how and when it evolved in different segments of our society (see Burgess and Wallin 1953, Chap. 3; Fass 1977; Rothman 1984; Modell 1983).

It is clear at least that major parts of what we associate with the process of dating were already widely accepted in the period after World War I. The more recent evolution of dating in America is almost as much *terra incognita* as the earlier origins of this practice, however (but see Ehrmann 1959; Burchinal 1964;

17

Gagnon and Greenblat 1978). While conducting this research, I occasionally asked friends and acquaintainces how they thought dating had changed, and I usually got only the vaguest of replies. Most people felt that dating today was very different from the days when their parents were young, but they were unable to state precisely what had changed, with one or two exceptions. The major change people are aware of is that sexual intercourse is a more common part of dating activities than in the past. In addition premarital cohabitation is becoming more and more widespread. From these changes some people generalize that a process of liberalization (or moral decay, depending on your point of view) must characterize the evolution of dating in America. According to this viewpoint, over the years parents have lost control, and young people have started dating earlier, have begun sexual activities at younger ages, have more casually tried and discarded large numbers of dating partners, and in general have experienced a variety of romantic and sexual experiences, so that marriage itself is viewed as less special than it once was. But these are hunches, rather than conclusions based on concrete evidence.

In this chapter data are presented to check a variety of hunches about our contemporary American mate choice process. There are two primary reasons why such data are of interest. First, the topic of continuity and change in premarital relations is a "blank spot" in the study of social change in America. We know something about recent trends in such aspects of family life as marriage ages, divorce rates, and fertility levels, but, as discussed in Chapter 1, we don't know much about what has happened to dating behavior. So there is some intrinsic interest in finding out how aspects of dating have or have not changed, and how any trends detected in this realm relate to broader social changes occurring in American society. The second reason for interest in dating trends concerns this study's focus on the link between premarital relations and marital success. Dating is an activity with a variety of purposes. For young people just beginning to participate in this activity, dating may be seen primarily or exclusively in recreational terms, devoted simply to testing one's attractiveness to the opposite sex and having fun, as the term "dating game" implies. However, eventually dating relationships tend to become more sustained and serious, and at some point dating begins to be seen more directly in terms of the goal of selecting a mate. In other words, the progression begins that is implied in our title, *Dating, Mating, and Marriage.* For this reason a central question of interest in the current study is whether some kinds of experiences in the dating stage are more conducive to a "wise" choice of a mate and subsequent marital success than others. If we can detect consistent trends over time in dating experiences, and if we find that the trends discovered are potentially threatening to marital success (or for that matter, are potentially conducive to marital success), we will have built a logical link between such dating trends and our "big question," the health of American marriage as an institution. Although the final testing of ideas about the impact of dating experiences on marital outcomes will not occur until later, in

Chapter 7, I want to consider here a variety of arguments about how these earlier experiences might be expected to have an important impact one way or the other.

How might variations in the timing and intimacy of dating be important? Quite contrary claims have been made in previous writing on this topic. On the one hand, there is what might be called the "educational" or, perhaps more appropriately, "marketplace learning" conception of dating. According to this conception, which might be considered the "orthodox" rationale for our dating culture, making a "wise" selection of a mate requires a considerable amount of knowledge and experience. Even though at one level Americans believe that marriage should be based upon love, and that in the best of circumstances, "love conquers all," still at another level we recognize that it doesn't make sense to rush to the altar with the first person who makes your heart beat faster. Rather, through dating, which provides an opportunity for explorations into romantic intimacy without requiring rapid escalation toward marriage, you can acquire knowledge of what sort of person you are attracted to and what sort of person you might be suited to when it comes time to eventually choose a marital partner. Through experience with a series of dates and steadies, you can gain awareness that will help you make a better choice of someone you might be able to live with "happily ever after".

While this conception might suggest a highly rational process, in which individuals gradually develop a detailed mental "check list" that they will use to screen dating partners to see if they might be suitable marriage targets, this need not be the case. Rather, it might be assumed that this sort of "comparison shopping" experience penetrates to a subconscious level, so that when one meets "Mr. Right" or "Ms. Right" the appropriate strong romantic attraction will be triggered spontaneously, leaving no need to consult a trait check-list.[1] The implication of these ideas, in terms of marriage, is that the emergence and elaboration of our dating culture was a "good thing." In general, according to this conception, individuals who have gained more experience in the dating stage, by having dated more individuals and by having the opportunity to consider a wider range of potential marriage partners, should be able to make a better choice when it comes time to select someone to wed.

But numbers of dates, steadies or marital prospects, are not the only consideration, according to this scenario. Another logical implication is that the better you get to know any one dating partner, and indeed the more the level of intimacy with that partner approaches what would occur once you marry, the better able you will be to judge whether that partner would be suitable as a spouse. So not only experience with a variety of dating partners, but also development of a high level of premarital intimacy with at least some of them, is seen as part of the useful learning process made possible by our dating culture. This sort of argument may be recognized as one that sexually active or even cohabiting young people use to try to calm their anxious parents: "After all, Mom and Dad, it wouldn't make sense to marry without knowing how sexually compatible we are and how we could get along on an intimate, day-to-day basis, would it?" So according to this justifying rationale, tendencies toward more prolonged dating with more partners, and toward intimacy with the most serious partners, should be conducive to "good" mate choice decisions. In contrast, individuals who start dating late, who only date one or a few individuals, and who head for the altar without getting to know their eventual spouses quite intimately should be more likely to make "bad" decisions and end up unhappily married.

This view on the positive functions of dating variety and premarital intimacy has not gone unchallenged. In addition to objections based on moral and religious grounds, there are a number of criticisms from a more pragmatic viewpoint. Critics pose a number of reasons for doubting that dating variety and intimacy help individuals to make a wise choice of an eventual spouse, as assumed by the "marketplace learning" scenario. One of the major criticisms attacks the assumption that through dating and progressively higher levels of intimacy you become better prepared for an eventual choice of a mate. In part the objection to this view concerns the idea that having had alternative romantic partners, including very intimate ones, does not, in fact, prepare you very well to make the exclusive and life-long commitment to a spouse that marriage is supposed to entail. In other words, rather than preparing you to feel that you have selected Mr. Right, extensive dating experiences may lead to a painful awareness of alternatives foregone, with a "grass is greener on the other side of the fence" sentiment always present in the back of your mind. As one prominent study of American high schools in the 1950s stated the matter:

> It seems unfortunate that so much of adolescents' energies must be spent in cultivating skills that serve them only at one point in life—in playing the courtship game. These skills and habits may be impediments to happiness in later life. The 'love of the chase' may linger after marriage for both male and female, making married life less content (Coleman 1961, p. 123).

If this alternative view is correct, then individuals who have had more limited dating experiences, and perhaps those who married their first sweethearts, should end up with the most satisfactory marriages, exactly the opposite of the prediction one is led to by the marketplace learning scenario.

There are additional criticisms of our dating culture that approach the matter from other angles. One version argues that the problem with the marketplace learning conception is that it makes false assumptions about what really motivates people in the dating stage. Critics question whether dating as it is normally practiced really provides for the kind of useful learning that the conventional rationale assumes. An alternative view is captured by the term, the "dating game." In this view other elements besides trying to find out who one would be suited to tend to dominate dating in America. In particular, concern to display popularity or to gain certain romantic and possibly sexual favors from partners leads young people to put on false fronts [what Douvan and Adelson (1966) call "dating personalities"] in order to impress dates and potential dates. With each individual manufacturing artificiality in order to impress their date, neither is in a very good position to learn what their partner is really like or whether they might be a suitable choice for a longer-term relationship.

The best known version of this criticism comes from the work of Willard Waller, who coined the term, "rating and dating," to convey the idea that competition among students for popularity dominates dating behavior and completely negates the kind of learning process that the orthodox scenario assumes takes place. (See Waller 1937 and the discussion in Lasch 1977, Chapter 3. For a critique of Waller's ideas, see Gordon 1981.) According to Waller, individuals are not motivated to date those who might be most suited to them, but those who are most likely to be defined as a "good date" or a "good catch" by peers. In such an environment, even if you could accurately assess the characteristics of your romantic partner by piercing through the superficiality of that partner's "dating personality," you would still end up dating the wrong person for the wrong reasons. When it comes time to pick a marriage partner, it will be very difficult to "switch gears" and select someone who is uniquely suited to your own needs and personality. In this version of the criticism of the marketplace learning scenario, extensive dating is at least not very conducive to a wise marital decision, if not actually being counterproductive.

Still other criticisms of our dating culture raise additional and somewhat related points—that early dating and early intimacy may lead to a younger age at marriage or may produce powerful emotions and urges that completely close out any sort of rational consideration of suitability. In either case the result is not likely to be a level-headed choice of a mate and a wise decision about when to marry. The resulting marriage is not likely to be as successful as one based upon a more gradual and constrained entry into premarital intimacy. High levels of absorption into dating and romantic concerns may also interfere with school learning and occupational training, resulting in poorer job placement and lower income, outcomes that will create considerable stress on a marriage relationship.[2]

Here, additional views on both sides of the issue could be discussed, but the general situation should be clear by now. There exist two conflicting arguments about whether various features of dating and premarital intimacy are conducive to marital success or not. The conventional rationale for our dating culture assumes that length of dating experience, variety in dating partners, and extensiveness of premarital intimacy are all useful preparations for a successful marriage. In the various criticisms of this scenario, it is argued that the opposite may more often be the case—that extensive dating and premarital intimacy may interfere with making a suitable choice of a marital partner. As noted earlier, these alternative points of view will not be tested until Chapter 7, but they form the background within which to consider what changes are visible in the dating experiences of women in our Detroit sample.

In the pages that follow, concrete evidence is offered to replace the speculations described earlier on whether the timing and nature of dating have changed. Our survey allows us to investigate whether various guesses about the evolution of dating in America over the last half century or so are accurate. Has everything become more free-wheeling in American dating, or are such claims incorrect? Since we interviewed women retrospectively about their dating experiences spanning a period of more than 60 years, we can begin to shed some light on what the actual changes in dating have been.[3]

In examining changes in dating patterns in the Detroit sample, I categorize the women we interviewed in terms of their years of marriage, as indicated in Chapter 1, rather than by age. By categorizing women by the year in which they first married I am, of course, ignoring the fact that the dating history these women are describing took place prior to their wedding, and that some women spent longer times in the dating stage than others. I simply want to establish whether women who married at successive points in time had similar or different experiences in their prior dating stage. In much of this analysis, it will be sufficient to divide respondents into three large groups, each representing a twenty-year time span of entry into marriage. These will be referred to as three major "marriage generations": those who were prewar brides, marrying in the years 1925–44 ($N = 66$); those who entered marriage during the "baby boom" years of 1945–1964 ($N = 180$); and those recent marriage cases who first wed during the years 1965–84 ($N = 209$).[4]

These categories, while nicely dividing the years of first marriage of the sample into three even slices, have the virtue of corresponding roughly to three different historical environments that are recognized in much previous writing on the American family. The first generation encompasses major disruptions brought on by the Great Depression and by World War II, which produced trials of strength for most American families (see Elder 1974). The second generation produced not only an unexpected baby boom, but also a high tide of general "familism" in American social life, with earlier and more universal marriage than before, a declining and then relatively stable divorce rate, the zenith of the "housewife syndrome" in America, and the explosion of life in suburbia— themes conveyed in the popular media of the time and in such popular television programs as "Father Knows Best." The third marriage generation encompasses a retreat from this familistic ethos, with declining birth rates, increasing divorce rates, and the rise of the feminist and sexual liberation movements. So the divisions in terms of which most comparisons will be made are not totally arbitrary.

At times I will want to use a finer time breakdown. Occasionally categories that divide women by their year of marriage into twelve groups, each of them five years in length, will be used, and I will refer to these groups as "marriage cohorts," (those who first married before 1929, in 1930–34, 1935–39, etc.). In places I will use the actual year of marriage to get the most detailed picture of trends. This chapter is concerned simply with determining trends in behavior in the dating stage. Questions about what sort of background characteristics are associated with early or late dating, premarital virginity, or other indicators of the American "dating regime" are deferred until Chapter 4.

Dating and Going Steady

The first question of interest is at what age women started dating in various periods. A direct question in a written supplement to our questionnaire asked women to report their age at the time they went on their first date, and it turns out, based on their replies, that there has not been any clear trend over time in the age of starting dating.[5] There is no clear correlation between marriage year and the age of first date, and in all three generations the median age at the time of the first date was 16. So in this respect, at least, in recent years women do not seem to be starting the dating process earlier.[6]

At this point it should be noted that the age at which women in our sample first married did change over time, but not in a simple fashion. As we know from many other studies of American marriage, ages of marriage dropped gradually during the 20th century until the mid-1950s, and since then they have been going up again (see, for example, the discussion in Cherlin 1981). In the Detroit sample this curvilinear pattern is also visible. In the prewar generation, the median age at first marriage was 21, then it dropped among baby-boom era brides to 20, and among recent cases it has risen again to 21.[7] The crude generational breakdown used here hides some of the recent increase; in the two final marriage cohorts (involving women who married after 1975) the mean age at marriage was over 23 years, matching national trends. The curvilinear trend in marriage ages, combined with the stable estimated age of beginning dating, means that the average number of years of potential dating—between the time of the first date and getting married—was about 5 years for women in the prewar cohorts, decreased to about 4 years during the baby-boom years, and is now back to 5 years or more. This changing length of time spent in the dating stage should be kept in mind when we consider other trends in dating behavior.

One other feature of the marriage ages in the Detroit sample should be noted. The ages of first marriages of the women we interviewed covered a very wide range, from 14 to 60! Even though there has been substantial publicity given to recent research claiming that women who pass the "prime marriage ages" may never succeed in marrying (see Bennett and Bloom 1986),[8] our data provide some support for the old saying that "it's never too late." Overall, 5% of the women in our sample first married at age 30 or later, and in addition to our champion who first married at age 60, there was another woman who finally made it to the altar at age 50. Both of these examples of the "never too late" phenomenon were wed in the late 1970s, indicating continued hope recently for women past the prime marriage ages.[9] So despite current concern that women who don't marry early may forfeit their chances, our data hint that the social convention that women should marry before it gets "too late" may be weakening.

Even though the age of starting dating has not gotten steadily earlier, other features of dating experience have changed. We asked our respondents to estimate how many different individuals they had ever gone out with on a date. The prewar brides on the average reported dating only 4–7 males, whereas the baby boomers estimated dating 10–14 and the youngest women in our sample gave figures averaging 12–15 males. It is possible that these figures exaggerate the trend, since older women may have forgotten some of the males they dated (and younger women may be more prone to brag by inflating the number they dated). Still, we suspect that there is a real trend underlying these figures, with younger women having had more dating partners before they married.[10]

The fact that women who married in more recent times report more males ever dated does not mean that "playing the field" has become more common than "going steady." Our respondents were asked about both their age at the time when they first went steady and about the number of "steadies" they had. It turns out that the age of starting to go steady has decreased steadily over time. Among prewar marriage cases, the median age of starting to go steady was 18, among baby-boom era brides it was 17, and among recent marriage cases the average age had dropped to 16. Whereas it was once common for young women to play the field for a couple of years before starting to go steady, in recent decades going steady starts almost immediately.

The number of individuals the average woman goes steady with before marriage has also increased somewhat in recent cohorts. Among prewar marriage cases a slight majority of women—55%—had not had any other steady boyfriends aside from the men they married. But this was true of only 34% of the women in the baby-boom marriage generation and only 25% of the women who married after 1965. In other words, the phenomenon of "marrying one's first sweetheart" seems less and less common, although it was still the pattern for one quarter of the youngest women in the sample. As one might expect, the average number of males ever gone steady with shows a corresponding increase, from 2.7 for the prewar generation through 3.5 for baby-boom era brides to 3.6 for the youngest respondents. (These averages include the eventual first husband.) Together these figures show that, while dating itself has not begun earlier in recent times, "serious dating" in the form of going steady begins earlier now. Since starting to go steady is seen by most as quite separate from preparing to marry, the fact that this stage begins earlier is not incompatible with our finding that women in this youngest generation ended up having had both more dates and more steady boyfriends prior to marriage than their older counterparts.[11]

How did parents react and adapt to these changes in dating behavior? Did they increasingly give their offspring free rein to do as they pleased in regard to the opposite sex? We don't have the best possible measures to answer these questions. We did ask our respondents the following two questions: "Did your parents ever try to influence who you went out with?" "Did they ever tell you they didn't want you to go out with a particular person?" It turns out that there is not a significant difference in the responses of women of different generations to these questions. In all three generations about half of our respondents reported that their parents had tried to influence who they went out with, and of those whose parents had played such a role, about three-quarters reported parents trying to forbid them going out with particular individuals. Unless we believe that the older women in our sample are selectively "forgetting" about such parental obstruction—a pattern that does not appear particularly plausible—these responses lead us to believe that parents have not significantly altered their concern about who their daughters go out with. [12]

In some cases this parental involvement and concern may even be expressed in some less subtle ways. For example, in one of our pretest interviews we asked a respondent how her parents conveyed to her that they were unhappy with the man she was dating. She replied that her mother pulled out a gun from a drawer, pointed it at her, and told her that if she tried to go out the door for her scheduled date she would shoot her dead! [13] On the other hand, the figures from our survey indicate that about half of even the older women felt that their parents gave them complete freedom to go out with anyone they wanted to. So our primary conclusion is that the women we interviewed reported a substantial and fairly constant (across generations) level of autonomy to make their own decisions about whom to date.

Premarital Sex

So far the picture we get is of a dating process that has changed only modestly. Reported parental supervision of dating has not changed much, and dating does not begin any earlier. However, going steady begins earlier, and both the number of males dated and the number of steadies have somewhat increased. But what of premarital sexual activity? Hasn't there been more of a revolution there? We asked a number of questions about this aspect of the dating process, but many of them were indirect. In other words, we didn't ask our respondents whether they had ever had sex before they got married. Instead, we asked them to report the age at which they first had sexual intercourse. By comparing their answers to this question with our data on the ages at which they got married, we can make a rough estimate of the proportion of women in the sample who engaged in premarital sex. It is a conservative estimate, since those women who lost their virginity in the weeks or months leading up to their wedding and who did not have another birthday before walking down the aisle would, according to this calculation, be classified incorrectly as virgins at marriage. So this measure will somewhat underestimate the proportion of nonvirgins at marriage. But since we are concerned here with comparisons across generations, this method should still give us a fairly clear picture of trends.

When we examine the proportion of the sample who had their first sexual experience at a younger age than when they were married, we do find a dramatic change across generations. Among the prewar brides, only 24% had already lost their virginity, according to our rough estimate. For the baby boom era brides this figure increases to 51%, and in the post-1965 cases to 72%. So the premarital loss of virginity has changed from being the experience of only a minority of women to that of the large majority of women. If we look at finer time divisions, the recent trend is even more striking. The percentage of nonvirgins at marriage, as computed by this method, increased from 56% among those married in the years 1965–69 to 67% among those who married in 1970–74, and then to 85% among those who married in 1975–79 and 88% among those who married in the years 1980–84. Keep in mind that these figures probably underestimate the extent of premarital sex in all generations. In other words, according to our estimates, it is probably the case that less than 10% of those women in the Detroit area who were marrying in the mid-1980s were still virgins.[14] Clearly a sexual revolution has taken place. From a situation in which "nice girls don't" we have moved to a new era in which "most girls do."

Is sexual experience beginning ever earlier, or is part of the increase in pre-marital sex simply due to the delay in marriage ages of women in recent years? From reports on the age of first sexual experience we can examine this question. In general our figures point to sex not only becoming more common prior to marriage, but beginning at an earlier age. In the prewar generation the median age of first sexual experience was about age 20. Among baby-boom era brides it dropped to about age 19, and in recent marriage cases to about age 18.[15]

One further implication of these trends is clear. Formerly it was the case that most women who engaged in premarital sex did so with their eventual husbands. Indeed, more than half of the women in both the Kinsey survey (Kinsey et al. 1953) in the 1940s and the Hunt survey in 1970 (Hunt 1974) who were not virgins at marriage had only had sex with their eventual husbands. This pattern has been interpreted as indicating that not only an exclusive romantic relationship (i.e., going steady), but even some sort of commitment to marry is seen by most women as necessary before they will engage in premarital sex (for those who do, in fact, lose their virginity prior to marriage). Hunt also argued, by comparing the similarity of the figures from his survey and from Kinsey's (see Hunt 1974, p. 151) that this situation had not changed over time, in spite of a major increase in premarital sexual activity among females.

However, our findings point to change, rather than continuity, in this realm. As women have reached increasing levels of intimacy at earlier ages, and with partners with whom there may be no explicit commitment to marry, it has become more likely that a woman will have had other sexual partners before her husband. We asked our respondents how old they were when they first started dating their eventual husbands, and by comparing this piece of information with their reports on their age when they first had sex, we can calculate an estimate of the proportion of respondents who had had sex already with another partner before their eventual husbands.[16] According to this calculation, the percentage of women who had other sexual partners prior to their eventual husbands rose from 3% among our prewar brides to 17% for brides of the baby boom era, and then to 33% among brides in the most recent generation.[17] As with our premarital sex estimates, if we examine more detailed time divisions, the recent increase is even more striking. Comparing the four marriage cohorts within our final marriage generation (those marrying in 1965–69, 1970–74, 1975–79, and 1980–84), the percentage of women who we estimate had prior sexual partners is 17%, 31%, 41%, and 51%. So not only are women who are virgins at marriage becoming increasingly scarce, but women who have lost their virginity before they start dating their eventual husbands are more and more the norm.

This trend does not imply necessarily that casual sex or sex with a variety of partners in the same time span is becoming accepted for women, either in attitudes or in behavior. We did not ask more detailed questions in this realm, so we cannot tell what proportion of our respondents engaged in premarital sex in anything other than an exclusive romantic setting (i.e., at least going steady).[18] But since an increasing proportion of women are having several steady relationships before they settle on a man to marry, and since sexual activity is increasingly accepted within a steady relationship, the net result is an increase in women whose sexual initiation precedes meeting and starting to date the man they will eventually marry.

Mapping Trends

From the various trends reviewed so far we can now construct profiles of how the average timing of the various stages in dating has changed across the generations in our sample (see Figure 2-1). In the prewar generation dating began, on the average, at about age 16; going steady followed a couple of years later, at age 18; and the first sexual experience followed at age 20 or so. However, for the majority of women sex began with marriage, at about age 21, rather than before.[19] In the baby-boom era, dating still began at about age 16, going steady followed at 17, and the first sexual experience two years later, at age 19. Still about half of the women, however, did not begin sexual relations until they married, and marriage occurred relatively early, below age 20 for half of the women in that generation. For the most recent generation in our sample, again dating began at age 16, but going steady began soon afterward, while these women were still 16. Then sexual relations began at about age 18, on the average, or about 3 years before the average woman in this generation married.

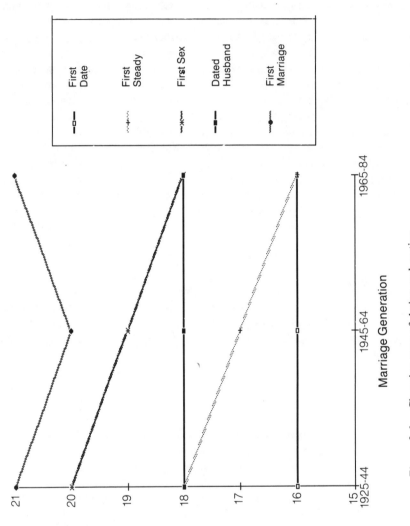

Figure 2.1. Changing ages of dating and mating

So the primary change in the dating process is not in beginning the whole process earlier, but in reaching deeper levels of intimacy at earlier stages in the dating process. Therefore, since the median age of first dating the eventual husband remained at about 18 for all three generations, the chart shows that intimacy was increasingly occurring not only prior to marriage, but prior to starting dating the first husband.[20]

The most dramatic expression of intimacy during the dating stage is premarital cohabitation, where a couple lives together as husband and wife, but without the benefit of matrimony. We know from studies by the U.S. Census Bureau and others that cohabitation has been increasing in recent years (see Spanier 1983; Eekelaar and Katz 1980), but to date there are few studies that can tell us what proportion of people do at some point live together before getting married. We asked about this directly, although again we do not have a perfect measure. The question used was, "Did you and your husband live together before you got married?" Responses to this question might slightly understate the extent of cohabitation, since women who lived with some other male before marriage but did not cohabit with their eventual spouse would not be counted as having cohabited. (Also some women, of course, might not admit to having cohabited.)

The shift across cohorts in responses to this premarital cohabitation question is particularly dramatic (see Figure 2-2). No women who married before the early 1950s admitted to having cohabited prior to marriage. Then among the cohorts who married between 1955 and 1974, between 5 and 10% cohabited. But in the final two marriage cohorts, the rate skyrockets—to 32% for those marrying in the period 1975–79 and then to 40% for those marrying in the years 1980–84. So cohabitation prior to marriage is now approaching becoming a majority phenomenon in the complex urban area that Detroit represents.[21] If this trend continues, and is duplicated in other places in the United States, then we can expect to see not only premarital sex but living together before marriage increasingly accepted as a normal part of the dating and mating process in American society.

At this point the reader may well wonder whether AIDS and other sexually transmitted diseases are not changing this situation fundamentally. There has been considerable discussion in the mass media of a new conservatism in American family life and sexual behavior generally in the 1980s, and even some advocates arising for what is called "the new celibacy." Could such general trends, and fear of contracting AIDS in particular, reverse the trends described here and produce an increase in the proportion of women (and perhaps also men) who remain virgins until marriage? Certainly it is not inconceivable that the trend toward premarital intimacy can be reversed, since this appears to have happened before in American history. Researchers have uncovered evidence suggesting that the current sexual revolution is the second in our history, rather than the first. An earlier major increase in premarital sexuality occurred at the end of the 18th century and early in the 19th century, but was followed by a retreat toward increasing premarital chastity during the Victorian era in the latter part of the

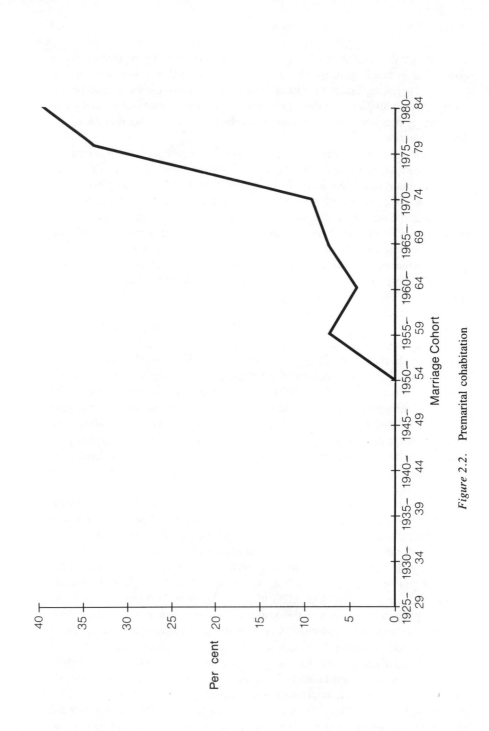

Figure 2.2. Premarital cohabitation

19th century (see Smith and Hindus 1975). Could this reversal be repeated as America approaches the end of the 20th century?

It would be nice if I could answer this question using data from the Detroit survey, but unfortunately we did not ask any questions in this survey about such things as fear of venereal disease. In any case, the timing of our interviews was such that fear of AIDS could not have been a major concern during the premarital years of the women we interviewed, since the disease had only been identified in the early 1980s. So my thoughts on this issue are largely speculative, rather than based on evidence from the Detroit survey.[22] At the time that I write these lines I see no clear signs that the trend toward premarital intimacy is being reversed. Insofar as unmarried individuals do not dismiss the danger of AIDS as irrelevant to them, because it is confined largely to "special" populations—drug addicts, homosexuals, and hemophiliacs—they are likely to become more cautious about "casual sex." But unless and until AIDS is seen as making greater inroads into the heterosexual population, individuals are not likely to feel that premarital sex in the context of an exclusive relationship with a steady or a future spouse is very dangerous.

Whether or not this perception is accurate or foolish, it seems to me that the dominant trend that emerges from the Detroit interviews—sexual intimacy incorporated into the dating and mating sequence as part of a romantic and exclusive relationship—is likely to continue to be interpreted as "safe sex." Popular attitudes toward premarital sexuality in this context remain quite liberal. Perhaps the AIDS scare may contribute to some greater hesitancy about beginning sexual activity, and therefore to an increase in the average age of the first sexual experience, and unmarried couples may more regularly choose condoms as their preferred means of birth control. But I do not anticipate any significant trend toward rising virginity at marriage unless AIDS spreads much more widely into the general population. The previous and long-standing convention that women, at least, might lose status and harm their chances for attracting a desirable marriage partner by giving up their virginity prior to marriage has been demolished, and I see no sign that this convention is being revived.

Approaching Marriage

For most Americans, even though dating initially begins without any clear connection to mate-selection, the eventual goal is to find someone to marry. Since we only interviewed women who had been married we have no direct evidence on the point; however, other research indicates that the increasing availability of premarital sex and cohabitation have not weakened the popularity of marriage as an institution. Very few individuals see our more liberal contemporary sexual mores as providing an acceptable alternative to marriage.[23] But has the way in which people select a partner changed? For instance, do people rush into marriage more nowadays? Is a formal engagement stage less common today than in the past? We asked a number of questions that allowed us to look at some features of the final stage of the dating process—the stage of selecting a suitable marriage partner and preparing to walk down the aisle.

One question that intrigued us was whether there had been any change in the number of "serious marital prospects"—the number of men that the average woman ever thought about marrying before she settled on her eventual husband. We asked respondents directly, "Before you married your (first) husband, were there any other men you seriously considered marrying?" (If so) "How many were there?" It turns out that change in this area has been slight. In the prewar marriage generation only 35% of all respondents had other "serious prospects." In the baby-boom generation the comparable figure was 47%, and among recent marriage cases 46%. There is a slight indication of an increase in the likelihood of having given other men serious consideration, but the trend is not statistically significant.

For those who did have other prospects, there is also not much sign of change in the number of alternatives considered. The mean number of other prospects considered is between 1.2 and 1.4 for each generation, with no clear trend. In spite of the tendency we have already commented on for going steady and sexual intimacy to begin at earlier ages, when women come to the process of actually selecting a spouse, they do not have a larger number of choices in recent years. Most women still go to the altar with the only man they seriously considered marrying, and even those who considered another usually had only one alternative. (But for the record, in our sample one woman claimed to have given five other men serious consideration.)[24]

We also inquired about how women first met their husbands. We were interested in whether they had met directly or whether they had been introduced. Allowing for some crudeness in the question, due to the possibility that "introduction" could have been defined in various ways by different respondents, still it is striking that there has been little change across generations in this aspect of mate choice. In the three major generations 58%, 54% and 58% of the women reported having met their spouse directly, so there is no clear trend visible.

We also examined more specifically how the couple had first met. In a follow-up to our initial question about whether the couple had met directly or had been introduced, we asked who had done the introducing, or where the couple had first met. The responses to these open questions are reported in Table 2.1. Just as there has been no clear change in the balance of introductions vs. direct meetings, these figures do not show any statistically significant overall trends. However, a few features of these percentages might be highlighted. First, in all generations introductions by friends and other nonfamily members were more common than introductions provided by family members, and a slight trend toward fewer family introductions is visible in the younger generations in the table. Blind dates are also less often mentioned by those in younger generations.

Table 2.1.   Generational Differences in First Meeting

How the Couple First Met	Marriage Generation		
	1925–1944	1945–1964	1965–1984
Introductions:	42.4%	46.1%	41.6%
Of which:			
By parents, older kin	2.8	3.9	2.4
By siblings, same age kin	12.7	11.2	11.0
By other kin	2.8	2.8	0.5
By friends, other non-kin	18.4	27.6	25.8
Blind date	5.7	0.6	1.9
Direct Meeting:	57.6	53.9	58.4
Of which:			
Known since childhood	0.0	2.8	1.4
In neighborhood	8.2	7.3	4.0
In church, church activity	3.3	1.7	1.9
In organization, club	4.9	1.1	1.0
In school, school activity	13.2	11.8	14.0
At work	11.5	10.6	14.0
At party, dance, wedding	0.0	7.9	5.3
At bar, dance hall	3.3	1.7	4.8
In public, chance meeting	13.2	7.9	10.6
Vacation, amusement spot	0.0	1.1	1.4
(*N*)	(66)	(180)	(209)

We recorded no cases at all of the much talked about modern replacements of the blind date—couples matched via computer dating or through classified personal ads. The neighborhood where one grew up, church activities, and clubs and other organizations are all somewhat less common as arenas for finding mates in the younger generations than in the oldest generation, and work organizations and parties and dances have become somewhat more promising venues.

It is rather difficult to put such data on how the couple first met in any kind of interpretive perspective, since we lack systematic data on this question for other times and places. I have attempted in Table 2.2 to piece together some figures from other studies that are somewhat comparable to ours. However, differences in samples, question wording, and coding procedures make this comparison almost impossible, and so any conclusions reached here can be only tentative. But several contrasts in these figures seem apparent. First, introductions of various kinds are more commonly mentioned in our data than in the other studies, although this may be an artifact of our asking about it directly.[25] Schools and places of work are the next most common places of meeting in our sample and are more common venues than in the French and English studies, but less common than in the Soviet study cited. Parties, dances, bars and other places of entertainment seem less common meeting places in our study than in the European samples examined in the table.

Table 2.2. Comparative Data on How Couples First Met

How the Couple First Met	Current Study	CT 1949–1950	France 1959	England 1969	USSR 1962
Introductions	43.4%	39.6%	17.0%	12.4%	8.7%
Of which:					
By family	16.3	n.a.	6.0	)	3.3
				12.4*	
By friends, non-kin	25.2	28.7	11.0	)	5.2
Blind date	2.0	10.9	n.a.	n.a.	n.a.
Direct Meeting:	56.6	60.4	83.0	87.6	91.5
Of which:					
From neighborhood, childhood	7.5	12.4	22.0	6.7	9.0
Church, church activity	2.0	2.4	n.a.	2.2	n.a.
Organization, club	1.6	1.9	6.0	n.a.	n.a.
School, school activity	13.1	7.0	)	4.5	17.5
			13.0*		
Work	12.2	12.4	)	14.6	21.0
Party, dance, wedding	5.8	12.4	17.0	32.6	5.7
Bar, dance hall	3.3	n.a.	n.a.	4.5	27.2
Public place, chance meeting	10.0	11.9	15.0	6.7	2.3
Vacation, amusement spot	1.1	n.a.	10.0	12.4	5.0
Other	n.a.	n.a.	n.a.	3.4	3.8
(N)	(455)	(715)	(1646)	(1037)	(500)

n.a. = not available   * = combination of category above and below
Sources:
Current study: respondents from all marriage generations together.
CT: white couples who married in New Haven in 1949–50, as identified by marriage licenses (both marrying for first time only), from Hollingshead 1952.
France: results of a national survey of married men and women reported in Girard 1974, p. 98.
England: results of a national survey of married men and women under 45, reported in Gorer 1971, p. 265 (percentages recomputed to total 100).
USSR: newly married couples identified through marriage registrations in Leningrad, as reported in Kharchev 1965.

Given the imprecision of this comparison, it is hard to know what to make of specific details. But two general observations do seem to be important. First, the similarities of our figures and those computed by Hollingshead from his study of New Haven marriages in 1949–50 do lend weight to the idea that there is an identifiable and relatively stable pattern by which marital partners are first brought together in America. Second, in a majority of cases the circumstances are other than those focused on in most of the mate-choice literature. Most research on mate choice in America is conducted among students and carries the implicit, if not explicit, assumption that schools and colleges are where most pairing off goes on in America. But only about one-eighth of our sample met directly in school or school activities.[26] Popular writings on finding a mate focus not only on schools, but also on the work place, on computer dating, on singles bars, and on vacation spots of the "Club Med" variety (see Godwin 1973; Mullan 1984). But these also are routes to mate choice used by only a small proportion of our sample to find a spouse. It would appear that future research on mate choice in America should look more in-depth at the introduction process, whether by family or friends, as the primary route to finding a spouse in our society. And other locales besides schools and offices deserve greater attention as well.

Perhaps our American ideology in regard to mate choice has blinded us in this realm. We are a society that believes in freedom of mate choice, and the idea of an arranged marriage is odd and repulsive. From this viewpoint it is only a short step to assuming that most couples in America should and do meet on their own. But in fact our data indicate that nearly half of all couples meet first via somebody else's introduction, rather than directly, and that the percentage who meet in this way has not changed much across generations. Of course, those doing the introducing are rarely the sort of hired matchmakers lampooned in "Fiddler on the Roof." Still, informal introductions turn out to be a very important, and a little studied, aspect of the dating and mating process in American society today.

We also investigated the "propinquity question." It is a standard theme of textbooks on American marriage that a large proportion of those who marry lived only a few blocks apart before they started dating (see, for example, Udry 1971, pp. 185–6). After all, without an arranged marriage system, people have to meet and get to know potential spouses, and your chances of doing so are much higher if you live near a prospect than if you live very far away. (Even if you meet via an introduction, it is unlikely that you will be introduced to a person living at a great distance.) Recent studies hint that propinquity—the closeness of prior residence—may no longer be so important a factor in mate selection in recent years. With more automobiles, increased college attendance, greater geographical mobility via jobs, and other developments, one can cast one's mate choice "net" somewhat wider. We asked our respondents how far apart they and their first husband had lived when they first started dating.[27] The median distance at the time of the first date as computed from this measure fluctuated somewhat, but did show a slight upward trend. In our prewar generation of women the median distance apart was 3 miles, and this increased to 4 miles for those in the baby-boom generation and 5 miles for women marrying since 1965. So there is some evidence for the view that propinquity is a somewhat less binding constraint than in the past, but still the fact that half of all recent brides lived less than 5 miles away from their future husbands when they started dating is notable.

Once they have found "Mr. Right," how long do women date him before they marry? Our data on this point are rather crude—we only have the age of the woman when she started going out with her eventual spouse and her age at the time she married, rather than a direct question about the number of months that she dated him. But our data suggest that here there has not been much change in the final stage of dating. The median number of years spent dating the eventual husband was 2 years in all three generations. In this case the median is a

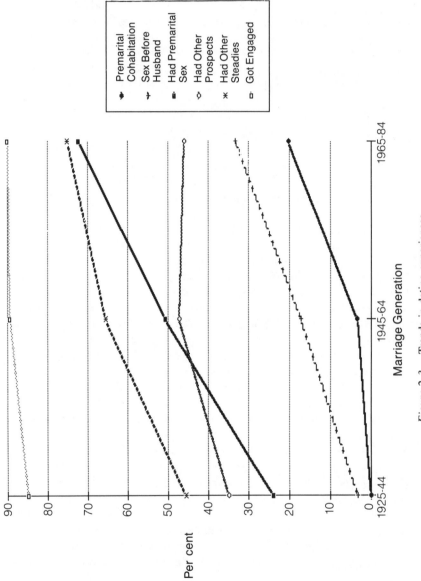

Figure 2.3. Trends in dating experiences

somewhat misleading statistic, and the mean number of years spent dating the eventual husband shows the same curvilinear trend we saw earlier in examining marriage ages—the averages were 2.5 years, 2.2 years, and 2.6 years for the three generations.[28] There has been some change over time, but there has not been a consistent tendency toward either hasty or delayed marriages. These figures provide no evidence that the average woman was "rushing into marriage," since even in the baby boom era when such hastiness was the subject of much public criticism, most women waited for two years or more before heading for the altar. In recent times, there are modest signs of further caution and delay before deciding to tie the knot.

If we consider the question of a formal engagement there is also not much sign of change. The great majority of women in all generations were formally engaged before they married. The figures for our three major generations were 85%, 89%, and 90% who had been engaged, and the slight increase here is not statistically significant. However, not all of those who considered themselves formally engaged received an engagement ring. And the proportion of women who reported receiving an engagement ring is higher in more recent generations—only 55% of prewar brides received a ring, but 71% of baby-boom era brides and 74% of recently married women did. Evidently, these figures provide testimony more to the increasing success of the diamond industry in promoting their products (see Epstein 1978) than to changes in underlying American mate choice customs. Assuming recollections are accurate, there has been a rather slight increase in the length of time spent in the engagement stage. The median number of months spent engaged is 8 for both the prewar generation and the baby-boom era brides, but 11 among those marrying since 1965.[29]

In various preceding sections of this chapter trends in the percentage of women in our sample who have had various premarital experiences were considered. The results are summarized graphically in Figure 2.3. The data in the figure show that in the prewar generation, only getting engaged was a majority experience. Since then having had other serious marital prospects and getting engaged have only become slightly more common, but having had other steadies besides the eventual husband and having engaged in premarital sex have become much more common experiences, such that they are now part of the "premarital regime" of the large majority of women when they marry. Additionally, as discussed earlier, both having had other sexual partners prior to dating the eventual husband and having cohabited with the eventual husband prior to marriage are rapidly becoming more common, and may well be majority phenomena for Detroit area women by the time this book is published. These figures display in yet another way the extent to which intimacy has become "normal" prior to the walk to the altar.

Conclusions

This chapter started by asking whether everything about the dating process in America has been getting earlier and more casual. The simple answer to this question is no. But that simple response is not very enlightening. In the preceding pages we have discovered both impressive continuities in dating behavior across generations and startling changes.

The major change in the dating regime that our data attest to is that premarital intimacy of various kinds—going steady, engaging in premarital sex, living together before marriage, having known other sexual partners before the husband—is occurring earlier, and to a higher proportion of young women, than in the past. The fact that more is involved in this trend than simply increasing premarital sexual activity leads me to refer to this as an "intimacy revolution," rather than simply a sexual revolution.[30]

This is really a striking set of changes in many ways. These trends testify, among other things, to dramatic alterations in the expectations surrounding the behavior of unmarried women, and to a decline in the sexual double standard. In earlier decades in this century premarital intimacy by males was often seen tolerantly as "sowing wild oats." No such tolerance existed for unmarried females. Virginity was seen as a prerequisite for a "good marriage," and young women who lost their virginity or simply developed a reputation of being fickle or "loose" placed their prospects on the marriage market in great jeopardy. As a result, young women tended invariably to become categorized, or stigmatized, into two groups: the "nice girls" who didn't (engage in premarital sex), and the "easy girls" who did. Young males anxious to sow their wild oats provided lots of attention for the "easy girls" as well as for professional prostitutes, but when it came time to select a girl for marriage they usually turned, instead, to one of the "nice girls."[31]

Clearly the situation has changed markedly. Young females are generally not expected to be virgins at marriage anymore, and engaging in sex or even having lived with a male prior to marriage no longer seems to harm a woman's chances of making a suitable marriage. (We have no data in this study on expectations, but from our figures it is clear that males who require a bride to be a virgin face an increasingly difficult search process.) It is probably the case that females are still more likely to be criticized than males for "sex without feeling" or for having more than one sexual partner at any particular time. In this sense some division between "nice girls" and "easy girls" still exists. But the categories have been redefined so that "nice girls" include those who are intimate, sexually and otherwise, but only in the context of an exclusive, romantic relationship. Promiscuity now has a narrower meaning of casual sex or sex that is not exclusively with one partner, rather than premarital sex per se. The assumptions that used to loom heavily over women—that intimacy before marriage indicated that as a wife she would be dissatisfied or unfaithful—no longer hold, for better or for worse.

This change clearly forms part of a more general process of alteration in the status of women relative to men. We should note, though, that we don't feel that the Women's Liberation Movement was primarily responsible for these changes.

The timing is simply wrong. The Women's Liberation Movement began to be a noticeable force in America in the mid-1960s, but the "intimacy revolution" clearly was underway well before that time. The same comment could be made about explanations of the sexual revolution in terms of the invention of the "pill" and other modern contraceptive devices and liberalized abortion rights. Again, the changes toward greater and earlier premarital intimacy were clearly underway even before the pill and legal abortion became available. Feminism and birth control options may have helped to accelerate changes that were already underway, changes that some analysts believe began even earlier than the time-span of our data, perhaps in the late 19th century (see Kinsey et al. 1953; Smith 1973; Degler 1974; Rothman 1984).

Our data don't speak directly to the reasons for this century-long pattern of change, but I would argue that factors such as increasing commercialization and affluence (particularly the rising financial autonomy of young people), growing privatization of family life and the decline of community controls, the assimilation of immigrants and the weakening of ethnic family controls, and the influence of Sigmund Freud's ideas on sexuality played more of a role in fostering the intimacy revolution than recent phenomena such as the pill and the Women's Liberation Movement. (See Smith and Hindus 1975; Shorter 1971.) This "intimacy revolution" is one of the most dramatic symbols of the decline in conventions noted at the outset of this study. Expectations that intimacy will be postponed until at least engagement, if not marriage, have fallen by the wayside in the face of a logic that says that whatever one does in an exclusive, romantic relationship must be "all right."

Part of the picture we have seen in this chapter is an "intimacy revolution" taking place in the lives of unmarried females over the last 60 years. However, our data also show us another side of the picture, a side in which there is much continuity with the past. Dating does not apparently start earlier than it used to. Parents still seem to hover at the sidelines, worrying about who their youngsters will go out with and whether they will make a "suitable" choice for a marriage partner. And even though premarital intimacy is much more common today, dating has not become an endless stage, or a replacement for marriage. For the vast majority of young people, intimacy in the dating stage serves simply as a further preliminary to the selection of a mate. The process of mate selection seems to be invested today with the same deliberation and ceremony as in the past. Most women end up selecting a mate from only one or two serious prospects. And 90% of them get formally engaged, and more of them than in earlier generations receive an engagement ring symbolizing their commitment. Both the dating stage and the engagement stage with the man they plan to marry are as long or longer, on the average, as was the case in earlier generations.

These elements of continuity modify our judgment about what has changed in the dating process. Startling as the inroads of intimacy into the process are, they don't add up to a fundamental alteration or challenge to the nature of "courting" in America. This increasing intimacy has not undermined, but has been incorporated into, a dating and mating sequence whose basic goals remain the same as before. The primary goal of this activity—to find a suitable mate—has not changed, although the rules about what one may do along the way have clearly been modified.

The basic argument I am making, then, is that the changes in the dating process are less revolutionary than they might at first appear. Even premarital cohabitation, shocking as it may be to the traditionally-minded, has come to be viewed as just one more stage in a sequence that will eventually lead to the altar. But the changes that have occurred in the dating process raise important questions. The implications of the intimacy revolution for moral and religious concerns will not be dealt with here, for they are not the proper terrain for a sociologist. But the sociologist can consider the social consequences implied by such changes, and in particular the consequences for those marriages which are formed at the end of this transformed dating process. Are those marriages likely to be better or worse as a result of increased premarital intimacy?

In some sense the intimacy revolution that our figures document is the logical culmination of our system of free mate choice based upon dating. Under the "marketplace learning" conception described earlier, it is assumed that the best mate selection is an informed selection, and that making such a selection requires familiarity with alternatives and also quasimarital intimacy with serious marriage prospects. According to this concept, the more constrained mate selection environment prior to the intimacy revolution was less sensible and more risky, a sentiment conveyed vividly by Sir Thomas More in *Utopia* when he compares mate selection unfavorably with buying a horse:

> when you're choosing a wife . . . you're unbelievably careless, you don't even bother to take
> it out of its wrappings. You judge the whole woman from a few squares inches of face, which
> is all you can see of her, and then proceed to marry her—at the risk of finding her most
> disagreeable, when you see what she's really like (quoted in MacFarlane 1985, p. 166).

When this sort of argument is pursued to its limits, premarital sex, cohabitation, and even sex with other potential marital prospects, can be seen not only as acceptable, but even as valuable preparation for a successful marriage.

Yet not only moralists, but many social scientists, raise questions about whether this intimacy revolution is a "good thing." As discussed earlier, these critics argue on a number of grounds that the kinds of changes that have been documented in this chapter—increasing numbers of dating partners, earlier pairing off with a steady boyfriend, and rising premarital sexuality—are not the building blocks of strong and satisfying marriages, and may in fact lead to more brittle conjugal bonds. An effort to resolve these important debates about the consequences of the intimacy revolution for marriage relations will be presented in Chapter 7.

Notes

1. In subsequent portions . this study I will no longer include references to both male options and female options, as in this passage. Instead I will refer to females dating and mating males, since our data come from interviews with married women. However, in most instances this is just a convenient shorthand, and the logic presented could apply to the male side of the dating game as well as to the female side. Some readers may find the use of marketplace terms and analogies offensive when talking about love and marriage. However, it is now a commonplace that the process of mate choice is in all societies governed by conditions in the "marriage market," even though the nature of what is exchanged in that market and who is in charge of making the exchanges differs from one society to another. (See the discussion in Goode 1964.) Therefore this study will often make use of such marketplace analogies.

2. The extreme version of this phenomenon is when premarital intimacy leads to pregnancy and a hasty, "shotgun" wedding. In the usual case the academic and career preparation of both the husband and wife are adversely affected, although the wife is affected more seriously.

3. My inquiry here focuses on changes in dating as an ongoing institution. As noted earlier, some analysts have argued that dating is on the decline or is even dying out (see Murstein 1980). I see no evidence from our research of any such dramatic change.

4. Four of our respondents had missing information in regard to their year of marriage, leaving 455 cases for analysis here. As noted earlier, only the year of first marriages, and dating experiences prior to such marriages, are considered here.

5. The actual wording used was, "How old were you when you first went on single dates?" The insertion of the word single was meant to convey the idea that we didn't want them to consider instances of going out with a mixed sex group of friends, with no pairing off as a couple. But we did not offer respondents a specific definition of what a date was, instead leaving it up to them to interpret the term as they chose. In general respondents did not seem to have trouble knowing what the term meant, or for that matter with being able to respond to other terms we used, such as "going steady."

6. This conclusion differs from that offered by some authors—see Gagnon and Greenblat (1978). Sociological studies done in America in earlier times occasionally pointed to the age of the onset of dating being younger than our data show. Burgess and Wallin (1953, p. 119) found that the median age of first date reported by their well-educated sample of Chicago area engaged couples interviewed in 1937–1939 was 15, and in a study of youths in a small Midwestern town in the next decade Hollingshead found that more than 90% of youths of both sexes had dated by the end of their fifteenth year (Hollingshead 1949, p. 225), implying an even younger median age at the onset of dating. A national survey of high school seniors conducted in 1960 also computed a median age at first date for females of about 15 (Bayer 1968, p. 629). Of course, with our sample the process of recall may produce an upward bias in our estimates from older respondents, but if so, one would have to conclude that the age of starting dating has gotten steadily later, rather than earlier. I have not been able to think of any explanation, in terms of bias in our estimates, which would be consistent with the idea that the actual age of beginning dating has gotten earlier in more recent years.

7. There is a minor complication to this pattern. The earliest cohort in our sample has the youngest average marriage age. The median marriage age computed for cohort 1 is 17. However, due to the small number of cases involved (5), and to what is technically called "sample truncation bias"—the fact that our sample upper age limit of 75 excluded women who married in the 1920s at older ages—we consider this pattern spurious and ignore the marriage age figures for our first cohort. We use medians in these calculations rather than means because the distribution of marriage ages is highly skewed. The median indicates the age by which 50% of the cases considered (e.g., women in our prewar marriage generation, minus the first cohort within that generation) had a given experience, while the mean is simply the arithmethic average of the ages at which each woman in that group of cases had the experience. The mean ages of first marriage for our three generations (again, minus the first cohort who married prior to 1930) are 20.5, 20.5, and 22.

8. In a June 2, 1986, *Newsweek* magazine story based on this research it was claimed that a 40 year-old woman's probability of marrying was "less than her chances of being shot by a terrorist." Subsequently, these researchers acknowledged that their projections were inaccurate, and projections by the U.S. Census Bureau yielded substantially higher estimates. For example, the latter estimates were for never married women who were college graduates, between 32 and 41% of those aged 35 could still expect to marry, and between 17 and 23% of those aged 40 could still expect the same. See the discussion in Cherlin forthcoming, Chapter 5.

9. Of course, there is an age truncation bias problem that prevents us from saying whether such unusually late first marriages are more or less common in recent times. Women who first married at such unusually late ages in the 1950s and earlier would presumably be deceased and not available for interview. It might also be noted that from other information in our questionnaire we know that the interviewee who first married at age 60 was still a virgin at marriage. Apparently there are other things besides getting married for which it is never too late.

10. Part of the increase is due to the later ages of marriage of recent years, giving women more time to meet a variety of dating partners. However, both the relatively late marriage ages of our oldest women, and the fact that our early-marrying baby boom era brides reported a relatively higher number of males dated (10–14, on the average) than prewar brides, indicate that this trend is not simply a consequence of changing marriage ages.

11. Burgess and Wallin's study of middle class, engaged couples interviewed in the late 1930s showed both an earlier age of going steady (76% by age 16) and fewer women with no other steadies than their eventual husband (30.7%) than our older marriage generations show (Burgess and Wallin 1953, pp. 120, 127). I do not have a ready explanation for this divergence, but it does provide an additional piece of evidence against the view that everything is starting earlier and getting more casual in recent years.

12. There are, of course, problems of both vagueness and recall that make our conclusions here tentative. Young people may not be aware of some of the more subtle ways parents try to influence their dating patterns, and over time the less blatant instances may drop from memories. One study by Sussman interviewed parents in the New Haven area in 1950, rather than their offspring, and found more than 80% of them reported active efforts to try to influence who their youngsters went out with (see Sussman 1953). Of course, the apparent constant level of parental involvement and concern about the dating patterns of their daughters may conceal a declining ability of parents to actually influence their offspring, which in turn produces increasing resignation among parents. We will see in Chapter 5 that in some respects the younger women in our sample were more likely to "marry out" of their ethnic or religious group than were the older women, which may give some indication that actual parental influence on mate choice decisions has declined somewhat.

13. The ending of the story is also interesting. I presume that she resisted going out the door immediately, but she did keep seeing the man her parents disliked and eventually married him. Obviously, she lived to tell the tale.

14. A 1970 survey using a national sample found that sex before marriage had increased from 31% among the oldest women in the sample to 81% among the youngest (see Hunt 1974, p. 150).

15. Data collected by Zelnick and Kanter from national samples of teenage females indicate that through the 1970s premarital sexual intercourse was becoming much more common, but that the average age of first intercourse was declining only slightly—from 16.4 years of age in their 1971 sample to 16.2 years in their 1979 sample (see Zelnick and Kanter 1980). These figures look much younger than those we have computed for our recent marriage cases, but they cannot be compared directly, since Zelnick and Kanter's study would not include cases who began intercourse only after their teens or at marriage, as ours does.

16. Again this may be a somewhat conservative estimate because, as with our general premarital sex estimate, women who had sex with another partner and then started dating their eventual husbands before passing another birthday would not be detected by this method as having had sex prior to dating their husbands.

17.   Or, to look at things in another way, we can consider only those women who we calculate had sex before marriage. Of those women, the proportion in our three marriage generations who we estimate had their first sex prior to starting dating their eventual husbands is 13%, 32%, and 46%. Or, to make the comparison with the Kinsey and Hunt studies clearer, the proportion of women who had premarital sex who did so only with their eventual husbands dropped from 87% to 68% and then 54%.

18.   Opinion polls overwhelmingly support the view that the permissiveness in regard to pre-marital sex extends to exclusive romantic relationships, but not to casual or multiple relationships (see the discussion in Hunt 1974).

19.   Since the figures in the chart report average, or median ages, they give the appearance of sexual relations beginning for most women prior to marriage, even for the first marriage generation. This appearance can be attributed to the fact that rarely, if ever, does a woman delay her first sexual experience until a year or more after her marriage. So the age of first sex figures are truncated or limited by the age at marriage, while there is no comparable lower limit. Thus the median age computation for first sex ends up being lower than for age at marriage, even though most women were not beginning sex until marriage in this first generation.

20.   If we use an alternative average tendency statistic, the mean, in place of the median, the typical age of first starting to date the eventual husband can be seen actually increasing within our sample—from 18.2 to 18.5 and then 19.5 in our three marriage generations. Use of means would make the same point as clearly—with age of first sex changing from occurring about two years after starting dating the eventual husband for the oldest generation (20.2 vs. 18.2) to occurring before starting dating the husband among the most recent marriage generation (19.0 vs. 19.5).

21.   A few figures on cohabitation elsewhere allow us to put these figures in perspective. National survey data from England yield figures of 3% premarital cohabiters among those who married in 1966, 10% among those marrying in 1971–1975, and 19% among those marrying in the late 1970s. In France the increase is said to be from 17% of those marrying in 1968–69 to 44% of those marrying in 1976–1977, and in Denmark and Sweden premarital cohabitation is claimed to already be a majority phenomenon (see Freeman and Lyon 1983, pp. 57–9). A recent study in Finland and Soviet Estonia found that about 70% of the newly married Finnish and Estonian couples had lived together prior to wedlock (see Haavio-Mannila and Rannik 1987). Several recent North American studies based on couples who married in the late 1970s or early 1980s yield estimates higher than ours, thus implying that premarital cohabitation has become a majority phenomenon already. Watson (1983) studied 84 couples in Victoria, Canada and computed a figure of 64.3% premarital cohabiters, and DeMaris and Leslie (1984) in a study of 309 recently married couples in Gainesville, Florida computed a figure of 71% premarital cohabiters. Gwartney-Gibbs (1986) studied marriage license applicants in a county in Oregon and determined that the percentage of couples who had cohabited prior to marriage had risen from 13% in 1970 to 53% in 1980. One possible explanation for the higher estimates in these other studies is that they are based on samples that include remarriages as well as first marriages, unlike the Detroit area estimates shown in Figure 2.2. Previous studies indicate that premarital cohabitation is more common among the formerly married than among those who have never married.

22.   In commenting on this issue I can rely to some extent on the results of surveys I have taken over the years among students in my family sociology courses at the University of Michigan.

23.   To be sure, marriage ages have risen in recent years, and as more people delay entry into marriage some of them may end up never marrying. Popular attitudes have changed, making a life without marrying more acceptable (see Thornton and Freedman 1983). However, to a considerable extent the rise in marriage ages and increase in the projected number of individuals who may never marry are only returning American society to patterns that were common earlier in our history, after a highly atypical period in the baby boom era of unusually young and nearly universal marriage. Compared to many other advanced industrial countries, America still has relatively young marriage and a high marriage rate. However, one portion of the American population represents a possible

exception to the argument that the availability of alternatives has not produced a general tendency to avoid marriage entirely, and that is the black population. From a pattern in the past in which blacks tended to marry earlier than whites and in equal or greater proportions, the period since the 1960s has seen a dramatic reversal and a rising trend toward both late marriage and non-marriage for blacks (see Espenshade 1985).

24.   A few other studies on this issue yield figures similar to ours. A study of three generations of married women in the Columbus, Ohio, area in 1949 yielded figures ranging from 24% to 42% who had one or more other marital prospects, with a slight tendency for such prospects to be more common among the youngest generation of women (see Koller 1951). An English national survey in 1969 found that 30% of the married women interviewed had other serious marital prospects. But in the latter study older women were more likely to have had other prospects than younger women (see Gorer 1971, pp. 22–23). One study in France in 1959 reveals a different picture, with 65% of the women interviewed there claiming to have had other serious prospects (see Girard 1974, p. 156). To cite a case at the opposite extreme, in a sample of ever-married Chinese women in the city of Chengdu who were interviewed for a research project on which the author is currently collaborating, only 6% of the respondents said that they had had other prospects besides the man they eventually married (see Whyte forthcoming).

25.   In other studies, if respondents were just asked how or where they had met their spouse, they might mention a place of first meeting even when an introduction had led to that meeting.

26.   However, the "introduction by friends" category may also conceal cases of introductions that took place within a school or college context.

27.   This was an open question, and answers were coded in tenths of a mile, with a city block treated as equal to one-tenth of a mile. See Appendix 2 for the details.

28.   The fact that median figures given here do not correspond to what one might assume from examining Figure 2.1 (where the apparent courting intervals are 3, 2, and 3 years) is attributable to the difference between computing separate medians for the two ages involved versus subtracting the ages first and then computing a single median figure.

29.   In Hollingshead's study of white couples who married for the first time in New Haven in 1949–1950, 84% of the women had received an engagement ring, 89% had had an engagement stage, and 10.3 months was the average length of engagement (with 28 months the average of the dating and engagement stages together). See Hollingshead 1952, p. 310.

30.   Earlier writers discussed some stages in the development of this intimacy revolution which our survey did not examine. For example, the rise in the incidence of petting within the context of dating from the 1920s onward was the subject of much commentary. See, for example, Kinsey et al. 1953; Hunt 1974; Fass 1977.

31.   For documentation of this syndrome in earlier times, see Whyte (1943); Hollingshead (1949); Schulman (1977).

Chapter 3

MATING

In the previous chapter we examined whether the stages of, and circumstances surrounding, dating had changed over time in the experience of our Detroit respondents. This chapter examines the culmination of the dating stage—the choice of a mate and the wedding celebration—and asks the same sort of question. In particular, I want to know whether the "intimacy revolution" already examined has had any impact on the way people enter into marriage.

Two sorts of changes have been suggested in popular writing about mate choice and weddings. On the one hand, you often hear that traditional weddings are less common now than in the past. Some speculate that premarital intimacy may have led to the wedding being seen as less of a major event and almost an anticlimax, particularly for those who have already been cohabiting. Therefore, perhaps young couples feel less need in recent times to solemnify their marriages in traditional ways. At the same time, the weakening of some conventional religious views and the rise of counter-cultural phenomena have apparently led to the proliferation of unconventional weddings, a favorite topic of commentary in our mass media. In such weddings the traditional bride in white walking down the aisle of a church has been replaced by couples marrying underwater in scuba gear, in the buff at a nudist colony, in jungle gear inside a lion cage, or on nationwide television for the entertainment of Johnny Carson show viewers. I want to examine here whether weddings have really changed as much as such mass media accounts might suggest.

Another possible change in the entry into marriage concerns not the wedding, but the attitudes and commitments that the bride and groom assume toward each other and toward marriage as an institution. In this regard two somewhat contradictory trends have been suggested. One view stems from the work of the pioneering family sociologist, Ernest Burgess, who described marriage evolving in America "from institution to companionship" (see Burgess and Locke 1945). The basic idea behind these terms is that until early in this century marriage was seen as an obligatory stage of life. It was entered into for procreation and other reasons, but with no strong emphasis on the likelihood of marriage providing personal happiness and fulfillment. Over the years, with growing affluence and other changes, the "companionship" ideal increasingly supplanted this "institutional" outlook. In the new orientation, marriage was aimed at finding a partner who could provide personal happiness. Implicit in this argument is the idea that expectations toward marriage have been raised, perhaps to an unrealistically high level. Idealized and romanticized notions of marriage may cloud the minds of those about to enter the institution, and the disappointment that must inevitably ensue may be one reason that marriages have become more brittle in recent years. This scenario assumes, then, that in recent times couples have had higher expectations and more unrealistic hopes in regard to marriage than had been the case in the past.

Yet another analysis of recent trends sees things quite differently. In this alternative account, the rise in the divorce rate has made it necessary for couples to adopt a more tentative and perhaps shallow commitment as they head down the aisle. The recent rapid increase in divorce is part of a longer and more gradual rise in the brittleness of marriages in America stretching back over a century, but as the likelihood of marriages surviving "till death do us part" has shrunk to something in the neighborhood of a 50/50 proposition, those about to enter this institution have adapted to the increased uncertainty. In some accounts, this rise in the divorce rate has led to an increasing switch from a simple monogamy assumption in America to a "serial monogamy" orientation (see, for example, Alpenfels 1970). In other words, even though you can only have one spouse at a time, you may anticipate having several spouses over your lifetime—perhaps a spouse for your young adult years, another for middle age, and still another for the retirement stage. In this sort of scenario, the walk down the aisle would be accompanied not by unrealistically high expectations, but rather by low ones and perhaps serious doubts. One can imagine brides and grooms thinking to themselves, "I feel like doing this now even though it probably won't last." The result would be a tentative or shallow commitment to a particular partner at the start of the marriage.[1]

In this chapter I will examine whether these and other suppositions about changes in the American way of mating have any basis in fact. Once again I will be comparing women across three marriage generations—those who first married in the years 1925–44, 1945–64, and 1965–84—to see how their experiences differed, with occasional use of finer chronological distinctions. Here I am only concerned with the first marriages of respondents. The nature of mating in remarriages will be considered later on in this study, in Chapter 8. As in the previous chapter, I do not have as much information as I might like, but three important aspects of the mating stage can be examined. First, have the circumstances in which women find themselves at the time of their weddings changed over time? Second, have there been changes in the attitudes and feelings that women hold as they prepare to walk down the aisle?[2] Third, have there been changes in the events and rituals of the wedding itself?

Circumstances on the Brink of Marriage

In Chapter 2 we saw that the circumstances our respondents found themselves in as they prepared to marry for the first time varied in important ways across marriage generations. For instance, recent brides were more likely to have been intimate before marriage and even to have cohabited with the man they were about to marry. The age of the woman when she married also varied across generations, being youngest for those who married in the years 1945–64 and older for both those who married before 1944 and those who married after 1965. There are a number of other aspects of the woman's situation at the time of the marriage that I wish to examine in this chapter.

One issue concerns where respondents were living at the time they were preparing to walk down the aisle. In the prewar generation, 40% of the women were still living at home as they prepared for their weddings. In the baby-boom years only 22% of the brides were still living at home, even though the average bride in that generation was marrying at a younger age than in the prewar era. Finally, among recent marriage cases only 12% of the women were living at home at the time they got married.[3] A variety of circumstances are involved in this change, including young women going off to college, simply getting a separate apartment, and, in a rising number of cases recently, moving in with a fiancé. But in any case, more and more women are residentially independent of their parents even before they enter into matrimony. Insofar as separate residence makes it more difficult for parents to supervise the dating activities of their offspring, this change might be expected to lead to less parental influence over the eventual choice of mates of younger women in our sample.

This growing trend for unmarried females to reside separately from parents is not explained by a decline in the proportion of women who had parents still together at the time of their marriages. In general about 69% of the brides in the whole sample had parents who attended their weddings as a couple, and there was no significant difference across marriage generations. One may suppose that the rising number of divorces among parents has been counterbalanced by the declining likelihood of parents dying during the premarital years, leading to a more or less constant proportion of parents of brides who could attend their daughters' weddings together.

The shift toward greater residential separation from parents prior to marriage is also not due to increasing employment of brides-to-be. In our sample as a whole about 69% of all respondents reported that they were working at the time of their weddings, and there is no sign of change of this percentage across marriage generations. Together with earlier figures, these data indicate that prior to World War II, it was not uncommon for young women to continue living with their parents even after they started employment outside of the home. In more recent times this situation has changed, however, and premarital employment is usually accompanied by separate residence.[4]

If we consider not the pattern of premarital employment, but the expectations respondents had about working after marriage, however, we can see signs of a dramatic, if not surprising, change. Admittedly recollections about one's "intentions" years and decades ago are imprecise. But when we asked, "Before you married did you want to be a full-time housewife, work outside the home some of

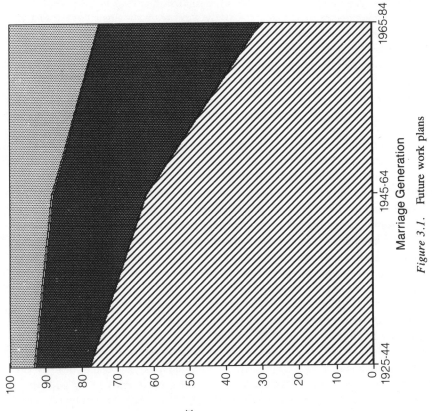

Per cent

1925-44   1945-64   1965-84

Marriage Generation

▨ Lifetime Career

■ Work Sometimes

▨ Housewife

Figure 3.1.   Future work plans

the time, or have a life-time career?" we got quite different responses from women in our three marriage generations. As one can see from Figure 3-1, there has been a dramatic decline in the proportion of brides who say they expected to be full-time housewives, from 78% to 62% to 30%. Correspondingly, the proportion of women expecting to work for pay some of the time has increased markedly, from 15% to 26% to 44% It should be noted, though, that these figures show that the proportion of women who reported the strongest work orientation at marriage—those who desired a life-time career—were still in a minority among recent marriage cases, constituting only 25% of the respondents in the final generation (compared to 7% among pre-war brides and 12% among baby-boomers).[5]

In spite of all of the changes in women's roles in American society, then, the most common expectation of recent brides is that they will work for a few years, take time off to raise children, and then resume working again later on. We do not have data for grooms, but you can bet that overwhelmingly they would say they wanted a life-time career and would not contemplate taking time off to raise young children. Both the prevailing pattern of interrupted work careers for married women (but not for married men) and the expectation of those women that they will not have a life-time career contribute to the much commented on earnings gap between men and women. Women who work full time still only earn about 60–70% (depending upon whose estimates you accept) as much as men in our society, and even if they have comparable educational credentials they are unlikely to earn as much. Expectations and a past history of continuous employment remain an important criterion for advancement in most lines of work in our society.[6]

There is little change across marriage generations in the employment situation of grooms at the time of the wedding. In all three generations about 85% of the grooms were employed full-time at the time they were married, and another 5% were working part-time. The only minor change of interest is that there was a slight increase from 3% to 8% in the proportion of grooms who were still in school in the post-World War II years, corresponding to the lower marriage ages and optimism about employment of the baby boom era. Among post-1965 marriage cases the proportion of student grooms drops back down to 4%. One other notable point about these figures is that in all periods they indicate that more grooms than brides were working at the time that they married (85% vs. 69%). Again such figures indicate that we are still some distance away from achieving a "unisex" work history pattern in America.

One further issue is whether there was parental approval of their daughter's choice of a spouse. If daughters are more independent prior to marriage than they used to be, one might expect them more often than in the past to choose men who would not be to their parents' liking. We asked respondents to tell us separately how their mother and father felt about them marrying their (first) husbands, and they were asked to respond using a five point scale: strongly approve, approve, neutral, disapprove, and strongly disapprove. If we can assume that their rec-ollections are roughly accurate, then their replies don't give us any basis for be-lieving that parental displeasure has increased. In all three generations, from 74% to 80% of both mothers and fathers were described as approving or strongly approving their daughter's marriage choice, and there was no significant dif-ference in this respect across generations. Similarly, the overwhelming majority of respondents—about 85%—perceived that their in-laws approved of their husbands' choice of them, again with no clear contrast across generations.[7]

Of course, such a simple question does not allow us to say whether such approval was willingly or grudgingly given, and perhaps parents in recent times have accepted the fact that they have little say in the matter and have voiced their approval even of selections whom they secretly despise. But at least in terms of the available evidence, there is no sign of greater generational conflict over mate choice recently than in the past, and in fact surprisingly little sign of such conflict in any generation.

One additional set of circumstances surrounding the marriage is of importance. Estimating the frequency of "shotgun weddings" in each generation—weddings precipitated by a pregnancy—and perhaps occurring earlier than desired, or even to a partner not seen as completely acceptable, is important. We did not ask about premarital pregnancies directly, but instead used a tactic that social scientists have taken over from village gossips: counting backward from the date of birth of the first child. In our questionnaire we asked for the exact date of birth of the first child and, in a separate part of the questionnaire, for the exact date of the wedding. I then somewhat arbitrarily assumed that births within the first 8 months of marriage were the product of premarital conceptions.[8] Of course, this technique is somewhat inexact, since dates may be misstated or falsified, and since the time honored explanation offered for early births—prematurity—might lead to "false positives," while miscarriages, still births, or abortions would contribute to an undercount.[9] Premarital *births* are less ambiguously categorized, being simply the cases in which the first birth occurred before the date of the wedding.

Even allowing for some lack of precision in our measure, the contrast across generations is striking (see Figure 3.2). Among prewar marriage cases 89% of first births are by this procedure considered postmaritally conceived, and the remaining 11% are all counted as premarital conceptions. There are no pre-marital births detected in this generation. In the baby boom era this situation changes markedly, as Figure 3.2 shows, and there is a modest further change seen among post-1965 marriages. The proportion of postmarital conceptions drops from 89% to 75% and then increases slightly to 78%. Approximately 25% of all first births among women who married after 1945 were premaritally con-ceived, according to this estimating procedure. However, the most striking trend seen in the figure is the increase in the proportion of premarital births—from 0 to 6% and then to 9%. One in eleven brides in the sample who married after 1965

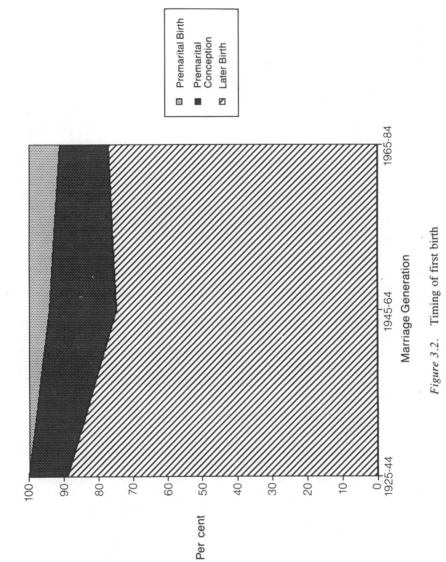

Figure 3.2. Timing of first birth

had already given birth prior to her wedding day.[10] And here the twenty-year grouping conceals further changes within the final marriage generation. The proportion of brides who had given birth "out of wedlock" in the five-year marriage cohorts within our final generation increased as follows: from 5% to 7% and then to 14% and finally 10%. In other words, of those who married within the last ten years, roughly one in eight had already given birth prior to getting married.[11]

These figures indicate a clear increase in both premarital conceptions and premarital births. However, two cautionary notes should be mentioned. First, it is likely that there is some general tendency to undercount cases of premarital conceptions and births by this method. In other words, the total number of cases of conception prior to marriage is likely to be greater than these figures indicate.[12] But that might not affect the verdict of a substantial increase across generations. However, it is also likely that some systematic bias is operating here that may lead to an exaggeration of the trend. I suspect, and other studies confirm, that older respondents are more likely to be embarrassed by premarital conceptions in their histories than younger respondents, and therefore they are more likely to take steps in responding to a questionnaire to conceal that history. If so, then this sort of reporting bias will lead to a sharper increase in the rates of premarital conceptions we calculate than really occurred.[13]

I cannot be certain that all of the increase shown in Figure 3.2 is "real," rather than being a product of reporting bias. However, there is enough other evidence of increasing rates of premarital conception and illegitimacy in America in recent years to allow me to state that the nature of the trend is quite certain, even if the specific percentages may be open to doubt. A major factor contributing to this trend is, of course, the intimacy revolution among the unmarried that was discussed in the previous chapter. There has also been a rise in the availability and use of contraceptives as well as in abortions over the same period, and one might have thought that these changes would make possible an intimacy revolution without a rise in premarital conceptions and births. Evidently this has not happened. Our figures are in line with national surveys that show rates of illegitimate births increasing by about 250% between 1940 and the late 1960s (see Smith 1973).[14]

Several explanations for the increase in premarital conceptions in spite of the contraceptive revolution are usually offered. Zelnick and Kanter (1980) argue that the rate of entry into premarital sex has simply risen faster than the increase in the rate of adoption of contraception among the unmarried. And many commentators argue that in today's more liberal sexual climate, premarital pregnancies and even premarital births are not as shameful as they once were. It is well to recall that in colonial times married couples who had an "early birth" were often subjected to a fine or to whipping (see Smith and Hindus 1975, p. 554.). Indeed, the trend we observe makes a term like "shotgun wedding" appear increasingly out of date and perhaps inappropriate. In recent times it is clear that pregnancy is less likely to lead to a rush to the altar than in the past. Abortion is, of course, one way to deal with a premarital pregnancy, but an increasing number of women are avoiding abortion and having the child "on their own." Only later will they perhaps marry the father, or some other alternative prospect.[15]

In sum, in the preceding pages we have seen that the circumstances brides found themselves in at the time they first married had altered in some respects but not in others. However, in the areas where change has occurred, it is dramatic. The employment status of the bride and groom, whether her parents were still together at the time of the wedding, and the degree of parental approval of the match did not vary much across marriage generations. However, in recent times brides have been more likely to be living on their own at the time of the wedding, more likely to be pregnant or to have already given birth, and more likely to be contemplating a life that includes at least extended periods of work outside the home.

Feelings Prior to the Wedding

I also wanted to determine whether the feelings of brides—toward marriage as an institution and toward the spouse they selected—had changed across generations with regard to the "higher expectations" or "serial monogamy" scenarios. Here I am on shaky ground, because we are dealing with retrospective reports about feelings the women had as brides, often years or even decades earlier. It is quite plausible that events since then, and in particular the subsequent fate of their marriages, may influence what they recollect today regarding their feelings when they first married. In this section a partial solution to this problem of biased recall is adopted. Figures are compared in two ways: first, by examining all of our respondents; and second, considering only those respondents whose first marriages did not end in divorce or separation. The assumption underlying this procedure is that in the second instance I will eliminate from the analysis those cases where current reports on premarital feelings are likely to be negatively biased.[16]

Respondents were asked a number of questions about their feelings at the time of their marriages. First, we asked the respondents how much in love they were with their grooms, and we presented them with a 7-point scale in which only the end-points were labeled. Scale point 1 was labeled "head over heels" and point 7 was labeled "not at all in love." Not surprisingly, women in all marriage generations clustered near the "head over heels in love" end of the scale. Forty-seven percent of all our respondents gave this reply, another 22% picked scale point 2, and a further 14% selected scale point 3. In other words, a total of 83% of our respondents gave answers indicating high degrees of love felt at the time of the marriage. At the other end, only 4% reponded that they had not been in love at all.[17] Furthermore, there is no clear difference across marriage generations in these love scores, whether or not we exclude the cases that ended in divorce or separation. These responses do not give us any basis for supposing that women who married recently had either more shallow commitments or idealized views of their partners.[18]

We further asked our respondents whether they sought advice about whether to marry their husbands, assuming that such requests for advice would indicate hesitancy or lack of complete commitment to the partner.[19] However, in this regard as well there is little difference across marriage generations. Nine percent of prewar brides, 18% of baby boom era brides, and 16% of recent brides report asking someone for advice, and so there is no consistent time trend.[20] Very few brides in any generation seem to seek out advice about whether to marry their chosen partner. However, when we asked respondents directly whether in the weeks prior to their marriages they had major doubts, minor doubts, or no doubts at all about their decision, there was a modest trend visible. The proportion with no doubts at all went down from 71% in our prewar generation and 70% among baby-boomers to 58% among our recent brides; the proportion reporting major doubts increased from 8% to 9% to 13% in this same comparison.[21] Whereas the major thrust of all of these figures is that now, as in the past, the great majority of women march down the aisle confident of their choice and deeply in love, still there is this one slight indication that the entertaining of doubts has become a little more common recently.

Finally, we asked our respondents directly, "When you first got married, do you feel that you had a realistic or unrealistic view of what married life would be like?" The answers to this question followed a curvilinear pattern across marriage generations. Seventy percent of the prewar brides claimed they had a realistic view, and 67% of our recent brides gave the same response. However, only 58% of our baby boom era brides felt that at marriage they had a realistic view about married life. Similarly, women of this middle generation reported the highest level of unrealistic views—36%, as opposed to 18% and 29% for our other two generations. (Neutral responses account for the remainder.) Various controls for the stability and quality of the subsequent marriage did not eliminate this curvilinear pattern (details not shown here). These results suggest, then, that the baby boom era may have been associated with somewhat less realistic expectations about the nature of marriage. This pattern is not too surprising, in view of the unusually young ages at marriage of many women in that generation. However, such figures do not provide much support for the overall "heightened expectations" argument. First, the recollected romantic feelings at the time of marriage do not show the pattern of increases across generations that the heightened expectations argument would lead us to expect. Second, the lack of realism reported by baby boom era brides has now been reversed, with more recent brides reporting that they had a good idea of what they were getting into.

I acknowledge that it is difficult now to accurately judge the state of mind (and heart) of our respondents when they first married years ago. Perhaps our questions are too crude and subjective, and the chances for intervening experiences to bias recollections too great to place complete faith in the results reported in this section. But these results do provide suggestive clues to feelings at the time of marriage that are worth pursuing in future research—through longitudinal studies of couples who are about to get married. There is some partial support in the responses to our "doubts" question for the "serial monogamy" argument, which assumes growing hesitancy and partial commitment at the time of the wedding. However, in responses to our "realism" question, there is some evidence for the alternative, "heightened expectations" argument, if only for baby boom era brides.

Perhaps these two scenarios are not, after all, so contradictory. It may be that in recent times people do expect more from a marriage partner, and precisely because of this fact, they may entertain some doubts that the chosen partner, or perhaps any partner, could satisfy their expectations. In other words, marriage itself may be idealized and persistently pursued even while particular partners are recognized as unlikely to be able to provide the idealized marital relationship that is being sought. Before following this analysis further, we must recognize that it receives only minor and very partial support from the Detroit area data. The main thrust of our results is that there is substantial continuity across generations in the feelings brides recall having as they prepared to walk down the aisle. And the predominant feelings include a strong love commitment, few if any doubts, and a perception that they know what marriage will be like. If we can trust the recollections reported here, neither the "unrealistic expectations" or "serial monogamy" argument is accurate as a characterization of the situation of the majority of brides in any recent generation.

The Wedding Ceremony

The culmination of dating and mating is, of course, the wedding itself. This section examines whether the nature of wedding activities and rituals has changed in recent times. The major question to consider here is whether weddings have become less traditional in form or whether entry into marriage is less dramatically marked by ritual than in the past. Consideration of this issue is an extension of the analysis in the previous chapter, where I questioned whether the intimacy revolution that has affected dating made marriage less "special" than it used to be. There I argued that greater premarital intimacy had been incorporated into our system of mate choice, rather than undermining it, but further evidence on this point can be obtained by examining what is happening to weddings. If traditional and elaborate weddings are being celebrated less today than in the past, such a trend might indicate that the meaning of marriage has begun to change.

The reader should note, however, that the term "traditional" is used in regard to wedding ceremonies in a limited sense. The contrast drawn is with the approved middle-class American wedding customs earlier in the 20th century—not exactly an ancient tradition. A look back in earlier American history reveals that in colonial times almost none of the rituals we associate with such "traditional" weddings existed. Weddings were originally civil, rather than religious; they were simple rather than elaborate in most cases; and they were not accompanied by bridal showers, honeymoons, or other elements that we take to be so familiar. It was only in the 19th century did the elements we associate with "traditional" weddings begin to be widely celebrated (see Demos 1970; Rothman 1984, Chapter 2).

One fundamental question about weddings in recent times is whether they are religious or civil. We asked respondents, "Were you married by a religious official—for example, by a minister, priest, or rabbi?" It turns out that the great majority of women in our sample—82%—answered yes to this question. There is no noticeable difference in this regard across marriage generations (or even if we examine finer time divisions). So there is no sign that civil weddings are becoming more common, as they might be expected to if a less formal and more casual attitude toward marriage was gaining hold.[22]

For more specific details, we then asked our respondents a follow-up question: "Where did the marriage take place?" We coded the answers to this open-ended question into four categories: (1) religious institutions (church, synagogue, etc.); (2) in the home; (3) city hall, justice of the peace office, etc.; and (4) other. At this stage there is a slight contrast across generations, but it points toward more church weddings rather than less. The proportion of all weddings that took place in church (category 1) increased from 68% in our first two marriage generations to 74% in the most recent one, while the proportion taking place at home or in "other" locales dropped from 17% to 12% to 10%.[23] It is interesting to note that only 5 women in the entire sample had weddings in "other" locales—in a park, in a hotel, etc. If the wedding is not held in a church or synagogue, it is almost always held either in a civil wedding locale (such as a justice of the peace's office) or in the home. The unorthodox wedding locales so often featured in the mass media—on horses at a rodeo, on a yacht at sea, while sky diving, etc.—are not a gro⋅ʻng trend in a representative population, but rather rare events. So neither civil weddings nor weddings in off-beat locales are making any detectable inroads into the traditional mode of marriage ceremonies in a church or synagogue.[24]

Weddings are often preceded by other ritual events. Traditional forms include one or more bridal showers—parties given by the friends of the bride to celebrate the upcoming "happy event" and to bestow gifts upon her. The rough counterpart for the groom, the bachelor party, has a different emotional tone. It is an occasion, usually on the night before the wedding, for the groom's friends to take him out drinking (preferably to excess) to mourn his last night as a bachelor. We asked our respondents separately about both of these events, and it turns out that each is substantially more common in recent weddings than in earlier ones. The proportion of our respondents who had at least one bridal shower was 39% for the prewar marriage generation, 57% for baby boom era brides, and 68% for recent marriage cases.[25] Regarding bachelor parties the same trend was visible. Among prewar brides only 14% reported bachelor parties being held for their grooms, while 36% of baby boom era brides and 51% of recent brides mentioned this event.[26]

The same picture of increasing elaborateness of weddings in recent years appears when we consider measures of the scale of the wedding celebrations themselves. We asked respondents to estimate how many people attended their wedding and, if a reception was held afterward, how many attended the reception. Although failing memories may make these reports subject to considerable error, the replies point to a possible increase in the scale of weddings. The median number of people estimated for prewar weddings was 30, for baby boom era weddings 50, and for recent weddings 80. Only 64% of our prewar respondents reported holding a wedding reception, whereas 78% of our baby boom era brides and 88% of recent brides indicated that they had wedding receptions. The number attending these receptions has increased even more than is the case in regard to the wedding itself—from a median of 50 in prewar weddings to 100 in the baby boom era and 150 recently.[27] So these figures point to weddings becoming more ceremonially elaborate, rather than less.[28]

Weddings that are ceremonially elaborate are also costly.[29] Have there been changes in who pays for the wedding? It is usually considered "traditional" for the bride's family to pay for most of the wedding expenses. When we inquired who had paid for the wedding, it turned out that the majority of weddings in all periods were not too traditional in this respect. In only 38% of the weddings did the bride's family handle most of the wedding expenses. In another 18% of the weddings the bride's parents shared the burden either with the bride and groom or with the groom's parents, or with both. Then in 37% of the cases the bride or the groom or both handled the expenditures themselves. (In the remaining 7% of the weddings either the groom's parents or some other relatives bore the main burden.) There is no significant difference across marriage generations in who pays, although there are some minor trends apparent. For example, the groom alone paying for the wedding has become slightly less common over time, while the couple together or the bride alone paying has become somewhat more common. In sum, in all periods it is about as common for the young couple to pay for their own wedding expenses as it is for the bride's parents to pay. As far as I can tell there have been no major changes in the pattern of payment for weddings.

The wedding and reception are customarily followed by a honeymoon. In this regard minor changes are visible in our data. There is a slight (but statistically nonsignificant) increase in the proportion of women reporting any sort of honeymoon—from 47% among prewar brides to 51% among baby boom era brides and 60% among recent brides. (For those married in the Detroit area the increase

is from 56% to 62% overall.) The amount of time spent on the average honeymoon has not changed across generations—the median number of days is 7 in all
three.[30] But with improved transportation, recent brides have been able to go
further than in the past. The number of honeymoons to other regions of the
country increased from 37% to 50% from prewar times to the post-1965 period,
and over the same period honeymoons outside of the U.S. increased from 3% to
12%. In sum, there is only a modest amount of change in regard to the honeymoon stage, but what change there is is in the direction of more elaborateness,
rather than less.

In Figure 3.3 a large amount of the material presented in this section is
summarized graphically. There the reader can see how common various parts of
the wedding ceremonial are relative to one another and whether there has been
any change over time. In terms of relative frequency of various ritual acts, there
are a few patterns to note which are not obvious from the chart. For example,
wedding receptions used to be held after almost all church weddings, but not
generally after civil weddings. Now receptions are expected for civil and religious ceremonies alike and, indeed, for all but the smallest and simplest weddings. Honeymoons also turn out to be more optional than is often thought. But
one pattern in the figure produces our dominant impression of these results. For
all of these stages in the wedding ritual, there has either been continuity or
increasing frequency of their performance in more recent generations. In the
experience of people in the Detroit area, weddings clearly have not become less
elaborate and more casual in recent years.[31] This general pattern provides additional evidence for the decline in conventions discussed in previous chapters. As
participation in a fuller set of wedding activities becomes more common, the
status barriers separating those who get married in the "proper fashion" from
those who do not have weakened.

Sooner or later, as the saying goes, the honeymoon is over. The final aspect of
the mating process to consider is where the couple live when they return from the
honeymoon. We asked respondents about their living arrangements in the first 6
months after their weddings. It turns out that in this realm there has been a
dramatic change. Of prewar couples, 42% started out their marriages living with
one or another set of parents at least part of the time. (And residence with the
groom's parents and the bride's parents was about equally likely.) This pattern
was still found for 30% of baby boom era marriages, but only in 10% of all
post-1965 marriages (see Figure 3.4). Correspondingly, the proportion of couples
who started their married lives in "their own place" increased from 47% to 64%
and then to 85%. (The remaining cases involved other circumstances, such as the
groom going off into military service.) Clearly the growing residential independence of women before their marriages is more than matched by a rising trend
toward residential independence after their weddings. While it used to be common to begin married life living with parents, that sort of arrangement has now
become much more unusual.[32]

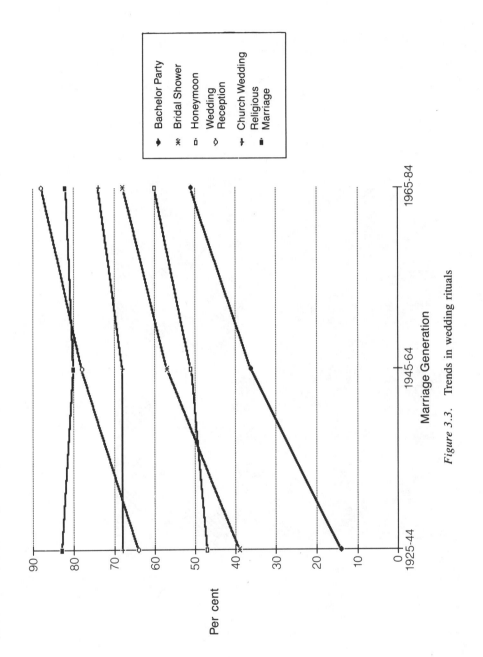

Legend:

♦ Bachelor Party
✳ Bridal Shower
▫ Honeymoon
◇ Wedding
  Reception
✝ Church Wedding
▪ Religious
  Marriage

Per cent

Marriage Generation

Figure 3.3. Trends in wedding rituals

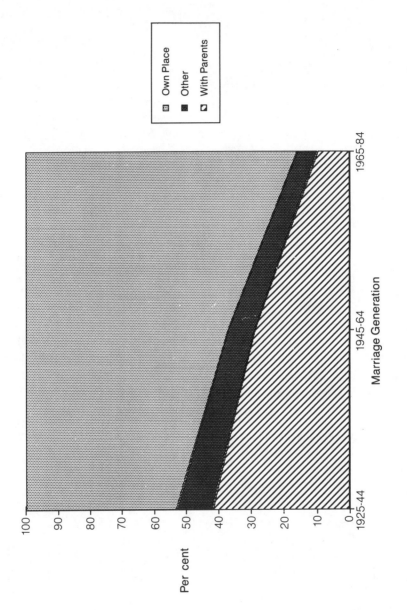

Figure 3.4. Couple's residence after wedding

Conclusions

This chapter began by asking whether weddings had become more simplified and casual, and whether the intimacy revolution had transformed the way marriage was viewed. On both counts the evidence presented here is negative. To be sure, we do see some signs of change in the experiences of different marriage generations. Women who married recently were more likely to be premaritally pregnant and to be living apart from their parents, both before and after the wedding. But the major message of this chapter is that "traditional" aspects of mating have persisted or have even increased. There is no indication in these results that weddings are becoming more casual or less traditional. Instead, they have become if anything more elaborate—stages of the wedding that used to be optional are more obligatory in recent years.

This persistence and elaboration of wedding rituals is striking and even in many ways puzzling. In an era in which fewer brides are virgins, increasing numbers are pregnant or already have had babies, and a significant portion are already living with their grooms-to-be, why is the fuss and bother (not to mention expense) of a formal wedding needed? While I have stressed the elements of continuity in recent weddings, it is certainly the case that this continuity on the surface conceals changes in interpretation. For instance, although we did not ask in our questionnaire about wedding garments, it is obvious that one would be foolish nowadays to assume that brides who wear white gowns are all virgins. Formal white wedding gowns are seen as the standard, regardless of the prior history of the bride.[33] Under changed circumstances, a number of interesting innovations in wedding rituals occur. For example, the newspaper advice columnist Abigail van Buren published a letter concerning a wedding invitation sent out, not by the bride's parents, but under the name of the 3 month old son of the bride- and groom-to-be.[34] Clearly the effort to reconcile the intimacy revolution with traditional wedding rituals results in combinations that some may find quite jarring. But our findings indicate that a full elaboration of wedding activities is expected, regardless of the premarital history of the couple.[35] Further, I stress that these trends can be interpreted in terms of the weakening of conventions—in this case, of the conventions that dictated who was and was not expected to engage in the full set of wedding rituals.[36]

Several reasons why weddings today are as elaborate, if not more so, as in the past can be suggested. In a certain sense the intimacy revolution makes wedding rituals still very important. Weddings, like other life-cycle rituals, symbolically mark the transition from one set of roles and expectations to another. In the past, virgins who were still living with their parents entered into marriage and became husband and wife. There was not much doubt about entering into a new set of roles and expectations. But now, with virginity no longer expected and premarital cohabitation on the rise, there is more ambiguity about what differentiates marriage from the premarital stage. Yet marriage remains different in crucial ways from cohabitation or other forms of premarital intimacy. Marriage is still viewed ideally as a permanent relationship, one with a deep set of mutual obligations between partners and expectations of sexual faithfulness. Wedding rituals help to symbolically stress the differences between two stages that seem so much alike; thus an elaborate wedding is intended to mark the fact that the couple is entering a fundamentally new status.

A wedding also assembles an audience of relatives and friends to give public recognition and support to that new status. As John Modell (1985, p. 86) states the case in explaining the American preference for religious weddings, "the ceremony marks marriage as an institution worthy of communal celebration and communal oversight." In one sense we might say that it is symbolically appropriate for the nonvirginal bride to wear a white wedding gown. For in a way she is becoming a virgin again, insofar as she is pledging, in front of the assembled guests, to give up her liberal premarital sexual behavior for the faithfulness that is still expected of wives (as it is of husbands).[37]

This discussion raises the question, though, of whether these symbolic statements via wedding ceremonies really make a difference. In other words, does having an elaborate wedding really strengthen the ritual specialness of the marital state and thus promote more stable and happier marriages? Or rather should the persistence of elaborate weddings be seen as an example of "cultural lag," of a failure of popular behavior to adapt to a new situation in which marriages no longer carry the same assumptions about deep obligations and faithfulness? In this sense are elaborate weddings an ineffective gesture left over from a bygone age? In Chapter 7 the question of whether the nature of the wedding celebrations makes any difference for the subsequent marital relationship will be considered.

The need to symbolically distinguish marriage from the dating or cohabiting stage is not the only reason for the persistence of elaborate weddings. The fact that in some respects weddings have not only been maintained but have become more elaborate alerts us to other considerations. Most of the members of our first marriage generation "tied the knot" during the depression or World War II. Perhaps the simplest explanation of the increases in wedding elaborateness that have taken place is that as "abnormal" times were replaced by postwar peace and rising prosperity, more couples and families found themselves in a situation in which an elaborate wedding was possible and desirable. Increasingly, working-class and minority group families were able to copy the wedding customs of the American middle class. During postwar conditions there were fewer excuses one could use to opt out of the full cycle of wedding activities.

Weddings do more, after all, than demarcate two stages in the life of the couple. They also are a symbolic way of asserting and displaying the status of the families involved. During more settled times and with greater affluence, more families are able to enter status competition via wedding celebrations. Wedding announcements in the newspapers serve to convey such status claims to the general public not invited to the festivities. In this sort of argument, what governs the nature of the wedding is not so much the premarital history of the couple, but such things as the economic status and the community position of the families involved. If this is the case, then our finding that wedding celebrations have escalated in elaborateness is really not very surprising after all.[39]

As a final note, I should clarify the argument just made by stating that the expenditures on a large wedding are not simply a wasteful form of conspicuous consumption. For the couple there is often real economic benefit received in the form of wedding gifts—toasters, blenders, dishes, and so forth (not to mention cash)—brought by the wedding guests. When the senior generation bears the main burden of paying the expenses, then a wedding may be seen as a way one generation indirectly endows another with the furnishings for a new home, as the parents pay and the bride and groom receive (the wedding gifts). Even if the young couple is paying many of the bills for the wedding, it is at least debatable whether in a pure economic sense they are suffering a loss or making a profit. In any case, the trend toward immediate separate residence after the wedding, which we saw in Figure 3.4, provides another support for elaborate weddings. When you intend to set up a new household, then finding a mechanism for furnishing that household as completely as possible is important, and the gift-giving that is obligatory at a formal wedding is one ready-made mechanism. "Bridal registries" that department stores establish to enable couples to specify what silver pattern, glassware, and so forth they want to receive, and which are designed at the same time to avoid having them end up with, e.g., five toasters, make this consideration quite explicit.

This discussion may appear rather crass, however I am suggesting that an elaborate wedding serves several functions. It serves notice that the couple is entering into a new set of roles and obligations associated with marriage, it mobilizes community support behind their new status, it enables the families involved to display their status to the surrounding community, and it makes it easier for newly marrying couples to establish an independent household. It is in the context of these multiple motives, and in spite of the intimacy revolution, that the increasing elaborateness of weddings observed here makes sense.

Notes

1. One might imagine this sort of thinking leading to alienation from marriage as an institution, rather than just from a particular partner. There is some sign in other societies, such as the Soviet Union, of a growing number of divorced people who don't remarry and don't intend to (see Shlapentokh 1984, Chapter 8). Most studies in American society suggest that those who divorce generally wish to remarry, and that as the divorce rate has gone up the remarriage rate has also risen. However, not all of those who wish to remarry will succeed in doing so, and some recent studies suggest modest declines in the proportions of divorced persons who will remarry (see, for example, Thornton and Freedman, 1983; Norton and Moorman 1987). The rise in the divorce rate showed signs of tapering off or even reversing in the mid-1980s, and if that trend continues the scenario outlined here of "serial monogamy" would become less plausible.

2.   In dealing with this question it is, of course, unfortunate that I don't have comparable information from married men.

3.   These figures may somewhat overstate the percentage of women still living at home, since they are based upon separate questions about the age when the woman left home and her age at marriage. Those who left home and then got married subsequently within the same year would therefore be counted incorrectly as having lived at home until marriage. One popular book on weddings gives a much higher figure of brides living at home until marriage circa 1970–67%, but this is apparently due to being based upon surveys conducted by bridal magazines, whose readers may be atypically traditional or family-bound (see Seligson 1973, p. 38). On the general trend toward earlier departure from the home in the U.S. in this century, see Goldscheider and LeBourdais 1986. This trend is not incompatible with another that has received publicity in recent years—"boomerang children," who leave home but then return to take up residence in the parental home once again at a later stage. On the latter trend, see Heer, Hodge, and Felson (1985); Glick and Lin (1986).

4.   Unfortunately, I don't have information about whether this change means that the financial relations between working daughters and their parents have changed. One might guess that this increase in separate residence means that unmarried daughters are less likely to contribute any part of their earnings to their parents now, but it is not clear how common such contributions occurred in the past.

5.   The crude grouping of women into generations 20 years in length does not conceal a more marked trend in this case. Looking at the four marriage cohorts in this final generation, the proportion wanting life-time careers was 14%, 34%, 30% and 26%. In other words, the women within this generation who married most recently were not consistently the ones most likely to want a career.

6.   In these regards, of course, there is nothing distinctive or deficient about America compared with other industrial societies, where roughly the same kinds of earnings gaps exist (see the discussion in Whyte 1984).

7.   For comparison purposes, one survey conducted in France in 1959 found that the percentage of families favorable or very favorable toward their son or daughter's choice of a spouse was in the range 77–81% (see Girard 1974, p. 121).

8.   See Smith and Hindus (1975) for a summary of studies using this sort of technique.

9.   One study that compared dates given to interviewers with data collected from marriage and birth registrations and hospital records found a worrisome undercount that the seemingly precise questionnaire reports yielded (see Coombs et al. 1970). It should also be noted that 5% of our respondents who had children did not provide information on the date of first birth or marriage or both, and one may suppose that some of them may be embarrassed women who conceived or gave birth premaritally. It seems likely, then, that our figures somewhat underestimate the percentage of premarital conceptions. They may still be suitable for gauging trends across time.

10.   For comparison purposes, we note that a study of a national sample of brides in France in 1959 estimated that 4% had given birth prior to the wedding, 15% within the first 8 months afterward, and the remaining 81% subsequently (see Girard 1974, p. 167).

11.   We don't know in what proportion of these cases the father was the eventual husband, or some other male.

12.   However, I might note that there is a fairly close correspondence between our premarital conception figures and those derived by more precise methods by Coombs et al. (1970) using DAS and other data circa 1960. They calculate 19–20% premarital conceptions from information on birth and marriage dates and then revise this to 25% using actual records rather than respondent accounts. We estimate that 24% of the marriages between 1955 and 1964 in our sample involved premarital conceptions ($N = 92$), a figure that agrees quite closely with that derived from direct records checks.

13.   See Smith (1973) on the influence of this bias in other studies.

14.   However, it has also been observed that "teenage pregnancies" have declined, apparently in substantial part due to increases in abortion and in contraception (see Vinovskis 1988). But births out of wedlock among those over age 20 have not shown the same decline, and for women of all ages

premarital pregnancy is less likely now than in the past to lead to marriage; therefore the overall number of births out of wedlock has continued to increase, even as teenage pregnancies have declined.

15. Women who had babies "out of wedlock" and did not subsequently marry at all were not eligible for inclusion in our study, in which only ever-married women were interviewed. Thus our data understate the scale of the phenomenon of births to unmarried women. As noted in Appendix 1, the increasing number of women in the Detroit area who had never married was a major reason why our sample fell short of the target number of 500 cases.

16. Women who have been widowed are included with those still married to their first husbands under this second procedure on the assumption that they will not share this sort of negative bias. Of course, even women who are still married to their first husbands may have their recollections influenced by the current state of their marital relations, and therefore biases can be positive as well as negative. Thus the conclusions reached in this section should be viewed as tentative.

17. If I exclude the cases of marriages that ended in divorce or separation, the percentages with high love scores increase to 51%, 24%, and 15%, and those not in love at all drop to 2%. For comparison purposes, one study of engaged couples in the late 1930s in the Chicago area reported that only 25% of the women said they were head over heels in love. But a 7 point scale was not used, and 68% chose the next category, "very much so," (see Burgess and Wallin 1953, p. 170).

18. Even when the stability and quality of the marriage were partialled out, there was no significant correlation between these retrospective love scores and the year a woman married. (Results not shown here. The measures of marriage stability and quality used in this study are discussed in Chapter 7.)

19. One English study of marriages in the 1950s found that those individuals who had sought advice before the wedding were more, rather than less, likely to have marital difficulties later on. The researcher suggests that such advice seeking indicates awareness of potential problems (see Pierce 1963, p. 228).

20. The small differences in percentages are not statistically significant. If cases of divorce or separation are excluded, the figures drop to 7%, 16%, and 16%.

21. Omission of cases of divorces and separations does not affect this trend. In the remainder of the sample the proportion with "no doubts" goes from 73% in the prewar generation to 62% in the recent generation, and the proportion with "major doubts" goes from 5% to 10% in this same comparison. The correlation of a three category "doubts" score with actual year of marriage is not reduced when the stability or quality of the marriage is partialled out (results not shown here). These retrospective estimates may understate the general level of doubts in all periods. One study of engaged couples in the Chicago area in the late 1930s indicated that nearly half admitted some "hesitation" about marrying their fiancés (see Burgess and Wallin 1953, p. 180).

22. Various studies in the U.S. in the 1930s and 1940s found from 70% to 96% of the couples surveyed had religious ceremonies (see Burgess and Wallin 1953, p. 17). More systematic data shows that in 1965 in the United States 80.6% of the weddings were religious, in 1975, 79% were religous, and in 1983 (the last year available to me) 75.9% were religious. In Michigan the percentage of religious weddings in those same three years was 77.6%, 83.9%, and 84.6% (see U.S. Department of Health and Human Services 1965; 1975; 1983). These figures do not take us back as far as the Detroit survey data do, but they hint that while there may be a slight trend toward more civil marriages in the United States generally, in Michigan the trend is modestly in the reverse direction, with an increasing proportion of religious weddings. If we consider a longer span of time, Modell (1985) argues that nationally, American weddings have fluctuated in the range of 75–80% religious since the 1930s, with no clear trend. In a French study in 1959 (Girard 1974, p. 134) it was found that 90% of the couples surveyed had had religious weddings. However, in England there has been a long-term decline in religious weddings, and civil weddings have risen from under 10% all weddings in the mid-19th century to nearly 50% in 1970 (see Leonard 1980, p. 212).

23. The proportion of weddings in a court or justice of the peace office fluctuated from 15% to 21% to 17%. The differences across generations, it should be noted, are not large enough to be

statistically significant. These percentages for church weddings are lower than those for religious marriages because many weddings in the home are conducted by ministers. It might be noted that a study of weddings in the New Haven area in 1949–50 found that 81% of those involving first marriages were church weddings (see Hollingshead 1952, p. 311). The slightly higher figure than in our study may be due to the fact that New Haven is an even more heavily Catholic city than Detroit, with the obligation to marry in church felt more heavily by Catholics than by Protestants.

24. It should be noted, though, that in the 68% of our total sample in which the wedding took place in the Detroit area there is a slight (but not statistically significant) tendency for weddings in church to decrease across generations, while in our cases where the weddings took place elsewhere there is a similar slight tendency for weddings in church to increase across generations.

25. For those married in the Detroit area, the percentages were higher but also showed an increase—from 50% to 66% and then 73%. In Hollingshead's study of New Haven weddings in 1949–50 (1952, p. 311), 81% were marked by bridal showers. This higher figure may be due again to New Haven's Catholicism, or perhaps also in part to the greater recall problems of Detroit respondents.

26. Here the recall problem may exaggerate this trend, since brides do not attend bachelor parties and may not always be informed when they take place. But in this case Hollingshead's figure of 34% of 1949–50 New Haven weddings having bachelor parties (1952, p. 311) is quite close to our baby boom era figure.

27. For comparison purposes, in Hollingshead's study of couples marrying for the first time in New Haven in 1949–50, 88% were reported to have held receptions, and the average reception attendance was 166 (see Hollingshead 1952, p. 311).

28. Some other work on weddings also argues that elaborateness and expenditure have increased (see, for example, Seligson 1973). However, there is one important qualification in our data. In general, the weddings of those respondents who married in the Detroit area (68% of the total sample) were somewhat more elaborate and well-attended than those that took place in other locales. For example, even in earlier marriage generations about 88% of the women who married in the Detroit area held receptions. But in addition, the contrast between modest weddings in early generations and elaborate ones in recent generations is greater in those cases that occurred outside of the Detroit area. So from our data it looks as if weddings in the Detroit area have generally been more elaborate than in the other locales from which our respondents are likely to have come, and that the increasing elaborateness observed in the figures presented in this section is mainly a product of changes that occurred in those other locales. Within the portion of our sample who married in the Detroit area there is still some trend toward increasing elaborateness in weddings, but it is less marked than that observed within the portion of the sample who married elsewhere.

29. Due to the problems caused by inflation and failing memories, no effort was made to obtain estimates of the total cost of the weddings of respondents. I assume that in general, weddings with more ritual stages and with more people invited will be more expensive, and thus questions about these other aspects of wedding ceremonies can serve as indirect indicators of expenditures on getting married.

30. In Hollingshead's study of New Haven first marriages in 1949–50 he found that 95% were followed by a wedding trip, and that the average trip lasted 9 days (see Hollingshead 1952, p. 311).

31. I examined finer time divisions by 5 year marriage cohorts to see if I could detect another pattern suggested to me: that weddings got simpler and more casual during the "hippie" era of the 1960s, but have since become more traditional and elaborate. However, I could not detect any such temporary down-turn in percentages for the presence of various wedding rituals, although perhaps the sample is too small to be certain. So my main conclusion stands. As in other realms discussed in this chapter, the phenomena focused on by the mass media, such as simplified and unconventional weddings, seem to be peripheral to the experience of most of the population.

32. In studies outside of the U.S. this sort of immediate separate residence is much more unusual than in the Detroit area today. In a sample of Leningrad marriages in 1962, Kharchev found that 38%

of the couples planned to live with one or another set of parents (see Kharchev 1965, p. 145). Similarly, a study of weddings in Swansea, Wales, found that 42% of the cases involved postmarital residence with parents (see Leonard 1980, p. 228). And Rosser and Harris (1965, p. 250), who did research in the same area, claim that residence with parents has increased over time in Swansea, due to the housing shortage. Similarly, a study of recent marriage cases in urban China found that 41% of the time, the newly married couple lived with one or another set of parents—in this case generally the husband's (see Whyte 1984, p. 234).

33.   There is increasing debate about whether a formal white wedding gown is appropriate in a second marriage. In other words, this sort of gown does not even necessarily indicate that the bride is marrying for the first time.

34.   "Dear Abby," *The Ann Arbor News,* August 7, 1985, p. E-1.

35.   In Chapter 4 we will see, however, that when all things are held constant, couples who have cohabited and brides who are pregnant are likely to have less elaborate weddings than others.

36.   Of course, this trend might be viewed in another light as representing and strengthening a new convention—that virtually everybody is expected to have an elaborate wedding. However, the important distinction is that the links between social status and certain kinds of premarital and wedding behavior have weakened. Precisely by becoming more widespread, if not obligatory, elaborate weddings show that the old conventions that made such weddings the preserve of prosperous families and virginal brides are no longer with us.

37.   In spite of mass media discussion of "open marriages" and other behaviors that are said to indicate a weakening of the expectation of marital fidelity, research indicates that in this regard there is little sign of changes in American society. Now, as in the past, overwhelming majorities of both men and women feel that extramarital sex is wrong under any circumstances. (Although now, as in the past, many do not, in fact, remain faithful.) See Hunt 1974, Chapter 5; Thompson 1983.

38.   It might be argued that Detroit has been affected by a severe economic down-turn in recent years, so that some sort of reduction in wedding elaborateness ought to be visible. But the argument advanced here does not imply that people react immediately and automatically to economic trends, and it is well known that families in decline may try to hide that fact by spending beyond their means on a wedding. But the problems of the Detroit area may help to explain why the increase in elaborateness of marriages that occurred in that area has been, as noted earlier, less marked than in the weddings of those who married in other locales.

Chapter 4

Variations in Dating and Mating

The previous two chapters have contained a broad descriptive overview of how the experiences of women in different marriage generations in our sample contrasted (or did not contrast). In presenting this overview, numerous questions about the sources of variation in dating and mating experiences were unresolved. What sort of women start dating early? Who is most likely to engage in premarital sex? Have the factors that influence whether a woman marries early or late changed over time? Are economic factors or the bride's sexual history more important in determining how elaborate the wedding is? In the present chapter I will attempt to examine many of these questions about variations in the mate choice process. However, there will be no attempt in the space available to examine every individual measure of dating and mating experiences covered in Chapters 2 and 3. Instead, the focus will be on what I consider the most important aspects of these experiences: the variety of dating partners experienced, the relative age of beginning various stages in dating and mating, the degree of sexual intimacy achieved prior to marriage, and the elaborateness of the wedding. In each case I will examine the statistical relationships between these mate choice experiences and a variety of background factors that may help explain variations in the nature of dating and mating.

What Causes Variations

Before proceeding to examine any results, I will first consider what background factors might be expected to influence how women go through the dating and mating process. Or, using social science jargon, what independent variables (background factors) do I hypothesize will be statistically related to our dependent variables (measures of dating and mating experiences)? Broadly speaking many, but not all, of the background influences to be considered can be categorized roughly under three labels—social class, traditionalism, and parental ties and controls.

Social class differences are perhaps the favorite explanatory tools of social scientists, and with good reason. Even though America may not have sharply delineated classes, where you stand in terms of factors such as education, income, and occupational status seems to be related to differences in life experiences, behavior, and attitudes (see, for instance, Kohn 1969; Jackman and Jackman 1983). How would social class position be expected to affect dating and mating behavior? Several possibilities are suggested by the existing literature.[1] First, middle and upper middle-class families are more likely than working class or poor families to socialize their children into an ethic of "delayed gratification," which emphasizes devoting one's energies to education and career preparation, rather than to the pleasures of romance and sex.[2] So women from such families, or who show signs of such "sublimation" through higher education, might be expected to start dating later, delay intimacy, and marry later.[3] However, the direction of causation may not always be clear. Women with high educational aspirations may, for instance, delay romantic entanglements and may be better informed and able to avoid premarital pregnancy. Conversely, women who become sexually involved and premaritally pregnant may have their educations cut short and their career aspirations undermined. Therefore if there is a relationship between delayed intimacy and social class, it may not be clear which is cause and which is effect. (One aspect of the intimacy revolution—cohabitation—is usually assumed to be the province particularly of college students. If so, this particular behavior would be associated with relatively high, rather than low, educational attainment.)

Social class may be related to dating and mating in other ways. People from higher social classes are likely to be viewed as more attractive dating partners and potential spouses than those from lower classes. Here desirability may be influenced by the social class background of the woman's family and by her possession of desirable personal characteristics and prospects, particularly in terms of education. Individuals so favored might be expected—other things being equal—to benefit in terms of popularity in the dating stage and to be in a strong position in the "marriage market." I assume that these advantages are associated with relatively higher numbers of dates, steadies, and marital prospects, but not necessarily with earlier marriage, since the "delayed gratification" argument leads me to expect well educated women to delay marriage even when they could find several "suitable" partners. Middle and upper-class families have more control over desirable resources that they can use to pressure their daughters not to rush into marriage; poorer families do not possess such resources, and may provide a home setting that daughters will want to "escape" from through an early marriage. Finally, when it comes to weddings, as discussed in Chapter 3, families in higher social classes can be expected to be both willing and able to engage in more elaborate weddings than those in lower classes. So existing thinking on the subject leads me to expect that women who either come from advantaged families or have relatively high personal status characteristics will delay entry into dating and sexual intimacy, marry relatively late, be more popular in the dating stage, and have more lavish weddings, in comparison with women who do not have these advantages.

A second grouping of influences I label "traditionalism"—and this denotes the idea that certain segments of the population subscribe to more conservative ideas about dating and mating than others—and that as a consequence individuals from such backgrounds will be less likely to join the intimacy revolution. Several types of traditional influences were examined in this study. First, it is assumed that Catholics may be less likely to engage in premarital intimacy, and perhaps slower to progress through the various stages of dating, than non-Catholics. But the fact that conservative views on sexual matters are associated not only with the Catholic Church, but also with some fundamentalist versions of Protestantism, leads me to examine other measures as well. Affiliation with a fundamentalist Protestant church while young may also inhibit premarital intimacy.[4] In addition, the intensity of one's religious faith may have a conservative influence on dating and premarital sexuality. Therefore we will examine whether affiliation with a fundamentalist denomination or high religiosity promote slower dating and less premarital intimacy.[5]

I also suspected that closeness to immigrant and ethnic roots might affect dating and sexual behavior in a comparable way. In spite of considerable variety among the groups that have come to America, most new arrivals possessed family roots that were somewhat more "patriarchal" or authoritarian than those found in "melting pot" America. Also many if not most immigrants came from cultures where there was no "dating culture" and where parents played an important role in selecting or approving marriage partners. So in families not far removed from their immigrant roots, energies that could have been devoted to romance and sexuality might be diverted into family quests for economic survival or simply controlled so that parental influence over mate choice would not be undermined. We asked our respondents about how many of their parents and grandparents were born overseas and about the strength of their own ethnic loyalties to a particular group, and I will use the results of these questions to measure the influence of "ethnic roots" on dating and mating.[6] However, not all immigrants came from equally conservative backgrounds, and it has been suggested that being of Italian or Polish background might inhibit premarital intimacy more than being of recent English or French extraction. While there is no good way to rate the conservatism of all nationalities, a crude three category measure based roughly on geography and cultural distance from American customs can be examined, with 1 = English, Scottish, and Irish; 2 = other Northern and Central European; and 3 = Southern and Eastern European. Finally, I also use a measure of whether respondents attended private or parochial schools when young. The assumption here is that such schools generally establish a more controlled atmosphere than is found in public schools, thus fostering more conservative dating and sexual behavior (rumors about "wild" girls in Catholic schools notwithstanding).[7]

Although variations in religion, religiosity, and. ethnic roots have been discussed here in terms of their possible influence on dating and premarital intimacy, these influences might affect the nature of wedding celebrations as well.

Catholics, true believers of any faith, and people with strong ethnic roots might be expected to hold more traditional and elaborate wedding celebrations than other people.

The third major factor that may affect dating and mating concerns parental controls and ties. Here there are several interrelated ideas. Let's assume that parents generally try to exert conservative pressure on their offspring—against rushing into dating and marriage, and particularly against rushing into sexual intimacy. But there are some family situations where that influence can be more effectively transmitted than in others. Assuming the parents are still married and have a close relationship with their daughter, and harmonious relations with each other (so that their daughter gets consistent messages), and that the daughter is still living at home and dependent upon her parents until she gets married, then we might anticipate that the family's conservative influence will be effectively communicated, and that dating, sexual intimacy, and marriage will be delayed. If, on the other hand, one or both parents have died or they are divorced, or the woman is not close to her parents or perceives them as in conflict and hostile toward her, or if she has left home at a young age to go off on her own, then we might anticipate that parental views would have less influence, and that more "liberal" dating and sexual behavior would be possible. At an extreme, some studies have suggested that young women who are in constant conflict with their parents or feel that their families are constantly interfering in their social life may even try to get pregnant or to find a boyfriend and elope so that they can escape from the oppressive atmosphere in the home.[8]

Some other aspects of the experiences of our respondents may also affect controls over dating and sexuality. Respondents who had mothers who worked outside the home may have been freer of maternal supervision and perhaps more likely to strive for independence in their own behavior—both considerations fostering liberalism in dating and sexuality. If a woman is already employed prior to marriage, that could give her greater independence from parental controls. Therefore, I suspect that most of these influences will affect dating behavior and sexual intimacy. However, they may also play a role in the form of the wedding celebrations. Where parent-daughter bonds are close and the chosen mate is approved of by the parents, and the parents are still together at the time of the marriage, the desire to hold a lavish wedding is likely to be greater than in families where these conditions are not present.

Some background characteristics do not neatly fit into any of these three major groupings of influences. In the analysis that follows a number of such characteristics will be listed together simply as "other" factors. For instance, I am particularly interested in whether the dating and mating experiences of the 75 blacks in our sample differed from the 380 whites.[9] Substantial literature suggests that in the past blacks tended to enter dating, sexual intimacy, and marriage earlier than whites and were more likely than whites to lose their virginity before marriage and experience a premarital conception or birth. On the other hand, recent studies indicate that the racial difference is declining and in some instances, such as the age of marriage, being reversed (see, for instance, Zelnick and Kanter 1980, Espenshade 1985). So one "other" influence to be investigated is race.

It is interesting to compare whether respondents who had high career aspirations when they were young, or who married men who had been married before, had different dating and mating experiences than women who did not have such qualities. Two other factors touched on in earlier chapters are the year of the marriage (which is obviously closely related to the age of the respondent) and whether or not the wedding took place in the Detroit area. Finally, I will examine the possibility that some early aspects of the dating experience have an independent effect on later stages of the process or on the nature of the entry into marriage. For instance, did respondents who began to date at an early age also marry at an early age? Does premarital sexual experience tend to hasten marriage (e.g., when pregnancy results) or delay marriage (since sexual desire and frustration will not lead to eagerness for an early marriage)? And, as discussed in Chapter 3, are those who have been sexually intimate before marriage likely to have simpler weddings than other women? These and a variety of other questions will be addressed through the analysis in the remainder of this chapter.[10]

Dating Popularity

One of the variations examined in Chapter 2 was how many individuals our respondents remembered ever dating, going steady with, or considering as marital prospects. It turns out that answers to these three separate items were interrelated—women who had had many different dating partners also tended to have a relatively high number of steadies and marital prospects. (The average intercorrelation among these items was $r = .44$.) Having combined these three measures together into a single scale that is labeled a Popularity Scale, I now proceed to examine how this scale is associated with various background measures.[11]

The statistical associations of this Popularity Scale with various factors that may influence variety in romantic partners are presented in Table 4.1. Since subsequent tables in this chapter will take the same general form as this one, I need to clarify how to interpret the figures in the table. Down the left hand side of the table are listed the various "independent variables" that may influence the "dependent variable"—in this case, scores on the Popularity Scale, which separates women who had few dates, steadies, and marital prospects from those who had many. These independent variables are grouped together into the rough conceptual groupings discussed in the introduction to this chapter: social class, traditionalism, parental ties and controls, and "other" measures. The actual question wording and coding for these measures are listed in Appendix 2. The first column in the table then lists the bivariate correlation statistic (Pearson's r)

Table 4.1. Influences Affecting Dating Variety

	Popularity Scale Scores	
	Bivariate r	Partial r
Social Class Measures:		
Respondent education	.23*	.20*
Father's education	.14*	
Social class origins	.17*	.06
Parent property income	.08	
Traditionalism Measures:		
Respondent Catholic	−.04	
Respondent fundamentalism	.01	
Respondent religiosity	−.03	
Foreign ancestry	.07	
Ethnic loyalty	.01	
Ethnic region	−.07	
Attended private schools	.00	
Parental Tie/Control Measures:		
Parents still together	.02	
Parents interfere in dating	.19*	.16*
Parent marriage happy	−.10*	−.11*
Close to parents	−.03	
Mother worked	.05	
Premaritally employed	.10*	.09
Married from home	−.05	
Other Measures:		
Respondent black	−.13*	−.10*
Age at first date	−.09	−.24*
Age at first marriage	.30*	.25*
Had premarital sex	.08	
Wed in Detroit area	.00	
Year of marriage	.19*	.07
(N)	(366–459)	(348)
		$R^2 = 25\%$

* = p < .05

for the association between each background measure and the Popularity Scale.[12] In general the larger the value of this correlation statistic, positive or negative, the greater our confidence that there is a "real" association between the independent and dependent variables. Asterisks are used to take into account varying sample size (caused by missing data) in judging how likely it is that such a correlation could have occurred by chance alone—less than one time in twenty, for those cases that are asterisked.[13]

However, a large and statistically significant correlation might still be spurious—in other words, due to the influence of some other confounding factor.

For instance, an apparent racial difference in dating or sexuality might be due per se not to race, but to social class, since blacks tend to be disproportionately located in lower social class positions. In this sort of situation one needs a "control" for the effect of social class to see whether the racial difference "holds up" under controls. This is done by using multiple regression in the following tables. The procedure involves selecting the variables that have strong bivariate correlations with the Popularity Scale and entering them into a multiple regression equation, which enables us to determine whether each has an independent influence on our Popularity Scale, when the effect of all of the others is partialled out.[14] In the second column of Table 4.1, are listed the partial correlation coefficients that emerge as a result.[15] The R^2 figure shown at the bottom tells us how much of the variation in the scale is explained by all of the independent variables included in the regression equation when taken together.

We discover from examining Table 4.1 that the R^2 figure of 25% indicates that we have been only modestly successful in our sample in explaining variations in dating popularity of women. About ¾ of the variation in Popularity scale scores remains unexplained, although by the standards of much social science research this is not bad. Perhaps the failure to explain more of the variation in dating popularity is not surprising, since writers on romance assume that personal qualities (not measured here) should have more influence on popularity than social background factors.

As seen in Table 4.1, women from higher social class families and with more education tend to be more popular than other women. This effect is not eliminated entirely when other factors, such as the age at which the woman married or her race, are controlled for statistically. The table indicates that none of our "traditionalism" measures has a strong influence on Popularity Scale scores. This is not very surprising. I do expect traditionalism to affect the timing of dating and premarital sexuality, but I did not have a clear prediction that women from more traditional families would differ in their number of dating partners, steadies, or marital prospects. The various measures of parental ties and controls demonstrate generally weak and inconsistent results. There are at best very few indications that women whose parents tried to influence their dating patterns, viewed their parents' marriages as unhappy, and were premaritally employed had more dating variety than other women. But most measures of parental ties and controls are not related to variations in popularity. Again this may not be surprising, since it is not clear why parental controls should particularly affect things like dating variety and the number of prospects.[16]

Black respondents are likely to report somewhat lower numbers of dates, steadies, and marital prospects, and this relationship is only slightly weakened by controls for other variables. The only other patterns that hold up under controls are quite understandable, but nonetheless important. Respondents who began dating early and married late are likely to have had more dating partners, steadies, and marital prospects, than women who had a more truncated dating stage.[17]

This finding may provide comfort for "wall-flowers," for it states that the longer you spend "at risk" of being asked out, the more likely you are to have dates and serious relationships. (However, these figures are statistical averages, and they do not, unfortunately, tell us what will happen to any particular individual.)

Moralists will be pleased to note that engaging in premarital sex is not associated with significantly greater popularity in the dating stage. However, loss of virginity does not harm a woman's dating popularity either—the effect is, in fact, a weak positive one. Finally, the increasing scores in recent times on this measure of dating popularity, which were commented on in Chapter 2, also lose significance when we apply controls for other influences (see the final row in the table). Much of the higher number of dates, steadies, and marital prospects claimed by women who married in recent years can probably be explained as the result of an increased number of years spent in the dating stage, rather than indicating more "hectic" dating activity at any one point in time, now or in comparison with the past.

In sum, only a few of the factors considered were modestly related to Popularity Scale scores. First, you are likely to have had greater variety in your romantic partners if you started dating early and ended late (through a late age at marriage) and if you came from a higher social class and received more education, and second if you are white rather than black. However, much of the variation in the number of romantic partners is not explained by the factors considered here.

Precociousness vs. Lateness in Dating and Mating

Since the time spent "at risk" of having dating partners appears to be important, we need to consider what factors influence the timing of various stages in the mate choice process. In the previous two chapters a variety of measures supplied by our respondents were examined that indicate the timing they experienced. It turns out—and this is an important feature that will be discussed more extensively later—that various indicators of early vs. late experiences are intertwined. Women who dated early also tended to go steady early, having sex early, and also marry early. I could, then, have formed a single scale of early vs. late experiences, but instead I chose to analyze three separate measures, in order to gain more insight into the timing of the various stages in the dating process. First, I combined responses to the age of the first date and the age of the first steady questions (intercorrelated at $r = .56$) into a single scale which I call a "Lateness in Dating Scale." Second, responses to the question about the age of first sexual experience were examined. Lastly, I examined separately the age of first marriage of respondents. All three measures are included in Table 4.2.

In Table 4.2 we can see that social class variables have fairly consistent associations with lateness in first sex and in marriage, but a much weaker

Table 4.2. Influences Affecting Dating and Mating Timing

	Lateness in Dating		Age of First Sex		Age of Marriage	
	r	par. r	r	par. r	r	par. r
Social Class Measures:						
Respondent education	.09*	.04	.23*	.17*	.28*	.17*
Father's education	-.05		.07		.11*	
Social class origins	.04		.15*		.12*	
Parent property income	.09	-.00	.16*	.06	.16*	-.04
Traditionalism Measures:						
Respondent Catholic	.08		.19*	.04	.19*	.01
Respondent fundamentalism	.13*	.17*	.11*	-.01	.03	
Respondent religiosity	.12*	-.01	.20*	.12*	.07	
Foreign ancestry	.11*	-.02	.24*	.10	.21*	.11
Ethnic loyalty	.08		.11*	-.04	.07	
Ethnic region	.08		.06		.07	
Private schools	.16*	.07	.29*	.08	.27*	.09
Parental Tie/Control Measures:						
Parents together	-.02		.07		.00	
Dating interference	-.07		-.05		-.04	
Parent marriage happy	.08		.12*		.06	
Close to parents	.15*	.14*	.21*	.19*	.11*	.14*
Mother worked	-.09	-.04	-.18*	-.19*	-.13*	-.08
Premaritally employed	.29*	.20*	.35*	.19*	.33*	.19*
Parental approval	.20*	.11*	.20*	.03	.21*	.08
Married from home	n.a.		.01		n.a.	

(continued)

Table 4.2.   (Continued)

	Lateness in Dating	Age of First Sex		Age of Marriage	
Other Measures:					
Respondent black	.03	-.19*	-.17*	-.13*	-.01
Lateness in dating	n.a.	.66*	.57*	.57*	.51*
Age of first sex	.66*	n.a.		.69*	.28*
Had premarital sex	-.14*	-.33*		.17*	.28*
Premarital pregnancy	-.15*	-.22*		-.05	
Popularity scale	-.05	.16*	.24*	.30*	.28*
Work aspirations	.14*	.06		.17*	-.00
Wed in Detroit	.11*	.10*	.06	.13*	-.02
Year of marriage	-.05	-.08	-.16*	.21*	.15*
(N)	(360-450)	(354-443)	(276)	(362-454)	(295)
	$R^2 = 18\%$		$R^2 = 58\%$		$R^2 = 51\%$

n.a. = not appropriate   * = $p < .05$

association with lateness in dating and going steady (as shown in columns 1 and 2 of the table).[18] Also, when other variables are controlled statistically, the influence of the respondent's educational level and parental class position (as indicated by parental property income) is somewhat weakened in each case. Generally there is a weaker social class influence on the timing of dating and mating than expected.

Traditionalism measures also appear initially to be fairly consistently related to lateness in dating and mating. Catholics, members of fundamentalist Protestant churches, people high in religiosity, those with close ethnic roots, and those who attended private or parochial schools are slower than others in passing through these various stages. However, once other factors are taken into account (in the regression analyses in columns 2, 4, and 6 of the table), most of these influences are sharply reduced or disappear. Having been raised in a very religious atmosphere may have a small independent influence on delaying the loss of virginity, and being raised in a fundamentalist church may delay dating, but otherwise none of the associations survive our statistical tests. Again, these results indicate less powerful influence from sources of traditionalism than I had expected to find.[19]

It is particularly interesting, in view of the Catholic Church's well-known conservative stand in regard to sexual morality, to note that being raised a Catholic does not have an independent influence on delaying the loss of virginity, once other factors are taken into account, and that the apparent delaying effect of attending private (usually parochial) schools also disappears under statistical controls. These figures testify to the increasing incorporation of Catholics into American life as they get further from their ethnic roots, a process commented upon by many observers (see, for example, Jones and Westoff 1979; Alwin 1986.)[20]

Most of the associations dealing with parental ties and controls, in the third panel of Table 4.2, are weak or become weak once we control for other factors. There are modest indications that closeness to parents and premarital employment are associated with delays in dating, loss of virginity, and marriage, and that maternal employment is associated with earlier loss of virginity, while parental approval of the woman's mate choice decision is associated with at least later onset of dating.[21] However, in several of these cases the direction of causation is in doubt. Perhaps rather than causing delays in dating, sexual initiation, and marriage, employment prior to marriage is more a result of such delays. Obviously a woman who married at 16 had a lesser chance of being employed at the time she married than one who married at 30. In general there is only modest evidence in these figures that close ties to, and controls from, parents *cause* dating, entry into sexual relations, and marriages to occur later. The one pattern that is closest to my original expectation is that women who felt close to their parents were slower to date, lose their virginity, and marry, even when other influences are taken into account.

In the bottom panel of the table several important patterns emerge. The only racial difference that persists under controls is that black respondents lost their virginity earlier than white ones. And even in this case, the association between race and age of first sex is no longer significant for respondents who married after 1965, a finding that supports the claim presented by Zelnick and Kanter (1980) that the racial differences in female premarital sexuality are decreasing.[22] Thus we can more or less discount the influence of race in explaining the timing of dating and mating, at least in recent years.[23]

In the bottom panel of the table we also note that the apparent tendency for women who married in Detroit to become sexually involved, and to marry later than other respondents drops out under statistical controls (although a tendency for such women to start dating later remains), and that those women with high job aspirations delay the onset of dating but not other stages of the process. In the bottom row of the table we also see that the year of first marriage is modestly associated with the timing of dating, sex, and mating, even when other factors are taken into account, implying slightly earlier dating, going steady, and loss of virginity for recent brides, but later marriage.[24] The figures in the bottom panel of the table also reveal important influences on the timing of dating and mating from other aspects of earlier experiences, and these require some extended commentary.

I am less successful in explaining the full range of variation in lateness in dating and going steady than in explaining differences in popularity scores (Table 4.1). Only 18% of the variation in the Lateness in Dating Scale can be attributed to the variables inserted into the regression equation.[25] Using a fairly wide range of standard sociological predictors, I am only able to explain a limited amount about the timing of entering the dating process. This relative lack of success may be due both to dating onset being explained by other factors we have not measured, such as personal qualities of the women and the quirks of the males who initiated such dates, as well as to the substantial amount of random error in such retrospective data.

Once the dating process has begun, however, the woman's experience in this process appears to have a powerful influence on the timing of subsequent stages. I can do a much better job of explaining variations in the timing of these later stages *if prior dating experiences are taken into account*. For example, it is possible to explain more than half of the variation in the age of first sexual experience ($R^2 = 58\%$). The overwhelmingly strongest predictor of when a woman began her sexual activity is the timing of her onset of dating and going steady. The single measure of Lateness in Dating alone explains more than half of the variation in age of first sexual experience (or more than one-quarter of the overall variance in this measure). High scores on the Popularity Scale are also modestly associated with delay of entry into sexual intercourse.[26] In other words, far and away the most important influences on when the respondent began having sexual intercourse are the nature and timing of her entry into less intimate stages of the dating process, rather than social class, racial, religious, or other influences. I would hesitate about advising parents who are concerned about daughters losing their virginity to lock them up and forbid them from going out on dates, since once they do a process of "escalation" will set in and the game will be over. But these findings do suggest that the timing of the stages of dating represents an important influence which is generally ignored in research on sexuality and mate choice.

This point is further underscored by examining the last two columns in the table dealing with the age of first marriage. In the bottom panel of the figures is further evidence of the independent influence of earlier stages in the dating process. Again lateness in entering the dating process has a very strong influence on delays in getting married, an influence that is not much diminished by other controls. We see there as well that Popularity Scale scores retain a noticeable influence on age at marriage even under statistical controls, although this is simply the opposite side of the relationship already seen in Table 4.1. The suggestion is that having a more active social life and a greater variety of partners may lead one not to rush into marriage, or may simply require a longer time in order to select a spouse, even though the direction of causation may still be questioned. Respondents who had engaged in premarital sex were also likely to marry later than other women, and premarital conception unexpectedly was not significantly associated with earlier marriage.[27]

A wit might note these figures and argue that parents who are more concerned about delaying their daughter's marriage than about preserving the latter's virginity might be well advised to look approvingly on premarital sexual activity. Be that as it may, these three measures of premarital behavior, lateness in dating, premarital sexual experience, and dating popularity, each have a stronger independent influence on the age of first marriage than any of our other measures, and together they account for the largest part of the 51% of the variance in marriage age that this regression analysis explains.[28] In comparison, the standard factors that are used most often by sociologists to explain when women marry, including educational level, premarital employment, and career aspirations, turn out to be less important influences. Again I stress that this is a major finding from this research. In the future, research on age at marriage and other aspects of mate choice would be well-advised to consider the influence of experiences in the earlier, dating stage.[29]

Premarital Sexual Intimacy

In Table 4.2 I examined one aspect of sexual intimacy, the age at which sexual intercourse was first experienced. Three other measures of premarital sexual intimacy examined are: whether or not the woman lost her virginity prior to marriage, if there was a premarital conception or birth, and whether she lived with her husband prior to marriage.[30] I examined the associations of these three

Table 4.3. Influences Affecting Premarital Intimacy

	Premarital Sex		Premarital Pregnancy		Premarital Cohabitation	
	r	par. r	r	par. r	r	par. r
Social Class Measures:						
Respondent education	.06		-.17*	-.11	.02	
Father's education	.09*	-.05	-.11*	-.00	-.01	
Social class origins	-.01		-.10*	-.00	-.01	
Parent property income	.02		-.05		-.03	
Traditionalism Measures:						
Respondent Catholic	-.03		-.21*	-.15*	-.04	
Respondent fundamentalism	-.13*	-.09	.00		-.00	
Respondent religiosity	-.16*	-.13*	-.07		-.13*	-.06
Foreign ancestry	-.05		-.12*	.12	-.06	
Ethnic loyalty	-.03		-.07		-.10*	.04
Ethnic region	-.01		-.14*	-.06	-.02	
Private schools	-.06		-.13*	.06	-.19*	-.10

Parental Tie/Control Measures

	1	2	3	4	5	6
Parents together	−.11*	−.14*	−.16*	−.08	−.19*	−.10
Dating interference	.04		−.05		.01	
Parent marriage happy	.06		−.05		−.13*	−.09
Close to parents	−.17*	−.04	.06		−.14*	−.01
Mother worked	.11*	.02	.05		.16*	.04
Premaritally employed	.00		−.22*	−.11	−.02	
Parental approval	n.a.		−.10	−.03	.12*	
Married from home	−.25*	−.17*	.05		n.a.	.15*
Other Measures:						
Respondent black	.05		.29*	.24*	.02	
Lateness in dating	−.14*	−.23*	−.15*	−.06	−.03	
Age of first sex	n.a.		n.a.		−.17*	−.27*
Age at marriage	.17*	.18*	−.05		.12*	.26*
Work aspirations	.16*	.10	−.11*	−.19*	.18*	.04
Wed in Detroit	.08		.07		.01	
Year of marriage	.38*	.20*	.10*	.23*	.34*	.19*
(N)	(350–438)	(311)	(322–405)	(281)	(366–459)	(297)
	$R^2 = 26\%$	$R^2 = 26\%$	$R^2 = 21\%$	$R^2 = 21\%$	$R^2 = 25\%$	$R^2 = 25\%$

n.a. = not appropriate   * = $p < .05$

measures with various background factors in Table 4.3. After examining the figures in this table, I will periodically refer back to the data on age of first sex in columns 3–4 of Table 4.2, in order to arrive at a comprehensive view of various aspects of premarital sexual intimacy. (Keep in mind, though, that a high score on age of first sex indicates less premarital intimacy, whereas high scores on the three measures in Table 4.3 indicate more intimacy.)

A number of interesting patterns are visible in these results. First, social class effects appear even less important when we consider the full range of measures of premarital sexual intimacy. More educated women start their sexual activity at a slightly later age than less educated ones (see Table 4.2) and may be less likely to premaritally conceive. But they are not any less (or for that matter more) likely to eventually engage in premarital sex or to cohabit before marrying. The negative finding on cohabitation deserves comment. I have noted that, while many aspects of sexual precociousness have been considered the province of the lower classes, cohabitation has often been depicted as a custom spreading from America's college campuses. But in this study there is no clear relationship between educational levels and cohabitation.[31] The rapid rise of cohabitation seems to be occurring in all classes, and not primarily among the upper middle class or the college educated.

The patterns in regard to education are, in fact, consistent in general ways with patterns found by Alfred Kinsey more than thirty years ago. Kinsey found that uneducated women began sexual activity at an earlier age than educated women. Also uneducated women also married at a younger age than educated women. The net result in Kinsey's data was that more educated women actually achieved higher rates of eventual premarital sexual experience than less well educated women—they in a sense "caught up and passed" the latter in their longer period "at risk" of engaging in premarital sex.[32] In our data the two tendencies (for early sex and early marriage) actually cancel each other out, and there is no net association between educational attainment and premarital sex. Other social class influences have no independent influence on any of our measures of premarital sexual activity. Social class appears to be of minor and selective importance in explaining variations in premarital intimacy.

The second panel in Table 4.3 indicates that the effect of traditional influences is also rather modest and selective. Catholics turn out to be less likely to premaritally conceive than non-Catholics, but not to differ significantly in age of first sex (from Table 4.2), eventual premarital sexual experience, or cohabitation. This pattern is ironic, in view of the Catholic Church's highly publicized stance against "artificial" contraception. One might speculate that either the rhythm method is much more effective than its critics contend or that the Church's stand on contraception may have made young Catholic women more aware of the issue, and therefore more likely than others to seek protection by using contraceptives. (Unfortunately, we do not have any questions in the survey about use of contraceptives that would enable me to test this speculation.)

The respondent's reported religiosity while she was young is associated with later beginning of sexual activity and with less likelihood of ever having had sex before marriage. But youth religiosity is not significantly associated with less likelihood of premaritally conceiving or, once other factors have been taken into account, with less likelihood of living together prior to marriage. The apparent conservative influence of fundamentalism, closeness to ethnic roots, and ethnic region is also eliminated when other factors are taken into account. Here, as in previous tables, the effect of traditional influences is less and more selective than previous writing on the topic would suggest.

The same sort of picture emerges when we consider measures of parental ties and controls in panel 3 of the table. Closeness to parents, maternal employment, and work before marriage for the bride, which were the only factors found to have an independent influence upon lateness in beginning sexual activity (Table 4.2), are found not to have an influence on the other three measures of sexual intimacy. Whether respondents ever engaged in premarital sex is associated with growing up in a "broken home" and having lived independently prior to marriage. In this case the continuous presence and supervision of both parents up until the woman's marriage, regardless of the nature of the relationship with the parents (note the reduction into insignificance of the correlation for closeness to parents), seems to have some, albeit modest, effect on the likelihood of remaining a virgin until marriage. But the premarital pregnancy measure is not significantly affected by any of these parental control measures once other factors have been controlled for, and the only predictor of cohabitation net of other influences is having parents who approved of the woman's choice of mate. Although this latter finding has some intuitive appeal (since parental approval is a frequent worry of cohabiters), this may just be a chance result. It is unclear why this one aspect of parental ties and controls, and not others, should affect the likelihood of cohabitation. In summary, the relationships with measures of parental ties and controls are so weak and inconsistent that they appear to play a marginal role in explaining variations in the degree of sexual intimacy achieved by our respondents. Undoubtedly this will be disturbing news to parents who hope to use close ties with, and controls over, their daughters as ways to induce more restrained premarital behavior.

Once again it is in the final panel of the table that we find the strongest associations. The effect of race appears similar to that of the woman's educational level. Black respondents begin sexual activity earlier (Table 4.2) and are significantly more likely to become premaritally pregnant than are white respondents (even when educational levels are controlled). But they are not any more (or less) likely to eventually engage in premarital sex or to live together prior to marriage. This pattern suggests that racial differences do not have as strong an overall impact on premarital sexual intimacy as previous writing has suggested. Aspirations for work after marriage are associated at the bivariate level with contradictory effects—more eventual premarital sex and cohabitation, but less likelihood of premarital conception. Once the effects of other influences are partialled out, only the negative relationship with premarital conception survives.

Measures of the timing of the mate choice process do have significant influences on our intimacy measures, but the associations are generally weaker than in the previous table. In other words, whether you are early or late in the first stages of dating is more closely related to whether you are early or late in subsequent stages than it is to whether or not you eventually experience various aspects of sexual intimacy. But as you would expect from earlier tables, whether or not the woman ever had premarital sex is influenced by whether she began dating and going steady early, and whether she married late. This pattern of association with the length of the period "at risk" of sexual intimacy is not consistent for the other two measures in the table. Early dating and going steady appear to be associated with a greater likelihood of premarital conception, but the association is weak and is no longer significant once controls are introduced.[33] Early dating and going steady do not apparently lead to greater likelihood of cohabiting before marriage. Also we can see the pattern noted in Table 4.2, in which premarital conception is not significantly associated with earlier marriage. Late marriage age and cohabitation are related as well, and in fact this relationship is strengthened once other factors are taken into account. But in this case the causation may well be the other way around, with cohabitation tending to delay entry into marriage, rather than with later marriage promoting cohabitation.

Even when other factors are taken into account, the year of marriage remains significantly associated with these measures of sexual intimacy (and with age of first sex, as reported in Table 4.2). This pattern strengthens the claim made earlier that a general "intimacy revolution" has been underway in American society, a shift that cannot be attributed to differences in the background traits of respondents across marriage generations. Also noted is the fact that the figures for R^2 at the bottom of the table testify to a return to more modest success (in comparison with Table 4.2) in explaining variations in these three aspects of sexual intimacy. In this case even by including measures of the timing of the stages of dating and mating, I can still explain only $\frac{1}{5}$–$\frac{1}{4}$ of the variation in these aspects of sexual intimacy. Social class effects, some traditional influences, certain aspects of parental ties and controls, and race, year, and the timing of dating and mating all have some relationship with sexual intimacy measures. But on the other hand no single predictor is consistently associated with all four of our premarital intimacy measures (including the age of first sex from Table 4.2).

Several conclusions emerge from this scrutiny of Table 4.3. First, these different aspects of premarital intimacy are not so closely associated that they respond to the same set of influences. In other words, there is not some set of influences that produces "sexual liberalism" in general, with that quality then manifested in different ways. Rather, the factors that explain the age of beginning sexual activity may not be indicators of whether a woman will later have a premarital conception or cohabit.[34] Each of these aspects of premarital sexual intimacy has a distinctive set of associated predictors. Only in the case of the age of first sexual activity have I been able to explain more than half of the variation in the sample, and that was primarily due to the strong influence of the timing of earlier dating stages on the timing of the loss of virginity.

Therefore, while able to document that an intimacy revolution has taken place that has transformed the nature of dating in America, I am not fully successful in explaining the variable participation of women in this revolution. But this modest success is itself an important statement. The figures in these tables provide evidence that the intimacy revolution is affecting the lives of women very broadly in all strata and subgroups, rather than being an experience mostly of one class, religion, or family circumstance. And in all cases a key predictor of whether a woman had joined this revolution is simply the year in which she first headed toward the altar.

The facts documented in the preceding pages, that a variety of social background factors (religion, social class, foreign ancestry, and race) are of modest and perhaps declining significance in explaining a women's participation in the intimacy revolution, provide additional evidence for the increased tolerance and weaker social differentiation in terms of "propriety" that were noted at the outset of this study. As the intimacy revolution has swept our society, confidence that there is only one proper way to enter marriage—as a virgin—has collapsed, and with this collapse has followed a weakening of the links between advantaged social status in America and premarital chastity. For better or for worse, "nice" girls increasingly do engage in premarital intimacy, and they feel less pressure than in the past to preserve their virginity as a way of preserving their social status (or that of their families) and their marriage chances.

The Nature of the Wedding

Finally we examine the sources of variation in the elaborateness and traditionality of the wedding celebrations. When I examined the various measures of wedding behavior discussed in Chapter 3, it turned out that 7 of them were closely enough related to each other to create a single wedding elaborateness scale (with an average item to item correlation of $r = .36$). Whether the woman was given an engagement ring, whether the wedding was a civil or religious ceremony, the estimated attendance at the wedding, whether there were bridal showers, and if the celebrations included a reception, a bachelor party, and a honeymoon—all of these things tended to be interrelated, such that some women had most or all of them, while others had few or none. In Table 4.4 I examine the associations of various background factors with this general measure of the degree of elaborateness of the nuptials.[35] In this case the list of background factors is somewhat expanded from earlier tables, since I anticipate that some features of the husband

Table 4.4. Influences Affecting Wedding Elaborateness

	Wedding Elaborateness Scale Scores	
	Bivariate	Partial
Social Class Measures:	r	r
Respondent education	.28*	
Father's education	.28*	
Groom's education	.40*	.10
Social class origins	.21*	.12
Groom social class	.22*	
Groom occupation	.31*	
Parent property income	.14*	
Traditionalism Measures:		
Respondent Catholic	.22*	−.11
Respondent fundamentalism	−.03	
Groom Catholic	.22*	
Respondent religiosity	.12*	.14*
Groom religiosity	.11*	
Foreign ancestry	.12*	.08
Ethnic loyalty	.03	
Ethnic region	.15*	−.00
Private schools	.22*	.09
Parental Tie/Control Measures:		
Parents together	.19*	.04
Dating interference	.04	
Parent marriage happy	.11*	−.08
Close to parents	−.02	
Mother worked	.01	
Premaritally employed	.29*	.20*
Parental approval	.12*	.29*
Married from home	−.05	
Other Measures:		
Respondent black	−.35*	−.22*
Had premarital sex	−.07	
Premarital pregnancy	−.38*	−.23*
Premarital cohabitation	−.15*	−.16*
Popularity scale	.09*	.14*
Age at first marriage	.08	
Husband remarrying	−.23*	−.29*
Couple pay for wedding	−.39*	−.23*
Couple to live separately	.27*	.16*
Wed in Detroit area	.28*	.35*
Year of marriage	.22*	.23*
(N)	(366–459)	(248)
		$R^2 = 58\%$

* = p < .05

and his family as well as those of the respondent will influence the nature of the wedding celebrations. (Additional "other" variables are also considered here.)

The figures in Table 4.4 show strong and consistent social class influences, with the expected pattern of higher class and better educated couples and families having more elaborate weddings clearly visible in the bivariate correlations in column 1. Interestingly, some of these correlations indicate that the husband's personal characteristics and those of his family may make more difference than the wife's. This pattern suggests that even though the bride's family may more often organize and finance the wedding than the groom's, in doing so the scale they aim for may be an effort to adjust to (or placate) the groom's family. If the groom is a "catch" or comes from a prominent family, then the bride's family may feel under obligation to spend beyond their means, but if she is "marrying down" then this may not be necessary. Before proceeding too far with these speculations, it must be noted that these correlations are substantially reduced and become statistically nonsignificant once I control for other influences (see column 2). Therefore, the net result is the same as in the earlier tables—social class is less of a factor, once other things are taken into account.

A similar verdict emerges from the figures dealing with traditional influences in the second panel of Table 4.4. Judged from the bivariate correlations in column 1, as expected, there appears to be a fairly consistent association between a traditional social background and elaborate weddings. Brides and grooms who were raised as Catholics, were very religious, had foreign born parents and/or grandparents, whose families came from more "traditional" regions of Europe, and who attended private or parochial schools tended to have more ritually elaborate weddings than did others. But once we take other influences into account, in the regression analysis reported in the second column of the table, only the religiosity effect is undiminished, and the effect of the bride's religion is actually reversed (indicating a nonsignificant tendency for brides raised as Protestants to have the more elaborate weddings, once other factors are taken into account).[36] So as with social class, once we consider other predictors, the influence of having been raised in a traditional family environment has a lesser impact on the nature and scale of the wedding than originally expected.[37]

An additional pattern not visible in Table 4.4 should also be noted. In Chapter 3, I suggested that one explanation for the rising scale of the average wedding might be a process of social homogenization. In the post-World War II normalcy that produced an increasingly middle-class dominated society, separate class, ethnic, and other subcultures might be weakening. If such a process has occurred, then families from various ethnic, racial, and religious subgroups in our society should be increasingly influenced by the dominant middle-class norms in weddings, which involve elaborate expenditures and a full complement of ritual stages (engagement, bridal showers, church weddings, receptions, honeymoons, etc.). If this speculation is correct, then we should expect that a variety of social background traits should be more strongly related to wedding elaborateness in earlier marriage generations than in the most recent one. I checked this prediction and found that it was borne out. In general, not only are such background traits not very good predictors of Wedding Elaborateness Scale scores in Table 4.4, but their influence is substantially less for women who married after 1965 than for women who married prior to that date (details not shown here).[38] An increasingly homogenized set of American wedding rituals has emerged which seem to influence couples and their families, no matter what their particular ethnic, class, or religious backgrounds.

The third panel in Table 4.4, dealing with parental ties and controls, produces a mixture of results. Several of these measures are not strongly related to wedding elaborateness, or do not have a significant correlation once other factors are taken into account (in column 2 of the table). It was a surprise, for instance, to learn that having parents who still lived together at the time of their daughter's wedding, having close relations with the parents, and having the bride still living with her parents prior to marriage did not produce a more elaborate wedding (once other influences were partialled out). Here two relationships survive the statistical tests posed. Not surprisingly, weddings are more elaborate when the parents approve of the groom their daughter has chosen, and the correlation in this case is actually strengthened by the imposition of controls for other influences. Brides who were already employed prior to marriage tended to have more elaborate weddings. The reasons for the latter finding are not entirely obvious. However, as discussed in Chapter 3, it is often the case that brides and grooms, and not just the bride's parents, help to pay for the wedding. Therefore in part these correlations may simply indicate that working brides have an ability to help finance more elaborate nuptials. It is probably also the case that working brides have developed a wider network of contacts and friends, and this network provides a larger pool of people who would be invited to a wedding and who may contribute to wedding elaborateness by holding bridal showers.

The final panel in the table reveals several more interesting patterns. Blacks tend to have less lavish wedding celebrations than whites, even when social class and other factors are taken into account. In addition, having cohabited prior to the wedding is associated with a somewhat more modest wedding. Having conceived or given birth premaritally is even more strongly correlated with a modest wedding, but being a virgin per se apparently makes no difference.[39] Generally, the degree of sexual intimacy prior to marriage has some negative effect on the scale of the wedding, but this is clearly not the major factor influencing its elaborateness. These findings require me to quality somewhat the comments made in Chapter 3. There I observed that dual trends over time of increased premarital intimacy and wedding elaboration were not totally contradictory, since being a virginal bride was of declining salience and even those who had cohabited would tend to feel a desire for the ritual markers involved in a formal wedding. Those statements are not inaccurate, and certainly cohabiters and even those who have given birth prior to marriage are not totally disqualified from engaging in an elaborate wedding. However, other things being equal, women who either lived with their intended prior to marriage or had premaritally conceived or given birth tended to have somewhat more modest weddings than other women.[40]

The bottom panel in Table 4.4 reveals other patterns as well. Women who have a large number of dates, steadies, and other marital prospects (as measured by the Popularity Scale) tend to have more elaborate weddings than others. I speculate that this finding may be a by-product of such women having broader networks of friends to be invited to a wedding. In other words, a large-scale wedding testifies to the general popularity of the bride (and groom), and not simply to success with the opposite sex. Also, women who marry later are only slightly more likely to have elaborate weddings than are women who marry earlier, and this association is not statistically significant.[41] However, whether it was the first marriage for the groom is important. (Recall that for all of our brides this was a first marriage.) In general, wedding celebrations are somewhat less elaborate the second (or third or whatever) time around (see Hollingshead 1952 and the discussion in Chapter 8 of the current study). Weddings are also significantly less elaborate if the couple has to foot the bill themselves than if either or both sets of parents are bearing the primary burden.[42]

Similarly, couples who establish a new household after the wedding are more likely than others to hold elaborate nuptials. This finding supports the observation in the previous chapter that one of the functions of a large wedding is to help the new couple to acquire the household items needed to live separately from parents. So the combination most likely to lead to a large and traditional wedding involves a couple relying on parents to pay for the wedding, but not relying on them for housing afterwards. In this sense, as observed earlier, a wedding is a mechanism by which the senior generation indirectly endows the junior generation.[43] Finally, weddings that were located in Detroit or were recent tended to be more elaborate, even when other factors are taken into account. The partial correlation figures in column 2 show that the apparent increasing elaborateness of weddings over time that was the focus of the previous chapter is not simply an artifact produced by differences across marriage generations and cohorts in the backgrounds of brides.

These findings add up to a fairly complex picture. Generally if you come from a favored social class position, have high religiosity, are employed and anticipate setting up a new household with your groom, and if your wedding was one held in the Detroit area in recent years, you will have had a more elaborate wedding than if none of these things was the case.[44] On the other hand, if the parents objected to the man chosen, the women was black, the couple had cohabited or the woman had premartially conceived, if the woman was marrying a "repeater" at the altar, of if the couple was financing the wedding themselves, then things tended to be more simple. Taking these factors into account, we can explain 58% of the variation (which is quite a high level) in the scale of the wedding celebrations.

Conclusions

In this chapter I have tried to determine the sources of variation in the dating and mating experiences of women in our sample. Initially I had assumed that by examining three primary influences on respondents—from their social class position, from a traditional family atmosphere, and from parental ties and controls—I could understand much of the variation in how women went through the mate choice process. Unfortunately, the world, or that portion of it represented in the Detroit data, was complicated. Very often I detected the associations I had expected, but in general they were fewer and occurred more irregularly than anticipated. When other factors were taken into account, many of these influences dropped from the picture.

Nevertheless, in most of the columns and tables reviewed in this chapter, measures that fell into the final, catch-all "other" category were more important in explaining results than were things like social class, religion, ethnic roots, or parental ties. Given the heterogeneity lumped into the "other" category, arriving at a coherent interpretation of what these findings mean is not easy. However, I would suggest that there are three primary conclusions revealed in the patterns within the final panels of these tables. First, being black rather than white makes a difference for many aspects of dating and mating, even when social class and other factors are taken into account. To be precise, black women in our sample tended to have a smaller variety of dating partners than white women, to begin sexual activity at younger ages, conceive a child premaritally, and to have a modest wedding. (However, black women were no more likely than white women to start dating or to marry at young ages, or to eventually lose their virginity prior to marriage or to cohabit.)

Second, a variety of what could be called "situational factors" are of considerable importance, particularly in terms of determining the scale of the wedding. Such factors involve distinctive experiences and constraints faced by women at the time, as opposed to more constant or enduring background factors, such as class and religion. I would include here not only influences listed in the "other" category, such as whether the husband was remarrying, the couple was paying for the wedding, and they were setting up a new household, but also influences that were heretofore considered as reflecting primarily parental ties and influence (in the third panel of each table). Examples of the latter include whether the bride was still living at home, if she was premaritally employed, and whether the parents approved of her mate choice decision. Generally these temporary, but immediate, circumstances seem to have more impact on dating and mating patterns than do enduring background characteristics. I have suggested that the greater importance of such situational factors than of social status traits provides evidence of the increasing "decoupling" of dating and mating behavior from their linkages with social status hierarchies in America.

Finally, and most important, the results reported here reveal that the timing and experiences of dating, mate choice, and marriage are interlinked in complex but important ways, and that experiences in earlier stages of this process can have a powerful impact on how women experience the later stages. The timing of the earlier stages affects the timing of the later stages very strongly, and also, in a lesser way, the likelihood of achieving high levels of intimacy in those later stages. The levels of intimacy reached may affect both the timing of the eventual marriage and the way in which that event is ritually marked with a wedding.

At first glance, it may appear that this conclusion is quite unexceptional, and even obvious. After all, humans all have histories and memories and do not confront each new experience as a *tabula rasa*. However, even if these results appear obvious, they are not. The first reason for this claim is that some previous research yields different results. For example, the finding that the timing of various stages of the dating sequence was highly intercorrelated implies that, no matter whether they began early or late, on average women in our sample tended to spend about the same period of time in each of the various stages. Some previous studies, though, suggested that individuals who begin the dating process relatively late feel worried about meeting expectations of marrying at a proper age and tend to "rush" more quickly through later stages, such as going steady and engagement, in their effort to "catch up" (see, for example, Lowrie 1961). The result, in these earlier studies, is a "telescoping" of the later stages, producing a shorter total amount of time between the onset of dating and first marriage. In our Detroit study, in contrast, there is no evidence of such telescoping, and as already noted, individuals who start the process later tend, on the average, also to finish later.[45] In a sense the pattern I find in the Detroit study is reassuring, in terms of what I called earlier the "marketplace learning" scenario of mate choice, since it seems to indicate that whenever individuals first experience various stages of dating and mating, they tend to take their time rather than rushing into the next stage.[46]

The second reason I stress the nonobviousness of the finding that previous timing and experiences influence the later stages of mate choice is that most research that has focused on things such as the onset of sexual activity, age at marriage, and the nature of wedding celebrations has ignored the timing and nature of premarital experiences. As noted earlier, much of this research focuses simply on "demographic" background factors, such as gender, social class, race, and religion. Considerable digging on my part, for example, turned up very few studies that reported such things as the age of beginning dating, much less used this as a predictor of later experiences in the mate choice process. The results of the Detroit study indicate, though, that demographic background factors are generally of less importance, if they are important at all, than the pattern of earlier experiences. So only when researchers take into account the sorts of timing and premarital history issues focused on in the current study will they have success in explaining why some people marry at younger ages than others and who submits to the expense and bother involved in staging an elaborate wedding.

There is an additional implication of these findings that the reader will see echoed in later chapters as well. In the general debate between sociologists who see individual behavior as determined (or even "overdetermined," see Wrong 1961) by social background vs. those who stress considerable personal autonomy, the pattern of results reviewed here points more to the autonomy side. Women in our Detroit sample appear to have been more than simply prisoners of their social backgrounds when it came to making decisions about dating and getting married.

Notes

1. The literature on this topic is enormous. See, for example, Hollingshead (1949); Kinsey et al. (1953); Rainwater (1964); and Pearlin (1971).

2. The upper class may have quite a different cultural pattern entirely. But there are so few women from upper-class families in our sample that middle and upper middle-class families will dominate the upper end of our class variables. To be more specific, only 4 respondents identified themselves as having grown up in upper-class homes, compared with 45 claiming upper-middle class origins and 158 middle-class origins. One other measure of upper-class origins is the possession of income from property or investments. In all 69 respondents recalled that their parents had some of this kind of income, but only 29 claimed that a substantial part of family income came from such investments. So depending on one's criteria, upper-class origin respondents constituted only 1% to 6% of our sample.

3. However, there is some research that suggests that women from higher classes begin dating earlier than others, even if they end up marrying later (see, for example, Bayer 1968).

4. Respondents who said they were raised as Protestants were asked what denomination they were. We used these denominations to categorize respondents into fundamentalist and nonfundamentalist denominations. For details, see Appendix 2.

5. We did not, unfortunately, use a very precise measure of religiosity. I have had to rely on a subjective question that asked our respondents, "How about your religious *feelings* when you were growing up? Would you say you were (1) very religious, (2) somewhat religious, (3) not very religious, or (4) not religious at all.

6. The two questions about where parents and grandparents were born were used to form one indicator of foreign born family members, which ranges from zero to six. The ethnic loyalty measure followed another question about what main nationality or ethnic group respondents considered they belonged to, and asked: "Do you have a strong sense or a weak sense of belonging to that group?" (The actual measure used includes three categories, with the middle one labeled "in between, medium.")

7. Attendance at a private school might reflect class influences as much as traditional family orientations. However, 89% of the private schools attended by women in our sample were parochial schools, so I assume that such attendance indicates traditional values more than family wealth. The actual measure used has three categories, with the second category being some attendance at both public and private schools and the third being exclusive attendance at private schools. (See Appendix 2.)

8. Most of these aspects of parental controls will be investigated in this chapter using the responses to individual questions. However, our measure of whether the parental family was intact was composed from two separate questions which inquired whether the respondent was raised by her own parents and whether her parents were still together at the time that she married. Respondents are divided into three categories—those not living with both parents even in childhood, those living with parents during childhood whose parents were not together at the time that they married, and those whose parents were together at both times. The measures used dealing with parental approval of the respondent's mate choice decision and respondent's closeness to her parents are also composed from two items and in each case represent averages from separate questions about the mother and the father. For details, see Appendix 2.

9. There were only 4 individuals in our sample who were classified as Asians or of other racial groups, and they will be omitted from the analysis of racial differences in this chapter.

10. Some other measures were available that will not be included in the tables in this chapter, because preliminary examination showed that they were not associated with variations in dating and mating. For example, we had our interviewers make subjective ratings of the apparent intelligence and attractiveness (for a woman of comparable age) of our respondents. Even though these ratings refer to the time of interview and not the time of first marriage, still it might be assumed that women rated high now would also have been seen as relatively intelligent and attractive as they entered the marriage market years before. But in general these measures were not strongly or consistently related to the measures of dating and mating considered in this chapter. I would not claim on the basis of this finding that beauty and intelligence do not count for anything in the marriage market, but only that there is no clear sign in these results, based upon questionable measures, that being blessed with such qualities leads to earlier marriage or even more lifetime dates, steadies, and marital prospects.

11. This and most other scales in this study were created by computing standardized scores for each item, to compensate for their differing variances, and then taking the mean of these standardized scores. See Appendix 2 for details.

12. The correlation coefficient can range from $+1$, which indicates a positive and perfect correlation, to -1, which indicates a perfect negative relationship. Quite a few of our variables are ordinal rather than interval, so that correlation statistics are not entirely appropriate. There is an extensive debate in the statistical and sociological literature about whether and when to use interval statistics with ordinal data, and about the suitability of significance tests in such cases. Given the large number of associations that will be inspected I will use correlation statistics and related interval statistics throughout this study for convenience, thus siding with the "pro" side in this debate. But the reader should keep in mind that I have adopted this short-cut.

13. An additional problem introduced by examining a table with more than twenty correlation statistics per column, as in this chapter. At least one correlation would be expected to surpass the conventional .05 significance level due to chance alone. Even though in all of the tables here the number of significant correlations is considerably larger than could be expected on chance grounds, still we need to keep in mind that some individual significant correlations might be "flukes."

14. Ordinary least squares regression is used here. In the case of social class variables, when several or all of such variables have strong associations with a dependent variable they are not all entered into the regression equation, since doing so would give rise to what are technically called multicollinearity problems. Rather my strategy is to select the social class variable with the strongest correlation for entry into the regression analysis, or in some cases to select two social class variables that are not themselves highly intercorrelated. (In practice this means using a measure of individual status, such as the respondent's education, and a measure of family class origins, such as subjective class background or parental investment income.) No annual income estimates are available for parents on either side in our retrospective data.

15. Customarily in reporting regression results either the standardized or unstandardized regression coefficients are presented, rather than partial correlation statistics. However, I have opted for presenting the partial correlation statistics because these give a more precise picture of whether controlling for other variables reduces the size of the initial bivariate correlation by a large measure or

not. In general the partial correlation coefficients are quite close in value to the standardized regression coefficients that are also produced by the computer, and comparisons within the column of partial correlations gives a clear picture of the relative importance of the remaining independent variables in explaining variations in measures of dating and mating behavior.

16.   The strongest association in this set, between parents trying to influence their daughters' dating practices and Popularity Scale scores, may simply indicate that actively dating women give their parents more to react to than others. It seems unlikely that parental interference actually would drive women to date more actively.

17.   This pattern conforms to the findings of Lowrie (1961), based on high school surveys, that those youths who had begun dating at an earlier age had a more active dating life at any given later age than their peers who had started dating later.

18.   Some earlier studies claim that women from higher class positions actually start dating earlier, rather than the later pattern that we find (see Lowrie 1961; Bayer 1968).

19.   One previous study, by Lowrie (1961), places major emphasis on ethnic roots as a factor delaying entry into dating, but there is no comparable effect visible in the table. Note also that these results do not indicate that daughters from immigrant families tend to marry very young—if anything, slightly the opposite is the case.

20.   The bivariate correlations between Catholicism and ages of dating, loss of virginity, and mating are only sizeable for pre-1964 marriage cases, and not among post-1965 brides, a pattern that provides support for this "melting pot" argument. To be specific, the three correlations for pre-1964 marriages are .20*, .33*, and .28*, and for post-1965 marriage −.04, .07, and .11.

21.   The finding in regard to the influence of premarital employment on loss of virginity is contrary to my expectation that such employment would foster independence and precocious behavior.

22.   Specifically, the correlation between race and age of first sex is −.32* for pre-1964 marriage cases and −.05 for post-1965 marriage cases.

23.   As noted earlier, in the case of age of marriage, other analysts have argued that in recent years there has been an actual reversal of previous patterns, from a situation in which blacks married at younger ages than whites to a current setting in which blacks tend to marry later (see Espenshade 1985). This trend is not yet visible in our data. However, the reader is reminded that a higher than expected proportion of sampled households in predominantly black neighborhoods in inner city Detroit did not contain any married women at all (see the discussion in Appendix 1).

24.   The year of marriage variable was included in all regressions because of my central interest in change over time, even though at the bivariate level in two out of three instances the correlation was not significant. The association of marriage year with the Lateness in Dating scale (with a partial correlation of $r = -.10$, just short of statistical significance) does not conflict with the observation in Chapter 2 that the median age of first date reported by women in all three generations had not decreased (i.e., was 16 in each case), both because the significant association seen here emerges only under controls for other variables and because the Lateness in Dating Scale combines age of first date with age of first steady (which has gotten earlier). It is also interesting to note that separately examining pre-1964 and post-1965 marriage cases (results not displayed here) reveals that the decline in the age of onset of dating stages and in the entry into sexual relations is concentrated in the earlier period, while the delay in marriage is concentrated in the later period.

25.   The variables for age at first sex, engaging in premarital sex, and premarital conception were not included in the regression equation in spite of their significant correlations in the first column of the table, since they were obviously not causally prior to the onset of dating.

26.   However, in this case we again may have doubts about the direction of the influence, since early entry into sexual activity may preclude "playing the field" and thus reduce the number of dating partners.

27.   Closer examination indicated that the correlation with premarital conception was a statistically significant $r = -.16*$ for those who married prior to 1965, but $r = .00$ for those who married

later. In other words, we see here confirmation of a shift commented upon in Chapter 3—the demise of the "shotgun wedding." Women who became premaritally pregnant in the earlier period were more likely to "rush into marriage," but this was not true for such women in recent times.

28. However, again issues may be raised about the direction of causation. For example, do women who are already sexually active move more slowly toward the altar, because sexual frustration does not influence their timetable, or do women who marry later have more time "at risk" of engaging in premarital sex?

29. A seminar paper by Anju Taj, one of the students in the Detroit Area Study seminar, first directed my attention to the important effects of dating variables on marriage timing. But these findings also fit well with the emerging "life course perspective," which has led sociologists, historians, and others to analyze life experience not simply in terms of standard kinds of demographic factors, but also in terms of issues of timing and sequences. See, for example, Hareven 1978; Elder 1987.

30. Another measure discussed in Chapter 2, whether a woman had sex before she started dating her husband, is not examined separately because it is so closely associated with our general premarital sex measure.

31. Examination of the table of educational attainment of our respondents vs. cohabitation reveals that women who were college graduates or who had some graduate education were less likely to have cohabited (6.1% and 10.7%, respectively), than women who had only completed high school (11.1%) or had had a few years of college (13.3%).

32. The estimates were that 30% of grade school educated women, 47% of high school graduates, and 60% of college graduates had experience premarital sex. This pattern was contrary to Kinsey's findings for males, where less educated men had higher rates of eventual premarital sexual experience than better educated ones (see Kinsey et al. 1953, p. 293).

33. An early first sexual experience does have a stronger association with the likelihood of premarital conception. I do not use both the Lateness in Dating scale and the age of first sex together in these regression equations due to the multicollinearity problem mentioned earlier, given how closely these two measures are intercorrelated (as seen in column 3 of Table 4.2).

34. These four measures of premarital sexual intimacy are intercorrelated, however, although loosely. With the age of first sexual experienced reversed, the average item-to-item correlation among these four measures is $r = .24$. The modest size of this intercorrelation led me to consider these four measures separately in this chapter, and enabled me to uncover their different determinants.

35. I initially expected that the lavishness—as represented by such things as the number attending—and the traditionality—as represented by bridal showers, etc., of the wedding might form separate complexes. However, a single complex emerged from my analysis. I label the resulting scale wedding elaborateness, but the reader should bear in mind that it includes having held various "traditional" rituals, and not simply having had a large and costly wedding.

36. Due to the intercorrelation in husband and wife religion and religiosity, the focus of Chapter 5, only the bride's characteristics were entered into the regression equation.

37. I should note, though, that the religion measures used compare only Protestants with Catholics and fundamentalist Protestants with nonfundamentalists. The Detroit sample is too small to investigate whether Quakers, Southern Baptists, or Jews have weddings that are more or less elaborate than other individuals.

38. Several regressions were examined. In general the personal status characteristics of the bride and groom retained more influence than the status characteristics of their parents and families. The influence of race on wedding elaborateness was only slightly weakened in the post-1965 period.

39. More detailed analysis revealed that for women who first married prior to 1964 there was a significant negative correlation ($r = -.23*$) between being a nonvirgin at marriage and wedding elaborateness, but that for post-1965 marriages this relationship had disappeared ($r = .01$). So it appears that virginity per se used to matter in deciding what sort of wedding to hold but is no longer a factor.

40.   In these cases the correlations between premarital conception or cohabitation and wedding elaborateness are not weaker for post-1965 marriage cases than earlier cases, so I cannot claim that these behaviors are on their way to becoming irrelevant to the scale of the nuptials.

41.   In both of these instances there are more positive correlations if we consider only women who married before 1965, but actually slightly negative correlations if we consider women who married recently (details not shown here).

42.   In a secondary analysis, not shown here, I examined associations with a measure of whether the parents on either side or the couple themselves had paid for the wedding. Once multivariate controls were introduced, I found that women whose parents objected to their chosen spouse, and women who left home prior to getting married, had a premarital conception, or whose groom was not getting married for the first time were more likely to have to do without parental funds, while women from wealthier families and women whose parents were still together at the time of the wedding were more likely to have the parents pay the wedding expenses.

43.   Of course, some direct endowment usually occurs as well, in the form of gifts from both sets of parents to the new couple.

44.   Social class position is included in this listing in spite of the fact that the partial correlations in column 2 fall short of statistical significance. This is done because of the overall consistency of the social class bivariate correlations, and also because the absence of an asterisk is due in part to the reduction in sample size that occurs in the regression analysis, (i.e., bivariate correlations for the full sample of $r = .10$ would surpass the $p = .05$ significance level). The results are interpreted as indicating that the social class effects are substantially reduced when other factors are taken into account, but not entirely eliminated.

45.   Obviously, the time any one individual spends in each stage is distinctive, and I am not claiming that there is some sort of built-in requirement that every person needs to spend two years going steady before getting engaged. What I am saying is simply that starting any one stage at a later age than others (whether it is dating, going steady, or whatever) does not result, on the average, in spending a briefer time in the subsequent mate choice stages.

46.   Since there has been relatively little prior research on this topic, and since there may be some doubt about the reliability of the recollected age data I used to construct these estimates of sequences, I state this lack of telescoping as a tentative finding and hope that other researchers will examine this question using other research designs. But I should note that, although the age of first date, first steady, and first sexual experience all came from a single self-administered instrument used with our questionnaire, the age at marriage and the length of engagement estimates come from other parts of the questionnaire and were based on other kinds of computations. Even if one might suspect that the lack of telescoping might be an artifact of listing several ages in a row on the self-administered form, that would not explain why there is also no telescoping involved in the length of engagement and timing of marriage (details not shown here). I doubt that the "fixed stage" pattern found in the current study is simply an artifact of a particular way we recorded ages and dates in our study. See Appendix 2 for details on question wording.

Chapter 5

WHO MARRIES WHOM?

One of the enduring questions in the study of mate choice concerns what is technically called *assortative mating*. In layman's language this is simply the question of who marries whom.[1] The question of who marries whom would appear to be bound up with the issue of how mate choice occurs, and in particular with the question: do young people or their parents control mate choice decisions (see Goode 1963). It seems reasonable to suppose that parents might have different criteria for their children's spouse selection than their children have. Even in colonial times, American mate selection was characterized by freedom of choice. Young couples usually took the initiative and did the selecting of their own marriage partners. Parental approval was expected, and some would even say required, but nonetheless the actual choice usually was made by the partners-to-be, rather than by their parents. Unlike many other agrarian societies, colonial America never had a system of arranged marriage, in which parents make the decisions about who their offspring will marry.[2]

Even though from the very beginning American customs have included this emphasis on freedom of mate choice, still it can be argued that our mating customs have changed. Over the last 300 years parental influence, exercised through mechanisms such as direct supervision and control over inheritable family property, has weakened. Parental approval has become more nominal, or even unnecessary. As noted in Chapter 2, the set of customs we call our "dating culture" emerged gradually toward the end of the nineteenth century and early in this century, and included, at its core, romantic associations among the young out of the range of direct parental supervision. Most social commentators would argue that over time the ethos of romantic love has become more highly emphasized as part of our method of mate selection.[3] If this belief is accurate, it implies that the choice of marital partners, which used to be in major ways based upon "rational" considerations, such as the intended's property, career prospects (for grooms, or domestic skills, for brides), health, reputation, and family background, has in recent decades become more and more an "irrational" process. In selecting a mate we are supposed to be guided by our hearts, rather than by our heads, and whoever can make our hearts go "pitter-patter" sufficiently should induce us to head toward the altar.

From this very brief overview of America's change from a basically free choice but rational and calculating pattern of mate selection to an even more "youth controlled" and romance-driven pattern, it might be assumed that the results of the process, in terms of who marries whom, would have changed markedly. Parental influence and rational calculation suggest that couples entering into marriage are likely to come from very similar backgrounds—upper-class women will marry upper-class men, Catholics will select Catholics, Polish-Americans will marry other Polish-Americans, and so forth.[4] But if the heart is in command, might not the results be quite different? Perhaps a Catholic will fall in love with a Jew, an upper-class male with a working class female, or a Pole with an Italian. Western culture, from *Romeo and Juliet* to the recent movie comedy, *Arthur,* is full of examples of love triumphing and producing "mismatches" (in terms of social backgrounds), even against determined parental and community opposition. Romantic love is seen as irrational and unpredictable. The popular novel, *The Godfather,* by Mario Puzo, captures this sentiment nicely by having Sicilian villagers shake their heads in pity at the sight of the love-sick refugee from American gang wars, Michael Corleone. His falling in love with a local peasant girl is described as having been struck by a "thunderbolt," with the result a total loss of self-control and good sense. If love is that irrational, we might suppose that under its influence mate selection would occur almost at random, in regard to the backgrounds of each partner (see, however, the arguments presented about the rationality of love in Heimer and Stinchcombe 1980).

However, when we examine the evidence, it becomes clear that even in recent years, mate choice in American society is very far from being a random process. For all of the changes that have occurred both in the nature of our society and in the customs surrounding mate choice, the most common pattern is to have "like marry like," in other words, for most couples to come from similar social backgrounds (a pattern sociologists refer to as "homogamy").[5] The maintenance of this pattern of status matching in mate choice, in the midst of "youth driven" marriage selection and the cult of romantic love, is the central puzzle with which this chapter is concerned. First, I will examine data from the Detroit survey to determine the extent of status matching and whether there are any signs of it weakening over time. Then I will examine some of the mechanisms that may help to perpetuate status matching in mate choice in American society even in the 1980s.

As in the previous chapters, my reason for interest in status matching in marriage goes beyond simple curiosity about trends. The degree of homogamy is often presumed to have an important impact on the outcome of a marriage. If the bride and groom come from similar backgrounds, public opinion and not a little previous research suggest that they will have an easier time building a successful marriage than if they are "mismatched." Popular culture is full of portrayals of the additional strain faced by those couples who come from contrasting backgrounds, as in the movie *Guess Who's Coming to Dinner?,* in which the daughter of the characters played by Katherine Hepburn and Spencer Tracy surprises her parents by bringing home a black fiancé (Sidney Poitier). However, it is not entirely clear how important status matching is for marital success, and whether all different kinds of matching (class, religious, ethnic, etc.) are equally important. Later on in this study, in Chapter 7, we will investigate the relative importance of various kinds of homogamy for the fate of a marriage. The issue of changes over time in status matching in marriage, which is the focus of the current chapter, forms a necessary background for that later discussion.

Trends in Assortative Mating: Race

The first and perhaps most obvious trait to consider, in terms of who marries whom, is race. In this realm the nonrandom nature of American mating is most obvious—the overwhelming majority of individuals end up marrying someone of the same racial background as themselves. Of our 459 respondents, 380 were judged by our interviewers to be white, 75 to be black, and 4 to be "Asians or other." Of the 380 white respondents, 375 had been married (in their first marriages) to whites, only 1 to a black, and 4 to individuals in the "Asians and other" category. *All* of the 75 black respondents had married black husbands. And 3 out of the 4 "Asian or other" women had married others in the same category, with the lone exception marrying a white.[6]

In sum, an overwhelming 98.7% of our respondents had as their (first) husbands individuals from the same racial group as themselves. Indeed, there were so few exceptions to this pattern that I cannot meaningfully examine with these data trends over time in racial intermarriage, or why some individuals marry homogamously with regard to race while others do not. In some larger-scale studies researchers have discovered a modest tendency for racial intermarriages to become more common in recent years (see, for example, Heer 1974). However, in the Detroit data racial intermarriages are decidedly rare in all three marriage generations.[7].

Ethnicity

We can examine whether nonblack respondents married others of the same ethnic or national origins as themselves or not. We asked respondents, "Aside from being American, what is your *main* nationality or ethnic group?" and we asked them basically the same question (but without the prefatory phrase) about their (first) husbands. Interviewers recorded the first ethnic group mentioned, or the group mentioned as the primary ethnic allegiance.[8] There are more than 50 single nationality categories that turn up using this method, and this proliferation makes meaningful analysis difficult. To simplify matters further, nationalities were grouped together by their geographical and cultural similarity into seven major categories: Anglo (English, Scottish, Welsh), Irish, Northern Europe (countries from France through Scandinavia), Central Europe (primarily Germany and Austria), Southern. Europe (countries from Portugal and Spain through Greece), Eastern Europe (countries from Poland down through the Balkans, plus most of the Soviet Union, but the Baltic republics of that country—Lithuania, Latvia, and Estonia—are grouped instead under Central Europe), and "Other" (mostly Latin America, but also some Asian countries).

Subdivided in this way, national origins are much less of an influence over mate choice than racial group. Overall, only 36% of nonblack respondents married men from the same group of national origins as themselves (details not shown here). It would also appear from this set of national origins categories that the tendency to "marry out" by mating with people from a different ethnic background has become more common in recent years. The percentage of women who married someone from the same ethnic grouping was 48% for the pre-1945 marriage cases, 45% for those married in the years 1945–64, and only 24% for those married since 1965.[9]

However, before we can be confident of the conclusion that the tendency to marry within ethnic groups has declined, we must perform another kind of analysis on these data on national origins. The reason we need to do this involves the fact that differences in the availability of women and men of various national origins across time in the sample (which affect the column and row totals, or "marginals" in such seven-by-seven tables) may produce misleading conclusions if we simply cite the total number of ethnically homogamous marriages (those who fall on the diagonals of such tables). To guard against this possibility, we utilize a technique called "log-linear analysis," which makes it possible to discount the effect of shifting marginal totals and see whether there is an underlying trend across marriage generations. In order to carry out this sort of analysis, I simplified nationality groupings still further, restricting my attention to European-origin groups and collapsing them into three broad groupings, Anglo/Irish, Northern and Central Europe, and Southern and Eastern Europe.[10]

The resulting tables for ethnic in-marriage and out-marriage over three marriage generations are presented in Table 5.1. With this much simplified table, the percentages of homogamous marriages are, of course, still higher, but they continue to display the time trend already detected. To be specific, in prewar marriages 58% of all respondents married men from the same broad set of national origin categories as themselves; for those married in the baby-boom generation a similar 57% married homogamously; but for the post-1965 marriages the homogamy figure was only 34%. (The figures for the diagonal of the lower panel of Table 5.1 total 35% due to rounding.)

When log-linear analysis was carried out on the figures in these subtables the model was tested which specified that the figures might be produced by shifting marginal totals and interactions among those marginals, with no "true" dif-

Table 5.1. Generational Contrasts in Ethnic Inmarriage (percentage of total)

	Wife Ethnic Group		
	Anglo/ Irish	North/ Central Europe	South/ Eastern Europe
1. Marriage Generation: 1925–44			
Husband Ethnic Group:			
Anglo/Irish	20	10	3
North/Central Europe	20	19	2
South/Eastern Europe (Subtable $N = 59$)	3	3	19
2. Marriage Generation: 1945–64			
Anglo/Irish	21	11	2
North/Central Europe	12	20	1
South/Eastern Europe (Subtable $N = 138$)	9	8	16
3. Marriage Generation: 1965–84			
Anglo/Irish	12	15	6
North/Central Europe	15	15	6
South/Eastern Europe (Subtable $N = 152$)	16	9	8

ference across tables. This test showed that I had to reject this explanation, and that a genuine change across generations was revealed in the table.[11] In other words, for reasons that are still not clear, there appears to be a real reduction in the tendency to marry within one's own ethnic origin group, and this reduction is concentrated within the last generation of marriages covered by our study. In fact, for women in our study who married after 1965, the percentage who married within these broad ethnic group boundaries (34%) is no greater than we would expect to find based upon chance alone. So in regard to ethnic group membership, I arrive at a conclusion radically different from what I described earlier in regard to race. Rather than forming an unyielding barrier, ethnic group boundaries seem in recent years to have become quite insignificant in the Detroit sample. Women now are not marrying within national origin boundaries any more than would be expected on a "random mating" basis.

Religion

A related characteristic which shapes the selection of mates is religion. Indeed, some assume that concern for remaining within one's faith is a primary motive lying behind the tendency toward ethnic homogamy. If this argument is correct, then Irish Catholics should be more reluctant to marry Scottish Protestants than to marry Polish Catholics, and Russians of the Orthodox faith should be unwilling to marry Russian Jews, in spite of their shared nationality. For the American scene, this sort of argument has led to what is known as the "triple melting pot" theory (see Kennedy 1952). The main point of this theory is to challenge the conventional view that American society is a single melting pot in which all national and ethnic loyalties are gradually eroding and will eventually produce a homogenized America with no clear ethnic groups. The triple melting pot theory implies that ethnic loyalties and boundaries are breaking down, as the single melting pot argument contends, but that religious loyalties and boundaries are holding firm. Thus over time what is emerging are two large and one small melting pots, each based upon a shared religious faith, Protestant, Catholic, or Jewish. So German Americans and Scottish Americans of Protestant faiths should be increasingly likely to marry each other, but neither would be likely to marry Irish or German Catholics, not to mention German or Russian Jews. I can use the Detroit data to examine whether, in fact, this triple melting pot theory is borne out.

Overall in the sample 65% of all respondents had married men of the same religious faiths as themselves. This conclusion is based on dividing the sample into three categories, Catholic, Protestant, and other.[12] This would appear to indicate a considerable degree of religious preference in mate selection, but given such large groupings we would expect a fair number of homogamous matches by chance alone—to be specific, about 42%.[13]

These figures represent the entire sample and do not tell us whether religious barriers to inter-marriage have remained firm over time. When we examine tables for each marriage generation, as we did earlier in regard to ethnic marriage patterns, we find that religious barriers also have weakened. Examining the subtables in Table 5.2, the overall percentages of religiously homogamous matches in the three marriage generations are 73%, 73%, and 57%. As in the earlier analysis of ethnic group membership, there is no noticeable difference between those who married before the end of World War II and the "baby boomers." However, among women who married after 1965 there is a noticeable drop in the tendency to marry within one's own religion.

As in the previous section, I made use of log-linear analysis to see whether this time trend was statistically significant. Again I found that this trend could not be explained by the shifting marginals of the tables.[14] This drop-off in religious homogamy appears to be "real," rather than a statistical artifact. Although the drop-off is not as striking as in the earlier analysis of ethnic group homogamy, and in recent times there is still some clear tendency to marry within one's religion, the decline in religious homogamy does undermine the "triple melting pot" argument. Apparently in the Detroit sample both ethnic group membership and religious faith are becoming less important in shaping who people marry, but

Table 5.2. Generational Contrasts in Religious Inmarriage (percentage of total)

	Wife Religion When Young		
	Catholic	*Protestant*	*Other*
1. Marriage Generation: 1925–44			
Husband's Religion:			
Catholic	24	5	0
Protestant	9	44	3
Other	3	8	5
(Subtable $N = 66$)			
2. Marriage Generation: 1945–64			
Catholic	29	11	1
Protestant	7	41	1
Other	1	6	3
(Subtable $N = 179$)			
3. Marriage Generation: 1965–84			
Catholic	26	15	2
Protestant	14	28	1
Other	3	8	3
(Subtable $N = 207$)			

only in the last couple of decades. If anything, these trends point instead to the more conventional, "single melting pot" argument, in which primordial characteristics rooted in family origin and history are becoming less important in today's America.[15]

Social Class

If factors such as ethnicity and religion are playing a less important role in influencing who marries whom, this could have one of several implications. It could mean, for instance, that arguments about the irrationality and unpredictability of romantic love are correct, and that status group barriers to intermarriage in America are declining in general (with the partial but crucial exception of racial barriers, as already noted). However, it may mean something quite different. Some previous analysts have suggested that ethnicity and religion, on the one hand, and social class on the other, are competing organizing principles of American social life. America has never had a strong socialist tradition or a unified labor movement, say partisans of this view, in part because the American working class is fragmented by ethnic and religious cleavages and animosities. But over time, as ethnicity and religious group membership lose some of their salience, perhaps social class will more and more dominate how Americans think about their places in society.[16] In terms of the topic at hand, this means that young people, and their families, will become less concerned with whether a potential marriage partner is of the "correct" ethnic group or religious faith, but they will continue to stress, and perhaps increasingly so, whether that prospect has the "correct" social class origins or personal status characteristics.

In order to examine these alternative possibilities, we used the Detroit data to see how much social class has shaped the choice of marital partners. However, it turns out that this is much more complicated to do than was the case with regard to race, ethnicity, and religion. There are two primary complicating factors. For one there are social class characteristics of the families in which the young couple grew up vs. those of the young couple themselves, and I don't have a ready idea about which of these is the most important for mate choice. In addition, social classes do not have clear boundaries, as do religious and ethnic groups, so what should be considered marriage within or outside of one's class is much more difficult to judge.[17] With these complexities in mind we will need to examine several different kinds of social class measures to see whether, together, they yield a picture of social class influences on mate choice becoming stronger, weakening, or remaining the same.

Let us first examine information about the families in which our respondents and the men they first married grew up. We asked each respondent which social class she would say her family belonged to when she was 16, and gave her five options to choose from—poor, working class, middle class, upper-middle class, and upper class. And we asked her to judge the social class origins of her first husband in terms of the same five categories. These questions provide rough measures of the subjective social class origins of the bride and groom. Overall for the entire sample about 58% of all respondents felt they had married men from families of the same social class levels as themselves. About 22% had married men from lower class levels and 20% men from higher class levels, figures that provide no support for the common view that there is a tendency for women in America to "marry up" to men from higher social class positions. If we examine contrasts across marriage generations (Table 5.3), we see a pattern that at first looks familiar—one of declining influence of social class origins. The percentages of respondents who had married men from the same class origins in the three generations was 62%, 65%, and 51% (52% in the third generation sub-table, due to rounding). In this case, however, when I simplified the table by using three class origin categories (poor/working, middle, and upper middle/upper) and carried out log-linear analysis, it turned out that the contrasts across generations were not significantly different from what we would expect by chance alone, based on the shifting marginal distributions in the tables (details not shown here).[18] I must conclude, then, that there is a slight, but not statistically significant, recent tendency for the subjective social class origins of the two families recently to be less salient in the selection of a marriage partner.

We have data in our questionnaire on one other social class characteristic of the

Table 5.3. Generational Contrasts in Class Origin Matching (percentage of total)

	Wife Class Origins				
	Poor	Working	Middle	Upper-Middle	Upper
1. Marriage Generation: 1925–44					
Husband Class Origins:					
Poor	5	5	0	0	0
Working	6	42	9	5	0
Middle	0	8	9	2	0
Upper-Middle	0	0	5	6	0
Upper	0	0	0	0	0
(Subtable N = 65)					
2. Marriage Generation: 1945–64					
Poor	6	5	1	1	0
Working	3	38	8	2	0
Middle	2	7	17	2	0
Upper-Middle	0	1	3	3	1
Upper	0	0	0	0	1
(Subtable N = 178)					
3. Marriage Generation: 1965–84					
Poor	1	5	1	0	0
Working	3	24	12	2	1
Middle	2	9	22	4	0
Upper-Middle	1	2	7	4	0
Upper	0	1	1	1	1
(Subtable N = 208)					

families of both the bride and groom—the occupations of their fathers. If I use our most detailed breakdown of occupations (into 10 categories), we discover that for the sample as a whole only 29% of our respondents married men whose fathers had the same type of job as their own fathers did (table not shown here).[19] However, if I am interested in social class this sort of calculation is not very useful, since some occupational categories may differ only slightly in prestige and pay. So instead of using this full distribution, I collapsed occupational types into three main categories: professional and managerial (categories 1–3 in the 10 category version), "other" (categories 4–5 and 9–10), and manual workers (categories 6–8). The intermediate category is something of a hodge-podge, but it mainly consists of lower white collar jobs that often entail slightly higher prestige, but lower pay, than the best of the blue collar jobs that fall in the third main category. Thus insofar as fathers' occupations help to determine general social class position, we may think of these broad categories as corresponding roughly to upper middle class, lower middle class, and working class. Using this

Table 5.4.   Generational Contrasts in Father Occupation Matching
(percentage of total)

	Wife's Father's Occupation		
	Professional/ Managerial	Other	Manual
1. Marriage Generation: 1925–44			
Husband's Father's Occupation:			
Professional/Managerial	9	7	2
Other	0	9	18
Manual	11	9	34
(Subtable *N* = 44)			
2. Marriage Generation: 1945–64			
Professional/Managerial	8	4	8
Other	3	8	9
Manual	14	11	36
(Subtable *N* = 143)			
3. Marriage Generation: 1965–84			
Professional/Managerial	14	4	14
Other	3	3	7
Manual	11	9	35
(Subtable *N* = 158)			

simpler division, I found that overall 51% of our respondents married men from the same social class origins as themselves.[20]

When we examine the three marriage generations separately (Table 5.4), we find that there is no detectable trend for occupational origin matching in marriage to increase or decrease. The percentage of women marrying men from the same family occupational origins is 52%, 51%, and 52% in the three generations. Log-linear analysis in this case confirms that there is no significant trend in assortative mating by fathers' occupational levels (details not shown here). These results provide no evidence that class origin barriers to marriage are either weakening or strengthening.

Of course, it might be argued that the sort of status criteria used in mate selection do not in most cases involve the comparison of the occupations of the two fathers, unless the fathers involved are wealthy members of America's upper class. What will matter most to a woman (and to her parents) is not what a prospect's father does for a living, but what the prospect himself does, or what his projected future occupation is (as perhaps indicated by his level of education). With regard to the woman, we can also raise some questions about what status characteristics will matter to any potential marriage partners. Will they care about the woman's occupation (if she has one) or her educational level, or will they be concerned mainly with the status of the family she comes from, as represented by the occupation of her father?[21] These considerations lead me to examine three other kinds of potential status matching in the sample of first marriages—the comparison between the husband's occupation and the respondent's father's occupation, between the husband's occupation and the respondent's, and between the husband's educational level and the respondent's educational level.

The results of all three of these comparisons tell pretty much the same story. Using the same three broad occupational categories, we find that 51% of the women married men whose occupations were in the same categories as those of these women's fathers, and that there was no significant time trend in this kind of status matching (tables not shown here).[22] For the comparison of the woman's occupation and her husband's the homogamous tendency was much lower—only 35%. This lower figure is due mainly to the sex-typing that is still prevalent in our labor force, since 74% of our respondents, but only 25% of their grooms, had jobs classified in our "other" category (mainly clerical, sales, and service jobs), while 53% of the grooms, but only 14% of our respondents, had blue collar jobs.[23] And again there is no significant trend toward stronger or weaker matching of the occupations of the bride and groom over time, according to log-linear analysis results (again, details omitted here).[24]

Finally, we can examine status matching in regard to the schooling obtained by respondents vis-à-vis their husbands. Using a six category division of educational attainment (primary, incomplete secondary, completed secondary, incomplete college, completed college, and post-graduate education), we find that overall 41% of our respondents married men who received the same amount of schooling that they did. About 30% of the women married better educated men, and 30% married less educated men, again showing no tendency for women to "marry up."[25] If we examine educational homogamy in each marriage generation (see Table 5.5), at first it appears that educational matching has become increasingly close. To be specific, the proportion of respondents who married men with the same amount of education as themselves (in terms of these six categories) rose from 32% to 36% and then 48%. But when I combined the schooling measures into three broad categories—less than high school graduation, high school graduation, and at least some college—in order to test this trend with log-linear analysis (details not shown here), the result was that the change over time was not statistically significant.[26] So there is evidence here for a modest increase in educational homogamy, but not a large enough increase to support an argument that educational matching has significantly more influence on mate choice now than in the past.

In general, the various social class measures reviewed produce a fairly consistent picture. Some show slight evidence of increased status matching in more recent times, while others show some evidence of decreased status matching. The slight decline in subjective class origin homogamy, combined with the

Table 5.5. Generational Contrasts in Educational Inmarriage (percentage of total)

	Wife's Education					
	Primary	Inc. H.S.	H.S. Grad.	Inc. Coll.	Coll. Grad.	Post-Graduate
1. Marriage Generation: 1925–44						
Husband's Education:						
Primary	10	14	8	0	0	0
Incomplete H.S.	0	5	8	3	0	2
H.S. Graduate	2	5	14	5	0	2
Incomplete College	2	0	3	2	2	0
College Graduate	0	2	5	2	0	2
Post-Graduate	0	0	0	0	5	2
(Subtable $N = 63$)						
2. Marriage Generation: 1945–64						
Primary	2	3	2	0	0	0
Incomplete H.S.	1	5	11	2	0	0
H.S. Graduate	2	4	22	9	1	1
Incomplete College	0	2	7	5	2	1
College Graduate	0	0	7	3	1	0
Post-Graduate	0	0	3	1	5	2
(Subtable $N = 179$)						
3. Marriage Generation: 1965–84						
Primary	0	1	2	0	0	0
Incomplete H.S.	0	2	7	3	0	0
H.S. Graduate	0	2	25	7	1	1
Incomplete College	0	1	12	10	1	1
College Graduate	0	1	2	7	5	2
Post-Graduate	0	0	0	2	1	5
(Subtable $N = 208$)						

modest increase in educational homogamy, provides some hint that over time personal status characteristic matching has been growing in importance relative to family class background matching. But none of these shifts are strong enough to allow us to conclude that they could not have occurred based on chance alone. So the weight of the evidence points to the conclusion that social class factors are important in the selection of a marriage mate, and that this importance has neither increased nor decreased significantly in recent times. Earlier we found that ethnic and religious factors in mate selection had declined recently in importance, but this change does not seem to have been part of a pattern in which social class influences on mate choice have increasingly replaced ethnic and religious choices. The evidence from the Detroit survey instead points to something like the following: Earlier in this century the issue of who marries whom was first and foremost influenced by race, and then perhaps by religion, and finally by ethnicity and social class. In recent times religion and ethnicity have declined in importance, while other influence have not changed much. So currently race remains the paramount barrier, religion and social class are still of some importance, and ethnic group membership has become relatively insignificant.[27] The declining strength of some of the status criteria that used to give powerful shape to mate selection does represent a broadening of options. But the continued strength of race and class, in particular, still make the process of mate selection very different from the random "love conquers all" pattern in which many Americans would like to believe.

Why Does "Like Marry Like?": Social Pressure

I have demonstrated that in a number of realms homogamy—the tendency of people to pick spouses from backgrounds similar to their own—is still important, although in regard to nationality and religion this pattern has somewhat weakened. But we still do not know why this pattern persists in the midst of our dating culture and emphasis on romantic love. And we also do not know why some people follow this tendency while others do not. In the pages that follow, I will test various ideas that people have put forward to explain why love, rather than conquering all, seems often to remain confined within the social cleavages of our society.

One source of the tendency to marry someone from a similar background may be social pressure. The discussion at the beginning of this chapter is based on this assumption. There it was argued that parents are more concerned with status than love, and an arranged marriage system should therefore produce high levels of homogamy. A totally youth-driven mate choice system, in this view, would result in less homogamy, as individual feelings and attractions overcome social barriers. Even though America has long had a predominantly free choice mating system, still parents have a variety of ways of making their views of a date or a marital prospect known.[28] In some cases parental feelings may be communicated subtly and indirectly—by a tone of voice, strained silence, or a slightly curled lip. In other cases, as discussed in Chapter 2, parental views are communicated more bluntly—by forbidding the offspring to see the person again, by quickly arranging a move to another locale or school, or even by threatening violence. And pressure to make a "wise" choice can come from other sources than parents. Friends, neighbors, and workmates may all convey approval of "suitable" dates and potential mates and disapproval of "mismatches." I am suggesting, then, that social pressure in general, and parental pressure in particular, may be an important factor fostering status matching in marriage.

How can we test the idea that social pressure is a primary mechanism that sustains homogamous choices of mates? If social pressure, and particularly pa-

Table 5.6.   Social Pressure Indicators and Mate Choice Homogamy
(bivariate correlation statistics)

	Class Origin Homog.	Father Job Homog.	Husb./ Father Job Homog.	Educ. Homog.	Relig. Identical	Ethnic Group Homog.
Social Pressure Indicators:						
Parental Interference Scale	−.11*	−.11*	.01	−.07	−.09	−.03
Family Conflicts Scale	−.11*	−.11	−.00	.10*	−.06	−.07
Youth Independence Scale	−.09	−.06	−.09	.02	−.05	−.20*
Broken Home Scale	−.03	−.07	−.02	−.03	−.00	.01
How Much in Love	−.03	−.00	−.09	.05	.08	.00
Age at First Marriage	−.08	−.10	−.04	−.07	.02	−.03
Premarital Cohabitation	−.08	−.04	.06	.02	−.14*	−.07
Premarital Pregnancy	−.06	.02	.08	−.01	−.01	−.00

*N*s range from 342 to 454; * = $p < .05$

rental pressure, is a major source of homogamy, we would expect that in cases where parents were active in exerting such pressure, and where daughters were closely tied to their parents and likely to be influenced by them, marriages would be quite homogamous. However, in cases in which the parents did not try to actively exert pressure, or where their daughters were alienated or independent, we would expect to find less homogamy. By looking at such contrasts within the Detroit sample we can see whether these predictions are accurate.

In Table 5.6 I examine the correlations between various homogamy measures and indicators of either parental pressure or daughter ties to her parents (assumed to lead to susceptibility to such pressure).[29] "Parental Interference" is a scale composed of various items indicating parental attempts to influence date selection and mate choice, actions presumed to foster homogamy. "Family Conflicts" is a scale composed of items indicating conflicts between the parents, and between them and their daughter, phenomena which should undermine homogamy. "Youth Independence" is a scale indicating financial and residential independence of the woman before and after the marriage, and this also should undermine homogamy. "Broken Home" is a scale that indicates whether one or both parents were absent when the respondent was growing up and when she married, with absence expected to lead to less homogamy. In addition, it is assumed that a late age of marriage, being very much in love, cohabitation before marriage, and premarital pregnancy all might indicate daughters who were less tied to parents and more likely to rebel against parental wishes. When I examine Table 5.6, however, it indicates that most of these expectations are not borne out. In general the correlations in the table are weak, and no single factor shows a strong and consistent tendency to affect various aspects of marital homogamy.[30] This pattern provides evidence for an important point that we will see again in later tables: The factors that lead women to marry men similar to themselves in one respect—say, religion—are not the same as those that produce homogamy in another, such as education. With so few correlations of any real strength in the table, it seems safe to conclude that social pressure is not a major determinant of the tendency for "like" to marry "like."

However, there is one pattern in Table 5.6 that requires further scrutiny. It appears that when parents try to influence their daughters' choices of dates and husbands, the daughters are *less*, rather than more, likely to marry someone from the same class origin (as shown by the modest, but statistically significant negative correlations between the Parental Interference Scale and both class origin and fathers' job homogamy). There are a couple of interpretations possible for this pattern. It could be that we are observing a "Romeo and Juliet effect," which involves the idea that parental disapproval, rather than having its intended effect, actually enhances romantic sentiment, thus making "mismatched" marriages more likely (see Driscoll, Davis, and Lipetz 1972). We cannot make an adequate test of this idea with these data, but it is worth noting that our respondents' retrospective judgments about how much in love they were at the time that they married are *positively* associated with parental approval ($r = .15*$ for mother's approval and $r = .12*$ for father's approval), whereas according to the "Romeo and Juliet effect" we might expect a negative correlation.

I suspect that the negative correlations between Parental Interference and some class homogamy measures have a simpler interpretation. My original hypothesis assumes that, other things being equal, parents approve of homogamous choices and disapprove of mismatches. If their disapproval is somewhat effective in discouraging marriages, then some daughters will think it over and end up marrying someone their parents approve of. Only if they go ahead and marry against parental advice will such mismatched marriages end up in our sample. In other words, the weak negative correlations between parental interference and some class homogamy measures may, then, simply indicate that parents are more likely to disapprove of such mismatches than of homogamous choices.[31] Perhaps examining marriages that did occur, as we have been doing, is not a sensible test of the social pressure explanation of homogamy, and what we should be doing is comparing how women are matched in terms of background traits to their husbands in comparison with how they were matched to other men they did not end up marrying.

Our questionnaire makes it possible to investigate this idea further, since we do have some information on other males respondents did not end up marrying. We asked each respondent whether there had been any other men she had seriously considered marrying. For those women who answered yes (205, or about 45% of the sample), we asked a series of follow-up questions about the one man they had been most serious about, and these provide a reduced set of background data similar to that collected for eventual husbands.

Table 5.7. Status Matching of the Other Marital Prospect and of the
First Husband Compared (percentage of the given categories)

	Ethnicity the Same	Religion the Same	Education the Same	Class Origin the Same
	5.7a: All Respondents Who Had Other Marital Prospects			
Other Prospect	33.3	59.2	40.6	53.4
First Husband	36.5	60.1	38.5	49.0

5.7b: Of Those, Distinguishing Instances of Parental Approval and Disapproval

	(Parent)							
	Dis.	App.	Dis.	App.	Dis.	App.	Dis.	App.
Other Prospect	14.5	43.5	49.0	65.1	37.8	42.5	49.1	55.1
First Husband	36.0	39.4	52.4	61.8	33.8	42.2	39.2	53.8

5.7c: Only Cases Where Parents Disapproved of Other Prospect

Other Prospect	33.3	59.2	40.6	53.4
First Husband	21.7	59.9	34.6	40.8

Previous research by Kerkhoff suggests that as women proceed from boy-friends to more serious relationships and finally engagement, they tend to narrow the "field of eligibles," and in the process the eventual fiancé often comes from more of a similar background than did the earlier boyfriends (see Kerkhoff 1964). (However, Kerkhoff was not concerned about whether social pressure was the particular mechanism that produced this tendency.) We can use the Detroit data to examine whether, in fact, respondents were more closely matched to their first husbands than they were to their "serious prospects." We find, in Table 5.7a, that there are only slight differences between eventual husbands and prospects, and in two cases the prospects were actually more closely matched than the husbands.[32]

What does this tell us about the role of parental approval, though? There are several problems with these figures. First, we have not taken into account the fact that parents were described as having approved of the large majority of prospects, as well as of husbands, and that the level of disapproval of prospects overall (28%) was only slightly higher than for husbands (24%).[33] If we examine separately the cases of parental approval and disapproval (Table 5.7b), we can see that parental disapproval was more likely if the couple was mismatched, but that is not surprising, and not a finding that would confirm the social pressure hypothesis. We also see from these figures that in all instances, it was the prospects that parents approved of, rather than the husbands, whether liked or not, who were most likely to be similar in background to the respondents, although in most instances the differences are very small. What we really need to know is whether the women whose prospects were disapproved of by their parents went on to marry men who were more closely matched to themselves. That comparison is shown in Table 5.7c, and it reveals that, where there is any difference, it runs in the opposite direction. Women whose parents disapproved of an earlier prospect were likely to marry men less like themselves than were the rejected earlier prospects. There is no evidence in these figures that parental pressure leads women to discard mismatched prospects and settle on more closely matched men for their eventual husbands.

I do not wish to claim here that parents never influence who their daughters marry. In some cases they clearly do, although only 1.5% of our respondents gave parental objections as the main reason for not marrying their "other prospect." Parents can and do exert some influence on the mate choice of their offspring, but when they do object it is likely to be on a number of grounds, and not simply because they want to promote homogamy. What these results show is that, even if parents have some influence, their pressure is not a major source of the tendency for "like to marry like." If anything, parental pressure designed to foster homogamy seems to be counterproductive. In general, both a general examination of social pressure-related indicators (Table 5.6) and a more specific examination of whether parental pressure fosters the rejection of "mismatched" prospects (Table 5.7) cast doubt on the idea that social pressure is a major mechanism by which homogamy is fostered.

Differential Association

If parental pressure is not a major source of the tendency for "like to marry like," how might this tendency be explained? One other explanation that has been offered focuses on the segregated nature of our society. America may be a melting pot, but if so it still has many unmelted lumps floating around in it. The "lumps" consist of neighborhoods, schools, workplaces, clubs, and other associations that are mainly composed of people of the same social class, ethnic group, race, or religion. The development of segregated social lives has been most extensively documented for America's very rich, but ethnic ghettos, parochial schools, restrictive housing covenants, and other features of American life make such segregation highly visible in most sectors of our society.[34] This extensive social segregation then produces what sociologists call tendencies for "differential association"—individuals will have many chances to meet and get to know people from backgrounds similar to their own, but relatively few to do so with people from very different backgrounds.[35] As a consequence, when choosing dates and considering marital prospects, it is likely that most of those you know and consider eligible will be from backgrounds similar to your own.

This tendency toward differential association is connected to a perennial finding of mate-choice research noted in Chapter 2, that "propinquity" plays a major role in mate choice. Numerous studies since the 1930s in American cities have found that a majority of newly married couples had lived only a few blocks from each other when they met. (The reader should recall, however, that in Chapter 2 I reported some evidence that recent brides in our sample had not lived as close to their grooms at the onset of dating as had earlier brides.) Some researchers have even suggested that this propinquity tendency works like gravity, with the likelihood of marrying being inversely proportional to the square of the distance between the residences of the two people! And given the tendency of most Americans to live among neighbors who have similar social backgrounds, propinquity tends to produce marital homogamy. The extreme instance can be illustrated by what I call the "missing Eskimo romance scenario." It might be the case that, in terms of personality and other factors, the individual most suited to marry Sally Jones of Detroit would be an Eskimo. However, since there are precious few Eskimos living in Detroit, she is never likely to know the romantic pleasures she is missing, and she will probably marry someone who comes from a much less exotic social background.

In its pure form, the "differential association" explanation of marital homogamy does not assume that pressure from parents or friends or strong sentiments of ethnic or class loyalty need occur for homogamy to be common. Perhaps family desires to avoid contact with "alien" groups and a wish to "mix with their own kind" do play a role in explaining why residential, school, and associational segregation occur in the first place. However, once this pattern of segregation is established, parents can afford to be quite "liberal" and not try to control the dating activities of their offspring. This is so because in a segregated society, few people from different social backgrounds will enter the social worlds of the offspring on a regular enough basis to become potential marital prospects—to enter what has been termed the "field of eligibles." Thus when it comes time to choose a marital partner, all of those whom one knows well enough to consider eligible are likely to come from similar backgrounds, and "marrying out" will be very unlikely. Indeed, research by Peter Blau and his associates (see, in particular, Blau and Schwartz 1984) indicates that variation in ethnic and religious ingroup sentiments plays little role in explaining the rates of intermarriage in American cities. What makes the most difference in intermarriage is simply the proportion of different groups that live in a city and the extent to which they are segregated, or integrated, with one another. So the second major mechanism explaining marital homogamy I want to consider is social segregation and the differential association tendencies to which this phenomenon gives rise.

How can we test this idea? Unfortunately, we cannot do so very precisely or directly. If differential association is the major explanation of variations in homogamy, we would expect that those individuals who have had a more limited range of social contacts prior to marriage, and with mostly similar people, would tend to marry homogamously. In contrast, those who have had a broader range of social contacts with a more heterogeneous range of people should be less likely to end up homogamously married. Ideally to test this supposition we would need to have detailed information on the racial/class/ethnic/religious composition of the neighborhoods, schools, workplaces, associations, and friendship networks of each respondent in the years prior to getting married. But it is impossible to get such detailed information with the sort of retrospective questionnaire used in the current study.[36] Instead, we have to content ourselves with a number of indirect but simpler measures that may tap differential association: Whether the first husband was introduced by someone or was first met directly (assuming that introductions are more likely to involve "matched" individuals); whether the woman had other steady boyfriends or not; how many years she spent dating prior to marriage; how far apart her first husband lived at the time that they first met (assuming, again, that those living close at hand are more likely to be homogamous); whether the respondent mostly grew up in a rural area, a small town, a small city, or a large city (assuming that chances for meeting dissimilar people are greater in larger communities); whether she attended a private or parochial school vs. a public school (assuming more heterogeneity in the latter); whether she recalls her neighborhood as homogeneous or heterogeneous; whether she recalls her friends as homogeneous or heterogeneous; and the number of states she lived in while growing up (assuming that geographical mobility leads to more diversity in social contacts).

In Table 5.8 the correlations of these indicators of differential association with various homogamy measures are displayed. The results are again rather disappointing. As with the earlier social pressure hypothesis investigation, no single measure influences all aspects of homogamy, and none of the correlations in the table is very strong. Whether the couple met directly or was introduced, whether

Table 5.8.   Differential Association Indicators and Marital Homogamy
(bivariate correlation statistics)

	Class Origin Homog.	Father Job Homog.	Husb./ Father Job Homog.	Educ. Homog.	Relig. Identical	Ethnic Group Homog.
Differential Association Indicators:						
Met Directly	.03	−.03	−.02	.00	−.06	.03
Other Steadies	−.15*	.03	.04	−.02	−.12*	−.13*
Years Dating	−.09	−.12*	−.03	−.15*	.01	−.04
Distance When Met	.03	−.01	−.12*	−.09	.04	.09
Size of Community	.00	.07	−.08	−.00	.04	.03
Private School	.04	−.13*	−.03	−.02	.05	.02
Neighbor Heterogeneity	−.05	−.08	.02	−.02	−.03	−.00
Friend Heterogeneity	.01	.05	.01	−.01	−.05	.01
States Lived In	−.07	−.03	.06	.02	.03	−.07

*N*s range from 346 to 454;   * = p < .05

the respondent grew up in a small or large community, whether she recalls homogeneous or heterogeneous neighborhoods and friends, and the number of states that she lived in while growing up are not significantly related to any of the homogamy measures. Also, contrary to my original prediction, those who attended private schools are somewhat more likely to marry men whose fathers have occupations that are different from their own fathers' than is the case for women who attended public schools. [37]

So most of my predictions in regard to differential association are not borne out. Still, there are more significant associations in the table than we would expect due to chance alone, and the table does show weak relations between several dating measures and homogamy. [38] Respondents who had had more than one steady boyfriend were, as predicted, more likely than others to marry men from different classes, religions, and ethnic groups. Women who spent more years in the dating stage were somewhat more likely to marry men from different parental occupational backgrounds and with dissimilar educational levels. And women who married men who lived further away from them were slightly more likely to have married men whose occupations were different from those held by their fathers. Still, even when taken together these findings provide only the weakest support for the idea that differential association is the major explanation of marital homogamy. Of course, our inability to measure differential association in the premarital years very well may explain these weak results, but until studies are conducted which solve the measurement problems, my conclusion must be primarily negative. At the aggregate or population level it may be the case, as Blau and others argue, that differential association is the best explanation for the degree of intermarriage that occurs in an entire community. But differential association does not appear to be a very powerful explanation for variation at the individual level—for why some women within a community such as Detroit married "one of their own" while others did not.

Values Selection

Yet a third potential source of homogamy has been referred to as "values selection." [39] The assumption here is that individuals in choosing someone to marry make use of their personal values, and by doing so they tend to select people who have values similar to their own. [40] It is also assumed that various subgroups in American society have somewhat different values; or, to put it in another way, that class position, race, ethnicity, and religion shape personal values in distinctive ways. [41]

If these two claims are true—that personal values play an important role in mate selection, and that values differ across subgroups in our society—then we can see how values selection could help explain marital homogamy. An individual would, while growing up, develop a distinctive set of personal values which to a considerable extent would reflect his or her class, ethnic, and other social background. Then in date selection and mate choice these values would act as "screening factors," ruling out individuals with incompatible values and leaving only those with compatible values (presumably mostly from similar social backgrounds) to choose from. Even if parents and friends exerted no pressure to marry homogamously, and even if there were lots of social contacts with individuals from different backgrounds, still the effect of values selection would be to produce a disproportionate number of couples who came from similar backgrounds.

Unfortunately, this notion cannot be adequately tested. Ideally we would measure important personal values that our respondents had prior to their first marriages, measures at the same time of the personal values of the men they married, and perhaps even measures of the values of other "marital prospects" that they didn't marry. But without a time machine we cannot obtain such measures. The best we could do was to ask our respondents a series of questions about their values at the time of the interview. We also asked them about their judgment of the values held by their husbands.[42]

I will test the idea that values selection promotes homogamy by indicating whether, in fact, the reported values of couples who are homogamous are more similar than those of couples who are not homogamous (in terms of social background). Several leaps of faith are involved in this test. I have to assume that women are accurately reporting their own values and that they are giving accurate reports of their husbands' values as well. I also have to assume that there is relative stability of values in any individual over time, so that values reported at the time of the interview are not very different from the values that would have been reported at the time of the marriage. In making this assumption I have to rule out other possibilities, such as that any similarity of values between spouses is primarily a product of the number of years they have lived together. (The idea that over time couples get more and more alike is a popular one, but I did test this idea and found that there was no significant relationship between the number of years a couple had been married and the degree of similarity of their reported values.) Still, it must be admitted that my test of the values similarity mechanism is a decidedly indirect and imperfect one.

Even if we assume that personal values play a role in fostering homogamy, that still leaves us with a research dilemma. What particular values are important in this regard? Individuals have all sorts of values—political, religious, familial, esthetic, and so forth—and any sort of comprehensive values inventory would have consumed all of our interviewing time. I decided in the Detroit questionnaire to focus on two important kinds of familial values, assuming that these would be more salient than other kinds of values in mate choice decisions. We asked our respondents to select which of seven personal qualities they thought was most important for a child to have—to be popular with others, to be ambitious to get ahead, to be obedient and well-behaved, to be interested in how and why things happen, to be considerate of others, to be independent and self reliant, or to have strong religious faith.[43] Then we asked her which trait her husband would choose as the most desirable. Similarity of values thus meant that the respondent claimed agreement between herself and her husband (which was the case for 44% of our sample). A similar procedure was carried out for a set of seven items dealing with traits needed for a successful marriage relationship—agreement on chores, satisfying each others needs, having a good income, being deeply in love, having common interests, being sexually faithful, and doing things together. (In this case 46% claimed agreement with their husbands on the most important quality.)

We also asked respondents two other sets of questions that are perhaps less centrally related to their personal values, but still seem related to the idea of "screening factors" that may play a role in mate choice. We asked respondents to list four activities they like to engage in when they have free time, and we then asked them what activities their husbands like to engage in in their free time. Again, these responses were used to construct a similarity score by counting how many activities were the same for both. In addition, we asked each respondent to rate herself in terms of ten character traits or habits, and then to do the same for her husband.[44] These responses were used to construct a trait similarity scale, which equalled the number of traits for which the respondent assigned herself and her spouse to the same descriptive category. Finally, I wanted to examine one special attitude item included in our questionnaire. We asked each respondent whether she strongly agreed, agreed, disagreed, or strongly disagreed with the following statement: "When the husband and wife come from different social backgrounds, the marriage is bound to have problems." I assume that if the woman's value system produces an inclination to agree with this sort of statement she would be likely to marry someone from a similar social background.

Table 5.9 presents the correlations between various measures of values similarities and of homogamy. The figures in the table are even weaker than those in previous tables, and the single significant association could have occurred by chance alone.[45] So these results provide no evidence at all that values similarity plays a screening role in promoting marital homogamy.

Of course, given the imperfect way in which I carried out this analysis, and particularly the fact that my values measures are for the time of the interview, rather than for the time prior to marriage, it might be argued that I have not given this idea a fair test. I looked into this possibility further by performing another kind of analysis. The values similarity prediction assumes that the various subgroups in our society have somewhat different values. But is that really the case? I conducted a brief analysis (results not displayed here) to see how the two sets of values items (for childrearing and marital success) were related to current background characteristics—the woman's ethnic group identification, level of education, the family's current class position, current religious identification, and husband's occupation. It turned out that none of these current background charac-

Table 5.9. Values Similarity Indicators and Marital Homogamy
(bivariate correlation statistics)

	Class Origin Homog.	Father Job Homog.	Husb./ Father Job Homog.	Educ. Homog.	Relig. Identical	Ethnic Group Homog.
Values Similarity Indicators:						
Agree on Child Values	.07	−.11	.01	.14*	.04	−.01
Agree on Marriage Values	.10	.06	−.08	.01	.03	−.04
Agree on Leisure	.06	−.09	−.04	.03	.06	−.09
Shared Personal Traits	.08	−.02	−.05	.05	.06	−.00
Believe Homogamy Important	.06	.09	.04	.08	−.06	−.11

*N*s range from 263–381 (respondents married once only included);   * = p < .05

teristics made a significant difference in the traits listed as important in a marriage, and only the perceived class level and the woman's educational level made some difference in childrearing values, with lower class and less educated women stressing obedience more than others, and middle class and better educated women stressing independence and being interested in how things work.[46] With these minor exceptions, in general I did not find much difference in these values across various current social background categories.

The findings in Table 5.9 leave us with two possible conclusions. It may be the case that I have not selected or measured properly the kinds of values that do play a role in fostering marital homogamy. The other possibility is that ethnic, religious, and class subgroups in our society do not differ consistently enough in their values for the values similarity mechanism to be a plausible explanation for the tendency for "like to marry like" in our society.[47] Given my own failure to find clear subgroup differences in values in the Detroit sample, I am inclined to favor the latter conclusion. Values similarity does not seem to play a major role in fostering marital homogamy. This does not mean that personal values play no role in influencing who will marry whom. It simply means that values may be highly variable and idiosyncratic, not predicted well by social background traits. Individuals may tend to marry people with values similar to themselves, but this does not mean that those selected will come from similar classes, religions, or ethnic groups.

Thus far we have been engaged in a rather discouraging analytical quest. We have examined three common explanations for why people tend to marry others who come from similar backgrounds—social pressure, differential association, and values selection. Although there are problems in measurement that prevent me from performing completely satisfactory tests of these ideas, still my conclusions are primarily negative. All three mechanisms seem to play either a minor role or no role at all in producing the levels of marital homogamy that exist in our

Table 5.10. Social Background Characteristics and Marital Homogamy
(bivariate correlation statistics)

	Class Origin Homog.	Father Job Homog.	Husb./ Father Job Homog.	Educ. Homog.	Relig. Identical	Ethnic Group Homog.
Social Background Characteristics:						
Respondent Class Origin	−.11*	−.14*	−.05	.09	−.11*	−.05
Father's Occupation	−.12*	−.26*	−.15*	−.01	−.06	−.13*
Father's Education	−.05	−.08	−.11*	.05	−.11*	−.16*
Respondent's Education	−.07	−.06	−.03	.01	.01	−.12*
Ethnic Roots Scale	.10*	−.07	−.05	.02	.06	.24*
Respondent Catholic	−.09	.06	.11*	.01	−.02	−.06
Respondent Religiosity	.01	−.12*	−.05	−.06	.10*	.04
Respondent is Black	.06	.11*	.09	−.01	.08	n.a.
Year First Married	−.13*	−.05	−.01	.10*	−.22*	−.22*

Ns range from 376–454;   n.a. = not applicable; * = $p < .05$

society. Before throwing in the towel, I want to examine a few other miscellaneous factors that may play a role in fostering marital homogamy. In particular, are there certain class or religious/ethnic groups that practice more homogamy than others? In earlier discussions I mentioned some arguments from previous research on this topic that implied that there are. For example, some previous work has suggested a trade-off between class and ethnic/religious factors in homogamy (e.g., Hechter 1978). People in higher class positions may be very anxious to marry within the same (or higher) class level, but less selective about ethnicity and religion. In lower class positions, in contrast, ethnic and religious boundaries may be seen as more important, and class levels less, since there are fewer class-related privileges to protect.

Table 5.10 presents correlations between class, ethnic, and religious background characteristics and various homogamy measures. The figures in the table are not entirely consistent, and again most of them are weak, but still they present a fairly consistent picture.[48] And that picture is somewhat different from the one suggested by earlier writings. Contrary to what was expected, it turns out that respondents who came from higher class positions were *less,* rather than more, likely than others to marry homogamously in terms of class.[49] We can also see that women from higher class positions are generally less likely to marry men of the same religion or ethnic background than women from less advantageous positions. In summary, then, there seems to be a weak but general association between higher class positions and less homogamy in all respects.

On the other hand, we can see in the table that strong ethnic roots are associated with ethnic inmarriage, and high religiosity is related to marrying within one's faith.[50] (Being a Catholic, however, was not associated with more religious homogamy than being a Protestant.) But these stronger homogamous tendencies are not consistently associated with less class homogamy. Rather, people with strong ethnic roots are also significantly more likely to marry within their class level than other people, Catholics are more likely to marry men with occupations similar to their fathers than are Protestants, and, contrary to my prediction, blacks are more likely to marry within the same class level than are whites. So I find a modest, although not entirely consistent, pattern for non-Wasp religious and ethnic affiliations of respondents to be associated with both class and religious/ethnic homogamy.[51] So rather than a trade-off between class and religious/ethnic factors operating in mate choice, what we see is that the two factors reinforce each other. Both low class and non-Wasp affiliations foster marital homogamy, while assimilated middle-class families display less homogamy across the board. However, it is not entirely clear whether this tendency is due to differences in sentiments toward intermarriage of these subgroups, or simply due to variations in availability of partners from smaller vs. larger subgroups.[52]

Conclusions

The effort to track down the sources of greater or lesser status matching in mate choice has taken me through a complex set of analyses with largely negative results. Although I have not been able to perform satisfactory tests in each case, I have found little evidence that social pressure, differential association, and values selection are major mechanisms that form the basis for "like to marry like" in our society.[53] I have found that people above the working class in America, and with more "Wasp-ish" characteristics, tend to be less homogamous than others. This finding suggests that the general pattern of ethnic assimilation and "bourgeois-ification" of American society may lie at the heart of the modest declines in religious and ethnic homogamy detected earlier in this chapter. But I don't have a ready explanation for how this trend influences patterns of mate choice. If it is not less social pressure, broader patterns of social association, or less restrictive values, then how can this lesser homogamy of the middle class and Wasps be explained?[54] I am left in the position of seeing evidence of an important social change in American mate choice patterns but not having a fully satisfactory explanation of why this is occurring. The Detroit data show that America is in the process of becoming modestly less rigidly stratified in terms of patterns of mate choice, but the hows and whys of this important change constitute a challenge for future researchers.

Notes

1.   There are many fascinating aspects of the question of who marries whom that I will not be able to pursue, such as questions about how personality traits, psychic needs, and explicit criteria for

choosing a mate influence the process. I will be concerned in this chapter only with the question of how the class, ethnic, and religious backgrounds of individuals influence their choice of partners.

2.   A considerable degree of freedom for young people existed in Northwestern Europe in general, and perhaps particularly in England, and this is one characteristic that differed from most agrarian societies in other parts of Europe and in Asia (see Macfarlane 1986). However, it may still be the case that frontier conditions and the inability of parents to control adult opportunities fostered even more autonomy for the young in this realm in colonial America (see the discussion in Demos 1970).

3.   On this shift, see Rothman (1984) and Modell (1983). Some works suggest that romantic love flowered within marriage relationships in colonial times in America, at least among the better-off classes, but it is less clear whether romantic love played a central role in selection of a mate (see Demos 1970).

4.   Of course, it should be pointed out that the rational component of mate choice involves an exchange, and that in this exchange it is not always equal "commodities" that are traded. Rational calculations may, for instance, lead a young and attractive woman from humble origins to enter into marriage with a much older man who is wealthy and prominent. Still, under the majority of circumstances I assume that parental pressure and rational calculations will tend to produce marriages of people of similar traits and backgrounds.

5.   For reviews of this tendency, consult Jacobsohn and Matheny (1962); Udry (1971). The phrase "like marries like" and the competing principle "opposites attract" are usually discussed in the context of personality characteristics, rather than social backgrounds. As noted earlier, I do not have data to address the question of assortative mating in terms of personality traits, although as I read the evidence from previous research it tends to support the "like marries like" formula more than "opposites attract" even in this realm (see Udry 1963; Adams 1979).

6.   The racial categorization of respondents was made by interviewers. The (first) husband's race, in contrast, was ascertained from a direct question within the questionnaire. See Appendix 2.

7.   Detroit may be slightly less likely than other comparable urban areas to have racial intermarriages, since there is a relatively higher degree of residential segregation by race and a wider income gap between blacks and whites than in some other cities (Reynolds Farley, personal communication). However, 32% of our respondents lived elsewhere when they first got married and these later migrants to the Detroit area were not any more likely to marry someone of another race than those who married in the Detroit area (details not shown here). Indeed, the single white respondent in our sample who married a black did so in Detroit.

8.   Where more than one national origin was volunteered our interviewers also recorded a second ethnic group (as in "Scotch-Irish" or "Polish and Italian"). For the sake of simplicity I will only be concerned here with the primary ethnic identification mentioned for both the respondent and her husband. It should be kept in mind that I do not have the husband's own report on his ethnic allegiance, but only the report from his wife (or ex-wife). Previous research tells us that reports on the ethnic group membership of others in the same family are subject to some degree of error (see Lieberson and Waters 1988).

9.   If I had not collapsed ethnic groups into these seven broad categories, the degree of ethnic homogamy in marriages in the sample would have been even lower—to be specific, only 25%. The percentage of women who married men from exactly the same ethnic group declines from 34% to 30% and then to 18% across the three marriage generations.

10.   My procedure for collapsing from more than fifty categories down to seven, and then from seven down to three, is influenced by research that argues that the status grouping of European national origin groups follows clear geographical lines in roughly the orders given, and that factors such as religion are of lesser importance than geographical origins in determining status (see Peach 1980).

11.   The Chi-square statistic for the deviation of the model $r + c + t + r.c + r.t + c.t$ (where r, c, and t are row, column, and time period totals for the subtables) from the fully specified model was 28.5, which is significant at the .001 level.

12.   The number of Jews in the sample is so small—9—that I cannot examine them separately. The "other" category includes, in addition, people of various Orthodox faiths and some who claimed no religion. For Protestants we did record which denomination they belonged to, but those data will not concern us here. In other words, a marriage between a Presbyterian and a Methodist, for example, will be considered as religiously homogamous, since both involve Protestants. In all cases the questions referred to the religion in which the woman was raised and the religious orientation of her (first) husband at the time of the marriage. Thus subsequent conversions, which might overstate the influence of religion on mate selection, are excluded from these data.

13.   In other words, since about 40% of the husbands in our sample were Catholics, and another 47% were Protestants, each respondent who belonged to one of these faiths had about these percentage chances of marrying a man of her own faith, even if her selection was completely random, and so the "excess" preference for marrying within the same faith is only on the order of 20+%, rather than 65%.

14.   The Chi-square statistic for the same model as utilized earlier in regard to ethnic groups was equal to 15.86, which is significant at the .05 level.

15.   My conclusion in regard to religion is echoed in the work of other analysts, and particularly in a recent study by Norval Glenn (see Glenn 1982). A reanalysis of Kennedy's New Haven data has also contradicted her triple melting pot argument (see Peach 1980). The current analysis does not allow me to examine in detail the experiences of small subgroups in our sample, and particularly of Jews. Jewish faith in the past was more of a barrier to religious intermarriage than Catholic or Protestant faith, but we do not have sufficient numbers in the sample to see whether the intermarriage of Jews is increasing. However, national data suggest that it is (see, for example, Bumpass 1970).

16.   An intriguing analysis that suggests a "tradeoff" between ethnicity and social class in assortative mating in America is presented in Hechter (1978).

17.   In these comments I am just scratching the surface of the complications of studying social class in America. There are also objective aspects of social class position, such as educational attainment, occupational status, and income, but also subjective factors, such as people's perceptions of their class level. For reviews of some of the complexities, see Gordon (1958); Duncan (1968); and Jackman and Jackman (1983).

18.   The Chi-square statistic for our model was only 8.246, which did not surpass the .05 significance level with 8 degrees of freedom.

19.   The categories are upper professional workers, middle and lower professionals and technical workers, managers and administrators, clerical workers, sales workers, craftsmen, operatives, laborers, service workers, and farmers and farm managers. Fathers in the military were omitted from these calculations, which thus refer only to those in the civilian labor force.

20.   In this case 25% of the women are counted as having "married down" to men from lower social class origins, and 24% as having married up. This pattern of equal movement up and down corresponds to the conclusion reached earlier in regard to the subjective social class ranking of the two families. For another study casting doubt on the idea that American women marry up, see Rubin (1968).

21.   It is assumed here, as is conventionally done, that at least until recently a family's social class position depended first and foremost upon the occupational position of the male "head of the family." As more and more married women have entered, or have returned to, the labor force, this assumption has been called into question. Recent studies seem to indicate, however, that the wife's occupation at best has only a marginal influence on the family's perceived status, which is still seen as based primarily on the husband's job (see Jackman and Jackman 1983). But since I do not have information about the occupations of mothers of the husbands of our respondents, that debate becomes academic for this analysis.

22.   To be more precise, the percentage of homogamous unions increased from 47% among our prewar marriages to 54% among the post-1965 marriages, but this increase was not quite large enough to be statistically significant.

23.   The occupations referred to are those that the respondent and her groom had at the time of the wedding. Some women were not in the labor force then, and the jobs of their grooms were often of a short term nature that did not represent their eventual occupational positions. Thus we might expect that this comparison would yield only modest evidence of status matching, even if sexual segregation were not so pronounced.

24.   In this case there was a slight decline in occupational status matching across the three generations, from 40% to 32%, but the change was not statistically significant.

25.   In fact, in the prewar marriage generation, women were more likely to marry down than to marry up, by 44% to 24%.

26.   In this case the percentage of educationally homogamous unions declines and then increases, registering percentages of 56%, 51% and 63% in the three marriage generations. But these changes are not large enough to differ significantly from what we would expect to find based upon shifting marginals in the tables. The apparent increase is largely attributable to the fact that in this third generation a higher percentage of both respondents and husbands had completed high school. The finding that educational homogamy has increased slightly, but not enough to be statistically significant, differs from an earlier analysis of this topic using other methods. Richard Rockwell, using data from the 1970 U.S. Census, argued that educational homogamy had declined since the turn of the century (see Rockwell 1976). However, the well known study by Blau and Duncan (1967), using data from a 1962 national sample, reached a conclusion closer to our own—that educational homogamy had not changed significantly.

27.   These generalizations refer, of course, to the population at large. They do not imply that there are no individuals for whom very different preferences, such as a heavy stress on ethnic similarity or no concern for racial similarity, apply.

28.   It has been argued by Marvin Sussman, in fact, that parents very regularly try to influence the mate choice process of their offspring, and particularly of daughters. See Sussman (1953); also Bates (1942); Leslie, Huston, and Johnson (1986).

29.   The homogamy measures used in this and the following tables are based upon the simplified versions used in the log-linear analyses earlier in this chapter. For details on their construction, see Appendix 2. Homogamy measures based upon more detailed categories were also examined briefly, and did not yield results substantially different from those reported here.

30.   Indeed, in examining a table such as this we would expect 2.4 of the correlations to be significant at our chosen .05 level, simply from the operation of chance variations alone. Since only 6 correlations in the table surpass this level, we must interpret them cautiously, since several of these could be due to chance rather than "real" associations.

31.   However, in this case I should expect consistently significant correlations for other homogamy measures, which we do not see in the table, although most correlations have negative signs.

32.   Percentages of homogamous unions are not the only way to display similarity, but other statistics would convey the same story.

33.   Here I am collapsing the categories "disapprove" and "strongly disapprove" in both cases, and I am taking an average of the separate scores for mother's and father's approval, in the case of the eventual husband. See Appendix 2.

34.   Numerous studies are available on these points. For a graphic picture of the various ways in which America's very wealthy manage to build social walls around themselves, see Birmingham (1969).

35.   Or when they do meet such people, it will not be on the basis of the sort of equality that is necessary for such things as friendship, romantic attraction, and mate selection to develop, but on the basis of inequality—as servants, gardeners, bosses, police, and so forth.

36.   Two factors are involved. First, many respondents find it hard to recall very precisely the social composition of neighborhoods and schools some decades ago. Second, since potentially we are dealing with multiple neighborhoods, schools, workplaces, and so forth, and for each there are questions about racial, class, religious, and ethnic homogeneity, it would take a great many questions

and probes to carry out a systematic inventory. This might be done through in-depth interviews with a small number of respondents, but not in one hour interviews with a large number of women.

37. Perhaps this result is related to the fact that "private" schools here involves a lumping together of private and parochial schools, with parochial schools being much more common in the experience of our respondents (28%) than were private schools (6%). In a parochial school the desire to be together with others of the same faith may lead to more mixing of children from different parental occupational backgrounds than is the case in most public schools, which take a class character from their surrounding neighborhoods. However, we would then expect to find a significant association between private schools and religious homogamy, but we don't see one in Table 5.8.

38. On the basis of chance alone we would expect less than 3 significant associations in a table of this size, and we find 7.

39. The role of values is stressed in a number of theories of the mate choice process (see, for example, Murstein 1976). The application to explaining homogamy is provided in Coombs (1962); see also Schellenberg (1962).

40. This does not imply that other factors do not also play a role, but only that values have an important influence.

41. Again there is much literature on this issue. For social class, see, in particular, Kohn (1969); for religion see Lenski (1961).

42. We did not have the opportunity to interview the husbands directly. We don't have any information about the values held by other marital prospects either.

43. Actually, we asked first for the three qualities respondents felt were most important, and then asked about which of these they considered the most important. Since the values similarity measure concerns whether the single most important quality was the same for both spouses, I focused here only on that single trait. A similarity measure based on all three values mentioned produced results not appreciably different from those reported here.

44. The list included neat and tidy, stubborn, outgoing, late, thrifty, hot tempered, a smoker, bossy, energetic, and a drinker. For all but the last they had to place themselves in one of three categories—e.g., very neat and tidy, fairly neat and tidy, not very neat and tidy. There were four categories for drinking behavior—heavy drinker, moderate drinker, occasional drinker, and do not drink at all, (see Appendix 2 for full details).

45. In fact, with a table of this size, we expect by chance alone to find 1.5 correlations significant at the .05 level, and we found only one.

46. These are precisely the class-related differences in childrearing values identified in the research program of Melvin Kohn (see Kohn 1969). However, I did not find the expected significant association between childrearing values and the husband's occupational level. Education and subjective class made little difference in regard to other childrearing values, and none of the other background characteristics tested were significantly related to variations in these childrearing values.

47. Some other research raises doubt about the idea that there are consistent American subcultures that can explain things such as marital homogamy (see, for example, Davis 1982).

48. I also examined crosstabulations of these variables in an effort to look for nonlinear patterns, but in general little interesting turned up not conveyed by the correlation statistics.

49. One qualification of these results, however, is that in the sample there are very few people who could properly be said to belong to America's small upper class, as noted in the previous chapter. For example, only 4 out of our 459 respondents said that the family in which they grew up had belonged to the upper class, and only 5 said that more than half of family income then had come from nonwage sources (investments, etc.). Some previous research has suggested that at the very top and the very bottom of America's class hierarchy there is more in-marriage than in the middle ranges. If this is the case, then by having the poor well represented in the sample (more than 8% of our respondents said that their families had been in this "sub-working class" location) but not the rich, our data will not show the high homogamy of America's upper class.

50. Ethnic roots is a scale composed from questions about how many parents were born over-

seas, how many grandparents were born overseas, and how strong a sense of belonging to a particular ethnic group the respondent felt while growing up, (see Appendix 2).

51.   One finding that does not fit this overall pattern is that respondents who were raised to be very religious were less likely than other women to marry men whose fathers came from the same status category as their own fathers.

52.   It is also worth noting that the correlations with year of marriage in the last row of the table echo my earlier analysis of changes over time. Both religion and ethnicity reveal declining homo-gamy, while the results for class variables are mixed—occupation-based measures show no clear trend, subjective class origins have become modestly less homogamous, while individual educational levels have become modestly more homogamous.

53.   In general the associations resulting from my tests are so weak that going further to multivari-ate analysis of the variations in marital homogamy is unwarranted.

54.   One possibility I considered is that an attitude favoring homogamous marriage may simply be less strong in America's middle and upper-middle class, with other factors, such as the personal character of the prospective spouse, considered more important. However, we saw earlier in Table 5.9 that agreement with our one questionnaire item about the importance of marital homogamy was not associated with greater actual homogamy, and in any case there were no significant differences among various subgroups in the degree of belief that homogamy was important in a marriage (details not shown here).

Chapter 6

CONTEMPORARY MARRIAGE PATTERNS

While initially dating is motivated primarily by social and recreational goals, in some sense the ultimate purpose of the prolonged dating and mating process in America is to prepare for marriage. To be more precise, our dating and mate selection customs are premised on the assumption that following them will help people to select "suitable" marriage partners, ideally partners with whom they can "live happily ever after." In American society, more than in many others, marriage, or the conjugal relationship, is the lynch-pin of the family system. Marriage in our society is seen as establishing a new family and not simply as adding an additional member to an ongoing family unit.[1] Questions about the health of, and prospects for, family life in America revolve centrally around the issue of the health and durability of marriages in our society. So in a sense all of the information that we have reviewed so far is prologue. What really matters is the marriage relations that dating and mating lead up to.

In Chapters 6 and 7 I will use information from the Detroit survey to discuss the nature of marriage relations as described by respondents. I defer until Chapter 7 a discussion of why some marriages fail while others succeed. In the present chapter I prepare the way for an examination of that topic by reporting the general patterning of marriage relations in the greater Detroit area, and how the conjugal bond varies across generations. In part I want to present a general description of the patterning of the marriage relationship. But I am also particularly interested in whether the nature of marriage has changed over time and with whether it is still changing.

Earlier in this study I examined how dating and mating had varied across three "marriage generations" within the Detroit sample. I am interested in a parallel question in the present chapter—how much does the nature of marital relations vary within our sample—and particularly when women who married long ago and more recently are compared. Popular discussions of changes in American marriage suggest a number of possible trends. Some observers argue that influences such as the increasing participation of married women in the work force and the women's liberation movement are fostering more equal relations between husbands and wives. Others argue that any such change is only part of a longer process of change in all modern societies in which the stress in marriage relations has shifted from childbearing and economic cooperation to companionship and psychological gratification. As noted earlier, Ernest Burgess and his colleagues (e.g., Burgess and Locke 1953) referred to this as a change in marriage from "institution" to "companionship." Across the ocean, British sociologists Young and Wilmott (1973) referred to this as the emergence of the "symmetrical family." Whatever the particular terminology used, in general the image conveyed is of a rigidly structured and not very rewarding set of marital roles being replaced by a more flexible set emphasizing the joint and equal tie between spouses and their mutual pursuit of happiness.

Other discussions of trends in marriage have a quite different tone. Some commentators see the stress on companionship, equality, and emotional gratification in modern marriages producing heightened expectations that are impossible to satisfy. They note that primarily psychological bases of marital bonds are inevitably weaker than the economic interdependence that was stressed in earlier times. Some also see increased participation in work by wives, growing hazards faced by children, and other trends as providing external pressures on marriage relations that are greater than existed in earlier times. In any case, social changes are seen as leading not, in fact, to more rewarding and symmetrical marriages, but to more divorce, and perhaps even in surviving marriages to more dissatisfaction and conflict than would have been the case in the past. So depending upon your point of view, social change has led to marriages that are in some general sense seen as better or more rewarding, or on the other hand to marriages that are worse or perhaps even to a view that marriage as an institution is "in trouble."[2] I will attempt to shed some light on this debate by analyzing contrasting patterns of marriages within the Detroit sample.

Before beginning this examination, I must acknowledge that the Detroit survey data are not ideally suited to fully resolving questions about social change, as noted in Chapter 1. The main reason for this, once again, is that these data are "cross-sectional." They were collected at one point in time, in the summer of 1984. With this sort of data it is not possible to disentangle different possible explanations for contrasts between younger and older women in our sample. If we find, for instance, that there is more sharing of chores between spouses among women who married recently than among women who married earlier, we might think that this indicates a trend in the making, that younger women, who are better educated and have grown up during the period of influence of the women's movement, are displaying a pattern of cooperation and equality that will become dominant in the future. However, this would not be a safe assumption. It could be that the older women in the sample used to have more sharing of chores in their marriages but no longer do so. Since we do not have information on how these older women divided chores in the earlier years of their marriages, we cannot be sure.

Similarly, it could be the case that the younger women in the sample in the future will fall into patterns that involve less sharing of chores by their husbands. We cannot know unless we go back and study these younger women again later. So we cannot be certain of whether contrasts between different generations in the sample indicate a "real" trend toward change unless we have "longitudinal" data.[3] In other words, we would need to conduct a study over time, instead of cross-sectionally. Since I do not have data from a study done over time, I will have to try to use other information in the study, such as on the life-cycle stage of each respondent, her age, and the number of years she has been married, to check impressions gained from comparing marriage generations.[4] I will not be able, even taking these other background traits into account, to resolve the issues of marriage change completely satisfactorily.

Since I am interested in the general patterns of marriage relations within the sample, I will not attempt to systematically investigate the impact of class, religious, ethnic, and other influences on the shape of conjugal relations. However, since both the work status of the wife and race are assumed in most writings on marriage relations to have a critical influence on the nature of the bond between spouses, I will give those two influences some attention. I will be interested in whether contrasts between generations in marriage patterns exist even if I control for the race and the working status of respondents.

The discussion to this point assumes that there will be major differences in the patterning of conjugal relations across marriage generations. But it will be interesting to see whether, for some aspects of the marriage relationship, there are no such clear contrasts. If we find, in fact, modest or negligible differences across generations, this would tend to indicate that neither the "improving" nor the "going to pot" arguments about American marriage is correct, and that what exists instead is basic continuity and consensus. (Although here again the Detroit data will not allow me to resolve issues of social change, or lack of change, with certainty.)

Marital History

In order to set the discussion in this chapter and the next in proper context, I summarize here basic factual information about the marital histories of the women we interviewed. The reader will recall that the Detroit sample included only women aged 18–75 who had been married at least once, and that the times when our respondents first married covered a span of 60 years, from 1925 to 1984. The basic facts about the marital histories of respondents are contained in the three panels of Figure 6.1. Of the 459 women we interviewed, 77.7% were currently married, 10.7% were divorced, 4.4% were separated, and 7.2% were widowed (see Figure 6.1a). The large majority of respondents—83.7%—had been married only once, but 12.6% had been married twice, 3.3% had been married three times, and two women (or 0.4%) were the champions within the sample in having been married four times (see Figure 6.1b).

Combining information on marital history and current status produces the division of the sample that is shown in Figure 6.1c. Almost two-thirds of all

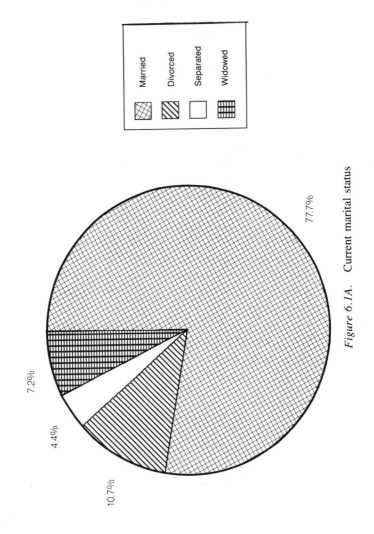

Figure 6.1A. Current marital status

Married

Divorced

Separated

Widowed

77.7%

7.2%

4.4%

10.7%

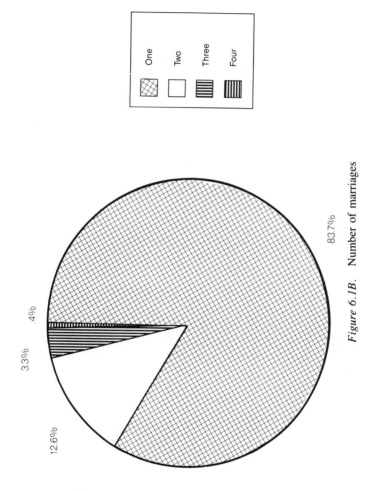

Figure 6.1B. Number of marriages

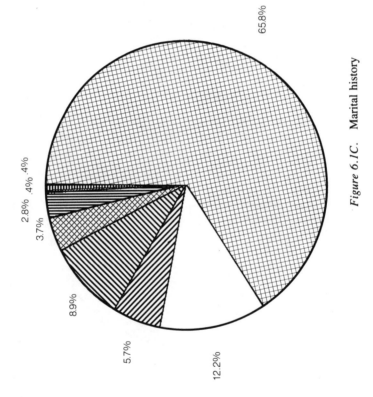

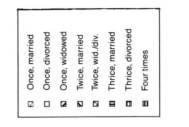

- Once, married
- Once, divorced
- Once, widowed
- Twice, married
- Twice, wid./div.
- Thrice, married
- Thrice, divorced
- Four times

65.8%

2.8% .4% .4%

3.7%

8.9%

5.7%

12.2%

Figure 6.1C. Marital history

respondents (65.8%) were still married to their first husbands, and another 17.9% had also been married only once, having been divorced (12.2%) or widowed (5.7%) without remarrying. Of those who had been married twice, most (41 out of 58, or 8.9% of the full sample) were still married, but the other 17 (or 3.7%) had been widowed or divorced and had not remarried a third time. Even smaller proportions were represented by the women who had been married three times and were still married (13, or 2.8% of the sample), those who were divorced from their third husbands (2 women, or 0.4%), and, as noted above, the two women who had been married four times. Sad to say, one of those two women who went to the altar four times divorced subsequently. Overall there is considerable variation in marital history represented within the Detroit sample, although clearly the dominant tendency is to have married only once.[5] Since in the present chapter I am primarily concerned with the general patterns in existing marriages, the information discussed here concerns only the 77.7% of the sample that is currently married. The issue of how first marriages and remarriages differ will be deferred until Chapter 8.

Marriage Values

What kinds of patterns are found in Detroit area marriages, and how do these patterns vary across generations? The first aspect of marriage to be considered involves not the actual patterning of conjugal relations, but the marriage qualities respondents feel are most important. We asked respondents to select, from a list of seven traits, those three qualities that would be most important in making a successful marriage. The seven traits listed were, "agree on chores," "satisfy each other's needs," "have a good income," "be deeply in love," "have common interests," "be sexually faithful," and "do things together." We then followed this question by asking each respondent to select which one quality she thought was the most important of all in making a successful marriage.[6]

There were some differences between the rank ordering produced by asking for the three most important values vs. one, but in general a clear order of relative importance emerges. (See Table 6.1, columns 1 and 2.) The most obvious pattern is that in their expressed values, respondents say that the emotional, rather than the practical, aspects of marriage are most important in producing success. The most heavily stressed trait is "satisfying each other's needs." In picking the single most important trait "being deeply in love" is ranked after satisfying each other's needs, but in selecting three traits it falls to fifth in the ranking, behind doing things together, having common interests, and being sexually faithful. Having a good income and agreeing on chores are claimed by most respondents to be much less important than these other traits in making a successful marriage. If one were to group the traits listed into three complexes— emotional involvement (satisfying each others needs and being deeply in love),

Table 6.1. Wives' Ranking of Seven Qualities for a Successful Marriage

Marriage Quality	All Wives		White Wives		Black Wives	
	Three Traits	*Most Basic*	*Three Traits*	*Most Basic*	*Three Traits*	*Most Basic*
Satisfy each other's needs	77.0%	39.8%	77.1%	41.7%	76.3%	27.0%
Do things together	61.0	9.6	60.3	8.9	68.4	16.2
Have common interests	58.4	13.8	59.7	12.1	47.4	24.3
Be sexually faithful	42.7	11.3	45.1	12.1	23.7	5.4
Be deeply in love	40.2	23.4	39.7	23.6	44.7	24.3
Have a good income	15.7	1.7	13.3	1.6	34.2	2.7
Agree on chores	3.9	0.3	3.8	0.0	2.6	0.0
N	356	354	315	314	38	37

togetherness (doing things together and having common interests), and family management (having a good income and agreeing on chores)—then in general respondents would rank the importance of these three complexes in exactly that order.[7] This general ordering of expressed values is not surprising, given the widespread belief in American society that marriage is or should be based upon one's heart rather than one's head—on love and emotional satisfaction—rather than on rational calculation. (Whether, in fact, this ranking of expressed values reflects the reality of what is most important in making a marriage work is a separate issue, and Chapter 7 will have some things to say about this issue.)

In general this ranking of familial values was fairly constant within the sample. I found no evidence that there was a significantly different ranking of marriage values across generations, or by women at different stages in the life cycle.[8] Whether a woman was working or not also had little impact on her ranking of these marital values. But there are some noticeable differences between how black and white women assess what makes a successful marriage, as shown in columns 3–6 of Table 6.1. Black wives are significantly more likely than white wives to list "having a good income" among the three most important qualities for a successful marriage, and they are much less likely than are white women to select sexual fidelity as one of the three most important qualities. In ranking the single most important trait of a successful marriage black wives were also somewhat less likely than their white counterparts to stress satisfying each other's needs, but somewhat more likely to stress having common interests and doing things together.[9] So there are modest indications that black wives have somewhat lower expectations of marriage, and in particular place less emphasis on emotional involvement and fidelity as necessary traits of a successful marriage, than is the case for white wives.[10] In subsequent sections I will examine the extent to which these racial differences in marriage values are related to differences in the actual patterning of conjugal relations.

This examination of marriage values points to a dominant conclusion. The ranking of qualities that go into a successful marriage is widely shared within the sample. Although there are modest differences between black and white wives, there is no clear evidence that major disparities in marriage values exist across generations, or that important changes in marital values are occurring in American society.[11]

Marital Involvement

Clearly most respondents feel that successful marriages are ones in which each partner's needs are satisfied, love and affection are mutually felt and expressed, and there is substantial sharing of interests and activities. To what extent do their own marriages live up to these standards? In Table 6.2 responses to seven questions about the present marital relationship are examined. In general the picture these figures portray is quite positive. From about half to more than two-thirds of all respondents rate their own marriages in the highest possible category, as characterized by doing things together most of the time, showing a great deal of affection, and so forth. Looked at from the other extreme, generally 10% or less of all respondents pick the lowest possible rating, the only minor exception to this generalization being that one respondent in six says that her husband does not often express his thoughts and feelings. In general, if we were to judge by responses to these questions alone, we would say that the large majority of wives we interviewed have high quality marriages.

Questions on aspects of "togetherness" in the marriage reveal a somewhat

Table 6.2. Descriptions of Positive Marital Interactions (Row Percentages)

	Very, Mostly	*Some, Sometimes*	*Rarely, Not Very*	*Total*	*N*
How much of free time spent together?	64.0	25.4	10.6	100	358
How much does husband confide about his thoughts and feelings?	45.8	37.9	16.3	100	356
How much does wife tell husband about her thoughts and feelings?	61.0	35.9	8.1	100	356
How affectionate is husband toward wife?	55.9	35.7	8.4	100	356
How affectionate is wife toward her husband?	50.4	42.3	7.3	100	357
How much concern does husband show for wife feelings and problems?	62.5	32.5	5.0	100	357
When disagreements, how often do they sit down and talk things out?	68.6	22.9	8.5	100	353

Table 6.3. Wives' Reports on "Togetherness" in Their Marriages
(Row Percentages)

					Total	N
		Joint Friendship				
	None	*One*	*Two*	*Three*		
Shared Friends:	17.9	12.8	21.8	47.4	100	358
Friends Married:	49.2	17.9	17.9	15.1	100.1	358
		Couple Joint Social Life				
		Several	*Several*			
	Weekly	*Per Month*	*Per Year*	*Rare*		
Joint Social Life:	15.6	37.1	34.3	13.0	100	353
		Talk to First with Problem				
		No	*Yes*			
Talk to Husband First:		48.4	51.6		100	339
		Wife and Husband Shared Values				
		Different	*Identical*			
Marriage Trait:		45.2	54.8		100	347
Child Trait:		54.1	45.9		100	351
		Shared Leisure Activities				
	None	*One*	*Two*	*Three*		
Number Shared:	37.4	38.0	15.9	8.8	100.1	353
		Kin Ties				
	Not	*Somewhat*	*Very*			
	Close	*Close*	*Close*			
With Wife's Kin:	12.1	38.4	49.4		99.9	354
With Husband's Kin:	21.9	42.7	35.4		100	354

more complicated picture (see Table 6.3). When asked how many of her three best friends were also friends of her husband, 47.4% of the wives we interviewed said all three were, and another 21.8% said that two out of three were (and only 17.9% said none of these three friends were). However, the image of the couple as the basic unit for forming friendships in middle class America is not fully borne out. Only 15.1% of interviewees said that all three of her best friends were the wives of friends of her husband, while 49.2% said that none of her best friends were married to friends of the husband. Evidently the most common basis for married women forming close friendships is not through joint social life with other couples. Instead it is more common for the wife to form her own friends independently, but to then become so close that the husband gets to know these friends well also, so that eventually they can be considered his friends as well. On a related note, only a little over half (52.7%) of the wives we interviewed said that they get together as a couple with friends several times a month or more often (and only 15.6% once a week or more often). The remainder get together as a couple with friends less frequently, with 13% saying that this happens once a year or less or hardly ever. So friendship ties and joint social life display less "merging" of the two spouses into one conjugal unit than we might have supposed, based on the figures dealing with communication, expressing affection, and so forth in Table 6.2.

We also asked wives, "When you have a personal problem you want to talk about, who do you speak to first?"[12] The most common response was to mention their husbands, but this was true only for 51.6% of currently married women. Almost half of all respondents said they would talk to someone else besides their husbands first—most often to a close female friend or relative.[13] Similarly, only a little over half of our respondents (54.8%) said that their husbands would pick the same trait as they would as the most important in making a successful marriage (from the traits listed in Table 6.1). Also, only 45.9% said their husbands would select the same trait as themselves from a similar list of qualities that a child should have. Looked at from the other direction, about half of the wives interviewed perceive that they do not share the same views as their husbands on what is important in making a successful marriage or raising a child. We inquired as well about the three favorite leisure time activities our respondents liked to engage in, and we also asked them to name the favorite leisure time activities of their husbands. Only 8.8% said that they and their husbands shared all three leisure activities in common, 15.9% said they shared two, 38% said they shared only one, and 37.4% said that their favorite leisure time activities were completely different from their husbands'. So the most common situation is for the husband and wife to have relatively few or even no leisure time activities that they share in common.[14]

The last two rows in the table concern matters that are not, strictly speaking, concerned with how much "togetherness" exists in the marriage. Instead they tap how embedded the couple is in kinship ties on both sides of the family. Comparing the pattern of responses reveals an expected slight bias in favor of closer ties with the wife's kin than the husband's, consistent with claims that American kinship has a somewhat "matricentric" slant, with maintaining kinship ties seen more as part of the woman's role than the man's (see Komarovsky 1962; Adams 1968). We can also see from these figures that most couples are far from being detached from kinship ties—there is not much sign here of the proverbial American "isolated nuclear family" (see Parsons 1949, 1955).

The responses reviewed in the last few paragraphs, based on the figures in Table 6.3, yield a picture not of couples intensely wrapped up in their conjugal relationship, but instead of many wives having friends, confidants, and activities that are at least partly independent from those of the husband. Still, lack of total conjugal involvement or merging of identity with one's spouse may not indicate an unsatisfying marriage, for most respondents may not have as their marital ideal a notion of intense conjugal involvement.[15] Recall from Table 6.1 that on average most wives stress satisfying each other's needs and being in love more than having common interests and doing things together as the qualities that make for a successful marriage. In fact when we asked wives to rate on a seven point scale (from 1 = very satisfied to 7 = very dissatisfied) how satisfied they were with their marriages, all things considered, most replied that they were fairly or very satisfied. In fact, 41.5% picked the "very satisfied" extreme end of the seven point scale, another 24.9% picked point "2," and 16.2% picked point "3." Overall, then, 82.6% of the wives interviewed gave positive ratings to their marriages, and only 9.2% gave negative ratings (with the remainder selecting the neutral "4" category). This finding accords with past survey results, most of which have found that large majorities of currently married persons say that their level of marital happiness or marital satisfaction is quite high.[16]

These figures give rise to another puzzle, since if most couples say their marriages are satisfying and happy, one may reasonably wonder why so many couples are getting divorced these days. This question will be considered later on in this chapter, but first I want to examine whether there are generational or other subgroup contrasts within the sample in regard to the questions dealing with marriage quality and involvement covered in Tables 6.2 and 6.3.

There are, it turns out, some important differences in how wives in different generations and stages in the life cycle describe their marriages. Women in earlier marriage generations are more likely than those recently married to say they spend most of their free time with their husbands,[17] but confiding a great deal in one's husband, showing affection toward the husband, receiving affection from him, and sitting down and talking over problems are significantly more common among women married recently than among older women. Talking first with the husband about a personal problem is also somewhat more common among recently married women, and particularly among those who have not yet had children. However, having friends who are also friends of the husband is more common among women who married earlier rather than recently. (Results not shown here.) Most other aspects of the conjugal pattern considered earlier do not show a clear pattern of differences across stages in the life cycle or across marriage generations. Taken together these results do not indicate that either the pattern of earlier or of more recent marriages is "better" in some general sense. However, they do indicate modest generational contrasts in the nature of the marital bond, with younger couples relying on communication and emotional exchanges more than common activities and shared friends, with older couples showing the opposite tendencies. I assume that these modest differences may reflect aging and progression through life stages rather than a process of basic change in the nature of marriage relations in America, but as noted earlier, I cannot test this hunch directly with the Detroit data.

When we turn to the seven point measure of overall satisfaction with marriage, we discover a pattern that has been noted by earlier researchers (see, for example, Rollins and Feldman 1970). If we use a life-cycle stage measure in place of the three marriage generations, we learn that 75% of young wives with no children give their marriages the top "very satisfied" rating, but for mothers of preschoolers this drops sharply to 39.7%. In later stages of the life cycle this drop continues, reaching a nadir of only 23.1% of mothers of teenagers saying they are very satisfied. Then wives in the final, "empty nest" life-cycle stage reverse the trend, with 48.2% saying that they are very satisfied. Overall, then, there is a curvilinear trend, with marital satisfaction appearing to decline in the early stages of the marriage and then partially recovering once the children have left home. In this instance there are some longitudinal studies that show that at least the pattern of declining marital satisfaction over the early stages of marriage is "real," and not simply the product of cross-sectional data (see, for example, Pineo 1961).

On balance the Detroit data do not provide a basis for judging that the patterning of marriage relations, in terms of mutual involvement and satisfaction, has changed in basic ways. There are some differences in the pattern of conjugal involvement between older and younger women in our sample, but these might be due to the influence of age and life-cycle stages, rather than showing that marriage relations themselves are being transformed in fundamental ways.

I also discovered that whether a woman was working outside the home or was a housewife did not make any clear difference in the sorts of patterning of marriage relations dealt with so far, nor in ratings of overall marital satisfaction (details not shown here). This is an important negative finding, since there has been much argument on both sides of this question. Those who applaud the trend toward increasing paid employment for married women claim that the drudgery associated with being a housewife produces emotional tension that has a negative effect on a marriage, and that women who enter the work force are able to establish relations with their husbands on a more equal and better footing. Critics of the trend toward increasing work by married women contend that the emotional and time burdens of work interfere with the involvement women can have in the conjugal bond, producing marriages that are less satisfactory.[18] Neither set of arguments finds support in the Detroit data, since patterns of expressing affection and concern, patterns of friendship and leisure activity, and the other aspects of marital involvement considered here do not differ significantly depending upon whether the wife works outside of the home or not.

Race, however, does appear to make a major difference in some of these same aspects of marriage relations. Black wives are significantly less likely than white wives (39.5% vs. 66.9%) to report that they spend most of their free time doing things together with their husbands, and there are weaker tendencies for black wives to report less confiding of thoughts and feelings (by both themselves and their husbands), less expressing of affection by their husbands, and less of a tendency to sit down and talk over disagreements, than is the case for white respondents (details not shown here).[19] An even more striking difference is visible in response to a question about whom a woman would talk to first if she had a personal problem. Of white wives 54.6% said they would talk to their husbands first, but only 20.6% of black wives gave this response. Black wives were also less likely than white wives to report that their best friends were also friends of their husbands or were married to friends of their husbands, and we found a weaker tendency for black wives to report less frequent joint social life as a couple than white wives (details not shown here). Perhaps understandably, in view of these contrasts, black wives were somewhat less likely than white wives (34.2% vs. 42.1%) to report that they were very satisfied with their marriages, and more likely (34.3% vs. 10.1%) to give their marriages a neutral or negative rating. These findings suggest a pattern of considerably less involvement and merging of identities into the conjugal unit among married blacks than among whites. Whether this contrast is a general cultural difference between blacks and whites or can be explained by other factors, such as the lower income level of blacks or higher unemployment in the black community, is a complex question that will be deferred until later on in this chapter.

The Division of Household Chores

The division of household chores between couples is often seen as a major point of tension in family life. Traditionally most domestic chores have been "sex-typed" and seen either as "women's work" or as "a man's job." Since the chores defined as women's work, such as cooking, cleaning, and doing the laundry, tend to involve more drudgery and have to be performed on a more regular basis than most men's chores, such as making household repairs, shoveling snow, or taking out the trash, wives usually end up bearing a much heavier burden of domestic chores than do their husbands. The general pattern, at least in the past, is for husbands to help out in "women's work" chores only in minor ways.

Furthermore, this pattern of women bearing the primary responsibility for household chores seems to exist even when the wife is, like her husband, employed full time outside of the home. In this case the wife often suffers from a "double burden" or "double shift," since after spending a full day at her paid job she has to come home to a demanding round of unpaid chores, which she may perform while her husband snoozes, watches television, or reads his evening paper. In previous work on this topic there is debate about whether paid employment for the wife has any impact at all on how much the husband does around the house. Skeptics say that it makes no real difference, with the chores remaining in the wife's hands. Even the nonskeptics or optimists claim only that husbands who have working wives help out a little more than do men married to housewives. Full sharing of the burden of household chores between husbands and wives is decidedly unusual, and cases of a working woman married to a "house-husband" are so rare that they give rise to feature stories in the news media.[20]

Why the domestic division of labor is so resistant to change is something of a puzzle.[21] But it seems to be much easier to change work roles outside the home than the division of chores within the home. In little more than a generation the United States has gone from having less than 15% of married women working outside the home to over 50%, but there has been nothing like this sort of dramatic change in how work is performed within the home (see Davis 1984). Still, I want to see whether in the Detroit data there are any signs of at least some changes in the household division of labor.

There are two major methods that have been used to measure the division of household chores. One technique involves the use of household time budget figures. Interviewees are asked to systematically record the number of minutes and hours spent each day on various tasks (e.g., working, eating, sleeping, and performing various household chores), and then the times spent by husbands and wives are compared. This technique makes possible quite precise estimates, but it is complex and difficult to administer in a survey, and so instead we utilized a simpler method pioneered in the research by Blood and Wolfe (1960). That technique involves presenting a list of household chores to respondents and then asking them to state for each whether they are performed by the "wife always," "wife more," "about the same," "husband more," or "husband always." This method yields a five point scale for each chore, but no estimates of the actual time spent on various tasks. Since the Blood and Wolfe study was based upon an earlier Detroit Area Study survey in 1955, and since the chore items in that survey were replicated in a later Detroit survey in 1971 (Duncan, Schuman, and Duncan 1973), the use of this method has the virtue of making it possible to compare some of the present results with those from these earlier studies.

We asked our respondents about seven household chores: Who does the grocery shopping? Who gets your husband his breakfast on work days? Who cooks dinner during the week? Who does the evening dishes? Who repairs things around the house? Who takes out the trash? Who keeps track of the money and bills?[22] The responses of all of the currently married women in our sample are displayed in Table 6.4. The first general impression conveyed by these figures is that household chores are for the most part still quite sex-typed. In only one chore area—getting the husband's breakfast—is it about as common for the husband to perform the chore as for the wife. Grocery shopping, cooking dinner, washing dishes, and keeping track of the money and bills are all to varying degrees predominantly female chores, while making home repairs and taking out the trash are predominantly male chores.[23] Perhaps equally important, for all of these tasks only about 10–20% of the respondents claimed that the husband and wife performed them equally (as shown in the "about the same" row in the table). So sharing of the burden of domestic chores is much less common than a clear division of labor, and in such a division the usual tendency is to follow traditional definitions of what is women's work and what is a man's job.

Is there any sign of change, though, in our data on the division of household chores? As a first step in considering this question, we can compare the chore division of couples in different generations and at different points in the family

Table 6.4.   Wives' Reports on the Division of Household Chores
(Column Percentages)

Chore Division	Grocery Shopping	Husband Breakfast	Cook Dinner	Wash Dishes	Home Repairs	Trash Disposal	Money and Bills
Wife Always	42.5%	33.5%	65.6%	51.9%	3.0%	6.9%	43.6%
Wife More	24.8	7.7	20.2	23.7	4.1	9.5	12.0
About the Same	22.5	9.6	11.4	15.9	11.5	22.3	20.1
Husband More	6.6	10.4	0.9	4.2	28.4	22.6	8.1
Husband Always	3.7	38.8	2.0	4.2	53.0	38.7	16.2
Total	100.1	100	100.1	99.9	100	100	100
N	351	260	352	308	338	305	358

life cycle. In performing this comparison I found that only in two of these seven tasks were there significant differences across generations or life-cycle stages— in regard to getting the husband's breakfast and making home repairs. Among women in the prewar marriage generation 50% said they always prepared their husband's breakfast, but this was the response of only 20.2% of our post-1965 brides. On the other side of the coin, only 23.7% of prewar generation wives said their husbands always prepared their own breakfasts, while 49.1% of recent brides said their husbands always did so.[24] Also the proportion of husbands who always made the repairs around the house dropped from over 60%, according to respondents in the prewar marriage generation, to less than 45% among those couples married since 1965. In both of these cases, then, younger couples appear to have a less sex-stereotyped division of labor than older couples. But no comparable contrasts are visible for the other five chores included in the list.

In this instance, as noted earlier, we can compare our results with two earlier surveys conducted in 1955 and 1971 with representative samples of Detroit area married women. This comparison should help to determine more accurately whether real change has occurred in the domestic division of labor, since it will not be confounded by possible life cycle and age effects, unlike the comparisons within the 1984 sample. Portraying the results of this comparison is more complex than reporting the findings of a single survey, and to make interpretation easier I followed the procedures used by Duncan, Schuman, and Duncan (1973) in reporting the 1971 survey, by utilizing a triangle diagram (see Figure 6.2.). In this diagram, the lower right hand corner indicates the wife always performing a given chore, the lower left hand corner indicates the husband always performing a chore, and the upper corner refers to shared performance (the middle three categories in the five point scales shown in Table 6.4.). The three axes thus show how far a given chore is from total wife monopoly, total husband monopoly, or total sharing. The lines and arrows sketched on the figure show (for those tasks asked about in all three surveys) how the distribution changed from the 1955

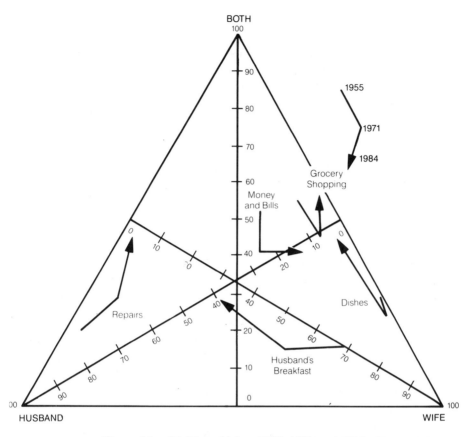

Figure 6.2. Division of labor: 1955, 1971, and 1984

survey to the 1971 survey, and then in turn to the 1984 survey. Movement to the lower right thus indicates increasing female monopolization of a task, movement to the lower left indicates increasing male monopolization, and movement upward indicates increased sharing.[25] The length of the arrow gives a rough indication of the magnitude of the change between surveys.

From Figure 6.2 we can see that there are a number of changes apparent when we compare the 1984 survey results with the earlier surveys. In only one case—preparing the husband's breakfast on work days—is there a clear shift from wives to husbands performing the task. However, in four out of the five tasks for which we have comparative data—all except keeping track of the money and bills—there is a change toward increased sharing of tasks. In the case of grocery shopping the change in this direction is quite small, but it reverses an apparent trend between the 1955 and 1971 surveys for this chore to become increasingly monopolized by wives. In the case of doing the evening dishes, making the husband's breakfast, and performing home repairs, the change in the direction of increased sharing of chores is quite large.[26]

These results lead me to qualify my earlier somewhat pessimistic conclusions. It is still the case that fully equal sharing of the sorts of household chores asked about is unusual. And between the 1955 and 1971 surveys no general trend toward more sharing of chores was detected. (See the discussion in Duncan, Schuman, and Duncan 1973, pp. 17–19 and in Duncan and Duncan 1978, pp. 196–202.) However, the 1984 data reveal at least modest increases in the extent of sharing of several domestic chores. Other than the item about preparing the husband's breakfast, the changes are not large enough to alter the general pattern in which some tasks are seen as men's jobs and others as women's work. But still our data do reveal some general movement toward increased sharing of domestic chores. Furthermore, the fact that this comparison of the 1984 results with earlier surveys reveals more significant differences than did my earlier comparison of women of different generations and life stages within the 1984 survey is also important. This pattern indicates that even among the older women in our 1984 sample, there is somewhat more sharing of chores than was visible among respondents of all ages in the 1955 and 1971 surveys.[27] In other words, somewhat greater sharing of chores is occurring to some extent among all age groups, rather than being restricted to young couples.

Such a change toward increased sharing of chores has been long awaited by advocates of sexual equality, and it was expected that both increasing numbers of married women working and general trends toward the acceptance of sex role equality in American society would help bring this change about. I want to consider now the relative importance of having a working wife vs. having a wife with egalitarian views in producing greater sharing of chores. In their pioneering study of this topic, Blood and Wolfe (1960) argued that ideology and traditionalism were not important influences on the division of household chores. What mattered was the relative "resources" held by each spouse, and working outside the home was one way in which a wife gained resources with which to obtain a fairer division of household chores. However, Blood and Wolfe did not have direct measures of sex role ideology, and so they tested the influence of ideology indirectly—by assuming that people of rural origins and Catholics held more conservative or traditional views than urbanites and Protestants, and then observing that neither factor affected the division of household chores.

In the Detroit survey we not only know whether the woman was currently employed outside of the home. We also asked two questions dealing directly with sex role attitudes, and I used the responses to these questions to construct a "feminism" scale.[28] So I can perform a more satisfactory test than Blood and Wolfe could of the relative influence of wife's work status vs. wife's sex role ideology on the division of chores. It should be noted that other researchers have investigated the influence of sex role ideology on chore division directly and have discovered at best only very weak support for the idea that egalitarian attitudes make a difference (see the discussion in Pleck 1985, Chapter 3).

When working wives were compared with housewives I found that they dif-fered significantly in terms of how some chores were divided, but not in terms of others. Working wives were significantly less likely than housewives to be the exclusive preparers of their husbands' breakfasts, the cooks for dinners, and the washers of dishes, and they were also somewhat more likely to report sharing the management of money and bills.[29] But there was no significant difference be-tween housewives and working wives on grocery shopping, making home re-pairs, or taking out the trash. Overall, however, and particularly in terms of traditional female chores, I find clear evidence that the relative contribution of husbands to household chores is somewhat greater in the case of working wives.[30]

I then examined whether women with more feminist attitudes differed in chore division from other women, and here as well I found that this was the case for some chores, but not for others. In this case women with feminist views were less likely than other women to be the exclusive preparers of their husbands' breakfasts or of dinners and they were somewhat more likely to play a helping or major role in making household repairs.[31] But feminist attitudes did not make a significant difference in who does the grocery shopping, who washes dishes, who takes out the trash, or who keeps track of the money and bills.

Since working women are more likely to hold feminist views than housewives (the correlation between work status and the feminism scale is $r = .26$), the next question is whether either of these findings could be spurious. Perhaps the apparent greater sharing of chores by couples in which the woman works is *really* caused by the feminist stances that working women tend to take; conversely, perhaps the apparent relationship between feminist views and sharing of chores is *really* caused by the fact that women scoring high on feminism tend dispropor-tionately to have jobs outside of the home. I attempted to resolve this question using a summary scale of the division of labor on four "female" chores—grocery shopping, preparing breakfast, cooking dinner, and washing dishes. Partial correlation analysis revealed that both feminist attitudes and work outside the home had a significant impact on this chore division scale, even when there was control for the other factor.[32] In other words, contrary to the claims in the Blood and Wolfe study, both working outside of the home and ideological factors (in this case, holding attitudes that favor sexual equality) have a noticeable impact on how household chores are divided.[33]

These results were checked further to see whether either correlation could be an artifact of age or time of marriage differences within the sample, with younger women more likely to insist on sharing of chores, to work outside the home, and to hold feminist attitudes. Regression analysis using age of the respondent and year of the marriage in addition to work status and feminist attitudes showed that these life stage variables did not produce a reduction in the coefficients of work status and feminism with chore division, and did not themselves have significant regression coefficients. (Results not shown here.) These findings indicate, then, that it is a woman's work status and her sex role ideology that affect how she and her husband divide the household chores, and not whether she is old or young. We would need to perform longitudinal research to be certain of the meaning of these findings, but in general they lead me to assume that both the increase in women working outside of the home in American society and the growing acceptance of egalitarian sex role ideologies have contributed to somewhat great-er sharing of domestic chores among couples of all ages. These results provide additional confidence that the modest increases in sharing of household chores are not simply a temporary phenomenon, typical of young couples, but likely to disappear as soon as children and the process of aging produce a reversion to traditional patterns.[34]

I wondered, finally, whether there were any differences between blacks and whites regarding how household chores were divided. I discovered that there were some, but that these did not fit into an easily interpretable pattern. To be specific, grocery shopping and keeping track of the money and bills are both significantly more likely to be shared by both spouses among blacks than among whites, while the husband preparing his own breakfast is significantly more common among whites, as is sharing in taking out the trash.[35] Overall, there is no clear tendency to have more sharing of chores, or more help from the hus-band, in one race rather than another. Why the particular tasks likely to be shared differ between races remains a puzzle.

In general the evidence presented here indicates that modest increases have occurred over time in the sharing of at least certain household chores. Does this mean that chore division is becoming less of a source of dispute within contem-porary marriages? We asked respondents to tell us "in general how satisfied are you with how the chores are divided in your family," and we used the same seven point scale (from 1 = very satisfied to 7 = very dissatisfied) that we used in examining general marriage satisfaction. The distribution of responses to this "chore satisfaction" question did not show quite as high a level of overall satisfaction as was the case when women were asked about their marriage rela-tionship in general, but still most women declared themselves fairly satisfied. In all 36% chose the highest, "very satisfied" point on the scale, and 19.8% chose point 2, and 17.9% point 3. Thus overall, 73.7% of all wives expressed varying degrees of satisfaction with chore division, and only 17.3% expressed varying degrees of dissatisfaction. (The remaining 8.9% chose the neutral fourth point on the scale.) So although household chores are still quite unevenly shared, with the burden falling more heavily on wives than husbands, most wives do not express dissatisfaction with this situation.[36]

When we examine contrasts across marriages generations and stages in the life cycle, we discover no differences in satisfaction with chore division that were statistically significant. However, the differences that were observed consistently were in the direction of younger wives being more dissatisfied than older wives. For example, 56.1% of prewar brides, but only 29.2% of recent brides, chose the highest, "very satisfied" rating to indicate their feelings about chore division in their homes. I noted earlier that there is slightly more sharing of domestic chores among these younger couples than among older ones, but this does not make such younger women on balance more satisfied—if anything the reverse is the case.[37] I suspect that this pattern indicates that younger women's expectations about husbands sharing chores are somewhat higher than is the case for older women. So even if their husbands cooperate a little more, the gap between actual sharing and their expectations will often be larger than is the case for older women. I do not have comparable data on satisfaction with the division of household chores from earlier Detroit surveys, so it is not possible to make confident statements about changes over time. But internal analysis within the sample gives me no reason to suppose that chore division is becoming less of a source of marital disputes than was the case in the past, in spite of the modest increases in sharing of chore performance.

It is vital, however, not to overstate the importance of the remaining and very considerable inequalities in household chore efforts as a source of marital unhappiness and strife. Although I will not directly consider the impact of unequal chore division on marital discord until Chapter 7, the reader should keep in mind that most wives we interviewed ranked sharing of chores quite low among those qualities making for a successful marriage (see Table 6.1), and I have just noted that most wives say they are satisfied with how chores are handled in their families, even though in the great majority of cases they are far from being shared equally. Our data indicate, in fact, that most wives tend to regard unequal chore division either as a given or as a relatively minor irritant.[38] Even though modest changes are occurring in the division of household chores, this is not the major battleground over which the future of marriage is being fought.[39]

Money and Power in Marriage

Studying the division of chores within American marriages is complex, but determining how marital power is divided is even more difficult. Such an elusive and multi-faceted phenomenon as marital power is difficult to study even through direct observation of the intimate corners of a couple's life over an extended period of time. Couples may be able to agree in describing how they divide the chores but unable to say who has the most power in the marriage. Trying to study marital power via a few questions on a questionnaire may thus seem hopeless or even foolhardy. Nevertheless, given the importance of power relations in marriage, family sociologists keep trying to penetrate this mysterious terrain, and the current study is no exception.[40]

We asked our respondents a series of questions dealing with control over money and family finances and with who wins out in marital disputes, and I will use responses to these questions to describe what was learned about power relations in Detroit area marriages.[41] Money is included in the discussion along

Table 6.5. Wives' Reports on the Control of Money and Power (Row Percentages)

					Total	N
Work Status						
Housewife		*Employed*				
41.2		58.8			100	323
Relative Income						
Wife More		*Similar*		*Husband $9000+ more*		
11.0		24.3		64.7	100	337
Manage Wife's Income						
	Wife		*Husband*			
Wife	*Control*	*Shared*	*Control*			
Control All	*More*	*Control*	*More*			
20.5	10.0	66.1	3.3		100	239
Manage Husband's Income						
	Husband		*Wife*			
Husband	*Control*	*Shared*	*Control*			
Control All	*More*	*Control*	*More*			
5.9	12.6	60.7	20.8		100	341
Manage Money and Bills						
Wife	*Wife*	*About*	*Husband*			
Always	*More*	*the Same*	*More*	*Husband Always*		
43.6	12.0	20.1	8.1	16.2	100	358
Power in Money Disputes						
Wife	*Wife*	*About*	*Husband*	*Husband*		
Always	*More*	*the Same*	*More*	*Always*		
2.5	13.7	69.6	12.0	2.2	100	358
Power in Chore Disputes						
Wife	*Wife*	*About*	*Husband*	*Husband*		
Always	*More*	*the Same*	*More*	*Always*		
2.2	6.7	76.0	12.3	2.8	100	358
Power in Child Discipline Disputes						
Wife	*Wife*	*About*	*Husband*	*Husband*		
Always	*More*	*the Same*	*More*	*Always*		
4.2	15.6	69.8	8.7	1.7	100	358
Power in Disputes about Having Sex						
Wife	*Wife*	*About*	*Husband*	*Husband*		
Always	*More*	*the Same*	*More*	*Always*		
3.1	7.5	76.8	10.6	2.0	100	358
Power in "Other" Disputes						
Wife	*Wife*	*About*	*Husband*	*Husband*		
Always	*More*	*the Same*	*More*	*Always*		
4.3	8.6	65.8	14.7	6.6	100	348

with power because many previous works on American marriage have argued that finances play a central role in defining marital power. Disputes over financial matters are one of the most common sources, if not *the* most common source, of marital conflict, and control over money, in the form of providing income and determining how funds will be spent, is often seen as a central aspect of marital power. Therefore, in the following pages I consider money and power in marriages together and investigate their relationship.[42]

In Table 6.5 the frequency distributions of wives in regard to the various money and power-related questions included in the survey are presented. Overall 58.8% of the wives interviewed were currently employed outside of the home. The table does not show another fact—that another 10.3% of wives had some income during the previous year, even though they were not regularly employed outside of the home. So only 30.9% of the wives interviewed had no income in 1983 and were therefore totally dependent upon the incomes of their husbands (or other family members). Even though almost 70% of all wives had some income, it is clear from the second row of the table that most women earned far less than their husbands. To be specific, the figures show that only 11% of wives earned more than their husbands, while another 24.3% had earnings that were roughly equal to or only moderately less than their husbands (defined here as within $9000 of the husband's annual income). Almost two-thirds of all wives— 64.7%—thus earned considerably less than their husbands.[43]

Is this differential in incomes a source of greater power of husbands within marriage? That differences in income of the spouses should have this effect is widely assumed, for example, in resource and exchange theories, in Marxist theory, and in feminist writings. A number of previous studies have reported that there is a clear relationship between relative earnings and marital power. For example, Blumstein and Schwartz (1983, p. 53) conclude bluntly, "Money establishes the balance of power in relationships."[44] However, I began to have some doubts about this association when I looked at the other figures in Table 6.5. First, we can see that most women who earn an income do not keep control over all or the bulk of their earnings themselves, but instead pool their income into a joint account that their husband can also draw upon (see row 3). Furthermore, this is also the most common pattern with regard to the husband and his earnings. Most wives (60.7%) report that their husband's earnings are pooled in this fashion as well. And in this case when the husband's income is not pooled it is slightly more common for it to be turned over mostly to the wife to manage than for the husband to keep control of it himself (see row 4). Overall, the most common pattern is for the income of both spouses to be pooled and used jointly, but the next most common pattern is for some portion at least of earnings of either or both spouses to be left in the hands of the wife to manage.

Clearly this pattern is not one you would expect to find if the husband were determined to translate his greater earnings into power within the marriage. While there are few other studies that have asked this sort of question, the patterns found here contrast sharply with a study done earlier in England. In a national survey in 1969 only 15% of the wives interviewed in that country said that they and their husbands practiced pooling and could draw on a joint account. Eleven percent of wives said that their husbands turned over their whole pay packet to them to manage and received spending money in return, but the most common pattern—reported by 55% of the wives—was for husbands to keep control over their own pay packet and just give their wives some housekeeping money. One out of six of the wives who received a housekeeping allowance did not even know how much her husband's pay was (Gorer 1971, pp. 92, 286; see also Pahl 1982).[45] So even when Detroit area wives do not contribute a major share to family earnings, they usually play a much more equal role than was apparent in the English study in managing the family's finances. This finding is consistent with what we learned earlier—as reported again in row 5 of Table 6.5—regarding how women describe "who keeps track of the money and bills in the family." Keeping track of money and bills is more likely to be handled by the wife than it is either to be shared or handled by the husband.

It would appear, then, that the financial power in the hands of most wives is considerably greater than their relative earnings might lead one to expect. However, it might be argued that managing the family purse is a bothersome task that is delegated to, or left by default in the hands of, the wife. And that when it comes to making decisions on spending money, the husband as the primary earner in most marriages might dominate, thus revealing his underlying greater power. However, the figures in row 6 of Table 6.5 cast doubt on this view. We asked all respondents about who usually gets their way when they and their husbands have disagreements about how much money to spend on various things. The pattern of responses indicates that most wives perceive that they have roughly equal influence on disputed spending decisions. Furthermore, when there is a power disparity in regard to spending decisions, at least as many wives feel that they win out as say their husbands hold more power. In sum, when it comes to earnings, husbands tend to dominate, but I see no signs here that the greater earning power of husbands is translated into dominance in the realm of family finances. In fact, if anything wives have a slight edge when it comes to control over the family finances.

The doubt about the impact of the husband's greater income is increased when we examine, in the lower panel of Table 6.5, the pattern of responses to the other areas of marital disagreements that were discussed. The pattern of replies to these questions is basically the same as in regard to disagreements about spending money. We asked who gets their way in the event of disagreements about who should do which household chores, disciplining the children, having sex, or in "other" realms. In each case about two-thirds or more of the wives replied either that they had no such disputes or that when they did have them they and their husbands had about the same ability to get their own way.[46] To be sure, we did not ask about who gets their way in a number of other areas of the marriage relationship. Still if we take these responses by wives at face value, they indicate that power in Detroit marriages is more equally shared than is the burden of chores, and that it is more equally shared than we might expect in terms of the relative earnings of the two spouses.

Furthermore, I examined the statistical associations between a measure of the relative earnings of the two spouses (reported in row 2 of Table 6.5) and various measures of money management and marital power (reported in rows 3–10). In general none of the associations between the relative earnings of husband vs. wife and these measures of financial management and marital power were significant (results not shown here). I also constructed a scale of marital power, using the items about influence in spending money, deciding who should perform which chores, having sex, and resolving "other" disputes, and that scale also had no significant relationship with the measure of the relative earnings of the husband and wife ($r = .06$, $N = 337$).[47] So when the husband has high earnings relative to his wife this does translate into a somewhat lower level of participation in domestic chores, as discussed in the previous section, but it does not lead to dominance in the marital power relationship. Conversely, when the wife has high earnings relative to her husband, this also does not mean that she will gain in power relative to her husband. The predominant pattern is for marital disputes to be handled in a manner which is disengaged from who earns the most, so that each partner has roughly an equal say in how things are resolved.[48]

The finding that relative incomes of the husband and wife are unrelated to the marital power distribution, even when it comes to financial matters, is quite surprising. As noted earlier, many different theories and a number of previous empirical studies all argue that there is such a direct relative earnings/marital power linkage. Why we have not found the pattern reported in earlier studies is not clear, but in part the difference may have to do with how marital power is measured. Conceptualizing and defining marital power is almost as difficult as measuring it, and a variety of approaches have been tried. My own approach may be understood most easily by comparison with the methodology used in the earlier Detroit survey by Blood and Wolfe. In general it is desirable to replicate earlier surveys done in the same locale in order to investigate social change, and I did so, as noted in the previous section, with some of the chore division questions used by Blood and Wolfe. However, when it came to marital power I decided not to replicate their questions, and I need to explain here why not, and how I did proceed.

In the Blood and Wolfe survey in Detroit in 1955, wives were asked to tell who makes the final decisions in regard to eight different matters: what car to get, whether or not to buy life insurance, what house or apartment to take, what job the husband should take, whether the wife should go to work or quit work, how much money the family can afford to spend per week on food, what doctor to have when someone is sick, and where to go on a vacation. No effort was made to determine how often these decisions occurred, or even if they occurred at all,[49] or whether they were the subject of debate or disagreement between the spouses. So no distinction would be made between a husband buying a car because both he and his wife agreed that it was his prerogative to make that decision and the husband doing so because they fought long and hard over which car to buy, and the husband won the argument. To be more precise, the sorts of questions asked did not deal with what I take to be a central aspect of power, in marriage or any other relationship—the ability to get one's way or impose one's will even against resistance.[50] So I felt that power should be measured not simply by an algebraic sum of who makes the decisions in a variety of areas, but by tapping who gets their way in the event of disagreements between spouses.

Therefore, we asked respondents first about whether they had disagreements with their husbands about several key issues—money, chores, child discipline, having sex, and "other" matters—and then we asked them who, in the event of such a disagreement, tends to get their way. Thus our measures of marital power, in contrast to those used by Blood and Wolfe, tap not the distribution of decisions about which both partners may agree (due to delegation, mutual agreement, etc.), but rather who wins out in the even of marital conflict. It turns out that with this sort of marital power index, most Detroit area wives judge their marriages to be fairly egalitarian.[51] Even in the third or so of marriages where equal say in resolving disputes is not reported, the husband is the "winner" no more commonly than the wife, and the relative earnings of the two do not seem to affect who will have more influence. I might guess, then, that earnings disparities may contribute to more kinds of decisions being mutually accepted as the province of the higher income spouse (as found by Blood and Wolfe and others), but that when marital disagreements occur they do not tend to get resolved on this basis. In sum, I do not find that money establishes the balance of power in Detroit area marriages.[52]

We asked respondents about two other aspects of the division of power in their marriages. We asked them "When you have disagreements [with your spouse], in general how satisfied are you with the amount of 'say' or influence you have?" and we presented them with another 7 point scale (from 1 = "very satisfied" to 7 = "very dissatisfied") to use to report their assessment. The pattern of responses to this item was very similar to the comparable item we asked about satisfaction with the division of household chores. Somewhat fewer wives (24.9% versus 36%) chose the extreme "very satisfied" point on the scale than was the case in assessing chore division, but still 69.8% of all wives expressed varying degrees of satisfaction with their influence in the marriage, while only 16.9% expressed varying degrees of dissatisfaction (with the remaining 13.3% giving neutral responses). This pattern of general satisfaction with marital power is also reflected in the responses given to another question about whether, in the event of a disagreement with their husbands, wives reported that the two of them would sit down and talk things out (reported earlier in Table 6.2, row 7). A substantial majority (68.6%) of all wives reported that this was almost always or often the case, and only 8.5% said that this rarely happened.

The general impression conveyed by all of our data on money and power is that in spite of clear differences in economic resources that favor husbands, most wives feel that their marriages are fairly egalitarian in terms of power and are characterized by a good deal of give and take and consultation. There are few wives who portray themselves as powerless and subordinated compared to their autocratic husbands.[53] But exactly what the mechanisms are that enable wives to maintain such equality in spite of clear disparities in economic resources are not clear from our data.[54]

If marital power is not a product of the relative incomes of the two spouses, what does affect it? In general I was not very successful in tracking down an answer to this question. Two contrary predictions have been made in regard to the effects of age or recency of marriage. On the one hand, it is often suggested that women who married "in the old days" were brought up to believe that the man is the boss, while younger wives might expect and demand equality. On the other hand, some observers have claimed that aging has a "matriarchal" effect, with older women having a more dominant voice in their marriages, especially after their husbands retire. Neither of these predictions was borne out in our data. Women who married recently did not have significantly more marital power in general than did women who married earlier, nor is stage in the life cycle significantly related to marital power.[55] But by the same token older wives did not exercise any more marital power than younger ones. (Evidence for these and other "negative" findings is not shown here.)

Some previous studies, and particularly the famous "Moynihan Report" (1965), have claimed that black marriages are more "matriarchal" than white ones, but I found no consistent differences between the races with our marital power measures.[56] I have already noted that the relative income of the two spouses is not related to various marital power measures, and the same negative finding results when I look at the correlation between whether the wife works or not and marital power. (The correlation with the summary marital power scale and the wife's work status is $r = -.02$.) Women holding feminist attitudes were also no more likely than other women to report that they had a great deal of say in the event of conflicts with their husbands. Other possible influences, such as the wife's educational level, the strength of her ethnic roots, her religion, and how many children she has had, also did not have a significant association with marital power measures. Unless this general pattern of negative findings is caused by defects in the marital power measures used, they suggest that marital power as we have conceived of it (involving who wins out in the event of a conflict with the spouse, rather than the pattern of dividing family decisions) is not influenced much by standard kinds of social background variables. Influences we have not measured, such as distinctive personality traits of the spouses or events in the past history of the marriage, seem likely candidates in explaining how power is divided in marriages.[57]

Not all aspects of marital power and financial relations are so immune to the influence of social background factors. One striking finding is that shared control over the earnings of both the husband and the wife is much less common among black couples than among white ones. To be specific, only 48.1% of black wives reported shared control of the wife's earnings vs. 71.9% of white wives, and the percentages for shared control of the husband's earnings were 31.4% vs. 64.4%. How much this lower level of sharing reflects greater hesitancy among black couples to commit themselves to a full "merger" into the conjugal relationship or simply less use of banks and joint bank accounts by black couples is uncertain.[58] There was also a weak tendency for Catholic wives to more often report shared control of their own earnings than did Protestant wives (80.4% vs. 62.4%), but no religious difference was detected for how the husband's earnings were handled.

In regard to satisfaction with one's say in marriage and descriptions of how disputes are dealt with, there are several patterns that emerge from the data (detailed results not shown here). In general women who married more recently, are younger, are better educated, and who have few or no children, are all more likely than other women to report both satisfaction with their power and to claim that disagreements are talked out with their husbands. (Talking out differences was also reported more by white than black wives and more by wives with high incomes, although neither race nor income was related to the satisfaction measure.)

Putting these findings together, I return to my central concern with the question of changes over time. I see no evidence in these data that the power of wives in Detroit marriages is on the increase, or for that matter no evidence that it is on the decline. What may have changed is not so much the pattern of who wins out in the event of a disagreement, but how those disagreements are handled. Younger and better educated couples are more likely to report that disagreements lead to mutual discussion and negotiations.[59] With our data it is not possible to know whether this is a growing trend, or whether it is a feature of new marriages that will be less typical when the marriage has added burdens and children. But in any case the result of this pattern is that younger women feel somewhat more satisfied with the say they have in their marriages. (Recall that the opposite was the case in regard to chore division, where younger wives were more dissatisfied.) Their satisfaction seems, if anything, to be due more to the way in which disagreements are resolved than to the degree to which they get their own way. (In fact, the correlation between satisfaction with marital power and reporting that disagreements are talked out is much higher than between satisfaction and the overall marital power scale: .58 vs. .14.) Young wives may not have any more say than do other women, but they feel better about the fact that their views are taken into account.

One implication of this pattern of findings is that marital power does not appear to be a growing source of marital discord. Unlike in our earlier discussion of household chores, this is the case not only because most wives are satisfied with the current situation, but also because they do not report much real imbalance existing. As already noted, most of the wives we interviewed see their marriages as a give-and-take relationship in which they do not feel particularly disadvantaged.

Marriage Problems

In the previous sections of this chapter I reviewed materials on the satisfactions provided by marriage and on the division of labor and power within the conjugal relationship, and for the most part my conclusions have been fairly "upbeat." In most respects Detroit area wives seem to be fairly satisfied with their marriage relationships, and with the possible exception of the unequal burden of household chores, they would seem to have marriages that should produce satisfaction. In the next few pages several kinds of marriage problems will be considered, leading to a more complicated picture. From the material reviewed so far the reader might suppose that only a small portion of the currently married women interviewed (5 to 15%) have poor quality marriages, but as I review questions about marital problems it will become clear that this is an underestimate.

Consideration of marital problems is, of course, limited by the questions on the topic that were included in the questionnaire. There are only three types of questions available, and the pattern of responses of Detroit area wives to them is shown in Table 6.6. As noted in the earlier section on marital power, we asked

Table 6.6. Wives' Reports of Marital Problems (Row Percentages)

				Total	N
Marital Disagreements					
	None	*Minor*	*Serious*		
Over Spending Money	43.6	47.8	8.7	100.1	358
Over Chore Division	62.6	32.1	5.3	100	358
Over Child Discipline	35.8	51.8	12.6	99.9	301
Over Having Sex	63.8	31.3	4.8	99.9	351
Wife Abuse					
		No	*Yes*		
Husband Ever Insult or Swear?		48.3	51.7	100	350
Husband Ever Stomp Out of House?		54.4	45.6	100	349
Husband Ever Push, Grab, or Shove?		77.8	22.2	100	351
Husband Ever Kick, Bite, or Hit?		92.9	7.1	100	351
Husband Ever Beat Wife Up?		95.7	4.3	100	351
Marriage Worries					
Never Thought Marriage in Trouble	*Has Thought Marriage in Trouble*	*Divorce Has Crossed Mind*	*Has Separated*		
46.1	11.0	34.3	8.7	100.1	356

about the existence and severity of several kinds of marital disagreements as a prelude to asking who, in the event of such a disagreement, usually gets their way. The responses to these "prelude" questions are shown in the top panel of the table. Serious conflicts in any of the four areas specifically asked about are acknowledged by relatively few wives, but minor disagreements are reported by one-third to one-half of all wives, depending upon the question. Within the realms we asked about, how to discipline the children was the most common source of disputes, followed by how much money to spend, with both the division of chores and how often to have sex less commonly given as sources of marital disagreements.[60] These responses make it possible to construct a marital conflict severity scale which will be used in later analyses.

In the middle panel of Table 6.6, responses wives gave to a special self-administered set of questions on spouse abuse are displayed.[61] By comparing the different items one can get a clearer idea about the degree of conflict within marriages, since at the extreme end, at least, the various acts form a step-like progression of increasing severity.[62] It appears that about half of all wives report that their husbands never so much as insulted them, swore at them, or walked off in a huff.[63] But slightly more than one wife in five reported having been pushed, grabbed, or shoved by an irate husband on at least one occasion, and much smaller numbers reported having been kicked, bitten, or hit with a fist (7.1%) or beaten up (4.3%).[64] The figures in the table indicate that severe physical abuse is relatively uncommon among currently married women, but that at least some strong verbal abuse is a feature of many marriages. (We did not ask about whether the wives used any of these forms of abuse against their husbands, although other research indicates that such abuse is at least as common as wife abuse. See, for example, Steinmetz 1977–78; Straus, Gelles, and Steinmetz 1980.)

The final, "marriage worries" item in the table is actually a composite developed from three separate questions asked in sequence: "Have you ever thought your marriage might be in trouble?" "Did the thought of getting a divorce or separation ever cross your mind?" and "Did you ever separate?" Considered together the responses to these questions again give us a way of viewing various levels of marital problems.[65] From the table the reader can see that slightly more than half of all wives have at least had worries that their marriages might be in trouble, more than one-third have at some point contemplated divorce or separation, and 8.7% have actually experienced a separation.

Combined, the figures in Table 6.6 yield a fairly consistent picture. Very severe marital conflict seems to be confined to the 5–15% of the sample that we would have expected, given the responses to the kinds of questions considered in earlier sections of this chapter. But at the same time perhaps another 30–40% of wives report a variety of conflicts and problems, and even though these are less severe, they have led a substantial share of wives to contemplate divorce or separation.[66] In other words, for many women it does not require a severe level of abuse or dissatisfaction to lead to worries about the marriage or thoughts about divorce. It needs to be stressed again that I am considering in this chapter only currently married women. Those women whose marital problems led them to divorce are not included in these figures. (Those who have remarried are included here, but only in terms of their feelings about their current marriages.)

These questions about marital problems lead me to reduce my rough estimate of the proportion of wives who feel everything is fine in their marriages. Rather than something like two-thirds to three-fourths fitting this category, perhaps it is more in the range of 35–50%. After making this revision the recent brittleness of American marriages does not appear so puzzling. Evidently even while large majorities of American wives report that they are fairly satisfied with their marriages, this does not mean the absence of all worries and problems, or any firm assurance that those marriages will all survive. I am suggesting here, and will develop the argument more fully in Chapter 7, that having a satisfying marriage and having a marriage devoid of problems are not exactly the same thing, and that it is important to consider separately both the level of satisfactions and the level of problems.

What sorts of wives report the most marital problems? I can briefly consider this question by using three summary measures drawn from the questions in Table 6.6: a scale of the level of marital disagreements, a wife abuse scale, and the question about the level of marital worries.[67] The level of marital disagreements seems to be greatest among younger women who have married recently, and also among wives who currently have many children at home. (Detailed results for these and other patterns discussed in this paragraph are not shown here.) Other factors, such as race, income, education, feminist attitudes, and the age at which the wives first married were not related to the marital disagreements scale. Wives were most likely to report being abused if they married young, had many children at home, had been married more than once, and had weak ethnic roots.[68] Again, other factors such as age of the respondent or recency of marriage, race, education, or income were not significantly associated with the level of wife abuse.[69] Finally, the level of marital worries was significantly higher among blacks than among whites and also among women with feminist attitudes, with many children at home, and who married when young.[70] When these factors were taken into account (through multiple regression, results not displayed here), factors such as age or recency of marriage, education, work status and income did not significantly affect the level of marital problems. Overall the factors that seem most consistently important in explaining the level of marital problems seem to be marrying at a young age and having a large number of children at home to cope with.[71]

There is no clear evidence that indicates a major deterioration or major improvement in the nature of the marriage relationship over time in our society, although insofar as women have been marrying later in recent years and having fewer children, this might indicate that primary sources of marital problems are in the process of being ameliorated (see also the discussion in Straus 1977; Straus and Gelles 1986).

Conclusions

Several primary conclusions emerge from the welter of specific findings about marriages reviewed in this chapter. First, even though our cross-sectional survey data are not ideally suited to measuring changes in marriage patterns, in general we find few important differences across marriage cohorts, or when comparing women of different ages or at different life-cycle stages. If fundamental changes in the nature of American marriage were underway, we might expect to find many such differences, but in fact we find fewer contrasts between women of different generations in marriage relations than were reported earlier (in Chapters 2 and 3) in regard to the patterns of dating and mating. It would appear that the stages leading up to marriage have undergone major changes, but that these alterations have not "spilled over" to produce comparable shifts in the nature of the conjugal relationship. Younger wives are slightly more likely to express dissatisfaction with the division of chores than are older wives; however, on the other hand they are also somewhat more likely to report that marital disagreements are discussed and to express satisfaction with their "say" in the marriage. But even in contrasts such as these, we cannot be certain that we see new social trends in the making, rather than features affected by stages in the life cycle, with younger wives likely to change to resemble older ones as they raise children and bear family burdens.

However, the finding of minimal contrasts between generations in the patterning of marriages could be interpreted in two different ways. On the one hand it could indicate a basic continuity in the patterns of marriage in America and how wives evaluate those patterns. If we assume that changes in marriage will show up through "cohort replacement," this would be a reasonable interpretation. Cohort replacement involves the idea that new social trends affect young women particularly, while older women, who grew up in different times and are set in their ways, will be resistant to such trends. But as the younger women age and older women die off, the new patterns will gradually become dominant (or will be replaced by still newer trends that get started among even younger women). If this is the sort of change mechanism operating, then the scarcity of major contrasts in marriage patterns between younger and older women would seem to indicate that no major changes are underway.

However, it is possible that cohort replacement, which assumes that people are socialized into certain values and patterns and then persist in them throughout their lives, is not an accurate view of how changes in conjugal relations are occurring. Perhaps instead general economic, cultural, and social trends are having an impact on women of all ages. Therefore even older women do not remain "set in their ways," but adapt their marriages to a changing social environment. If that is the case, then my failure to find many or major contrasts between the marriages of women of different generations would not mean that marriage patterns are basically stable and unchanging. Instead it might simply indicate that marriages of women of all ages are being altered by new social trends.

In only one instance do the data reviewed in this chapter allow us to choose between these two conceptions of the change process. That instance concerns the division of household chores. In that case we found evidence of changes in the pattern of chore division being experienced by women of all ages, and not solely by the youngest wives in the sample. There is a pattern of somewhat less sex-typed household chore performance visible in the 1984 data that is not primarily the result of a cohort replacement change process, and is not visible primarily among recently married women.

We cannot be certain whether the same dynamics would be visible in other realms of marital relations considered in this chapter, since we don't have comparable data from earlier Detroit surveys dealing with those other realms. But assuming that this pattern of change is not distinctive to the realm of household chores, I am led to a conclusion that is more complex than simple continuity. On the one hand there is little sign of the dramatic changes in marriage that are suggested by terms such as a shift from "institutional to companionate marriage" or "marriage increasingly in trouble." But modest changes are underway and are affecting older as well as younger wives. The "typical" marriage that we find in this study is a complex mixture of elements—high levels of mutual concern, communication, and affection; high satisfaction with the marriage overall; perceived equality in power; somewhat distinct patterns of friendship and leisure activity for each spouse; a still largely sex-typed division of chores (in spite of modestly increased sharing); an awareness of a range of at least minor disagreements; and a nagging concern about whether the marriage will last. No conclusion that existing marriages are better or worse than those in earlier eras seems adequate.

Much of the evidence reviewed in this chapter has been negative. Whether the wife has a job outside the home or not, how feminist her attitudes are, and the relative income of the two spouses have some effects on how chores are divided, but not on much else about the marriage relationship.[72] The one consistent pattern that does emerge is that black marriages are different in significant ways (but not in all respects) from white marriages. I did not find any evidence for the supposed "matriarchal" nature of black marriages that dominated earlier writings on the topic, and in fact the division of power and of household chores were the realms in which black and white marriages seemed most similar.[73] However, in many other respects I found that the black wives in the sample differed from the white wives—in holding somewhat different marital values (e.g., stressing a good income more and sexual fidelity less), exhibiting less mutuality and to-getherness (in spending free time together, confiding, speaking to the husband first about a problem, and so forth), less often pooling income into a joint account, and in general expressing less satisfaction with the marriage and being more likely to have experienced a marital separation. In general these differences point to a more incomplete "merger" of the two spouses into the conjugal rela-tionship in black than in white marriages, producing a greater maintenance of separate activities and resources. I have no detailed evidence on the reasons for these differences, although given the greater brittleness of black as compared to white marriages (19.7% if the first marriages of white respondents had ended in divorce compared to 58.7% of the first marriages of black respondents), it is not hard to see why rational black wives would be hesitant to invest all of their energies in marital togetherness.

Are these really differences between whites and blacks, though, or are they instead reflections of social class? Blacks tend to have lower incomes than whites, and they are more likely to experience unemployment and other conse-quences of a lower-class position. And segregation of roles and less satisfying and more brittle marriages are generally more typical of working and lower classes than of middle- and upper-classes in American society (see Rubin 1976). So perhaps it is the low-class position of many blacks that explains the dif-ferences found, rather than race per se. I checked this possibility by controlling the relationship between race and various marriage measures for class-linked variables—the husband's income, total income, unemployment of the husband, the wife's educational level, and the subjective social class position reported by the wife. In general none of these controls weakened the statistical association between race and various measures of marriage patterns.[74] My tentative conclu-sion is that the racial differences noted in this chapter are not a product of class differences between whites and blacks. But whether they are simply a product of the greater instability of black marriages or reflect deeper cultural differences between the races in America is unclear.[75]

One final note concerns theories used to interpret marriage relations. In pre-vious sections of this chapter I have referred to resource and exchange theories and to the views of what some call the "new home economics" (see in particular the works of Gary Becker 1973, 1981). These various perspectives differ some-what, but they all lead to a view of marriage in which each spouse brings certain assets to the relationship and tries to use these in a rational fashion to pursue his or her advantage. The new home economics, for instance, approaches family life from a basic "homo economicus" standpoint, seeing individuals weighing costs and benefits in order to decide whether to marry, divorce, or have children or how to divide the household chores. In extreme form this point of view can lead to marriage being seen simply as one of many arenas in which individuals compete to advance their interests.

In discussing chore division I found some support for this view in the Detroit data, but still that support was only partial. Wives who are employed or who earn a lot relative to their husbands do a somewhat smaller proportion of the housework than other women, but in most cases they still do much more than their husbands do. There is no exact calibration of the chore burden to accord with the financial resources of each spouse or the "opportunity costs" of their diverting their attention from their workplaces to tend to burdens at home. In other realms there is much less evidence that this sort of rational dynamic is working, and I pointed this out in particular in my discussion of marital power. Marriage is more than simply a combination of two interest-maximizing spouses, and often partners defer to their spouses in the interests of the marriage relationship itself, even when it might not seem "rational" to do so. (See comments along similar lines in Heimer and Stinchcombe 1980.)

Perhaps it is obvious that marriage is different from other organizational settings, and that institutional and cultural forces that produce what might be called a "marriage mystique" lead wives and husbands to behave differently toward one another than they would toward a business associate or even a friend. But in view of the recent popularity of models of marriage based upon individualistic competition, it is worth stressing that most contemporary marriages do not really operate in this way.[76] The marriage relationship continues to be more than the sum of its parts, and this fact helps to explain the continuing allure of married life in America society, in spite of the brittleness of the marital bond and the ability to satisfy many human needs outside of the marriage relationship.

Notes

1. Anthropologists make the distinction between kinship and family systems that stress conjugal vs. consanguineal ties, and America is clearly one example of a society that has always placed the main emphasis on the conjugal bond. The classic work describing how industrialization and other forms of social change foster change around the world toward the "conjugal family" as an ideal type is Goode 1963. At the other extreme, there is at least one culture on record, the Nayar in 19th century India, which placed total emphasis on consanguineal ties (in that case matrilineal descent ties) and did not even recognize marriage as an institution (see Gough 1960).

2. The same conflicting views have been voiced even about the rising divorce rate. Optimists argue that in general this trend indicates that it is easier to get out of unrewarding and unhappy marriages than in the past, and that since most divorced individuals do remarry, they are able to use divorce to leave a bad marriage and enter another one, which hopefully will be better. The pessimists note instead that increased marital brittleness increases the economic and psychological trauma for both adults and children, even if remarriage does eventually occur, that a significant minority of those who divorce do not remarry, and that remarriages are not generally better—being even more brittle, for instance, than first marriages. (But see my assessment of remarriages in the Detroit survey in Chapter 8.)

3. A classic article on the problems caused by confusion between these different possible interpretations is Ryder 1965.

4. In one case, concerning the division of household chores, we will be able to compare the present results with those reported from earlier Detroit Area Study surveys, and this will give us a

clearer picture of any changes underway. Even though those earlier studies used different respondents, if two surveys using comparable and representative samples from the same locale reveal different findings, this is a surer sign of a real social change than are the contrasts between generations within any one cross-sectional sample.

5.   The reader may wonder how this large proportion of women married only once squares with recent estimates that perhaps 50% of marriages in America are terminated by divorce. The answer is that such 50% projections are based upon the trends in divorce from year to year of couples who married in the late 1970s and early 1980s, whereas our sample includes large numbers of women who married before the 1960s, when the likelihood of getting a divorce was much less. In addition, some of the women in our sample who have not been divorced may do so in the future. I do not know and have not attempted to project what proportion of the youngest women in our sample will eventually divorce, but the variety of ages contained in the sample explains why it is quite possible to find, as I do, that about two-thirds of the women in our sample are still married to their first husbands, even if the likelihood of divorce among the younger women may eventually approach the level suggested in such "fifty-fifty" estimates.

6.   The precise wording used for this and other questions discussed in this chapter is given in Appendix 2. We also asked respondents to judge which three traits, and which single trait, their husbands would pick as the most important, and I use the responses to both sets of questions to help construct a measure of spouse "values similarity" that will be used later on. For the moment I am interested only in the reports of wives about their own values.

7.   Being sexually faithful does not fall obviously into one of these three complexes, and this trait ends up in fourth place in the ranking given by all respondents.

8.   There were tendencies for older women to stress mutual satisfaction of needs more than younger women, and for younger women in contrast to place more emphasis on being deeply in love, but neither of these tendencies was statistically significant.

9.   These latter tendencies are not statistically significant. The differences in percentages are fairly large (for example, between 42% for whites and 27% for blacks selecting satisfying each other's needs), but because there are only 38 currently married black women in the sample, the racial contrast does not pass the conventional significance test level of $p = .05$. In a case such as this I feel the percentage differences should be noted as suggestive of real differences that could be looked for in a larger sample. (Women classified as neither white nor black—Asians or others—are excluded from this and other racial comparisons in this study.)

10.   It would be misleading, however, to argue that black wives are mostly concerned with the practical side of marriage. Even if they rank having a good income more highly than white wives, it is picked as the most important quality for a successful marriage by few black wives. And there is no clear racial difference in the ranking of being deeply in love as the single most important trait. So at most there are modest differences in emphasis between black and white wives in evaluating what makes for a successful marriage, and not two completely different views.

11.   If, however, major changes in American values are occurring that are affecting women of all ages, then the sort of generational comparison carried out here would not provide evidence of such changes, and it would be misleading to conclude from the absence of generational contrasts that no changes are occurring. My examination of this question of marital values is limited by the traits included in the questionnaire. A variety of traits of importance to a marriage, such as communication, expressing affection, and so forth, were not included in the list of values respondents were asked to select from.

12.   Grammatical lapses—not saying "to whom do you speak first"—are recommended in survey research in order to avoid sounding pedantic.

13.   Of course, if the problem is one caused by the husband, it is understandable that he might not be the one talked to first.

14.   This final pattern of answers raises a minor puzzle, since it seems to conflict with the responses to an item included in Table 6.2, which showed that almost two-thirds of the wives

interviewed said they did things together with their husbands most of the time when they had free time. In part the discrepancy may be caused by the fact that people can do things together without doing the same thing, as when she sews while he watches a football game on television. But probably the major reason for the discrepancy is that the second question about free time asks not about what people actually do, but about what they like to do. In response, people may list things like going hunting, traveling, or going to the movies, even if they do not spend much of their actual free time engaged in these "favorite" leisure activities. So this second question about leisure activities taps preferences or values, rather than the actual time spent engaged in various activities. To put matters in a different way, if husbands and wives could spend all of their free time engaged in the leisure pursuits they enjoy most, they would spend much less of their free time together than they actually do. More mundane leisure activities, such as watching television, relaxing, and reading, occupy more of actual free time than do many preferred leisure pursuits, and the former often are engaged in together with one's spouse.

15. I am suggesting here that many couples may not have as high expectations of their marriage as the advice columns and some family sociologists imply or recommend. A well known study of middle-class marriages by Cuber and Haroff (1963) classified couples into five types of marriages, with "vital relationships" and "total relationships," involving intense immersion in the marital bond, described as desirable but rare. The more common middle category, which the authors call "passive congenial," since it involves little zest but also little conflict, is clearly seen by Cuber and Haroff as less desirable, but may be seen by women in such marriages as quite acceptable and even satisfying.

16. For example, in a 1982 poll conducted by the National Opinion Research Corporation, 96% of respondents described their marriages as happy, and in the same year 79% of 5,000 readers of *Better Homes and Gardens* polled said that their expectations of happiness in marriage were being fulfilled. Figures cited in Davis 1985, p. 15.

17. The percentage giving this response was 80.5% among those married prior to World War II, 69.2% among the "baby boom" brides, and 55.6% among those married since 1965.

18. Of course, working husbands would have the same problem, but critics argue that having a wife at work simply makes even more complex the problem of establishing involving and mutually rewarding marital ties.

19. These latter differences fall short of the conventional $p = .05$ statistical significance level, but the percentage differences seem worthy of note in any case. As noted earlier, these comparisons involve only currently married black women, and there are so few of such women in our sample (38) that it takes a very striking contrast to surpass this significance level.

20. Joseph Pleck argues that the discrepancy between past studies which show that husbands of working wives help out more and studies that do not show them helping out more is due to varying methods used. Studies that ask about proportional contributions of each spouse tend to show husbands of working wives helping out somewhat more, but research that asks about absolute contributions of each spouse (such as time budget studies) do not show this pattern. Pleck argues that what is really happening is that working wives spend less time and effort on household chores than do housewives, while husbands are not affected by the wife's work status. Thus proportional measures show that the husband's relative contribution when he has a working wife is greater—overall, according to one estimate, 25% of all household chore efforts vs. 15%—but the difference is produced by lower efforts from the wife, not more efforts from the husband (see Pleck 1985, Chapter 2).

21. Sociological studies in the Soviet Union, China, and the Israeli kibbutz find that in these societies men do not help out much with domestic chores, even though these socialist societies have much more universal participation in work by women than does the United States, and have official ideologies that advocate total sexual equality. For a discussion of some of the evidence, see Whyte (1984).

22. Two of these items, dealing with cooking dinner and taking out the trash, were not asked in the 1955 and 1971 Detroit surveys, and in our 1984 survey we left out one task asked about in both of

those surveys—who straightens up the living room when company is coming—as well as two tasks asked about only in the 1955 survey—who mows the lawn and who shovels the sidewalk.

23.   It might be noted that keeping track of the money and bills may have a somewhat different meaning than the other chores listed. It is not simply a tedious task, but perhaps also an aspect of family management that gives the person who performs it some power within the marriage. So the fact that women tend to perform this task more than men may not indicate simply another burden that they have to bear. The topic of financial management will be dealt with further in the next section.

24.   The same contrast emerged in comparing women at different stages of the family life cycle. Not a single wife in the pre-children stage said she always prepared her husband's breakfast, while 42.2% of wives in the empty nest stage said they always did so, and the proportions in these same stages who said their husbands always fixed their own breakfasts dropped from 68.8% to 31.9%. Note the relatively small N in column 2 of the table, which indicates that in many families no breakfast is prepared for the husband. He either skips the meal entirely, or grabs something on the way to work.

25.   The reader may wonder why I don't simply make a chart showing how the average score on a task—ranging from 1 to 5—has changed across surveys. The reason is that there are two quite different ways in which sex stereotyped scores—near 1 or near 5—can become less so (by becoming closer to the average score, 3). This could occur through an increase in the proportion of respondents who claim chores are shared—by indicating categories 2, 3, or 4. But it could also occur by having an increasing shift to both extremes of the distribution—with a major proportion of the sample indicating a task is monopolized by the wife (point 1) and another major portion indicating that the same task is monopolized by the husband (point 5). Both of these tendencies would yield average scores near 3, but they would have quite different implications. The triangle diagram allows me to distinguish sharing of chores from both male and female monopolization.

26.   I have not computed significance tests on these differences, but in the Duncan, Schuman, and Duncan book it is reported that only the change from 1955 to 1971 in doing the dishes was not statistically significant. Graphically the size of all of the changes between the 1971 and 1984 surveys is larger than that particular shift between 1955 and 1971, indicating that all of the changes shown for our survey are unlikely to be explained by chance factors alone.

27.   This pattern was confirmed graphically for the case of prewar brides in our sample, but the results are not shown here.

28.   These questions asked respondents to indicate whether they strongly agreed, agreed, disagreed, or strongly disagreed with the following statements: "It is much better for everyone involved if the man is the achiever outside the home and the woman takes care of the home and family." "A woman can live a full and happy life without marrying." The second item was reversed, so that a high score in both cases indicates a nontraditional response, and then the scale was simply computed as the mean of the standardized scores of the two questions. For use in tabular analysis I then divided the scores into three levels, indicating low, medium, and high feminist sentiments.

29.   For example, only 26.2% of husbands of housewives prepared their own breakfasts, but 51.2% of husbands of working wives did so; 60.2% of housewives reported that they always washed the dishes, but only 45.6% of working wives gave this response.

30.   We need to keep in mind, however, Pleck's observation (1985) that, since we don't have any information about the absolute efforts of either spouse on such chores, this apparent greater share could be produced simply by working wives decreasing their chore contribution, with husbands not helping out any more at all.

31.   For example, 46.3% of women low on feminism said they always prepared their husbands' breakfasts, but only 19.2% of women high on feminism gave this response; only 7.7% of women low on feminism said they did at least as great a share of the home repairs as their husbands, but 26% of women high on feminism made this claim. Of course, one can question how beneficial it is to a woman to take on a new household chore such as home repairs, even if it is one that has been labeled a man's job. Also, I cannot be certain of the direction of causation in the feminism/chore division

relationship. It seems less plausible, but it is nonetheless possible, that women who experience more equal chore division will adopt more feminist attitudes, rather than having their attitudes influence their chore participation.

32. The correlation between the feminism scale and the chore division scale was reduced slightly, from .23 to .20, when the effect of work status was partialled out; similarly, the correlation between the wife's work status and chore division was reduced slightly, from .20 to .15, when the effect of feminist attitudes was partialled out. Both correlations remained statistically significant.

33. These results also show a stronger association between feminist attitudes and chore participation than have many previous studies that employ direct tests of the influence of such attitudes, such as Pleck 1985. I am uncertain about why my results on this point are stronger, but the possibility can at least be entertained that it has taken some time for the effects of the major changes in sex role attitudes that have been occurring in American society to be fully felt. In spite of some speculations about a conservative trend in public opinion since the 1970s, recent research indicates that expressed sex-role attitudes of Americans have continued to become more liberal or "unisex" (see Mason and Lu 1988). And some recent empirical studies have discovered a significant association between feminist attitudes and family chore division, as I have described for the Detroit survey. See, for example, Kamo (1988).

34. I did perform some additional regression analyses on the chore division scale. These analyses revealed that more educated wives tended to have domestic chores shared more equally, that high income husbands shared less in the chores, and that wives who had little power in the marriage (as measured by a marital power scale to be described in the next section) ended up doing more chores. For women who worked the most important feature about their work, in terms of influence on division of chores within the home, was how high an income they earned. These findings tend to support the views associated with the "new home economics" (e.g., Becker 1973, 1981), which argues that chore division tends to reflect inversely the pattern of income earning ability outside the home. In other words, couples are seen in this theory as rationally deciding that the partner who will be stuck with most of the household chores is the one who can earn the least from labor outside of the home. The number of years a woman has worked outside of the home since marriage also has an independent influence on chore division in the home, even after the woman's income is taken into account, but neither her nor her husband's occupational status group has such an independent effect. Other factors considered that did not have a clear impact on chore division scale scores, in addition to age and year of marriage, were the husband's educational level, the number of children at home, current subjective class position, and race (see below). Taking into account feminist attitudes, the woman's work status or her income, her educational level, the marital power distribution, and the husband's income level together only explained about 14% of the variation in the household chore division scale. This modest level of success indicates again the difficulty of transforming the division of household labor, since even those factors that I have identified as having an impact on this realm do not have a very strong or dependable impact (detailed results not shown here).

35. In all 44.2% of the white wives but only 27.8% of the black wives said they did all of the grocery shopping, and 18.3% of whites compared with 36.8% of blacks said they shared equally in money management. And 42.2% of white husbands are said to always get their own breakfasts compared to only 14.8% of black husbands, while taking out the trash is the exclusive domain of 37.1% of the white husbands, in contrast to 55.6% of the black husbands.

36. The apparent discrepancy between wives who said they did all or most of the listed chores and yet were still quite satisfied with chore division in their homes was the source of discomfort to some of our interviewers. Particularly the more ardent feminists among the students conducting interviews had to stifle urges to ask women why they were satisfied with such an inequitable situation.

37. The correlation between the chore division scale and satisfaction with the division of chores is positive, but quite modest in size—$r = .16$. In other words, the connection between how women feel about chore division in their homes and the actual degree of sharing of chores is quite tenuous.

38.   Similarly, Pleck found in national survey data that even of employed wives, only about one third would like their husbands to help out more with housework. Most wives can thus be seen as satisfied with an unequal division of household labor. Why it is that women are not upset with this unequal division of chores is a topic that deserves further study. But among the factors usually suggested are perceptions by wives that husbands are not competent enough to perform "female" chores well (although on husbands' parts this may reflect "learned incapacity"), and the fact that many wives accept the definition of these chores as women's work and continue to perceive performing them as an important source of their status as wives and mothers.

39.   My conclusion differs, therefore, from that offered in some feminist analyses of housework, such as Mainardi 1970 and Hartmann 1981.

40.   For a number of essays on the topic, see Cromwell and Olson 1975; for a critique of many existing studies of marital power, consult Scanzoni (1979); Kranichfeld (1987).

41.   I recognize that these are not the only domains of marital power, but nonetheless they seem to me and to others who have studied the topic to be central, and therefore I focus on them. See further discussion of my choice of aspects of marital power below.

42.   Studies of family financial arrangements are rather rare, in spite of the obvious importance of money matters in American marriages. The usual reason given for the scarcity of studies on the topic is that it is difficult to acquire data on family finances. As Alfred Kinsey noted, Americans tend to be more willing to describe the intimate details of their sex lives than they are to tell you how much money they make. In our Detroit survey we obtained only 3 "no answer" responses to a question about how often a woman and her husband have arguments about having sex, but 10–27 "no answer" responses to various income questions. See the discussion in Blumstein and Schwartz (1983, pp. 51–3).

43.   This figure includes 27% of all wives who earned no income at all and 37.7% who earned some, but more than $9,000 per year less than their husbands did. It should be noted that we did not ask respondents for exact dollar incomes, but showed them a card with income ranges of $3,000 (except at the upper end of the scale—see Appendix 2 for details). Thus having the same income really means having an income within the same range, such as $12,000–14,999, and not exact equality.

44.   To be more precise, they studied four kinds of couples: married couples, heterosexual cohabiting couples, gay men, and lesbians, and they found that relative earnings were related to power within the relationship for all but lesbian couples. The relative income-power association was also reported earlier by Blood and Wolfe (1960, pp. 31ff).

45.   Only 8 women, or about 2% of the wives in the Detroit sample, gave "don't know" as their answer to our question about their husband's income. In the English study there is a further 5% of wives who reported other, idiosyncratic arrangements for handling their husbands' earnings.

46.   To be more precise, we asked first about whether couples had serious, minor, or no disagreements in each of these areas, and then about who got their way when disagreements occurred. From 35% to 65% of wives reported that they had no disagreements, and in the figures in Table 6.4 these responses are lumped together with "about the same" in the follow-up question about who gets their way, which was only asked if at least minor disagreements in an area were reported. I also analyzed data from this section, treating these "no disagreement" cases as missing data, and the results were substantially the same as reported here, although of course the predominance of the "about the same" category was lessened. The final row in the panel of the table dealing with power relations, concerning "other" disagreements, stems from a follow-up question we used in an effort to compensate for the fact that we were only asking about four specific areas of possible marital disputes. We asked respondents what else they and their husband disagreed about, and for the first item mentioned, we asked who usually got their way. The most frequently mentioned "other" disagreements concerned uses of free time, relations with in-laws, and personal habits of a spouse (e.g., drinking too much).

47.   Since the relative income measure used in the table includes only three crude income categories, I tried this analysis again using the full 16 categories of our measures of husbands' and

wives' incomes. The result was an even weaker relationship between relative income and the marital power scale ($r = .03$).

48.   One important qualification needs to be noted about these data. I do not have reports from the husbands, but only from the wives. Could these figures reflect a "false consciousness" about marital power that women hold, while their husbands would report power distributions that are less equitable and favor themselves? I cannot be certain since I do not have the data, but previous research suggests that if there is a bias in the reports from spouses about marital power, it is in the direction of each partner claiming they have less power than their partner credits them with having (see Quarm 1977). If that is the case I would not expect wives to exaggerate how much power they have, or husbands to yield a much more male dominant picture of marital power. In other words, if we went by reports from husbands we might expect to find a more "wife dominant" picture of marital power than is shown in Table 6.5.

49.   Some critics argue, for instance, that among poor black families, decisions such as buying insurance and taking a vacation may never or rarely be faced.

50.   Sociologists will recognize the Weberian origins of this conception of power (see Bendix 1960, p. 290).

51.   This equal pattern contrasts with Blood and Wolfe's (1960) finding that decisions on his job and what car to buy, and to a lesser extent buying insurance, tended to be left to the husband, while decisions on her work, calling a doctor, and spending on food were mainly left to the wife, with only buying a house and deciding where to go on vacation primarily shared decisions (see Blood and Wolfe 1960, p. 21).

52.   The Blumstein and Schwartz (1983) study which makes this claim does not use the Blood and Wolfe methodology, nor the one used here. Insofar as I can tell from their book, marital power was measured with a single question, "In general who has more say about important decisions affecting your relationship, you or your partner?" with responses recorded on a 9 point scale running from 1 = "I much more" to 9 = "he much more." The vagueness of this single item makes it unclear whether it implies ability to impose one's will on the partner or not and what areas of the relationship it refers to.

53.   The picture conveyed is therefore quite different from that given in some ethnographic descriptions of American marriages, particularly in the working class. See, in particular, Rubin (1976).

54.   Of course, writers using an "exchange" or "resources" perspective on American marriage have usually emphasized that wives and husbands have different kinds of resources they use in marital negotiations. For example, husbands may exchange their resources as a breadwinner for the attractiveness and social graces offered by the wife (see, for example, Scanzoni 1982). However, the limited attempt we could make to test this idea, by correlating interviewer ratings of the attractiveness of our respondents with our marital power measures, did not provide any evidence for it (details not shown here). And it remains somewhat surprising, in terms of exchange theory, that even the husband's earnings, not to mention the wife's earnings and the relationship between the two, have no significant association with our various marital power measures.

55.   The one partial exception to this generalization is that in more recent marriage generations more wives report that they get their way in the event of a disagreement about having sex than was the case for earlier marriage generations.

56.   Details are not shown here; however, the only partial exception is that among blacks more wives report that in the event of a disagreement about having sex they tend to get their way. It might be noted that the earlier claims about the "matriarchal" nature of intact black marriages (see Moynihan 1965) have been criticized on several grounds, particularly as being an artifact of only one or two questions (e.g., buying life insurance) in the marital power measures used in the Blood and Wolfe study cited by Moynihan (see Quarm 1977).

57.   To be more precise, we did include one set of rough measures of several personality traits in our questionnaire. Respondents were asked to rate themselves, and then their husbands, in terms of a

number of different personality traits. And it turns out that there are small but statistically significant correlations between reporting that the husband is stubborn and that he is bossy and our marital power scale ($r = .15$ and $.13$, respectively). However, I am not confident enough that this is an accurate and independent measure of the husband's personality to assert that I have "proved" that personality traits affect marital power more than social background factors.

58.   Although I have no direct evidence, I assume that maintaining separate control over earnings is more likely when earnings are kept at home rather than in a bank.

59.   Multiple regression analysis (results not shown) indicated that both education and age have independent effects on reporting that differences are mutually discussed.

60.   We also asked a follow-up question, as noted earlier, about whether there were any other areas where the respondent and her husband had disagreements. Overall 52% of the wives interviewed reported that they had disagreements in some other area not inquired about specifically, although in this instance we did not find out if the disagreements were minor or serious. Considering the various answers given, it turns out that reporting no disagreements with the husband in any area is fairly uncommon. Only about 15% of the wives we interviewed denied having any disagreements with their husbands (including such "other" disagreements).

61.   The questions were on a separate page which was given to each respondent to fill out in writing, rather than to respond to verbally. She was told to place the sheet in a special envelope when she had finished, a device to try to minimize the discomfort that some respondents might feel from talking about this realm or even having written answers immediately scrutinized. The first two items are shown here in reverse order from how they appeared on the self-administered form, in order to display them in a consistent order in terms of frequency. For the full wording of these questions, see Appendix 2.

62.   In the jargon of social science, the more severe items form a Guttman-scale pattern.

63.   Actually, the responses to the single items are somewhat misleading, since some women were insulted, but did not have husbands stomp out of the house, while others experienced the reverse pattern. Considering all items together, only 35% of all wives said that they never experienced any of the kinds of treatment included in the list. Obviously these items provide only a crude scale of spouse abuse since, among other things, they only indicate whether certain kinds of behavior had ever occurred, and not how often they had occurred, or how recently.

64.   In the full sample the percentages experiencing extremes of abuse were somewhat higher—about 7% reported having been beaten up. But as might be expected, some of such women had decided to end their abusive marriages, so that they are reporting about their former husbands. The figures in Table 6.6, as throughout this chapter, refer only to currently married women, and thus they somewhat understate the extent to which all ever-married women have experienced abuse.

65.   Previous research indicates that this sort of multi-level indicator provides a good predictor for the likelihood of divorce subsequently (see Booth et al. 1983).

66.   The variable about the degree of marital worries, a scale of spouse abuse, and the scale for the severity of marital conflicts are all intercorrelated, with the average correlation $r = .34$. In Chapter 7 I will use this fact to construct a marital problems scale that will be used in my effort to determine what factors affect the quality and survival of marriages.

67.   As in other parts of this study, the scales were composed of the mean of the standardized scores of each item included. For details, see Appendix 2.

68.   Inspection of the individual items in this scale indicates, however, that they operate in different ways. Marrying young, having many children at home, and having weak ethnic roots are significantly associated only with the "milder" forms of abuse, up through and including "push, grab, and shove." Being married multiple times, on the other hand, is significantly associated only with the two more extreme forms of abuse—"kick, bite, or hit" and beating the wife up, and why this differential pattern should occur is something of a puzzle. See the discussion of remarriages in Chapter 8.

69.   Some of the literature on spouse abuse suggests that the strains associated with unemploy-

ment of the husband are particularly likely to lead to violence against other family members. However, in our data there was no significant difference between reports by wives of employed vs. unemployed men in terms of our spouse abuse measures, and if anything the pattern ran in the other direction. In fact, none of the unemployed or marginally employed husbands in our sample ($N = 24$) was reported to ever have beaten his wife.

70. For blacks, the primary difference seems to be a substantially higher frequency of having experienced a marital separation. Overall 28.9% of the black wives had been separated at some point, compared to only 6.3% of the white wives.

71. The correlations between the number of children ever born and the marital problems measures were not significant. It is the number of children currently living at home, rather than fertility per se, that makes the difference. Even when the factors indicated in this paragraph are taken into account, I can only explain a modest amount of the variation in the levels of marital problems reported by respondents (generally under 10%).

72. Feminist attitudes are also related, though, to lower levels of reported mutual expressions of concern and affection between spouses, and to reporting more worries about whether the marriage is in trouble. It is unclear in this case what is cause and what is effect.

73. To be more precise, no significant differences were found between white and black marriages in power distribution, and although some differences were found in the patterns of chore division, these did not indicate a pattern of sex-typing being more common in one race or the other.

74. These controls were carried out through partial correlation analysis. Results are not shown here. Detailed analysis of the predictors of composite scale scores for both marriage quality and marriage problems will be presented in Chapter 7.

75. I should also stress again that the racial comparisons in this chapter are based on only 38 wives in the case of blacks, so that I am uncertain how much confidence I can place in these findings. Hopefully future research using larger samples can delve further into the question of racial differences in marriage patterns and their sources.

76. Again, this should not be that surprising, since the family is, after all, the original and perhaps the only really successful "communist" society—in the sense of being an organization in which rewards are distributed according to needs rather than according to contributions or resources. Some scholars have attempted to adapt the rational actor model to these realities of marriage by modifying its assumptions. Heimer and Stinchcombe (1980), for example, describe love and marriage as establishing a "joint utility function" such that each partner takes the other's needs and feelings into account in his or her behavior.

Chapter 7

WHAT MAKES FOR A SUCCESSFUL MARRIAGE?

For decades researchers have tried to fathom what makes the difference between a good and a bad marriage, and between couples who divorce and those who stay together. Some early researchers on American family life hoped to be able to scientifically predict which marriages would succeed or fail, and by so doing make it possible for couples contemplating a trip down the aisle to know in advance whether they had a high or low chance of "living happily ever after." This optimism proved unwarranted. Studies that tried to predict marital success (e.g., Locke 1951) were not themselves notably successful. Some critics of this sort of research said, "I told you so." To such critics, marital success depended upon "unpredictables" and "unmeasurables," such as romantic love, personality quirks of each partner, and unique personal histories. Some critics even opposed carrying out research on the background factors affecting marital success, saying that this would take much of the mystery and romance out of marriage (see Rubin 1977).

In spite of this sort of critical response, family researchers have not given up their quest for enlightenment about what makes for successful or unsuccessful marriages. Indeed, as the divorce rate has risen in American society, the need to explain the factors lying behind marital failures has been more keenly felt. Over the years a body of research has accumulated that makes it possible to point to several factors that do influence the fate of marriages (see, for example, Stephens 1968; Lewis and Spanier 1979). Researchers are not in a position to predict whether any particular couple will live happily ever after, or even to fully explain divorce trends in our society generally. Nonetheless, they have been able to point to a variety of background factors that make marital success more or less likely. In this chapter a wide range of these factors will be examined to see whether they help to explain the marital histories of women in the Detroit sample.

Good and Bad Marriages

Up to now I have referred rather vaguely to "good vs. bad marriages" or to marriages that are successful or unsuccessful. Before we can examine the evidence on the fate of marriages, I must be more precise about what differentiates marriages, and about how I have measured marital success and failure. It turns out that this is not an easy thing to do. While it might be nice to use a single measure of marital success, examination of both previous research and the Detroit data convinced me that it was not advisable to do so. Instead I ended up using three different measures of the fate of marriages.

Conventionally, the literature on this topic distinguishes between marital stability and marriage quality. Marital stability refers simply to whether the couple stays together vs. divorcing or separating.[1] But some couples stay together in spite of the fact that they are miserable; others may divorce even if they are not totally miserable and may in some respects have a relationship that others would envy. Because of the crudeness of instability as a measure of the fate of a marriage, researchers have introduced the "umbrella" term *marriage quality* to refer to a variety of features of existing marriages—the level of marital communication, affection, companionship, satisfaction, and related factors on the one hand, and the relative absence of severe conflict, spouse abuse, and simple dissatisfaction on the other. (For a review of the ideas and research evidence lying behind these two concepts, see Lewis and Spanier 1979.) Researchers have devised and tested multiple item questionnaire-based inventories to construct a variety of "marriage quality scales," with the assumption being that a "low quality" marriage is more likely than others to end in divorce, but that the association between stability and quality will not be perfect. (For examples of such marriage quality inventories, see Locke and Wallace 1959; Orden and Bradburn 1968; Spanier 1976.)

Recently a new wrinkle has been added to the issue of how to measure marital success or failure. Johnson et al. (1986) have argued that marriage quality should be divided into two elements. In analyzing multiple items dealing with marriage quality, they discovered that two separate factors emerged. One referred to positive qualities of the marital relationship, and the other to worries and marital conflicts. To oversimplify somewhat, their study suggests that "good marriage quality" traits, such as communication, understanding, and affection, and "bad marriage traits," such as conflicts and anxieties about the relationship, are at least partially independent aspects of a marriage. So it is possible to have couples who love each other and communicate intensely but also fight like cats and dogs. On the other hand you can have what Cuber and Haroff (1963) termed a "devitalized" marriage—a relationship devoid of either affection or of conflict. These sorts of combinations are common enough, say Johnson et al., that it would be misleading to use a single global measure of marital quality. (For earlier and related ideas, see Bradburn 1969; Gilford and Bengston 1979.)

As indicated in Chapter 6, when I examined the Detroit data I found much the same pattern that Johnson et al. described. Items dealing with positive marital quality clustered together, but were not closely enough associated with items dealing with marital problems and conflicts to warrant combining them into a single scale.[2] For this reason I constructed two separate scales, which will be called a "Marriage Quality Scale" and a "Marriage Problems Scale."[3] So in the remainder of this chapter I will be concerned with whether various background characteristics and experiences affect marital instability, marriage quality, and marriage problems, and it will become clear (as expected from previous research) that some background factors affect only one or two of these measures of the marriage relationship, rather than all three.

In the following pages, I will conduct two analysis stages. First I will consider the major types of predictors of marital success and failure that have been suggested in the literature and see whether or not measures that tap these realms are associated with the three indicators of marital success. Those predictors that survive this first scrutiny will then be entered into multivariate analyses to see if, when other measures are controlled, they still have an independent influence on the fate of the marriage relationship. Throughout this chapter I will be examining only those women who have been married only once ($N = 302$). The stability, quality, and problems of remarriages will be considered in the following chapter. As in other parts of this study, my approach is eclectic to almost a "kitchen sink" degree. I will consider a wide variety of predictors of marital success, rather than simply test a pet theory or two.

Even though the reader may feel that an exhaustive listing of predictors of marital success is contained in the pages that follow, there are some important influences that cannot be examined here. How happy or unhappy people will be with their marital relationship, and whether they will contemplate divorce, depends upon both the mix of satisfactions and dissatisfactions in the current marriage and the perception of available alternatives to that marriage (see Udry 1981). Whether the marriage will last also depends not only on the wife's assessment of these things, but also on the husband's. In the current study we have no information on the husband's assessment of the marriage, now or prior to any divorce that occurred. Even for wives, we only have information about a variety of features of their current marital relationship, and not about their awareness of any alternatives to that relationship.[4] Therefore even the extensive consideration of predictors of marital success that follows can only claim to present a partial and incomplete picture.

Premarital History and the Fate of the Marriage

One of the central concerns of this study is how premarital relationships have changed and whether the nature of premarital experiences has an identifiable impact on the fate of the marriage. Thus it seems appropriate to start the survey of predictors of marital success by considering what the impact of premarital experiences might be. How could the nature of a woman's dating and mating process affect her subsequent marriage relationship?

Earlier in this study the ages at which respondents began dating was examined. Previous research does not provide a clear prediction about whether starting dating early is "good" or "bad," in terms of the fate of the marriage relationship that results at the end of the dating stage.[5] However, other features of the dating stage have been identified as important. Marrying very young has been indicated quite consistently as producing less stable marriages, and probably lower quality relationships in those marriages that do survive.[6] Therefore I want to examine the age of first marriage of respondents in relation to the three measures of marital outcomes. Some studies also suggest that knowing the eventual spouse for a short time is less likely to lead to marital success than knowing him for a longer time (one year is sometimes indicated as an important dividing line). I also want to examine whether the length of this final courtship is related to the fate of the marriage.[7]

With regard to the number of dates and steadies a woman had prior to marriage, there is little previous research to go on, and two contrary predictions are possible, as indicated in Chapter 2. Those who have had many dating partners, steadies, and even alternative marital prospects have an extensive basis for saying, "If only I had married so-and-so," while those who married their first sweetheart would not know what they had missed. This logic would lead to a prediction that those with extensive dating experiences with other partners would be more likely to have unhappy or unstable marriages than women with more limited experiences. On the other hand, our dating culture is premised upon a contrary logic. Dating is seen as a process that will enable individuals to gain social experience with the opposite sex. As you grow older and date a variety of partners, it is hoped or assumed that you are learning more about what sorts of people you could and could not be happily married to. As previously discussed in this study, this sort of learning experience should, as a consequence, produce a "wiser choice" and presumably a more stable and higher quality marriage among those who have had extensive experience in dating than among those who marry the first fellow who comes along. So we end up with two contrary predictions; extensive dating experience may be related to poor marital outcomes, or then again it might be related to good marital outcomes.

Several aspects of premarital sexuality have also been mentioned by researchers as influencing the fate of the eventual marriage. The one feature most often discussed is premarital pregnancy. It is argued that premarital pregnancy may precipitate a hasty and ill-considered marriage, and that as a result couples who go to the altar in a "shotgun wedding" situation will have poorer prospects than other couples. A related concern is that a baby will arrive very soon after the wedding (if not before), thus making it necessary for the couple to adapt to the demands of a baby before they have adjusted to married life with each other. Thus a special strain on marital relations can be expected with a premarital pregnancy.[8]

It is less clear how we should expect premarital sexual relations or cohabitation prior to marriage that does not lead to a premarital pregnancy to affect the fate of a marriage. Again, contrary predictions have been advanced. As noted earlier in this study, in sociological research done thirty or forty years ago, it was often argued that having had premarital sex would have a harmful influence on the subsequent marriage. If sexual intercourse had been engaged in with other partners besides the eventual spouse the same logic previously discussed in regard to dating experience promoting a "grass is greener" mentality might apply. For this reason we will examine separately those respondents who had other sexual partners before their first husbands.[9] But even if sexual relations only involved the spouse-to-be, some past studies indicated that this could have a harmful effect (see, for example, Burgess and Wallin 1953, p. 518). The underlying logic was one often used by both parents and religious leaders over the years, that sex prior to marriage would make marriage "less special," and that those who indulged would develop less respect for marriage as an institution.

However, over time in American society there has been growing acceptance of a contrary logic, as discussed earlier. To oversimplify somewhat, premarital sex is increasingly treated as a more intimate stage of the learning process that is involved in dating. Marriage will involve sexual compatibility and therefore, it is increasingly argued (more by unmarried young people, to be sure, than by their parents) that selection of the "right mate" requires determining in advance whether the couple can be sexually compatible. Some would even extend this argument to justify the "beneficial" effect of a variety of premarital sexual partners on a subsequent marriage relationship. By gaining sexual experience one would, in this view, be in a better position to make "the right choice" in terms of sexual compatibility when selecting someone to marry. So again we confront contrary arguments; that premarital sexual experience can harm the subsequent marriage relationship or can improve it. The same two sets of arguments can and have been raised in regard to premarital cohabitation. Critics say that the practice will tend to make marriage less special, while advocates claim that it provides a sort of "ultimate test" of whether one is suited or not suited to marry a given individual.

There is another aspect of dating and mating that will be examined as well. I am interested in whether the elaborateness of the wedding is in any way associated with the fate of the marriage. Admittedly in this case my interest stems not so much from previous research as from customary lore surrounding weddings. Certainly older relatives, and many mothers in particular, try to create the impression that a marriage that is not begun with a traditional and elaborate wedding is in some vague but important way less likely to succeed.[10] But perhaps there are some cogent reasons behind such feelings. As noted in Chapter 3, an elaborate wedding provides a public ritual demarcation of movement from the single into the married state, and reinforcement for giving up single ways and single attitudes. It provides an occasion for relatives and friends on both sides to gather and publicly celebrate the occasion, thus indicating their approval and support for the marriage relationship. In some wedding rituals, those attending are called upon to pledge support and assistance to the new couple. As discussed earlier, an elaborate wedding also tends to bring forth a copious flow of presents that help to endow the new couple with items that will ease their adjustment to the married state. (Think of the strain, after all, of having to begin married life with no toasters.) Finally, an elaborate wedding may produce at least some pause and embarrassment if the couple should subsequently decide that it was all a big mistake and want to divorce. (Do the toasters all have to be returned?) For all of these reasons, then, we might expect that elaborate weddings will have at least some reinforcing effect on the marriages that they establish. Couples who elope, marry in simple civil ceremonies, or go with a friend or two to city hall or a justice of the peace would in these terms be starting off their married lives less auspiciously.

The reader may have noted that up to now I have left out of the discussion one factor that would seem of considerable importance in predicting marital success: love. Indeed, in our culture it is often assumed that love can "conquer all." Or, as the Beatles' song lyric put it, "all you need is love." If a couple is enough in love, we would like to believe, then they will do whatever it takes to make the marriage a success. No matter how important this idea may be in our culture, it is not an easy notion to test. The kinds of deep, inner feelings we refer to in talking about romantic love are not easily captured by simple questions in a survey. And in this case, we face the additional problem that the Detroit respondents are all married women, rather than brides-to-be, and they may not be able to recall accurately how much in love they were when they first married, years or even decades ago.[11] For these reasons I will not be able to perform a very satisfactory test on the influence of premarital love feelings on the subsequent fate of the marriages of Detroit respondents. However, since our questionnaire did ask respondents to try to recall how much in love they had been prior to first marrying (as described in Chapter 3), I cannot resist the urge to see whether this measure adds anything to my ability to explain marital outcomes in the Detroit study. The reader should join the author in examining the associations between this love indicator and marital outcomes while preserving some skepticism about what is really being measured.

Table 7.1 presents the bivariate correlations between these various measures of premarital experiences and the three indicators of the fate of the (first) marriage. In the table we see that only three aspects of dating and mating have a consistent impact on all three measures of marital success. Marrying young is associated with marital instability, and for those who remain married, with lower quality marriages and more marital problems. Having an elaborate wedding also shows a surprisingly strong association (surprising in terms of the semi-whimsical basis of this hypothesis; the actual correlations are modest in size) with marital stability, high marriage quality, and fewer marriage problems. The recollected level of premarital love feelings also is associated with marital stability and with high quality and low problems, although, as just discussed, we cannot be totally confident that these recollections are unbiased.

Table 7.1.   Correlations of Dating and Mating Patterns with Marriage Outcomes

Dating and Mating Behavior	Divorced or Separated (1st marriage)	Marriage Quality Scale	Marriage Problems Scale
Popularity Scale	.07	.03	.00
Courting Interval	−.12*	−.00	−.05
Wife Marriage Age	−.21*	.12*	−.21*
Premarital Sex	.04	−.03	.10
Sex Before Husband	.07	−.01	.07
Cohabitation	.04	.01	.10
Premarital Pregnancy	.20*	−.04	.14*
Love	−.29*	.30*	−.14*
Wedding Elaborateness	−.26*	.16*	−.15*
Median *N*	439	301	301

* = p < .05

The figures in the table also show that premarital intimacy does not have a consistent impact on marital success. Respondents who were premaritally pregnant were more likely to get divorced and those who did not divorce reported more problems than other women, although their quality scores were not significantly lower. The other three premarital sexuality measures show generally weak and nonsignificant associations with the marital outcome scales. So both those who claim that premarital intimacy makes the marriage less special and those who argue that it provides a positive learning experience will not find much support for their views in these results.[12] Evidently it is primarily the strains associated with premarital pregnancy and early childbearing, rather than any aspect of premarital sexual activity per se, that have a harmful effect on the subsequent marriage relationship.[13]

Finally, we see in Table 7.1 weak and generally nonsignificant associations with the remaining measures of dating history. Having had a variety of dates, steadies, and prospects, as tapped by the Popularity Scale, does not seem to have any effect one way or the other, and a long period of dating the first husband prior to marriage may be very weakly associated with a more stable marriage, but not with any difference in the quality or level of problems in a marriage.

Overall, the results in the table raise serious questions about the major premise of our American dating culture—what I called earlier the "marketplace learning" scenario. We like to believe that, in the American system of free mate choice, individuals participate in our dating culture in order to acquire valuable experience that will help them pick a suitable mate and have a successful marriage. The popular scenario assumes that having a variety of dates, getting to know serious prospects for an extended period of time, and, perhaps, developing a high level of intimacy with such prospects will help pave the way for a successful mate choice and marriage. However, from the figures in Table 7.1 it would appear that those women who married their first sweethearts had marriages that were no less successful than women who had had extensive dating experiences; that women who married soon after meeting their intended were as satisfied with their marriages as were women who had extended courtships and engagements; and that women who married as virgins were no less happy with the outcome than women who tested their sexual compatibility with their fiancés or with others first. In general, with the possible exception of the association between a longer courting interval and marital stability, there does not seem to be a clear pattern of association between the extent of experience in the dating stage and marital success.[14]

However, the figures in Table 7.1 do not provide any evidence for the alternative scenario discussed in Chapter 2. There I summarized a different set of arguments—that the process of dating, by beginning at very young ages and by being distorted by social pressures and concerns for popularity, ends up being counter-productive, in terms of the search for the most suitable mate. A related argument concerning premarital sexuality is often made by anxious parents. Youths who "forget themselves" and become sexually involved prior to marriage may mistake physical attraction for love and compatibility, and their passion may lead them to make an inappropriate choice for a marriage partner. If these sorts of "rating and dating" and "loss of control" arguments, or for that matter the "grass is greener" view described earlier in this chapter, are correct, we might expect to find that those who were most involved in dating activities and premarital intimacy would consistently have the least successful marriages. But that is not what the figures in the table show. Instead, the figures point more in the direction of the dating process being irrelevant to subsequent marital success one way or the other.

What does this pattern of findings mean? Does it indicate that we might do as well by drawing lots or flipping a coin to pick a mate as by going through a prolonged dating process? This troubling question will be deferred until the concluding chapter in order to move on to a consideration of other influences on marital success.

Homogamy and Marital Success

Chapter 5 reviewed evidence about the extent of "status matching" in the marriages of the Detroit sample, and I concluded that in terms of race and class there had not been much change over time, while both ethnicity and religion had become less important as mate selection "filters." Still, many Americans believe that marriages are more likely to be successful if the partners come from similar backgrounds. (Indeed, in our study we asked respondents to agree or disagree with the following statement: "When the husband and wife come from different social backgrounds, the marriage is bound to have problems." Fifty-four percent of our respondents agreed with this statement.) There is also a fair amount of empirical support for this view in past studies (see the reviews by Stephens 1968; Lewis and Spanier 1979). The reasons given for this association are complex. In part, it is assumed that people from different backgrounds will have different values, habits, and perhaps even personalities, and that these differences will make it difficult to get along in a marriage relationship.[15] (The effects of values and personality differences will be considered more directly in a subsequent section of this chapter.) It is also assumed that when the partners come from different backgrounds there is more likely to be opposition to the match from parents and other relatives, and that this opposition will create an extra strain on the marital relationship. (Again, the importance of parental opposition will be considered directly in a subsequent section.) Finally, in the case of at least some kinds of "mismatches" (e.g., interracial marriages, a young groom and an older bride) it is assumed that couples will experience general discrimination and community isolation, and that as a result the marriage will suffer from more strain than is normal for married couples. For a variety of reasons, then, we expect homogamous marriages to be of higher quality, and nonhomogamous ones to be more unstable and more beset by problems and conflicts.[16]

In Table 7.2 the associations between a variety of aspects of homogamy and indicators of the fate of the marriage are examined.[17] In general the figures in the table provide very little support for the idea that homogamy is important in making a good marriage. There are marginally significant associations in the table between class origin homogamy (as measured by the subjective class identifications of the respondent's family and of her groom's family) and higher quality marriages and fewer marriage problems, but various objective class-related indicators, which compare the occupations of the respondent's father, her spouse's father, and the spouse himself, as well as the educational levels of both spouses, show no similar pattern. There is also a weak correlation between religious homogamy and marital stability, but otherwise no indication that religious or

Table 7.2. Correlations of Homogamy Measures with Marriage Outcomes

Homogamy Measures	Divorced or Separated (1st marriage)	Marriage Quality Scale	Marriage Problems Scale
Subjective Class Origins	.02	.14*	−.16*
Educational	−.03	.05	.02
Fathers' Occupations	.02	−.01	.01
Father/1st Husband Occupations	.08	−.03	−.00
Same Religion	−.09*	−.03	−.00
Same Ethnic Groups	−.02	−.08	−.02
Median *N*	419	301	301

* = $p < .05$

ethnic endogamy makes any particular difference for the fate of the marriage.[18] Thus in examining these relationships we are led to doubt that there is any systematic impact of social background mismatches on the fate of the marriages involved. This is a surprising "nonresult" in view of the widespread popular belief, supported by some past research, that homogamy is important to a marriage.[19]

Intrigued by this pattern of negative findings, I examined another possibility, that women who had "married down" would be unhappy about their marriages, but that women whose mismatches involved "marrying up"—to a higher status male—would if anything be unusually happy about their marital outcomes.[20] This possibility was examined (results not shown here), as well as a prediction suggested in an earlier study (Pearlin 1975) that women who had had high aspirations for social mobility and ended up marrying down (to a lower class origin male) would have less satisfactory marital outcomes. Even these more specific predictions received little support in the Detroit data. I am forced to conclude, then, that with a couple of possible minor exceptions, the closeness or distance between the social background characteristics of the bride and groom has very little to do with how their marriage will fare.[21]

Social Ties and Marital Success

The existing literature on marital outcomes also includes a number of claims that social ties and social support have an effect on the durability and quality of the marriage relationship. First, there is some support for the notion that marital instability may be transmitted from generation to generation and that individuals who grew up in "broken homes" or in conflict-laden families are more likely to have unhappy and brittle marriages themselves. Conversely, those whose parents had happy marriages may see these as models, leading to greater success in their own marriages. We can examine this possibility by looking at the relationship between scales tapping whether respondents grew up in intact families and the degree of conflict in family relationships on the one hand and measures of marital success on the other.[22] Another set of social ties factors concerns parental approval of one's choice of a marriage partner. Some studies indicate that individuals who marry partners their parents disapprove of are less likely than others to have successful marriages, perhaps due to the extra strains caused by this lack of social support (see Sussman 1953). We can examine this possibility by looking at the relationship of the degree of parental approval of the first husbands chosen and measures of marriage outcomes.

There are also a number of suggestions that the pattern of social ties a couple has after they are married may have an independent influence on the fate of their marriage. The classic study on this point is Elizabeth Bott's *Family and Social Network* (1957), in which she found that when the husband and wife had tightly-knit and separate friendship networks the marital bond was likely to be brittle, whereas if the husband and wife had loosely-knit and overlapping social ties the marriage was likely to be durable. The logic behind this finding was subsequently amplified into a general theory of divorce by Ackerman (1963). He argued that couples who were embedded in "disjunctive affiliations"—separate and competing sets of social ties and obligations—were likely to have brittle marriages, whereas couples who were embedded in "conjunctive affiliations"— overlapping and reinforcing social ties and obligations—were likely to have stable marriages.[23] On the one hand "conjunctive affiliations" brings to mind the American middle-class ideal of "togetherness," in which spouses share activities, interests, and friends and conduct most of their social life with other similar couples who are not seen particularly as "his friends" or "her friends." On the other hand "disjunctive affiliations" brings to mind a pattern generally more common in the working class, in which each spouse has separate activities, friends, and social obligations, and in which he spends much of his social life off with "the boys," while she spends much of hers off with "her friends." The former situation, it is presumed, reinforces the marital bond, while the latter situation undermines it.

Finally, some have suggested that simply the presence or absence of social support, as shown by close ties with kin and an ample friendship network, may have a positive impact on the marriage relationship. If such social ties are lacking, so the argument goes, then all of the emotional needs of each partner have to be met by the spouse, and this situation of having all of one's "emotional eggs in one basket" can put a special strain on the marital relationship. We can examine the influence of social ties after marriage by using measures of closeness to kin on both sides of the family, a measure of the number of close friends named, whether there is a web of friendships linking the wife's friends, and a scale measuring the number of friends the husband and wife share.

In Table 7.3 the associations between various measures of social ties and support and marital success are examined. Several of the ideas discussed receive at least modest support from the figures in the table. Parental opposition to the respondent's dating and mating activities is associated with poor marital outcomes according to all three measures, and conflicts between the respondent's parents and between them and her produce a similar effect, although the association with marital instability is quite weak. Not growing up in an intact home has a similar impact, but only the correlation with marital instability is statistically significant. Close kinship ties on both sides of the family seem to occur with higher quality marriages with fewer problems, and a full and close-knit friendship network and friends shared with the husband seem to be associated with slightly higher marriage quality scores, but only shared friendship is related to fewer marital problems.[24] Of course, one can ask in these latter instances what causes what. Perhaps people with conflict-prone marriages tend to alienate their relatives and friends, rather than having the absence of social support foster

Table 7.3. Correlations of Social Ties Measures with Marriage Outcomes

Social Ties Measures	Divorced or Separated (1st marriage)	Marriage Quality Scale	Marriage Problems Scale
Parental Opposition	.22*	−.23*	.31*
Family Conflicts	.11*	−.31*	.22*
Broken Home	.14*	−.07	.10
Mutual Friends Scale	n.a.	.19*	−.15*
Friendship Web	n.a.	.12*	−.04
Number of Friends	n.a.	.10	−.03
Ties with Wife's Kin	n.a.	.17*	−.20*
Ties with Husband's Kin	n.a.	.19*	−.24*
Median N	454	302	302

* = p < .05

n.a. = Not applicable, information only available for those currently married.

marital conflict. We cannot resolve this question here, but for the moment I simply observe that several of these social ties measures do show the expected associations with measures of marital success.

Resources and Marital Success

Another broad category of explanations of marital success and failure has been referred to in terms of "resources" (see, for example, Lewis and Spanier 1979, p. 277). The underlying idea here is that achieving marital success requires income, assets, status, access to opportunities, and so forth. Individuals who lack such resources may feel under great strain because of their deficiency (for example, the failure of the "breadwinner" to be able to provide for his family), and in general both spouses will feel low levels of commitment to maintaining the unrewarding relationship. Conversely, individuals who have succeeded in acquiring such resources will feel more satisfied, and that satisfaction is likely to have a positive spill-over onto their feelings about their marital relationships. Their desires to maintain their resources and maintain their marriages will become intertwined, fostering more durable marriage bonds. These sorts of arguments lead to the expectation that people who are disadvantaged in various ways—in terms of education, income, social class origins, racial group, and so forth—will have more difficulty developing successful marriages than will individuals without such disadvantages. In general it has been observed that in societies with relative freedom to divorce, divorce rates are inversely related to social class position (see Goode 1962).

This general approach of explaining marital success in terms of resources vs.

Table 7.4. Correlation of Resources Measures with Marital Outcomes

Resources Measures	Divorced or Separated (1st marriage)	Marriage Quality Scale	Marriage Problems Scale
Respondent Black	.33*	−.15*	.11*
Wife Class Origins	.01	.15*	−.14*
Parent Investment Income	.02	.10	−.04
Wife's Father's Occupation	−.03	.06	−.10
Wife's Education	−.08	.11	−.07
1st Husband Class Origins	−.05	.04	−.08
1st Husband's Education	−.14*	.12*	−.06
1st Husband's Occupation at Time of Marriage	−.18*	.07	−.01
Current Class	n.a.	.02	−.02
Wife's Current Income	n.a.	.02	.06
Present Husband Income	n.a.	.06	−.04
Total Current Income	n.a.	.08	−.02
Wife Current Occupation	n.a.	−.07	.06
Husband Current Occupation	n.a.	.12	.08
Husband Unemployed	n.a.	.01	.04
Satisfaction with Living Standard	n.a.	.19*	−.26*
Median *N*	455	300	300

* = p < .05
n.a. = Not applicable, no data for the period just prior to the divorce.

disadvantages can be applied at two points in time. On the one hand we can examine the kinds of advantages or disadvantages that spouses had prior to marriage and how these affected all three marital success measures. We can also examine how the current status and resources of those couples who are still married is related to their reports about marriage quality and problems. In the fashion that is conventional with sociologists, I examine here a range of "SES" (socioeconomic status) indicators and how they relate to marital success measures.

When we examine these associations in Table 7.4, it turns out that there is surprisingly weak support for the resources approach to explaining marital success. Blacks in the sample had less successful marriages than whites according to all three of these measures, as we might anticipate from the discussion in Chapter 6, but the effect is much stronger for marital instability than it is for marital quality or problems.[25] There is also a weak tendency visible in the first column of the table for first husbands who were well educated and had high status jobs to have had more stable marriages, but the characteristics of their wives (our respondents) and other SES measures had no significant impact on the likelihood of divorce. There also are significant associations in the table between both husband's education and wife's class origin and marriage quality, but these correlations are quite weak.

Perhaps the most surprising finding is that current SES position, no matter how measured (see the bottom half of the table), is not related to marital quality or problems—contrary to the assumption that relative status and control over resources plays a central role in marital satisfaction in American society. Even having an unemployed husband—a factor usually seen as a common source of serious stress in American marriages—does not show up here as an influence on marriage quality and problems. The only even modestly strong correlations in the lower part of the table are those between satisfaction with the family's current standard of living and high marriage quality and fewer marriage problems. However, given the fact that none of the objective indicators of current class position shows a similar pattern, I am led to speculate that the figures in this final row of the table reveal a different pattern of causation than assumed. Rather than economic success or failure "spilling over" and affecting perceptions of the nature of one's marriage, what may be happening here is that marital happiness or unhappiness is spilling over to affect how satisfied one is with one's standard of living.

There seems only the weakest of evidence in these data for the notion that social class position has a general and strong impact on marital success, and because of this fact it also seems unlikely that the higher marital instability of the blacks in the sample is due simply to the greater economic disadvantages suffered by blacks.[26] But it is unclear at this point what other influences could be operating to produce the moderately strong correlations between race and marital success shown in this table.

Wife Autonomy and Marital Success

Another common explanation for marital instability involves the degree of autonomy or independence of the wife. The underlying idea here is that marriage in America as in most other societies tends to be an asymmetrical relationship from which husbands benefit more than wives. Wives are often dependent upon the husband financially, and even when women work they tend to do most of the domestic chores anyway, with little help from their husbands, as noted in the previous chapter. Traditionally, at least, husbands also had more active lives outside of, and apart from, the family, while wives' social horizons tended to be more narrowly confined to family burdens and activities. All of these phenomena are sometimes argued to make marriage a positive and healthy relationship for husbands, but a somewhat stressful and even harmful relationship for wives (see, for example, the discussion in Bernard 1972). Even if women feel miserable about their marriages, their economic dependence on their husbands may lead them to decide to endure, rather than to divorce.

Insofar as these observations are accurate, they may help explain particular aspects of recent divorce trends. The increased independence of wives, manifested particularly in their rising rates of participation in work outside the home, is seen by many as a primary factor contributing to the upsurge in the divorce rate in America and other modern societies in recent times. Researchers have also found that women who contribute a higher share of household income are more likely to divorce than women who contribute a lower share, and working women are more likely to divorce than housewives (see, for example, Hannan, Tuma, and Groeneveld 1978). Studies of this topic argue that increased female autonomy is responsible for these findings. Wives who become less dependent upon their husbands are no longer willing to tolerate an unhappy marriage, and are more willing to contemplate embarking on life on their own. But the autonomy is not only financial—women who work outside the home or who have other activities that are unconnected to their husbands may develop social ties and obligations that conflict with their conjugal obligations—the phenomenon of "disjunctive affiliations" discussed in a previous section.

The argument just summarized concerns only marital instability. What would be the impact of female autonomy on marriage quality and problems? The answer to this question is unclear, and again contrary predictions could be made. Perhaps by having work skills and experience and a source of independent income a wife will be able to consider the possibility of life on her own and therefore will be more likely to notice the shortcomings in her own marriage. A wife who is totally dependent upon her husband financially, on the other hand, may simply close her mind to any defects in her relationship with her spouse. If this set of speculations is correct, then we would expect wives with jobs and incomes to rate their marriages lower than would housewives. However, a variety of arguments to the contrary exist. Women who are totally dependent upon their husbands may stay married no matter how miserable they are, while more autonomous wives who are unhappy will readily divorce. Thus autonomous wives who are still married will feel good about their marriages, or at least better than do dependent wives. In addition, as noted in Chapter 6, champions of female employment argue that a wife who has a job and an income of her own may have more pride in herself than a housewife and may feel that her work gives her an opportunity to establish more of an equal partnership with her husband. If these sorts of considerations hold true, we would expect autonomous wives to have more successful marriages than dependent wives.

In Table 7.5 we examine the possibility that female independence in various forms affects marital success. The first measure, a scale of female independence, concerns the woman at the time she first married; whether she was employed, living apart from her parents, and whether at marriage she and her husband set up an independent household. The other measures concern the subsequent work activities of the wife; whether she is currently working, what proportion of the years since she got married she has worked, and what share of the total family income her earnings constitute.

In Table 7.5 we see no consistent support for the idea that independence of the

Table 7.5. Correlations of Female Independence Measures with Marital Outcomes

Female Independence Measures	Divorced or Separated (1st marriage)	Marriage Quality Scale	Marriage Problems Scale
Female Independence Scale	−.08	.01	.05
Wife Currently Employed	n.a.	.02	−.11
Years Worked/Years Since First Married	n.a.	−.12*	.08
Wife Share of Family Income	n.a.	−.02	.06
Median *N*	459	283	283

* = p < .05

n.a. = Not applicable, no information on period just before divorce.

wife, or greater relative control over resources, is related to marital success. To be sure, I cannot perform a fully satisfactory test of this idea because I do not have longitudinal data, and this means that there is no information about the work status and relative income just prior to divorce of those respondents who were divorced from their first husbands. Thus we cannot examine the impact of most of these female autonomy measures on marital instability. It is interesting, however, that the coefficient in the upper left hand corner of the table indicates that female independence prior to marriage is weakly related to less, rather than more, marital instability.[28] The correlations elsewhere in the table are uniformly weak, and only the trend for years working since marriage to be associated with poorer marriage quality barely surpasses the .05 statistical significance level. Although this single finding points toward female employment being "harmful" to marital success, the second correlation in the final column of the table, which is almost as large, points in the opposite direction, with wives who are currently employed reporting somewhat fewer problems.

There is some danger in over-interpreting results in a table such as this, in which all of the correlations are so weak. Nevertheless, one additional pattern of interest turned up through more detailed analysis. The figures in the final row of the table conceal an interesting contrast across marriage generations. For women who married prior to 1965 the correlation between the wife's income share and marriage quality was $r = -.16*$, and with marriage problems was $r = .21*$. For women who first got married after that year the same correlations were .17* and −.09. In other words, there are modest signs here that for older women in the sample contributing a high share of the family income is associated with an unsatisfying marriage, while for younger women this is associated with a satisfying marriage. It is unclear whether this contrast is a sign of the demise of expectations that the husband be the "breadwinner" or is simply connected to differences between life stages, so that younger women will become more resentful if they still are contributing a major share of family income decades after the marriage.[29] So while perhaps the safest conclusion to be drawn from Table 7.5 is that autonomy of the wife does not have a consistently positive or negative impact on marital success, there are at least weak indications here that, for younger women in particular, autonomy before marriage and financial contributions by the wife afterward may have a positive impact on the marriage.

Traditionalism and Marital Success

The next item in my inventory of predictors of marital success is termed broadly "traditionalism." The underlying notion here is that individuals who have been reared in conservative religious or ethnic traditions will see questions of marriage and divorce in a distinctive light. In particular, they are less likely to see divorce as an acceptable way to escape from an unhappy marriage, and they may be motivated to work harder in comparison to other couples to make their marriages work. Individuals such as this may see marital problems as their lot in life that must be endured, whereas more "secularized" or "cosmopolitan" individuals would see the same problems as things that must be resolved or escaped from (through divorce). And of course there are some religions (Catholicism) and some ethnic traditions (e.g., Chinese) that have traditionally made divorce and remarriage very difficult, and individuals who are embedded in such religious or ethnic subcultures may simply fear the social pressure and ostracism that they would feel if they contemplated ending their marriages. So it seems important to examine whether various measures of traditionalism in the backgrounds of our respondents (and of the men they first married) are related to marital outcomes.[30]

A variety of indicators of traditionalism are available, and as in earlier sections, some of these refer to the period prior to marriage, while others refer to the current situation. In Table 7.6 we can examine whether the respondent and her first husband were raised as Catholics or not, whether either belonged to a fundamentalist Protestant church, and the depth of religious feelings of each partner prior to marriage.[31] We also have an "ethnic roots scale" which includes items indicating how many of the parents and grandparents of each respondent were born abroad and the depth of her identification with a particular ethnic group, as well as a measure of the ethnic region her ancestors came from (Northern, Central, or Southern and Eastern Europe). Then in terms of current characteristics, we have items tapping whether the respondent is currently a Catholic, whether she now belongs to a fundamentalist church, and her reported current depth of religious feelings. We also have a "liberal attitudes scale," which contains items designed to tap a range of nontraditional attitudes currently.[32]

The figures in Table 7.6 show some general, although inconsistent, support for the idea that traditionalism is associated with marital stability, and perhaps slightly with marriage quality and the absence of marital problems as well. Being raised as a Catholic is associated with less divorce, and more strong ethnic roots, coming

Table 7.6. Correlations of Traditionalism Measures with Marital Outcomes

Traditionalism Measures	Divorced or Separated (1st marriage)	Marriage Quality Scale	Marriage Problems Scale
Wife Raised a Catholic	−.22*	.10	−.05
Wife Fundamentalism	−.04	−.03	−.03
1st Husband Raised a Catholic	−.11*	.11	−.01
1st Husband Fundamentalism	.04	−.07	.05
Wife Religiosity in Youth	−.04	.15*	−.04
1st Husband Youth Religiosity	−.20*	.08	−.11
Wife Currently a Catholic	n.a.	.05	.07
Wife Current Fundamentalism	n.a.	−.04	−.03
Wife Current Religiosity	n.a.	.16*	−.06
Wife Ethnic Roots Scale	−.18*	.08	−.17*
Wife Ethnic Region	−.16*	.02	.03
Wife Liberal Attitude Scale	.17*	−.13*	.13*
Median *N*	440	276	276

* = p < .05

n.a. = Not applicable, divorce preceded period of traditionalism measure.

from a more "conservative" ethnic region, and high youth religiosity of the husband are also associated with marital stability. In general the signs are in the predicted directions, but the only significant associations of premarital traits and our other two marital measures were between the respondent's religiosity and marital quality, and between her ethnic roots and the absence of marital problems. Catholicism in one's upbringing and currently does not seem to make a significant difference for marriage quality or problems, but if the respondent claims to be deeply religious currently she is more likely than others to report a high quality marriage. Liberal attitudes in regard to family matters and sex roles are weakly associated with instability, poorer quality marriages, and more marital problems.[33] So although the figures in the table are not that strong or consistent, they do provide some general support for the notion that traditionalism helps to foster marital success.

The Life Cycle and Marital Success

One of the most intensively researched explanations of marital difficulties concerns stages in the life cycle. Researchers contend that some of the other claimed causes of marital success or failure may be artifacts of underlying general tendencies in the development of marriages over time. By mixing together people who have been married for shorter and longer times, the influence of the "natural evolution" of marriage relations may be obscured. However, there are ongoing debates about what the pattern is of this natural evolution of marriages. There are two competing scenarios, the "linear decline" and the "curvilinear" pattern. Advocates of the pattern of linear decline argue that the emphasis on romantic love as a mode of mate choice in America produces a high degree of excitement and attraction prior to marriage, but that once the marital knot is tied "there is nowhere to go but down." In other words, as couples settle into mundane routines and have to adapt to each other's quirks, their degree of marital satisfaction and involvement will inevitably decline.[34] In fact there is a fair amount of evidence that various indicators of marital quality tend to decline over the course of a marriage (see, for example, Pineo 1961; Renne 1970).

The curvilinear trend scenario is based on a different set of assumptions. The general trend toward declining marital satisfaction, advocates of this view contend, is not due simply to growing boredom over the marriage getting into a rut. Rather, it is due to the strains caused by events in the family life cycle, and in particular by those associated with having and raising children. So marital satisfaction and other measures of marriage quality can be expected to decline during the years of childrearing, perhaps reaching a nadir in the children's teenage years, but then in the postparental or "empty nest" stage, when the children have left home, there will be an improvement in the marriage relationship. In fact a number of studies have found evidence for this sort of a "U curve" in marriage satisfaction over the family life cycle (see, for example, Spanier et al. 1975; Gilford and Bengston 1979; Lupri and Frideres 1981.) Some evidence in favor of the U-curve view was presented in Chapter 6, but I will now examine the issue in more detail.

Testing these possibilities is a little more complex than testing other ideas in this chapter because of the predicted curvilinear relationship between the stage in the life cycle and marital outcomes. We know that marital stability does not fit either the proposed linear deterioration or U curve patterns; instead, divorce is most likely in the early years of marriage and becomes more or less steadily less likely the longer the couple has stayed together.[35] So my interest in examining the linear and curvilinear predictions will only concern the trends in marriage quality and problems of those first marriages that have not ended in divorce. Measures of the wife's age and the length of her marriage enable us to see how these are related to marriage quality and problems scores.

We can also examine the correlations between marriage quality and problems scores and indicators of childbearing burdens—the total number of children given birth to, the number of children still at home, the number of preschoolers at home, and the number of teenagers at home. Children are usually seen as having somewhat contradictory effects on a marriage. On the one hand, previous research generally finds that the presence of children makes divorce less likely, although with the rise in the divorce rate, "staying together for the sake of the children" is not the imperative it once was.[36] On the other hand, having and raising children puts a strain on marital relations and is seen (by advocates of the curvilinear trend, in particular) as a primary reason for declining marital satisfaction and rising marital problems after the early married years are over. But researchers differ on whether contending with a young baby or a teenager is more stressful. Regardless of which stage of childrearing is the most stressful, if we find that women in the "empty nest" phase after the last child has left home report higher quality marriages with fewer problems than women who still have children at home, that would lend support to the curvilinear scenario.

However, to provide a full test of the curvilinear pattern, I cannot look at simple correlations as I have been doing, since those would reveal only a linear, not a curvilinear, relationship. Since a curvilinear pattern could be represented by a quadratic rather than a linear equation, we need to compare the simple regression of length of first marriage on the two marital success scores with a regression containing not only the length of the marriage but the square of this number, and similarly for the age of the respondent. We can also investigate the curvilinear hypothesis by employing a more precise measure of the actual life cycle stage of our various respondents. By utilizing information on the age and number of years of marriage of each respondent, the number of children currently at home, and their various ages, I constructed a life-cycle stage measure, in which early marriage prior to children, preschoolers at home, primary schoolers at home, teenagers at home, and the "empty nest" stage after all children have left home are distinguished.[37] Through regression analysis and graphical inspection I can determine how the actual life stage relates to marriage quality and marriage problems.

Looking first at the simple correlation results in columns 1 and 3 of Table 7.7, there is modest support for the linear deterioration argument in regard to marriage quality, although the various items dealing with children (in the last four

Table 7.7. Correlations of Life Cycle Measures with Marital Outcomes

Life Cycle Measures	Marriage Quality Scale		Marriage Problems Scale	
	(r)	(partial)	(r)	(partial)
Years Since 1st Marriage	−.19*	−.05	−.10	.04
Years Squared	n.a.	−.01	n.a.	−.08
Wife's Current Age	−.15*	−.04	−.17*	.07
Age Squared	n.a.	.02	n.a.	−.09
Life-Cycle Stage	−.15*	−.14*	−.13*	.15*
Stage Squared	n.a.	.12*	n.a.	−.17*
Number of Children Born	−.10		.02	
Number of Children at Home	−.01		.18*	
Number of Preschoolers at Home	.03		.13*	
Number of Teenagers at Home	−.05		.07	
Median N	302	301	302	301

* = p < .05
n.a. = Not applicable

rows) do not have a significant effect. In regard to marital problems we see what appear to be contradictory results. On the one hand there seem to be fewer marital problems reported by both older women and by women in later stages of the life cycle. (The trend is the same for length of marriage, but the correlation is not quite statistically significant.) However, both the number of preschoolers at home and the number of total children at home are associated with increased marital problems. (Curiously, teenagers do not appear in these figures to be as "harmful" to marital relations as do younger children.)

The effects of age, length of marriage, and life-cycle stage can be examined further through regression analysis, which allows us to search for curvilinear tendencies. The results of this analysis are shown in the abbreviated second and fourth columns of Table 7.7.[38] For both the age of the respondent and for the number of years married to the first husband the effect of adding a quadratic term in the same equation with the nonquadratic term (e.g., both length of marriage squared and length of marriage) is to "wash out" the original linear relationships; neither coefficient remained statistically significant, and there was no clear gain in explanatory power. Thus age and length of marriage per se seem to have modest and largely linear effects on both marriage quality and problems—their effect is to reduce both. This is not, however, what the "linear decline" prediction leads us to expect. According to that prediction, we might expect that in longer-lived marriages quality scores will be low and problems scores will be high. Instead we find a tendency for both scores to be low. To oversimplify somewhat, the impression one gains from these figures is that both the highs and lows of married life may be particularly intense in the early years, and those who survive beyond the early years will settle into a pattern that is less intense in both directions.[39] It is in these figures that we can see most clearly the importance of considering positive features of the marriage relationship and marital problems separately, since declining quality does not imply increasing problems.

The figures dealing with the family life-cycle measure, however, reveal a more complex picture. In this case the addition of a quadratic term leads to both associations being statistically significant, and to an increase in the explanatory power of the regression equation. In other words, if we consider not only the age of the woman or the number of years she has been married, but her stage in the family life cycle, we find clear support for the curvilinear pattern in marital relationships. To be specific, reports of the positive features of the marriage relationship, as measured by the marriage quality scale, start high and then tend to decline during the early stages of the family life cycle, and then at least level off toward the end, when the last child has left home. For marital problems, on the other hand, what emerges is a sort of "inverted U curve" pattern. Initially, marital problems are low in the childless stage. Then marital problem levels increase in the early stages of marriage, presumably in part because of the extra strains associated with coping with young children. However, at the end of the life cycle there is a strong trend toward fewer marital problems.[40] So the overall

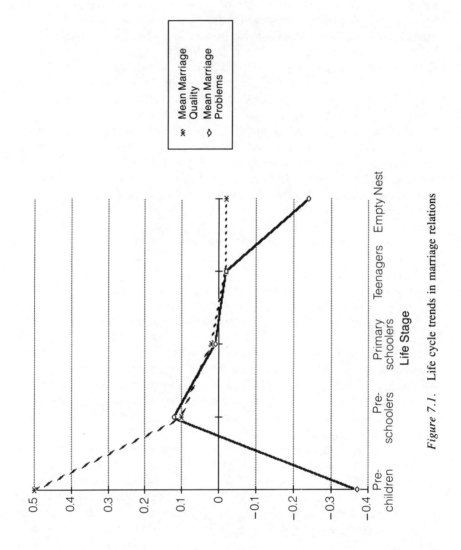

Figure 7.1. Life cycle trends in marriage relations

pattern, as previously noted, is toward both lower quality and lower marital problems at later stages in the life cycle, but the route to these eventual destinations is quite different.

The impact of different stages in the life cycle can be understood more readily from a graph than from regression coefficients. If I could assume that these differences represent trends that could be expected to occur over the course of the life of the average woman in the sample (a risky assumption, given the cross-sectional nature of these data), then the contrasting trends would be those displayed in Figure 7.1. From the figure we can see that the curvilinear trend is more pronounced in regard to marital problems than in regard to marriage quality scores. Marital problems appear to steadily decline after the pre-schooler stage. But in the case of marriage quality we seem to have an arresting of the long-term trend toward lower quality marriage relationships in the empty nest phase, but not a return to the sort of positive reports that characterize women in earlier life stages. In other words, it would appear that in the final, empty nest phase of married life conjugal relations settle into a pattern that tends to lack intensity of either a positive or a negative sort.

From Figure 7.1 we can see that there is no simple answer to the question of whether coping with infants or teenagers is more stressful to a marital relationship. Women who are raising preschoolers report more problems in their conjugal relationship and also higher marriage quality than women who are raising teenagers. If coping with teenagers seems the most difficult stage, this may be due to the fact that by the time adolescents have to be dealt with, the high quality and satisfactions of the early years of the marriage have dissipated.[41]

Type of Marriage Pattern and Marital Success

As the last general factor in my inventory of things that explain marital success or failure, I want to consider specific patterns in the marriage relationship. The underlying assumption here is that, depending on how couples structure their conjugal life, they will be more or less successful in building a stable and satisfying marriage. This sort of general approach represents what might be seen as the optimist's view of marriage, or the view to be found in marital advice manuals and popular magazines. The view is optimistic because it assumes that the kinds of background factors I have been considering in earlier sections do not rigidly determine the fate of the marriage. If only a couple will work to establish suitable habits and relations, they can live happily ever after, no matter how favorable or unfavorable to success are their backgrounds.

I want to see, then, whether there are clear patterns of association between how the marriage is structured and measures of marital outcomes. However, in doing this I have to guard against testing ideas that are true by definition. In other words, since I have constructed the marriage quality scale from items dealing with communication, expressing affection, and showing concern, and since the marriage problems scale includes items regarding worries about the marriage, spouse abuse, and the severity of marital conflicts, by definition couples who communicate well and who do not engage in constant conflict will show up as having successful marriages. My task in this section, then, is to consider some other aspects of the marital relationship that are conceptually distinct from those I have included in these marriage outcome scales, and see what impact these have on marital success.

In the Detroit data there are several measures (all described in Chapter 6) that I feel tap such distinctive aspects of the marriage relationship. First, we have a scale that summarizes the pattern of chore division in the marriage. As noted in Chapter 6, this is composed of items dealing with who does the grocery shopping, who cooks breakfast, who cooks dinner, and who does the evening dishes. A high score on this scale means that the husband does a fair amount of the chores, and I assume that in such cases the wife will be pleased with her marital relationship. I also constructed a similar scale dealing with the division of power in the family, composed of four items indicating who gets their way in disputes over spending money, who should do the chores, how often to have sex, and in "other disputes" (see the discussion in Chapter 6). In this case a high score means the wife often gets her way, and I assume that this will increase her satisfaction with the marriage relationship. We also asked about how the earnings of the wife and the husband were handled—in each case whether they were completely or mainly controlled by the husband, whether control was shared, or whether they were mainly or completely controlled by the wife. Again I assume that greater control over both his earnings and hers by the wife will be associated with her having positive feelings about the marriage.

Finally, we have a number of measures of "commonality" of the couple which I assume may promote positive feelings about the marriage. First, we have a scale intended to measure the perceived similarity or difference in the personality characteristics and habits of the partners. We asked each respondent to rate herself in terms of ten of such traits and habits; for example, is she very stubborn, somewhat stubborn, or not very stubborn.[42] Then we asked each to rate her husband in terms of the same ten characteristics. Then the shared habits and traits scale score is simply the number of these traits on which she judged her husband to be the same as herself. We also asked each respondent to tell which of seven traits she would most want a child to have and which of seven characteristics would be most important in making a successful marriage.[43] In both cases we then asked her to select which characteristic her husband would be most likely to select, and I assume that when she says he would pick the same trait as herself this is an indication of shared values. The mean of these two scores is then used as a shared values scale.[44] We also asked about up to three activities that the respondent liked to engage in during her spare time, and then about the same number of activities her husband liked to engage in during his spare time. In

Table 7.8.   Correlations between Marriage Patterns and Marriage Outcomes

Marriage Pattern Measures	Divorced or Separated (1st Marriage)	Marriage Quality Scale	Marriage Problems Scale
Chore Division Scale	−.12*	.03	−.04
Marital Power Scale	−.31*	.06	−.19*
Wife Manages Her Earnings	n.a.	−.31*	.24*
Wife Manages His Earnings	n.a.	.20*	−.20*
Shared Habits and Traits	−.16*	.30*	−.33*
Shared Family Values Scale	−.29*	.28*	−.21*
Shared Leisure Activities	−.21*	.27*	−.14*
Frequency of Joint Social Life	n.a.	.32*	−.12*
Median *N*	379	299	299

* = p < .05

n.a. = Not available, data collected only for those currently married.

Note: Column 1 involves all of those who have been married only once.

parallel to the other measures, these questions allow me to construct a scale ranging from zero to three, tapping the extent to which the couple's preferred leisure activities are the same. Finally, we asked a question about how often she and her husband get together as a couple with friends; from once a year or less to once a week or more. In all of these cases, I expect more similarity and commonality to produce more successful marriages.

In Table 7.8 we can see how these various aspects of the marriage relationship are related to marital success. The pattern of chore division, it turns out, does not have a significant relationship with either our quality measure or our marital problems scale, and only a weak association with lower divorce.[45] This result is somewhat surprising, given the considerable attention that has been paid to the unequal burden of chores, and particularly to the "double shift," as a primary source of strain on marriage relations borne by working women. However, as already indicated in Chapter 6, unequal chore division may be an adaptation that most wives treat as "normal" or "natural" and for the most part do not question. The figures in Table 7.8 reinforce this conclusion by showing the relative unimportance of chore division as a predictor of marital success.[46]

Marital power, on the other hand, seems related in the expected fashion to marital instability and problems, but not to marital quality. Women who perceive themselves as having a good deal of influence in the event of disputes with their husbands are less likely to divorce or to report marital problems than other women, but this apparently does not lead them to report high levels of communication, understanding, and other markers of positive marital quality.[47]

The two items about who controls the purse-strings reveal a curious pattern. I cannot investigate the influence of this factor on divorce, since these questions were only asked of currently married women about their present marriages. But the figures in the table indicate that when women have control over their husbands' earnings the impact on the marriage is positive, as indicated by high quality and low problems scores. However, when women have considerable control over their own earnings the effect seems to be just the opposite; such cases typically have lower quality scores and higher problem scores.

I do not have an adequate explanation for this intriguing pattern and at this point I can only speculate. Given the prevailing pattern of husbands having higher incomes, turning over his earnings to his wife could underline the unity of the couple and their commitment to shared control. If, on the other hand, she retains substantial control over her own earnings, then the implication would be quite different. What this might symbolize is the separateness of each partner and the unwillingness of the wife to merge her resources with her husband's. What is cause and what is effect in this case is not clear. It may be the case that a stressful marriage will prompt a woman to try to maintain separate control over at least some portion of her earnings, perhaps in anticipation of a marital breakdown and the need to become self-reliant financially. Some hint of this pattern is contained in the finding in the previous chapter that black wives are both more likely to have unstable marriages and less likely to put their earnings into a shared account than are white wives. In other words, I am not saying that the wife controlling her own earnings "causes" marital discord, but only that the two things seem to occur together. The Detroit data suggest, then, that control by the wife over her husband's earnings and her own have quite different implications, contrary to my original prediction, and that only the former is associated with a successful marriage.[48]

The last four rows of Table 7.8 show that shared personality traits, shared values, shared leisure activities, and an active joint social life are all associated in expected ways with marital outcomes. I am not certain how much trust can be placed in these figures, since they are all based on reports from the wives, rather than separate reports from the wife and the husband. However, in the case of the first column in the table there may be some biased retrospective reporting of how little the divorced women had in common with their former husbands. But assuming that these figures portray an underlying reality, they indicate that shared character traits, values, leisure pursuits, and social lives are more important to the success of a marriage than shared social backgrounds. (See the earlier discussion of homogamy and marital success.) What remains to be seen is whether these and other influences have an impact on marital relations even when other factors have been taken into account.

In the final section of this chapter I want to investigate which of the factors that seem, according to the preceding tables, to have an impact on at least one of the measures of marital success continues to show such influence, even when other variables are controlled for statistically. In other words, in a parallel fashion to the analysis presented in Chapter 4, it is now time to see whether any of the predictors that did "pass the test" by having a significant impact on at least one of the three measures of marital outcomes might nonetheless be spurious factors, with their influence attributable to other predictors. To examine this question it is necessary to perform multivariate analysis. As I do so, I will be particularly interested in the question of whether social background factors or the contemporary ways in which the marital relationship is patterned exercise more powerful influences on the fate of the marriage.

Multiple Influences on Marital Outcomes

In this section I present the results of multivariate analyses of the three separate measures of marital outcomes. Because multivariate analysis of the divorce measure has some special complications, I leave that for last and consider first the predictors of Marital Quality Scale and Marital Problems Scale scores. In both instances the technique used is ordinary least squares multiple regression.[49] As throughout this chapter, this analysis of marital quality and problems only concerns women whose first marriages are still intact.[50]

Table 7.9 displays the results of several variants of equations designed to explain scores on the Marriage Quality Scale. I present in the left hand column the original bivariate correlation statistics of this scale with relatively important predictors, and these are simply the figures reported in Tables 7.1–7.8.[51] In column 2 I present what I call Model 1, which is the most inclusive model. All of the variables that my review of bivariate relationships showed had some significant association with the Marriage Quality Scale scores were used in an attempt to predict scores on this scale for all women still married to their first husbands.[52] Here I present the partial correlation statistics from the regression analysis, rather than the regression coefficients themselves, as this will make comparisons easier with the bivariate correlation statistics in the first column. By comparison across columns, the reader can see to what extent the original relationship is weakened (or strengthened) when other variables in the model are controlled for statistically.

In the third column I present Model 2. This was derived simply by dropping predictor variables that in Model 1 turned out to have very little association with Marriage Quality Scale scores, once other predictors had been controlled for statistically, and then adding money management measures into the regression equation. This model leaves me with fourteen predictor variables (although several of them have fairly weak associations with marriage quality), and together these explain more than half (51.5%) of the variation in the scores on that scale (as shown by the R^2 coefficient in the bottom row of the table). The final column in the table presents the most reduced or "efficient" model, obtained by dropping the weaker predictors from model two. The result still contains twelve predictor measures, and together they allow me to explain about half (50.4%) of the variation in Marriage Quality Scale scores.

What do we learn from this statistical complexity? For the most part, the

Table 7.9. Regression Analyses of Marriage Quality Scale Scores

| | | Marriage Quality Scale Score | | |
| | | Model 1 | Model 2 | Model 3 |
Predictor:	R	Partial R	Partial R	Partial R
Wife Marriage Age	.12*	.09	.13	.13
Wedding Elaborateness	.16*	−.03		
Love	.30*	.28*	.25*	.27*
Class Origin Homogamy	.14*	.15*	.13	.10
Parental Opposition	−.23*	−.03		
Family Conflicts	−.31*	−.32*	−.32*	−.33*
Mutual Friends Scale	.19*	.06		
Ties with Husband's Kin	.19*	.11	.20*	.18*
Respondent Black	−.15*	−.18*	−.15	−.16*
Wife Class Origins	.15*	.06		
1st Husband Education	.12*	−.04		
Standard of Living Satisfaction	.19*	.08		
Years Worked/Years Married	−.12*	−.04		
Wife Current Religiosity	.16*	.05		
Wife Liberal Attitudes	−.13*	−.11	−.15	−.13
Life-Cycle Stage	−.14*	−.14*	−.22*	−.23*
Stage Squared	.12*	.11		
Shared Personal Traits	.30*	.13	.20*	.20*
Shared Family Values Scale	.28*	.22*	.13	.18*
Shared Leisure Activities	.27*	.12	.10	
Joint Social Life	.32*	.10	.18*	.18*
Wife Manages Her Earnings	−.31*		−.25*	−.28*
Wife Manages His Earnings	.20*		.08	
N	302	206	153	161
R^2		47.7%	51.5%	50.4%

$* = p < .05$

Note: All calculations are based on women still married to their first husbands.

results of my earlier review of many different approaches to explaining marital success and failure are reconfirmed. Several categories of predictors that have been used in much prior research on this topic have now disappeared from view entirely, or are represented in only marginal strength at best. Homogamy of marital partners does not appear to matter in predicting marriage quality, except possibly for a weak negative effect of differences in subjective class origins. Female independence measures did not even make it into the regression analysis. From all of the resource measures, only the race of the respondent appears to have any clear independent effect, and this takes the form of a tendency for blacks to have somewhat lower marriage quality scores. Similarly, all measures of traditionalism disappear from view, although the wife's current religiosity and the liberalism of her attitudes have generally nonsignificant associations in the expected direction with marriage quality scores.

When all of this explanatory chaff has been cleared away, only selected components of the explanations reviewed earlier in this chapter appear to make much difference for marriage quality. Two features of dating and mating remain important. Although this is a fairly weak effect, women who married relatively late report better marriages than other women.[53] Also, if we can trust recollected reports of the woman's feelings as she prepared to walk down the aisle, being very much in love then also helps to make for a successful marriage. However, as noted in my previous discussions, other aspects of dating and mating do not have much impact on current marriage quality. (The intriguing finding from Table 7.1, that women who have more elaborate weddings go on to have more successful marriages, disappears here when we control for other predictors.) About as important as being very much in love is having grown up in a close and loving home. Women who had severe conflicts with their parents, and whose parents also frequently fought, report poorer quality marriages today. Having close ties to relatives (in this case the husband's) also retains its original positive association with marriage quality. Liberal attitudes also retain a weak association with poor marriage quality, even though the smaller numbers in the regression models make it appear that this association could be due to chance alone. The linear effect of the length of the marriage on marriage quality also survives, with women married longer generally offering lower quality assessments.[54]

However, the largest number of separate predictors that show an independent influence on marriage quality come from what I have called current marriage pattern indicators.[55] Having many habits and traits in common with the husband, sharing similar childrearing and marriage values, having leisure activities that are the same as one's spouse's, engaging in frequent joint social activities with friends, all of these aspects of marital togetherness are related to higher marriage quality, even when each of the others, as well as other factors, is controlled for statistically (even though not all attain statistical significance in every model). Finally, women who emphasize their fiscal separateness in a marriage through their independent control over their own earnings tend to report lower quality scores than other women. (The association between the wife having some control over her husband's earnings and *higher* marriage quality scores, which I commented upon earlier, is visible but much weaker.)

If I tried to reduce the findings in this table to a recipe for building a high quality marriage, the advice offered here would be fairly simple. It helps if you marry at a mature age, if you are very much in love, if you are white and come from a close and loving home, and also if you are in the early stages of your marriage. But what matters most seems to be whether you can build a pattern of joint activities and orientations and shared participation and control with your spouse. The reader at this point may feel that it is not surprising that these factors are important in producing a successful marriage, but what should be surprising

Table 7.10. Regression Analyses of Marriage Problems Scale Scores

| | | Marriage Problems Scale Score | | |
| | | Model 1 | Model 2 | Model 3 |
Predictor:	R	Partial R	Partial R	Partial R
Wife Marriage Age	−.21*	−.13	−.14	−.19*
Premarital Pregnancy	.14*	.02		
Wedding Elaborateness	−.15*	−.07		
Love	−.14*	−.14*	−.21*	−.21*
Class Origin Homogamy	−.16*	−.12	−.10	−.12
Parental Opposition	.31*	.24*	.29*	.28*
Family Conflicts	.22*	.07	.06	
Mutual Friends Scale	−.15*	−.03		
Ties with Husband's Kin	−.24*	−.11	−.03	
Respondent Black	.11*	.10	.06	
Wife Class Origins	−.14*	−.12	−.03	
Standard of Living Satisfaction	−.26*	−.10	−.10	−.20*
Wife Ethnic Roots Scale	−.17*	.02		
Wife Liberal Attitudes	.13*	.04		
Life-Cycle Stage	.15*	.16*	.18*	+.15*
Stage Squared	−.17*	−.17*	−.21*	−.17*
Number of Children at Home	.18*	−.07		
Marital Power Scale	−.19*	−.11	−.12	−.21*
Shared Personal Traits	−.33*	−.15*	−.09	−.15*
Shared Family Values Scale	−.21*	−.19*	−.20*	−.20*
Shared Leisure Activities	−.14*	−.02		
Joint Social Life	−.12*	.09	.04	
Wife Manages Her Earnings	.24*		.19*	.17*
Wife Manages His Earnings	−.20*		−.01	
N	302	229	154	182
R^2		38.8%	41.4%	41.4%

$* = p < .05$

Note: All calculations are based on women still married to their first husbands.

is the large number of other factors that have been claimed to be important but are not, such as a good income, coming from similar backgrounds, or having deep religious faith. I will return to the importance of these findings once the results of other regression analyses are presented.

In Table 7.10 I present the results of regression analyses of scores on the Marriage Problems Scale. The analysis and the format of the table parallel the examination of Marriage Quality Scale scores in Table 7.9. The predictor variables included in these models are in some cases different, although a glance will show that there is a considerable degree of overlap with Table 7.9. And the results are substantially similar as well. Again, measures of resources, traditionalism, female independence, and homogamy do not generally display any independent influence on the level of marital problems reported.[56]

Few dating and mating measures influence the level of marital problems. Women who marry at relatively late ages tend to report fewer problems than other women, and the same is true for women who recall being very much in love prior to the wedding. But again the effect of having had an elaborate wedding disappears when other predictors are controlled for, and measures of such things as variety in dating partners and premarital sexuality did not even make it past the earlier analysis of bivariate correlations.

Of the several aspects of social ties and support that seemed to affect the level of marital problems reported, only one survives this new statistical test. Having had parents who interfered with the woman's dating and opposed her choice of a mate is related to marital problems, but the associations of family conflicts, mutual friends, and ties to kin with marital problems all disappear when other predictors are controlled for. In regard to the life cycle, the figures in the table provide quite clear and consistent evidence for the curvilinear argument, with marital problems reaching their highest levels in the early stages of marriage (when the positive life-cycle stage coefficient governs the regression equation) and then much reduced levels in the later stages of life (when the negative life cycle stage squared coefficient dominates the equation). However, this tendency does not seem to be due primarily to the burdens of coping with childrearing, as I had supposed, since this pattern in regard to the life cycle is visible even when the number of children in the home is controlled for statistically (in model 1). At this point I do not have a ready explanation for why this curvilinear pattern should exist, if it is not explained by the burdens of raising children.[57]

Finally, once again the largest number of predictors of marriage problems come from within the set of contemporary marriage pattern measures. In this case shared habits and traits and shared values seem to promote fewer marital problems, but neither shared leisure interests nor an active joint social life plays an independent role. Those aspects of the marriage pattern that concern power are relatively important in explaining marriage problem scores. Again, the wife's independent control over her own earnings is associated with more marital problems. Also, her report that she has a substantial say in resolving common disputes in the marriage (as measured by the Marital Power Scale) is associated with fewer reports of marital problems. Together these various predictors explain a somewhat lower proportion of the variation in marriage problems scores than was the case in my earlier treatment of marriage quality, but still a quite acceptable level of 39–41%, depending on which model is chosen.

In sum, even though some particulars are different (for example, as noted earlier, later stages in the life cycle are associated with lower quality scores, but not therefore with higher marital problems scores), the general pattern of findings is quite consistent whether I consider the level of problems or reports of the positive qualities of existing marriage relationships. Standard socioeconomic, religious, and other background factors do not appear to have much importance in comparison to the ways in which the conjugal relationship is structured and the nature of the woman's ties to her natal family, as well as such factors as the age at which she married and the stage of the life cycle she is currently in. But are the factors that explain how good or bad continuing marriages are the same as those that explain why some marriages dissolve while others do not? To address this question I must carry out a comparable analysis of whether or not the first marriages of the Detroit respondents ended in divorce or separation.

In my earlier review of explanations of marital success and failure, it became clear that the Detroit data are less well suited to discovering the determinants of divorce or separation than of the quality or extent of problems in existing marriages. The major problem is that the Detroit study was a cross-sectional one, and even though we asked many retrospective questions about the earlier experiences and marital histories of respondents, these did not fully provide what we would need to know in order to test several important explanations of marital instability. In particular, we did not ask about, and probably would have had difficulty getting accurate information on, various aspects of marital relations, income levels, kinship ties, and so forth in the period just prior to marital dissolution of those women whose first marriages ended in divorce, the period during which the influence of such factors would presumably have been most clearly visible.

We did ask some questions about chore division, marital power, and other aspects of marital relations of women who had been divorced, but if they had since remarried these questions were asked only about the current (or most recent) husband, and not about the first husband. (The reader should bear in mind that I am concerned here only with divorces or separations which ended the first marriages of respondents. Second or subsequent marriages will be considered in Chapter 8.) This means that we only have information about such aspects of first marriages that ended up in divorce for a small and perhaps atypical subset of respondents, those who did not remarry (56 women out of our total sample of 459).[58] For these women, answers to the relevant questions do refer to their first marriages, but even in these cases I suspect that jaundiced recollections of marriages that went sour may color and distort reports of what the marital relations were actually like. With these considerations in mind, it should be clear why I am not able to make as satisfactory an examination of explanations for divorce as for marriage quality and problems. Still, in spite of these serious limitations, it is worth examining what we can learn from multivariate analyses of marital instability. Table 7.11 presents results that in most respects parallel those seen earlier in Tables 7.9 and 7.10. One difference is that in this table we examine first all respondents (in Models 1 and 2) and then all respondents who have been married only once (in Models 3 and 4).

Another contrast with the previous two tables is that we employ a different form of regression in Table 7.11. Using ordinary linear regression when the dependent variable is dichotomous, as in this case (with 0 = not divorced or separated; 1 = divorced or separated), would yield inaccurate and misleading estimates. In this situation an alternative procedure called "logistic regression" is available (see Aldrich and Nelson 1984). That technique was used to test the

Table 7.11. Logistic Regression Analyses of Divorce or Separation from First Marriages

Predictor:	R	Divorce/Separation (all cases)		Divorce/Separation (married once only)	
		Model 1	Model 2	Model 3	Model 4
		Beta	Beta	Beta	Beta
Courting Interval	−.12**	−.03		.25	
Wife Marriage Age	−.21***	−.15	−.14**	−.08	
Premarital Pregnancy	.20***	.44		1.61*	.65
Wedding Elaborateness	−.26***	.25		.24	
Love	−.29***	−.37**	−.41**	−.10	−.13
Religious Homogamy	−.09*	−.29		−.87	
Parental Opposition	.22***	.91**	.52**	−.27	
Family Conflicts	.11*	.19		.94	.41
Broken Home	.14**	.57*	.08	−.56	.30
Respondent Black	.33***	1.09*	1.25***	2.75*	1.90**
1st Husband's Education	−.15**	−.11		−.10	
1st Husband's Occupation at Time of Marriage	−.18***	.02		.16	
Wife Raised a Catholic	−.22***	−.69	−.68*	.46	
1st Husband Youth Religiosity	−.20***	−.46	−.46**	−.83	−.22
Ethnic Roots Scale	−.18***	−.03		.35	
Wife Liberal Attitudes Scale	.17***	.55*	.50**	.69	.73*
Chore Division Scale	−.12*	n.a.	n.a.	.46	
Marital Power Scale	−.31***	n.a.	n.a.	−3.35***	−1.90***
Shared Personal Traits	−.16***	n.a.	n.a.	.00	
Shared Family Values Scale	−.29***	n.a.	n.a.	.08	
Shared Leisure Activities	−.21***	n.a.	n.a.	−1.28	−1.31**
N	459	242	387	201	279
Chi²		64.0***	97.3***	64.0***	80.9***
−2 Log likelihood		165.77	325.04	55.9	111.56
Degrees of freedom		16	8	16	10

* = p < .05;   ** = p < .01;   *** = p < .001
n.a. = Not applicable—questions concern present or most recent marriage, and for women married more than once they would not refer to the first marriage.

several models of predictors of marital instability that are displayed in Table 7.11. However, because this alternative procedure does not yield partial correlation coefficients, but only beta coefficients, the size of those coefficients cannot be directly compared with the bivariate correlation statistics listed in the first column of the table, as was the case in the previous two tables, nor even directly with other beta coefficients in the same column.[59] So when interpreting the values in the table the reader should pay more attention to the statistical significance levels displayed than to the relative sizes of the beta coefficients. (Additional statistical significance levels are displayed in this table to facilitate that comparison.)

In certain respects, the findings displayed in this table are similar to those in the previous two tables dealing with marital quality and problems, but with some important differences. Because of the lack of longitudinal data, we have not been able, for example, to give a full and fair analysis of the potential impact of the resources, female independence, or social ties mechanisms in influencing marital stability. The reader will see by glancing back at Tables 7.3, 7.4, and 7.5 that for the "divorced or separated" columns there are more "n.a." entries in these tables than correlation coefficients. But we have already determined (in Table 7.2) that homogamy plays little role in marital stability in the Detroit sample, and a number of other factors that are often seen as important in studying this topic— the socioeconomic backgrounds of the couple, the ethnic roots of the partners, and premarital pregnancy, for instance—again appear to make little difference once other factors are taken into account.

What does stand out in the table is the central importance of race in predicting marital instability. Even when other variables are taken into account in the "best models" (models 2 and 4), the blacks in the sample had notably more brittle marriages than the whites. The strength of this association between race and marital instability is in marked contrast to what was found in the previous two tables, where we saw that race had only a modest impact on marriage quality evaluations and no significant impact on marriage problems reports among currently married women, once other influences were taken into account. In other words, there appears to be a level of brittleness to the first marriages of blacks in the sample that is greater than we might anticipate from reports about the features of ongoing marriages of blacks and whites.[60]

Early on in this study I noted evidence from other research that blacks in recent years have had a lower rate of entry into first marriage than whites, and we see evidence in the present study that their marriages tend to be more brittle, and that once divorced or separated they are less likely than whites to remarry. Furthermore, insofar as I have been able to test for a number of possible reasons for these differences (e.g., lower socioeconomic backgrounds of blacks, higher rates of premarital pregnancies), they do not account for the remaining and quite substantial differences in marital instability found in the Detroit study. These differences in marital instability by race remain an intriguing phenomenon that cannot be pursued further here.

If we shift our attention to other parts of Table 7.11, several patterns become visible. First, it will be apparent to the reader that there are some important differences between the first two models and the last two models, with fewer predictors dominating the picture in the latter two. There appears to be a simple reason for the decline into unimportance of some predictors in models 3 and 4. It turns out that selectivity is operating to produce this result. Women who married at young ages, who were not completely in love, who were Protestants rather than Catholics, and who married men who were not very religious were (as shown in model 2) more likely than other women to get divorced. However, such women were also more likely to remarry than other divorced women who did not share these experiences.[61] For this reason, such women disappear from models 3 and 4 in the table, which concern only women who did not remarry, thus weakening the apparent importance of factors such as age of first marriage, romantic love, and religious affiliations. Because of the existence of this selectivity, and the resulting weaker explanatory power (as shown by the -2 log likelihood figures in the bottom row), primary attention will be given to models 1 and 2, rather than 3 and 4.[62]

The main lesson to be learned from the latter two, weaker models is that features of the subsequent patterning of the marriage relationship, which we saw as very important in predicting both marriage quality and marital problems in the previous two tables, are also important in explaining marital instability. In this case it appears that having had little power in decision making compared to one's husband is a very important predictor of marital instability, while sharing few leisure time activities in common has some negative impact.[63]

Examining models 1 and 2 more closely, then, several familiar patterns emerge. Marrying young does appear to be conducive to divorce, as well as to low quality and high problems in continuing marriages, even when other predictors are controlled for statistically. Not surprisingly, those respondents who have divorced or separated also report that they were less in love with their fiancés than is the case for other respondents. Parental opposition to the marriage and growing up in a broken home also seem to be related to marital instability, although in the "best model" (model 2) the effect of the broken home is no longer statistically significant. The greater instability of black marriages, as shown in row 9 of the table, has already been discussed. The final pattern visible is that elements of "traditionalism" are more consistently important than was the case in my earlier analysis of marriage quality and marital problems. Women raised as Catholics and women who married highly religious men (generally women who were themselves highly religious) were more likely than other women to still be married, even when other predictors are taken into account, and women with liberal attitudes about family matters were more likely to be divorced.[64] The influence of these last factors reinforces the importance of distinguishing marital stability from marriage quality and problems. For a given level of marital problems, women who were raised as Catholics or in a very religious environment seem more reluctant to resort to divorce than other women, even as women with liberal attitudes are more willing to contemplate ending their marriages.[65]

Conclusions

Although the specifics are different in each case, there is substantial overlap between the types of predictors that are important in explaining marriage quality, marital problems, and marriage stability. Of the dating and mating predictors, the wife's age at marriage and the recollected level of romantic love at the time of the wedding are both consistently related to all three marital success indicators, while predictors such as dating popularity, length of courting, and aspects of premarital sexuality do not appear important. Perceived similarity in class origins fosters marriage quality and inhibits marriage problems slightly, but does not have any significant impact on marital stability. However, it is difficult to understand what to make of this finding, since none of the objective measures of homogamy in social class has a comparable impact on marital success. Within the group of measures of social ties, parental opposition to dating and mate choice decisions, family conflict, and growing up in a broken home are to various degrees related to less successful marriages, although all three of these predictors do not have an independent influence in each case. Race has a fairly consistent impact as well, although the relationship between being black and marital problems is not statistically significant, once other predictors are taken into account. Traditionalism predictors have a clear independent influence only in promoting marital stability, although there is a weak tendency for liberal attitudes also to predict lower marriage quality scores. There is also a clear impact of life-cycle stages on marriage quality and marital problems, even when other predictors are taken into account.[66]

Finally, the largest number of predictors that survived all the tests performed here concerned the patterning of the marital relationship. To some degree measures of the marital power distribution, the pattern of money management, sharing of personal traits, family values, leisure activities, and joint social life all had independent effects on one or more of my three measures of marital success. In comparison, predictors that concern homogamy, socioeconomic status and resources, and female autonomy appear in general to be quite unimportant in explaining marital outcomes in this sample.

In spite of the limitations of the Detroit data, in general the analysis presented here seems to threaten the careers of those who still hope to develop a system for using background traits to predict the future prospects of marriages, and as a consequence the critics of this sort of enterprise have their claims strengthened. Or, to put the matter in other terms, my analysis strengthens what I have called the "optimist's view" of marital success. Many factors that have been identified in previous research as predictors of marital stability and quality, such as premarital pregnancy, religion, social class, homogamy, and the wife's income have turned out to have little or no significant impact on marital success, especially once other predictors are taken into account (in Tables 7.9 to 7.11). A few factors that are "givens," such as age at marriage, race, and poor relations with a woman's family, do have some impact, but even these explain only a small amount of the variation within the sample in marital outcomes. It is features of the organization of the marriage relationship which are not themselves "explained away by" such background factors that have the clearest and most consistent influence on marital outcomes and account for most of my ability to explain variation in the fate of marriages.

To be sure, some of these aspects of existing marriage patterns, such as the similarity of the habits and traits of the spouses or of their familial values, are not that easy to alter, and so the view presented here is not so optimistic that it would warrant writing cookbook-like marital advice manuals, which people could readily follow in order to live happily ever after. These findings do yield some general prescriptions, however, about which features of marital relations help to produce relatively satisfying and stable marriages. And in fact these prescriptions are not that different from the American middle class ideal of conjugal relations in the 1950s, summarized by the term "togetherness."[67] Generally speaking, having partners who share values, personality traits, habits, leisure interests, social lives, and friends (but not necessarily social backgrounds); perceptions by the wife that she is involved and influential in resolving disputes and has shared control over her husband's earnings (but not independent control over any earnings of her own); and reinforcement of their marital bond by supportive ties and interactions with parents and other kin on both sides—these seem to be the central elements in successful marriages of women in the Detroit sample. Couples who have, or can achieve, such conditions are more likely than others to have enviable marriages, even if they would appear in some respects to be "mismatched" or to have started out their married lives inauspiciously, in terms of the warnings drawn from previous research.

Notes

1. Widowhood is therefore in a sense considered "marital stability," since the marriage was not terminated by divorce or separation. In the present study I could measure marital stability of the first marriage relatively easily with a set of three questions: Are you now married, separated, divorced or widowed? How many times have you been married? (If married more than once:) How did your first marriage end—were you divorced, separated, or widowed? Women who were identified by these questions as having been divorced or separated from their first husbands (119 women in all out of 459) were considered to have had "unstable" marriages, with the rest considered "stable." Only the stability of first marriages will be dealt with in this chapter. The fate of remarriages will be examined in Chapter 8.

2. A graduate student in the Detroit Area Study training course, without being aware of the Johnson et al. study, independently came to the conclusion that two separate measures of marital quality were required, see Karl Landis, unpublished (1984).

3. The marriage quality scale was composed of the mean of the standardized scores of responses on seven items: the frequency of spending free time with the husband, the husband confiding in the respondent, the respondent confiding in the husband, the husband showing affection toward the respondent, the respondent showing affection toward her husband, and the frequency with which the husband showed concern for the respondent's feelings and problems (all with 4 response categories ranging from "a great deal" to "none at all"), and the degree of overall satisfaction of respondent with the marriage (measured on a seven point scale from "very satisfied" to "very dissatisfied)." The marriage problem scale was constructed from the mean of the standardized scores of responses on three items described in Chapter 6: a 4 level measure of marital worries, a 6 point scale of wife abuse, and a

marital disagreements scale composed of the means of five items. For further details on both scales and their component items, as well as on other measures used in this chapter, see Appendix 2.

4.   Even our inventory of questions about the current marital relationship is not exhaustive. Acts that may have a very destructive impact on a marriage, such as sexual infidelity, were not asked about in the Detroit questionnaire.

5.   Early onset of dating may be associated with a longer dating history with more partners or perhaps with early marriage, and dating variety and age at marriage are thought by some researchers to affect the marital outcome. However, more direct measures of dating variety (what I have called the Popularity Scale) and age at marriage capture such effects directly here, and I have no reason to think that the age of starting dating has an additional and independent effect on the fate of the marriage. Other aspects of dating and mating about which I have no predictions include whether the couple was introduced or met directly and whether they lived with parents or in their own home right after the wedding. These latter aspects of dating and mating, as well as the ages of beginning dating and going steady, will therefore be ignored.

6.   In most cases I will not attempt to make separate predictions about each of the three different measures of marital outcomes: instability, marriage quality, and marriage problems. Some of the available studies distinguish the first two concepts, but many do not, and the quality/problems distinction is too recent to have developed a literature around it. Thus I will make single predictions in most cases, but in examining the data I will be concerned with whether these predictions are borne out for three, two, only one, or none of these measures of marital outcomes.

7.   Unfortunately, I do not know how long the respondent and her first husband were acquainted, but only how old she was when she started dating him and when she married him, so my "courting interval" measure is technically the "years dating the eventual husband."

8.   It is unclear how much a premarital birth will cause significantly greater strain than a pre-marital conception that results in a birth after the wedding. The measure used here, as described in Chapter 2, has three steps—with postmarital conceptions coded as 1, premarital conceptions that result in postmarital births coded as 2, and premarital births coded as 3. Thus this measure implicitly assumes that a premarital birth has even more negative effects than a premarital conception that results in a postmarital birth. However, examination of a dichotomous version of this variable (with all premarital conceptions grouped together, regardless of when birth occurred) yielded very similar results to those reported here.

9.   As noted in Chapter 2, the measures of both premarital sex and of sexual relations prior to the first husband used here are indirect and rough. We did not ask either question directly, but computed the measures used here by comparing the answers to separate questions dealing with the respondent's age at marriage, her age when she first had sex, and her age when she first started dating her eventual husband.

10.   One sees this theme frequently in American popular culture as well. In the recent Oscar-winning movie, "Moonstruck," the character played by Cher insists on an elaborate formal wedding for what will be her second marriage because, in her view, to do otherwise would make the marriage less likely to last. Some early research indicated that marriages celebrated religiously were more likely to endure than civil marriages (see Locke 1951).

11.   Even more problematic is the fact that the subsequent fate of their marriages may bias the accounts these women give now of the state of their hearts prior to marriage. Insofar as this is the case, then the causal ordering of these two realms will actually be the reverse of what I am trying to test, with marital success or failure predicting reports about premarital love levels, rather than premarital love levels predicting marital success or failure.

12.   The strongest associations are between all three sexuality measures and greater marital problems, and between having had other sexual partners before the eventual husband and marital instability, but none of these associations is very strong or surpasses the .05 significance level. The weak positive associations with instability and problems might be taken as providing some support for those who adopt the traditional argument that premarital sex is harmful. But perhaps what is

involved here is not a cause and effect relationship, but rather selectivity, with individuals who have more liberal and skeptical views more likely both to engage in premarital intimacy and to contemplate divorce or to actually divorce. It might be noted that some other studies of the effects of cohabitation on the subsequent marital relationship find a much stronger impact in the same direction—with noncohabiters having better marriages (see Watson 1983; Booth and Johnson 1988; cf. White 1987). These pieces of evidence are hardly conclusive, but parents are entitled to be skeptical when their offspring try to convince them that cohabitation will lead to a better marriage. But of course if premarital cohabitation continues to increase as it has in the recent past, eventually becoming the norm, then I would not expect it to have even the weak "harmful" effect that appears to exist currently.

13. However, the inconclusive nature of the findings in relation to premarital sex, sex partners prior to the husband, and cohabitation may conceal important changes over time. A finer grained analysis (details not shown here) revealed some tendency for these measures to be more strongly associated with poor quality and high problem marriages among respondents who married long ago, but not among those marrying recently. For example, among prewar brides the association between having had premarital sex and marriage quality was $r = -.41$, while among post-1965 brides the same correlation was $r = .01$; the comparable correlations with the marital problems scale were .33 and $-.08$. In other words, in our data there is some indication that in earlier decades, when liberal premarital sexual behavior was unusual for females, women who participated had less satisfying marriages. In recent times, with premarital intimacy becoming more and more the rule, this harmful effect has disappeared, although there are no clear signs that premarital intimacy now promotes marital success.

14. Even this courting interval predictor is only significantly associated with less divorce for women who married prior to 1965, and not among women who married more recently (details not shown here). To be sure, marrying at a young age is associated with poorer marriages, as shown in row 3 of the table, but that finding can be attributed to other factors (such as psychological and financial immaturity), rather than to the fact that a young marriage age tends to mean a shorter period of time spent in the dating stage. Measures of the total length of time in the dating stage showed no clear association with marital outcomes, once the age at marriage was controlled for (details not shown here).

15. However, in Chapter 6 evidence was presented casting doubt on the assumption of consistent group differences in values.

16. This hypothesis seems to conflict with the popular saying that "opposites attract." However, there is also, of course, the contrary popular saying that "like marries like." In any case the factors that attract people to one another may not be the same as those that make it easy to stay together in a marriage. As noted in Chapter 5, one well known attempt to follow the logic of "opposites attract" in explaining mate choice, by Robert Winch, concerned personality traits more than social background characteristics, and has received little confirmation in subsequent research (see Winch 1958).

17. As noted in Chapter 5, there are too few interracial couples in the sample to examine the impact of interracial marriage. I also do not consider homogamy in terms of age here, although preliminary inspection of the data indicated no clear association of age disparities with marital outcomes measures. Previous research has noted that investigations of the impact of homogamy on marriage are made difficult by what is called the "specification" problem—the fact that what is assumed to be the impact of homogamy or heterogamy is actually confounded with the impact of the particular categories involved in various marriage combinations (see Glenn, Hoppe, and Weiner 1974). As I will report in subsequent sections, the separate class and other variables involved in our measures of homogamy seem to have little impact on marital outcomes, so I can afford to ignore that problem here.

18. All of the homogamy measures used here are based on those derived in Chapter 5. Thus "same religion" refers to only Catholics and Protestants marrying one of their own kind, with denominational differences ignored. Whereas, same ethnic group means marrying within the seven

different regional groupings of ethnic origins (e.g., France, Belgium, Holland, etc. in the Northern European grouping), rather than with someone from exactly the same nationality. (However, inspection of correlations for exact ethnic group matching and marital outcomes produced results not substantially different from those shown here.)

19.   The size of all of the correlations is very modest, and in a table of this size at least one correlation would be expected to surpass the .05 significance level on chance grounds alone. Thus at best there is only a slight indication that some kinds of homogamy make a difference. In this case a more detailed analysis did not find evidence that homogamy was more important to marital success in earlier marriage generations than recently (results not shown here).

20.   Of course, this assumption leaves the husband's views out of the picture, since marrying up for her is marrying down to him. But given the usual assumption, at least in the past, that the family's status is primarily determined by the characteristics of the husband, and not the wife, marrying down should be less stressful for the groom than for the bride. It is primarily for this reason that it is usually assumed that there is a built-in tendency for women to marry up, although I noted in Chapter 5 that no such general tendency is visible in the Detroit data.

21.   At one point in my effort to "tease" a positive result out of the data, I even created an "overall homogamy" measure that was a sum of these separate scales (as in Girard 1974), but that also failed to be significantly associated with my three measures of marital outcomes.

22.   Unfortunately, what I will call a "broken home" measure is based simply on whether when the respondent was young she was raised in a home with both parents and whether her parents were still together at the time that she first married. So widowhood of a parent, being raised in an orphanage, and other circumstances can lead to being counted as coming from a broken home by this measure, and it is not a precise indicator of parental divorce that I can use to investigate the transmission of marital instability from one generation to the next.

23.   To be more exact, Ackerman argued that the differences between preindustrial cultures with high and low divorce rates could be explained by the sorts of affiliations established around married couples in these cultures. He did not try to predict the fate of particular marriages.

24.   We cannot test the impact of these final social ties measures on marital instability, since we have data only for currently married women, and not information from the period prior to the divorce for those women who got divorced. The positive, albeit weak, association between a high quality marriage and a tight-knit friendship web of the respondent—tapped by asking how many of her close friends know one another—is slightly surprising, since Bott's work leads to the conclusion that loosely knit friendship ties are "better" for one's marriage. Bott tended to assume, however, that where each spouse's friendship ties were tightly knit they would not overlap, whereas we find that they often do— the association between these two separate traits is $r = .40$.

25.   More detailed analysis showed that while the association between race and marital instability was strong across all three marriage generations, marriage quality and problems scores differed by race only among older women. Black women who married after 1965 were not significantly different from white women in their ratings of the quality and problems in their marriages.

26.   This issue of whether the higher divorce rates of blacks are due primarily to income and other social class factors or to something else is admittedly a complex and controversial one (see the results presented in Heiss 1975).

27.   As noted earlier, we do not, unfortunately, have an exact measure of the proportion of family income contributed by the wife. For the wife, the husband, and the family as a whole we have a 16 category income measure (ranging from 0 to $75,000 plus), and the variable used in Table 7.5 is simply this categorical measure for the wife's earnings divided by the comparable measure for the family's income.

28.   For post-1965 marriages this coefficient is statistically significant—$r = -.15^*$.

29.   The wife contributing an important share of family income may, of course, stem not simply from her high earnings, but from the low earnings of her husband. And while low earnings of the husband may be excusable in the early years of a marriage, if the husband is still finishing school or is

just getting established in his career, this may be less true when he is in his forties and fifties. Indeed, more detailed analysis of the wife and husband income figures, which were used to construct this wife income share measure, shows the same sort of generational contrast, although with weaker correlations. The husband's income is related to high quality and low problems scores for older women and to low quality and high problems scores for younger women. The reverse is true for the wife's income—it fosters low quality and high problems scores for older women, but high quality and low problems scores for younger women (details not shown here).

30.   These arguments concern marital instability. The implications of conservative religious or ethnic traditions for perceptions of marriage quality and problems are not so clear.

31.   This last measure is a four point item; not religious at all, not very religious, somewhat religious, and very religious.

32.   Specifically, this latter scale was composed of the mean of the standardized scores on three items, each of which used a 5 point set of response categories (from "strongly agree" to "strongly disagree"). The statements used here were: "It is much better for everyone involved if the man is the achiever outside the home and the woman takes care of the home and family;" "Keeping the family going is a very important reason why sons and daughters should expect to marry and have children;" and "A woman can live a full and happy life without marrying." The third item was reversed, so that in all cases a high score means disagreement with traditional attitudes. The average inter-item correlation of the three items was .30. Note that this is a slightly broader scale than the "feminism" scale discussed in Chapter 6, which contained the first and third of these items, but not the second.

33.   Again, the direction of causation in these instances may be questioned. Perhaps marital difficulties lead women to question traditional assumptions about family life and women's roles, rather than it being the case that liberal attitudes in these realms lead women to be more critical of their marital relationships.

34.   This trend is sometimes used by social critics from countries with arranged marriage systems to argue the virtues of the latter custom over free mate choice, since in an arranged marriage if you start with no affection between the spouses at all "there is nowhere to go but up." See, however, the contrary evidence presented in Blood (1967). Comparing arranged and free choice marriages in Japan, Blood found that the arranged marriage cases started out "neutral" but over time exhibited the same declining satisfaction as the free choice marriages. Thus the result after several years was, in fact, more dissatisfaction in the case of the arranged marriages.

35.   Overall 119 out of the first marriages of our respondents had ended in divorce or separation. Of these divorces, 32.8% took place during the first four years of the marriage, and another 37% took place between years five and nine. Only 13.4% of the divorces had occurred in years 10–14, and another 8.4% in years 15–19, with even smaller percentages in marriages that lasted beyond 20 years.

36.   We cannot test the strength of this consideration with the Detroit data because we lack information on the number and ages of children at home prior to the divorce, for those women who have been divorced.

37.   I followed the conventions of previous research here in constructing this scale (see Campbell, Converse, and Rogers 1976), with only women under age 30 with no children assumed to be in the first stage, and with other stages demarcated by the age of the *youngest* child at home. Women over age 30 who have not had any children are thus omitted from the analysis.

38.   For both marriage quality and marriage problems I examined three separate regression equations, for length of marriage and its square, for age and its square, and for life-cycle stage and its square. In other words, the partial correlations reported in columns 2 and 4 in the table come not from regression analyses with all six variables included, but with only two variables included at a time.

39.   Since the Detroit data are cross-sectional, it may well be the case that couples with many problems will divorce, so that selective departure from marriage, rather than successful problem management, explains the lower scores on the marriage problems scale of older women who have been married longer. However, if that is the case we would also expect selective departure from

marriage to produce unusually high marriage quality scores among women married for many years, and the data do not show evidence of this pattern.

40.   Somewhat comparable trends are reported in Gilford and Bengston (1979). Given the possible selection bias problems in these cross-sectional data, as mentioned earlier, this pattern will have to be verified in future research applying a longitudinal design. Such a design would make it possible to collect reports on marriage quality and problems from the same women at multiple stages in the life cycle, rather than presuming that the scores of women in the earlier stages are comparable to those that would have been reported earlier by women who are now in the later stages.

41.   The reader should keep in mind that problems as measured here refers to problems in the relationship with the spouse, and not to problems between the mother and her children. See Appendix 2 for details. Also, since women are sorted into life-cycle stages here according to the ages of their youngest children, some of the women classified as in the preschooler stage may actually have teenagers as well to cope with, while the reverse is not the case. Thus part of the higher problems score of these stage 2 women may be attributable to the burden of other children besides their preschoolers.

42.   The traits included were neat and tidy, stubborn, outgoing, late, thrifty, hot-tempered, a smoker, bossy, energetic, and a drinker (see Appendix 2 for details).

43.   The child character traits were popular with others, ambitious to get ahead, obedient and well-behaved, interested in how and why things happen, considerate of others, independent and self-reliant, and has strong religious faith. As noted in Chapter 6, the marriage characteristics were agreeing on chores, satisfying each other's needs, having a good income, being deeply in love, having common interests, being sexually faithful, and doing things together.

44.   Admittedly these last two measures, the Shared Habits and Traits Scale and Shared Family Values Scale, do not quite fit into the optimist's view of marriage previously discussed, since such traits and values may be more difficult to change than family chore division or patterns of handling money.

45.   Even this weak association between high male chore participation and low divorce may be questionable. Since in this case the reports for divorced women are retrospective, I suspect that some of the women are exaggerating how little their former husbands did to help out around the home. Thus this weak association could be attributable to biased reporting.

46.   It might be noted that one other study of contemporary marriages found that where the couple shared chores relatively equally, the result was that there was *more*, rather than less, strain, with the husband griping about having to shoulder an unfair burden (see Blumstein and Schwartz 1983, p. 146). Since we did not interview the husbands, I cannot test whether this was the case in Detroit marriages.

47.   However, the correlation of the power scale with divorce may again be somewhat inflated through biased reporting by the women who have been divorced. In retrospect they may exaggerate how domineering their former husbands were.

48.   A recent study, it might be noted, presents a contrary view. Rosanna Hertz (1986), in a study of upper middle class dual career couples, argued that marriages benefited by having the wife keep her earnings separate, since in these cases she could feel positive about not having to get her husband's approval for every expenditure. Our much broader sample survey study casts doubt on this supposition. Similar conclusions to ours come from the study by Blumstein and Schwartz (1983), who argue that reluctance to pool incomes is related to lower commitment to the marriage.

49.   As in earlier chapters, there are a number of less than ideal features of the analysis. Although the two marital outcome scales have been created in such a manner that they can be considered interval in nature, as multiple regression requires, a number of the independent or predictor variables used are ordinal rather than interval, and the experts on such techniques have engaged in a lively debate on whether and under what circumstances use of ordinal variables in multiple regression is suitable. Also, given the large number of relationships I am interested in, and my desire not to follow a mindless pattern of throwing all of the variables considered in this chapter into the regression

"pot," I have had to make a decision to restrict my attention to only those instances in which a variable of theoretical interest showed a bivariate correlation with one of our scales that was statistically significant—generally that meant a correlation of about .11, given the size of the Detroit sample. But this means that there remains some possibility that "hidden associations" that might have emerged in a multiple regression analysis will not be discovered here. As is conventionally the case, the justification for these shortcuts is that the broad-ranging and preliminary nature of this analysis makes such procedures warranted and even perhaps necessary.

50.   One complication is that one of the explanatory variables that showed a relatively strong influence (see Table 7.8), the measure of how the wife's income is handled, is only available for the women in our sample who are currently employed ($N = 243$), and any regression models with this variable in them would have considerably less than half of the cases in the sample to work with. Preliminary analyses showed that regression models with this variable included produced somewhat different coefficients for some other variables than models that did not include this variable, but it was not clear whether this was due to the power of this one variable or to the distinctive nature of the employed and currently married women subsample of the data. In examining predictors of marriage quality and problems (the money management measures are not applicable to the third marital outcome measure, marital instability), I first carried out multiple regression using all other predictors except these money management measures. Then, after eliminating predictors which had weak regression coefficients and settling on the best, reduced model, I added one or both money management measure into the final models reported here (in models 2 and 3 in Tables 7.9 and 7.10).

51.   In the case of the life-cycle stage predictor and its square, the correlations listed in the first column of these tables are the partial correlations from the equations containing only these two predictors, as shown in Table 7.7.

52.   To be more precise, in instances where two or more closely related variables had significant bivariate correlations, only the strongest predictor is included in these regression analyses, in order to avoid problems of multicollinearity. However, as noted earlier, the two money management measures are omitted from this most inclusive model. I do not include in these regression analyses, and in those that follow, any interaction terms, since I do not have any a priori theoretical reasons to predict that particular interaction effects will exist.

53.   In the various regression models, the coefficient for the respondent's marriage age no longer has a statistically significant association with marriage quality. However, since the strength of the coefficient is not much altered from its bivariate level, this relationship is still worth mentioning. In other words, the main reason for the lack of statistical significance in the regression models is the smaller number of cases involved in those analyses, and not a substantial reduction in the strength of the correlation.

54.   The curvilinear effect of progression through life stages, with quality reports no longer declining in the empty nest stage, is still visible here, but weakly. The positive quadratic term—life cycle stage squared—indicates an improvement in marriage quality scores in later life, but the coefficient falls short of statistical significance, and was dropped from the final regression models.

55.   Initially I had supposed that many of these indicators would be closely related to one another. However, inspection of their intercorrelations revealed that this was not generally the case, and that there was no real problem with multicollinearity produced by including these variables together in the regression models.

56.   The correlation between homogamy in class origins and lower marital problems is only weakened slightly when other predictors are controlled for, but that weakening is enough to lead me to suspect that the coefficient in Models 2 and 3 might have occurred due to chance alone. Within the set of resources variables, being black is associated with somewhat more marital problems, even after other predictors are controlled for, but the racial difference is not quite statistically significant, and is dropped from the final model. The associations between low satisfaction with one's standard of living and marital problems are generally statistically significant, but as I indicated earlier, none of the objective indicators of resources or class position show a clear association with marital problems.

Thus the association between standard of living dissatisfaction and reported marital problems might best be interpreted as evidence of a general "grumpy" vs. "upbeat" orientation, rather than constituting proof that those with few resources will confront more marital problems.

57.   As noted earlier, one important other possibility is that this apparent curvilinear pattern is due to the selective process by which women with marital problems get divorced early on, leaving only those with relatively problem-free marriages in the empty nest stage. I have no way to test this possibility with the Detroit data, but as noted earlier, if these selectivity argument were correct I would expect to find higher marriage quality scores for women in the empty nest phase than I in fact find in these data.

58.   The number of women who had been divorced from their first husbands but had subsequently remarried was 75, or more than 57% of all of those who had divorced.

59.   The beta coefficients listed are in some ways analogous to unstandardized regression coefficients in ordinary linear regression, which have the same properties; unlike the correlation statistics, they can exceed 1, and they tell us about the effect of a unit change in the independent variable. Thus the size of various coefficients is not directly comparable (since the independent variables used have different ranges of values). The computer program used also does not yield a statistic comparable to the R^2 given at the bottom of the two previous tables, so I cannot compare in any precise way the proportion of variance explained in these various models for predicting marital instability. However, the -2 log likelihood ratio figures given at the bottom of the table, while not strictly comparable to the R^2 figures in the previous tables, do provide an estimate of the relative success in explaining marital instability across these four models.

60.   However, one might imagine that there is some sort of boundary level of low marriage quality and/or high marriage problems that will lead fairly automatically to divorce, and that a higher proportion of blacks than of whites will have marriages that pass this boundary level. Then poor quality marriages and frequent marriage problems would be more characteristic of blacks than of whites, but by producing a higher exit rate from marriage of blacks than of whites, the quality and problems levels of the marriages that survived of both races might not be so different. In other words, a contemporary judgment about the nature of continuing marriages of the two races may be quite misleading in terms of judging the nature of first marriages since their inception.

61.   For example, women who divorced and then remarried had average ages at first marriage of 19.1. Women who divorced and did not then remarry had average ages at first marriage of 20.4. (Women still in their first marriages had average ages at first marriage of 21.8.)

62.   Another reason for paying less attention to models 3 and 4 is the small and perhaps atypical number of divorced women involved, only 18 out of the 201 women used in the fullest specification in model 3.

63.   In these instances the size of the coefficients may be inflated somewhat by retrospective biases, as women whose marriages failed exaggerate how little say and how little in common they had with their former spouses. However, it is interesting to note that other features of the marriage patterning that might be expected to display similar biases, such as the measures of shared personal traits and shared family values, do not seem to have an independent influence on marital instability. (I cannot test here the impact on marital stability of one factor that emerged as very important in the previous two tables—the pattern of money management—because the relevant questions were only asked of those women currently married, and not about former marriage relations.)

64.   In the latter instance, though, there is some possibility that the failure of the marriage may influence a women to adopt liberal attitudes, rather than vice versa, as our analysis assumes.

65.   What is particularly striking is that all three factors—religion, religiosity, and liberal attitudes—are included in model 2, and each of them has an independent influence on marital stability, even when the other two, as well as other predictors, are controlled for statistically.

66.   It is clear from other evidence that life-cycle stages have a powerful impact on marital instability as well (see, for example, Booth et al. 1986), but I was not able to examine this effect directly with the Detroit data.

67. One final limitation of these data needs to be stressed again in regard to the general comments offered here. I do not have separate reports from the husbands, and it is entirely possible that at least some of the features that make marriage more satisfying to them are not ones of central importance to their wives, and vice versa.

Chapter 8

THE SECOND TIME AROUND

Married life customarily begins with a pledge to live happily ever after, but obviously not all marriages endure. Some end a few years later in widowhood or divorce, and a relatively high proportion of Americans whose marriages end prematurely go on to remarry. In the Detroit sample, as noted earlier, 65.8% of all respondents were still married to their original husbands, 17.9% had been widowed or divorced and had not remarried, and the remaining 16.3% had been remarried at least once.[1] This chapter will focus on those women who have remarried. I want to know how different the experiences and marriage patterns of these women are, in comparison with women who have been married only once.

There are two quite different kinds of arguments that have been made about remarriages in comparison with first marriages. One I will call the optimistic view. As I have repeatedly noted, our American dating culture is based upon the analogy of learning in a marketplace environment. It is assumed that a prolonged period of dating with a variety of partners will prepare individuals to make an informed and suitable selection of a marriage partner. This idea is captured nicely by the notion of picking "Mr. Right." But given the brittleness of first marriages in America, perhaps the process of premarital screening does not work the way it is supposed to in many cases. Either many women end up selecting Mr. Wrong instead of Mr. Right, or else one or both partners change after the wedding in such a way that they are no longer suited to one another.

When couples break up and remarry, the optimistic view assumes that the market-oriented learning process is continued. Experience in a failed marriage should enable former spouses to "learn from their mistakes," and the wisdom thus acquired should help them to make a better choice the second time around. Or perhaps it is not simply that they chose the wrong sort of person the first time and can select someone more suitable for remarriage, but that they have learned something about what it takes to make a marriage relationship work and can "try harder" the next time. In any case, the optimistic scenario follows the sentiment of the ballad of an earlier era in assuming that love is much more wonderful "the second time around." The optimistic view leads to a prediction, then, that most remarrying women will be more satisfied with their new conjugal relationships than their previous ones. Perhaps they will even be more satisfied than women in first marriages on the average, since the latter will include a fair proportion of women who have not yet had the "beneficial learning experience" of a failed marriage, or who for one reason or another are not willing to end very unhappy marriages.

Many analysts of remarriage have suggested quite a different and more pessimistic view. Perhaps people do not learn from their mistakes but instead keep repeating them. Certain individuals may tend to pick individuals who are not well suited to them, resulting in unhappy marriages, but if they divorce and remarry the same tendencies may lead them to pick another unsuitable partner the second time around. Or perhaps certain individuals have character flaws that make it hard for them to get along in a marriage relationship with anyone. If that is so, then such people should be overrepresented among those whose first marriages break up, and their subsequent marriages are also likely to be brittle. We have here an analogy with recidivism in criminal behavior—the notion that certain individuals for whatever reason are "prone" to divorce, and that any divorce statistics will be inflated by such "multiple offenders" on the marriage front.

In evidence of this sort of pessimistic scenario, there is one study (Dean and Gurak 1978) which discovered that individuals who had remarried tended to have had relatively low levels of status homogamy in relation to both their first spouses and their subsequent spouses, in comparison with individuals whose first marriages were still intact. The implication drawn in this study was that certain individuals are prone to making status mismatches in choosing a spouse, and that these mismatches help to explain the instability of their first marriages and make it more likely that their remarriages will also be brittle.[2] In fact many studies have documented a tendency for remarriages to be less stable than first marriages (see, for example, Cherlin 1978; 1981). So the pessimistic scenario leads to an expectation that remarriages may be less satisfying and more unstable than first marriages. In the pages that follow I will consider the evidence from the Detroit survey to see whether the optimistic or the pessimistic view is closer to the truth.

What if remarriage follows widowhood rather than divorce? In that case arguments can be found in favor of both the optimistic and pessimistic scenarios, but they seem less compelling. Perhaps simply having had a previous marriage will help one to pick a new marriage partner wisely, even if it is not a matter of "learning from one's mistakes." Or perhaps the later age at which remarriage tends to occur following widowhood and the difficulty widows have remarrying may make such women who do reenter marriage feel especially fortunate and may lead them to have lower demands and expectations than would otherwise be the case. On the other hand, perhaps cherished memories of one's deceased former spouse will interfere with establishing sufficient intimacy and trust with one's new partner. The remarried spouse may be regularly compared with the original and found wanting.[3] There is not much evidence one way or the other about the fate of remarriages following widowhood, and so I am uncertain how much credence to give to these speculations (see, however, the discussion in

Ihinger-Tallman and Pasley 1987). So the analysis that follows will focus mostly on remarried women whose first marriages were terminated by divorce.

Unfortunately, there are gaps in the Detroit data that prevent me from making as complete and systematic a test of these competing ideas as desirable. For those married more than once, we collected data not on features of each marital relationship, but only on the first and the most recent. So for those 17 women out of the total sample of 459 (3.7%) who had been married three or four times, the remarriages I will be able to examine are not, in fact, their second time around, but their third or fourth. Therefore, for most of the questions we asked about relations with the spouse, we only have information about one marriage, the current or most recent. This fact means that I cannot actually compare the pattern of conjugal relations of remarried women in their present marriage and in their earlier marriage. Instead I will have to compare these women's current marriages with those of a different set of women, the 65.8% of women in our sample who are still married to their first husbands. My tests of these competing scenarios will in some cases be rather indirect.

These data pose a stiffer and more suitable test of the optimistic scenario than would have been the case if we had asked about relations within the prior marriage as well as the current one. The ideal test of the optimistic scenario would require longitudinal data, not the sort of cross-sectional data available in this study. In other words, it would be necessary to collect data from a sample of women who are currently married, observe which of those women divorced and remarried in subsequent years, and then go back and ask them comparable questions about relations with their new spouses. Then if, other things being equal (such as the length of each marriage, the burden of children, etc.), the remarriage was more satisfying, I would have a strong case for claiming support for the optimistic scenario. But in the current cross-sectional design I can get at past marriage relations only through retrospective questions. And if we ask divorced women (whether or not they have remarried) what their relations with their former spouses were like, there is reason to think that they might give us a negative and perhaps distorted picture (distorted in comparison with what they would have said prior to their divorces). If such a process of distortion operates, it would lead us all too easily to conclude that remarriages are better than first marriages, as the optimistic scenario predicts. Since I lack longitudinal data, I am better advised to compare remarriages with intact first marriages. This comparison provides a stiff test of the optimistic scenario because I can assume that women still in their first marriages tend to have quite satisfying relations with their spouses, since many "bad marriages" have been removed from this comparison group via divorce. If the quality of remarriages is equal to or better than such intact first marriages, this would seem to indicate that the optimistic scenario is operating, although the evidence would still be less conclusive than if I had longitudinal data on the earlier marriage relations of these remarried women.

Homogamy in Remarriages

The two scenarios lead to quite contrary predictions about homogamy in first marriages and remarriages, and I can test these predictions directly, since we have information about some social background characteristics of both the first husbands and the most recent husbands of remarried respondents.[4] The optimistic scenario leads me to expect that there may be more similarity in the background traits of respondents and their most recent husbands than they had in relation to their first husbands. The newer choice should thus be "better," since the remarried husband should be more "suited" to her, in terms of coming from a more closely matched social background (ignoring, for the moment, the finding in the previous chapter that homogamy does not really do much to foster marital success in the Detroit sample). The pessimistic scenario argues that those women whose first marriages ended (by divorce, at least) were less well matched to their husbands than are women in continuing first marriages, and that they will tend to "repeat their mistakes" by remarrying to another husband from a different social background, as Dean and Gurak (1978) found. In other words, there should be no tendency visible for women to remarry more homogamously the second time around.

We can examine these predictions in regard to a variety of background characteristics.[5] There are too few cases of interracial marriages in the sample to make any meaningful statements about these two scenarios in regard to racial homogamy.[6] I considered first, whether women who divorced their first husbands and remarried subsequently were less closely matched to those first husbands in terms of other characteristics than women still in their first marriages. In general I did not find strong or statistically significant differences in homogamy when comparing the first marriages of women who remarried after divorce and intact first marriages (results not shown here). This conclusion should not be surprising, since it coincides with the finding reported in Chapter 7 that lack of homogamy was not a clear predictor of marital instability.[7]

What differences do exist, however, tend in several cases to be in the direction of less homogamy in the first marriages of those women who divorced and remarried. For example, with respondents and their spouses divided into six educational attainment categories (primary schooling, incomplete secondary, high school graduation, incomplete college, college graduation, and post-graduate education), 32.2% of the women who were divorced from their first husbands and remarried had the same level of education as their first husbands compared to 42.6% of those women still married to their first husbands. Similarly, 57.6% of those women who divorced and then remarried had the same general religious affiliation (Catholic, Protestant, other) as their first husbands, compared to 66.5% of respondents still married to their first husbands; and for a five category individual occupation group comparison (professional and managerial, clerical and sales, skilled worker, semiskilled worker, unskilled and service worker), the comparable percentages are 17.3% and 28.3%.[8] To summarize, at best there is only a very weak tendency for status mismatches to be more typical in the first marriages of women who divorced and remarried, in comparison with women who are still married to their first husbands.

If we compare the first and most recent husbands of women who divorced and remarried, again no very clear pattern emerges. In general the differences in homogamy between the two marriages were quite small, and in the case of education and age the subsequent husband was more closely matched, while in the case of religion and ethnicity the second husband was slightly less closely matched (details not shown here). Since none of these differences are statistically significant, the safest conclusion is that there is no clear tendency toward either greater homogamy or lesser homogamy "the second time around."

The pattern in regard to age matching deserves some comment.[9] In regard to age, women whose first marriages ended in divorce were less closely matched to those first husbands than were women who married only once ($r = .44$ vs. $r = .74$). The divorcing women who remarried tended to marry men who were more similar in age than were their first husbands ($r = .56$), and this finding would seem to support the optimistic scenario. The same apparent trend appears when we compute the average age gap between husbands and wives. For women married only once the gap is 3.2 years, for women whose first marriages ended in divorce the gap is 3.5 years, and when those same women remarried the average age gap between their new husbands and themselves is only 1.2 years. But the notion that age matching, at least, fits the optimistic scenario is thrown into question when we consider the standard deviations in the age gap between husband and wife in these three marital situations. The standard deviation in the age gap for both women who married only once and for the first marriages of multiply marrying women was about 4.4 years, but for the subsequent marriages of the latter women the figure was 8.3 years. In other words, although on the average remarrying women are closer to their new husbands in age than is generally the case in first marriages, there are also more extreme age mismatches among the remarried couples. At the extreme, there are cases in the sample of a subsequent husband being 25 years older and cases in which he was 17 years younger. This degree of variation suggests something quite different from the optimistic scenario, something we might designate as a third, "less choosy" scenario. Perhaps given the difficulty some women have in remarrying and their anxiety about being able to find a new husband, their definition of what is a "suitable" mate may expand. So men who come from backgrounds more dissimilar to them than their first husbands may be considered eligible. This is an intriguing alternative to the two initial scenarios, but aside from this partial support in terms of age matching, only the trends in religion and ethnicity provide weak support for it. So again the verdict of "not proven" seems required.

In sum, neither optimistic nor pessimistic scenario receives much support.

There is not a strong tendency for the most recent husband to be more closely matched in background than the first husband, as the optimistic scenario would predict. And while the degree of matching of women who have divorced is similar with their first and most recent husbands, as the pessimistic scenario leads me to expect, in neither case is the extent of homogamy significantly less than for women who are still married to their first husbands. The safest conclusion would seem to be that status matching operates at a fairly constant level no matter which time around it is, and that in any case, as I noted in Chapter 7, the closeness of this matching is not strongly related to whether the marriage will succeed or not.

I was also interested in whether women might have done better "the second time around" in a different sense. In the past some have argued that divorcées are discriminated against in the marriage market, compared to women who have never been married. The disadvantages faced by divorcées might be due to the fact that many have custody of children from their previous marriages, as well as to a lingering stigma from having had a "failed" marriage. If this sort of discrimination exists, we might expect such women to have to be less selective than never-married women in trying to find a new spouse, and those who succeed in remarrying might therefore end up with less desirable or lower status husbands than would women approaching the altar for the first time. However, a contrary tendency is also possible. Perhaps women will make use of divorce and remarriage to "trade up," by leaving their husbands for others who are more desirable, in social status or other terms.[10] In this version of the pessimistic/optimistic debate, what we want to know is whether women who divorce and remarry are downwardly mobile or upwardly mobile, in terms of a comparison of the social statuses of former and subsequent husbands.

I cannot investigate this question as fully as desired due to limitations in the Detroit survey data, but a partial test is possible. One aspect of socioeconomic status is education. If we use the same six levels of schooling employed throughout this study (see Appendix 2), it turns out that of all of the divorced women who remarried, 30.5% married new husbands who were less well educated than their first husbands, 35.6% married men with the same level of education, and 33.9% married better educated men. In terms of the educational level of husbands, then, upward mobility, downward mobility, and stability via remarriage are about equally likely, with only the slightest sign visible of any tendency to "trade up."

There is a different story to tell in regard to the husband's occupational status. In this case we know the occupations the first husbands of divorcées had *at the time of their marriage,* and we also know the current occupations of the second or most recent husbands. Unfortunately, we do not have information on the two things that would give us the most accurate test of occupational social mobility through remarriage: the occupations of the first husbands *at the time of the divorce* and the occupations of the subsequent husbands *at the time of the remar-*

riage. We cannot simply compare the information we have on the occupations at marriage of first husbands and the current occupations of new husbands, since there is an underlying tendency for men's jobs to improve over their lifetimes through a process of career mobility.[11]

We can utilize a method adapted from another study (see Mueller and Pope 1980) to construct a proxy that permits an indirect comparison of the occupations of prior and current husbands. The method is as follows: First, we determine the mean year of first marriage of all women who divorced their first husbands and subsequently remarried ($N = 63$). The result turns out to be 1958. Then we select all cases in our sample who married in a three year "window" on either side of this date, or in other words, from 1955 through 1961 ($N = 65$). We can then regard this group of respondents as a sort of "control group." By examining the occupations at marriage of the husbands of women in this control group and the current occupations of the same men, we can gain some idea of the underlying career mobility trend over this sort of time span. If the husbands of remarried divorcées have higher status occupations on average than do husbands in our control group, this would provide evidence of upward occupational mobility via remarriage; conversely, if they are in lower status jobs than husbands in the control group, that would indicate that remarrying divorcées tend to be downwardly mobile.

What results do we obtain from this elaborate and indirect test? If we use a five category grouping of occupations into professional and managerial, lower white collar, skilled worker, semiskilled worker, and unskilled and service worker groups, we find that 47.3% of the husbands in our control group (women who first married in the years 1955–61) have been occupationally stable, 38.2% have been upwardly mobile, and 14.5% have been downwardly mobile. In comparison with these figures, 28.9% of remarried divorcées have current husbands with the same occupational status as their first husbands, 60.5% have remarried to higher status husbands, and only 10.5% have remarried to lower status husbands. If we accept the accuracy of this proxy comparison, we conclude that in terms of the jobs held by husbands, divorcées do show some success in "trading up" to more successful husbands.[12] Perhaps, given the indirectness of this test and the much weaker results obtained in regard to education, we should interpret these figures skeptically. Still, there is no evidence here that on balance women who remarry do worse the second time around, and many manage to come out somewhat better. (See the similar conclusions in Mueller and Pope 1980.) The balance of the evidence on this point supports the optimistic view.

Weddings

What sort of ceremonies and celebrations are held when women remarry? Here there is a fairly clear prediction dictated by both common sense and past re-

Table 8.1.   Weddings in First Marriages and Remarriages

| | New Haven 1949–50 | | Detroit Women 1925–84 | | |
	Both First Time	Remarriages	Both First Time	Remarriages	Earlier Marriage
Years Courting	2.3	1.6	2.4	2.5	1.7
% Church Weddings	81.3	23.6	73.3	33.3	52.4
Number at Wedding	172.0	32.0	98.0	25.8	45.0
% with Reception	87.7	48.1	82.3	77.0	60.3
Number at Reception	166.0	32.5	157.5	54.5	85.1
% with Honeymoons	94.5	68.7	57.7	39.3	31.7
N	715	127	402	63	63

Note: The second column of figures averages in figures for women remarrying to men who have never married before ($N = 62$) and women remarrying to men who have been married before ($N = 65$) from the New Haven survey, since these two situations are not distinguished in the Detroit data. *Source:* Hollingshead (1952); 1984 Detroit Area Study survey.

search. I expect that in general remarriages will be celebrated with less fanfare and expense than first marriages. A number of factors point to this expectation. A remarriage may be considered less of a significant change in one's life than a first marriage, and thus less worthy of elaborate festivities. Parents and relatives who exert pressure in favor of an elaborate first wedding are less likely to be still alive and even if alive less motivated or able to pressure for an elaborate wedding "the second time around." In any case they are not as likely to help pay for a second wedding. In addition, perhaps some remaining stigma of having had a first marriage that "failed" may lead couples to feel that they should celebrate remarriages in more modest ways. Data from a study of New Haven marriages conducted in 1949–50 by August Hollingshead (1952) show quite clearly a tendency for the scale, ritual elaboration, and expenditures to be less on remarriages than on first marriages.

In Table 8.1 I present data from the Detroit survey that permit direct comparison with Hollingshead's New Haven data.[13] In general we can see from the table that the pattern of simplification in subsequent weddings is quite similar in both studies, with minor exceptions (compare column 1 with 2, and column 3 with 4). There are, however, a couple of minor contrasts between the two sets of results. Hollingshead's study suggests that people are quicker to head to the altar in remarriages than they were in their first marriages, producing a markedly shorter courting interval, but we found a slightly longer courting interval in Detroit remarriages than in first marriages (see row 1). Overall the first marriages in the current study appear to be somewhat less formal and elaborate, on the average, than those reported for New Haven, and as a consequence the "simplification effect" found in remarriages appears less extreme in the Detroit data.

This is particularly true in regard to holding a wedding reception and taking a honeymoon, which are not that much less common "the second time around" in the Detroit data (comparing columns 3 and 4).

Since the present data, unlike those used by Hollingshead, contain information on first marriages and remarriages of the same women, I can say something more here about how the contrasts in wedding customs looked to those women who married more than once. Dealing first with issues not covered in the table, I note that 63% of the Detroit multiple marrying women had met their first husbands directly, as opposed to via an introduction, while only 48% of them had met their most recent husbands directly. These figures suggest that women increase their reliance on friends and other intermediaries in their search for a new husband.[14] Second, of those women who remarried, 75% had a religious wedding the first time around, and only 53% did so in their remarriage. So there is a modest trend toward remarriages being more secular than first weddings.[15]

Other features of the first marriages of multiple marrying women in the sample are displayed in column 5 of Table 8.1. These figures reveal several things. First, women who divorced and remarried tended, on the average, to have had rather simplified weddings the first time around, compared to women who married only once (compare columns 3 and 5). This finding should not be surprising, since in Chapter 7, I reported that one of the things that distinguished stable from unstable first marriages was the degree of elaborateness of the wedding celebration. If we focus only on the women who did remarry (by comparing columns 4 and 5), my conclusion about the simplification effect in remarriages is modified somewhat. It appears to be true that these women were less likely to hold their weddings in church the second time around and that they invited fewer people to their wedding and to their reception. (They also took somewhat longer to head to the altar with the subsequent husband, unlike the "acceleration" that Hollingshead's data seem to imply.) However, these women were somewhat more likely to have held a wedding reception and to have taken a honeymoon when they remarried than was the case when they first got married.

What do all of these comparisons add up to? First, in general it is clear from both Hollingshead's study and from my own that there is a "simplification" tendency visible in the wedding customs followed for a remarriage. However, in addition to the reasons already suggested for this pattern, I have discovered another. One additional factor is selectivity, in terms of who is likely to divorce and remarry. It turns out that women who marry more than once tend disproportionately to have had somewhat simple weddings the first time around. So part of the simplification effect observed in the present study is due to the fact that those who are likely to stage elaborate weddings don't often get the chance to display this tendency a second time around, rather than simply because those who held elaborate celebrations the first time think it more suitable to be modest when remarrying. In any case this simplification effect is neither uniform nor inevitable. Some remarrying women, in fact, experienced even more elaborate weddings in their remarriages than they did the first time.[16]

Marriage Patterns and Marital Success

Is love really more wonderful "the second time around?" I can examine that question here by comparing remarriages in the Detroit sample with first marriages, using the indicators of marital success employed in Chapter 7. The first issue concerns the stability of remarriages. I have already noted that on this score the weight of the previous evidence favors the pessimistic view. Remarriages tend to be even more brittle than first marriages (see Cherlin 1978, 1981; Furstenberg and Spanier 1987). One study contends, for example, that the likelihood of eventual divorce is 7–10% higher in remarriages than in first marriages (Weed 1980). What do the Detroit data say on this issue?

When I examined the figures I discovered somewhat to my surprise that in the Detroit sample remarriages seem to be, if anything, more stable than first marriages. Viewed in the most simple fashion, 20% of remarried women whose first marriages had ended in divorce had the same fate befall their most recent marriages. In contrast, about 26% of first marriages in the sample had ended in divorce. However, this simple contrast could be misleading, since we know that the likelihood of divorce declines more or less steadily with the length of the marriage, and remarried women tend, on the average, to have been married for fewer years than women married only once. In order to correct for the influence of the length of the marriage, I constructed a graph showing the cumulative proportion of first marriages and remarriages that had ended in divorce for each year of marriage. The results are displayed in Figure 8.1.[17]

From the curves in Figure 8.1 it does appear that remarriages are slightly more stable if the first marriage ended in widowhood rather than divorce. However, the pattern that is most striking is that even remarriages preceded by divorce are more stable than first marriages. No matter whether it is two, five, ten, or twenty years after the wedding, a higher proportion of first marriages have ended in divorce than is the case for remarriages entered into by divorcing women. The number of remarriages in the sample is relatively small, so the modest differences shown might not be that reliable. Still, on balance these figures lead me to conclude that in the Detroit sample remarriages are at least as stable or even more stable than first marriages.[18] This finding provides another piece of evidence in favor of the optimistic view of remarriage.

We can also examine the patterns, quality, and problems of first marriages vs. remarriages as part of a continuing quest to see whether marriage is better "the second time around." Here again we can consider two competing views. The optimistic scenario implies that people shed difficult spouses and unrewarding marriages and try again. Assuming either that they learn from their mistakes or simply that they try harder the second time around, their relations with their subsequent spouses should be better and more satisfying. The negative scenario assumes instead that selective mechanisms are operating. People who get divorced from their first spouses tend to be, on the average, individuals who will

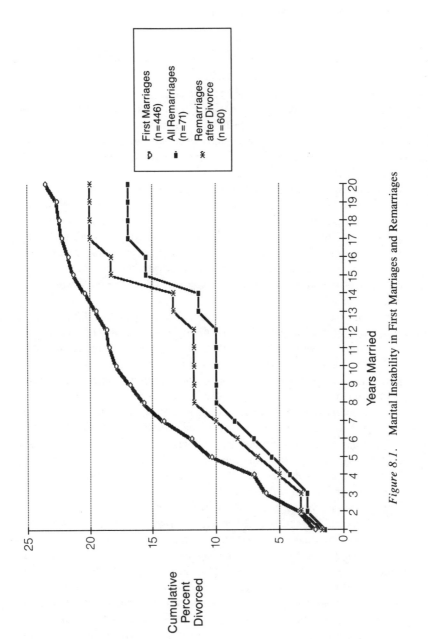

Figure 8.1. Marital Instability in First Marriages and Remarriages

find it difficult to have a stable and satisfying marriage with anyone. They may be difficult to live with; they may be too critical of the flaws in their partner; perhaps they are not suited to married life in the first place. For whatever reason, the pessimistic scenario leads me to expect that people who divorce and then remarry will tend to be unhappy the second time as well.

As noted earlier, I cannot test these ideas satisfactorily, since I lack reliable data on the patterns and quality of the earlier marriages of those women who have divorced and then remarried. Instead I will have to compare the intact marriages of women who have married only once with those women currently married to a subsequent spouse to see if there are any differences. The pessimistic scenario leads me to expect that there will be lower quality, and more problems, in the remarriages than in first marriages. What we would predict from this comparison by the optimistic scenario is less clear, since I don't have data on marriage patterns from earlier and current marriages for the same women. But I will assume that this scenario predicts that there will be no significant differences between continuing first marriages and remarriages. In other words, by ending an unhappy marriage and remarrying to someone "better," I assume that these women will manage to improve to some sort of "average" condition of continuing first marriages.[19]

Although I am particularly interested in how first marriages and remarriages compare in terms of quality and problems, the realms dealt with in Chapter 7, I decided to examine as well the full range of marriage pattern items discussed in Chapter 6. This seems appropriate, since I know that some aspects of how marriage relations are patterned do have an impact on how women evaluate the quality and problems of their marriages (see the discussion in Chapter 7). So if when women remarry they tend to structure their relations with their husbands in a manner different from women who have been married only once, this distinctive patterning might help explain any differences in evaluation of first and subsequent marriages. My initial question is broader than I have implied up to now: "In general, how does the pattern of the marriage relationship differ when we compare remarriages with first marriages?"

Considering the answer to this question required me to scan through a large number of tables and statistical coefficients, covering essentially all of the aspects of marriage relations discussed in the preceding two chapters—marital values, the division of chores, money management, marital power, patterns of communication and expression of feelings, marital worries, and so forth. In general this laborious review uncovered very few strong or statistically significant differences (results not shown here). So my primary conclusion is that there is not much difference in the patterning of remarriages in comparison with surviving first marriages. This general finding tends, as I have indicated, to lend support to the optimistic scenario, and to refute the pessimistic scenario. It appears that women who have divorced and remarried have "learned from their mistakes" or are trying harder, and that they have been able to construct with their new husbands relations that are in most respects quite similar to those of women who have had only one husband.

Given the scarcity of differences uncovered by this comparison, there is some risk in interpreting the few contrasts that did turn up, since they might have occurred due to chance alone.[20] Still, it may be worth examining the few differences that did emerge. First, there exists a weak tendency for somewhat more sharing of certain chores in remarriages than in intact first marriages (cooking dinner, washing dishes, and making home repairs, with the correlation with the marriage order number about $r = .11$ in each case). However, these tendencies are not strong or consistent enough to make a significant difference in the overall chore division scale (for which the correlation with marriage number is $r = .06$). There is also a modest tendency for women in remarriages to be slightly less likely than women in first marriages to say that they turn to their husbands first (rather than to a friend, a sibling, etc.) when they want to discuss a personal problem ($r = .12$). Since other questions about communications and discussing thoughts and feelings do not reveal any difference between first marriages and remarriages, this particular finding may be a statistical "fluke." Overall, the relationship between remarriages vs. first marriages on the one hand and my summary marriage quality scale is positive but not statistically significant $r = .05$.

The strongest and most consistent pattern of findings that does emerge from this comparison of first marriages and remarriages relates to the spouse abuse items, and here the pattern lends some support instead to the pessimistic scenario. In general respondents in remarriages were more likely to report various forms of spouse abuse than were women who had married only once, and these differences were particularly clear in the case of the most severe forms of abuse (as noted already in Chapter 6). To be specific, only 5.4% of women still married to their first husbands claimed that their husbands had ever hit, kicked, or bit them, and only 2.4% of these same women claimed to have been beaten up by their husbands. But for women in current remarriages the comparable figures were 17% and 15.1%. I do not know how many of these remarried women were abused in their earlier marriages, but it seems plausible here to suppose a pattern that the pessimistic scenario predicts—women in abusive marriages may leave and try again, but then they are likely to "repeat their mistakes" by picking a new husband who is also likely to abuse them.[21]

However, this pattern of association between spouse abuse and remarriages is not duplicated when I examine other areas of marriage problems, such as the frequency of marital disputes reported or the level of worries about the future of the marriage. As a result, the correlation between marriage order number and my overall marriage problems scale (which includes disputes and worries along with the spouse abuse scale) is not strong enough to be statistically significant ($r = .07$).[22] So I do not find a general pattern in which marriage problems are more severe in remarriages than in first marriages. With the possible exception of the question of spouse abuse, my conclusion is that remarriages and first marriages do not differ in important ways. In general this set of findings—a pattern of "no differences to speak of"—lends support to the optimistic scenario. I cannot say for certain that for remarrying women love is more wonderful the second time around, since I lack data on their earlier marriage relations.[23] But if we compare these women with women in the sample who have been married only once, I can conclude at least that they are not doing any worse.[24]

One final question of interest is whether the predictors of marriage quality and problems for remarriages are similar or not to those for first marriages. The predictors of marriage quality and problems for current or first marriages in general were reported in Chapter 7. I could not carry out as elaborate an analysis for those women in continuing remarriages because there are only 55 of such women in the sample (including widows who remarried), too few to support a detailed multivariate analysis. But I did examine a wide range of correlations with the summary marriage quality and marriage problems scales for remarriages and compared these with comparable correlations for first marriages (detailed results not shown here).

In general I found that the pattern of predictors of marriage quality and problems was similar for both first marriages and remarriages. For example, in both cases factors such as the degree of homogamy and social class made little difference in marital success, and in both cases features of the structure of the marriage relationship (such as agreement on family values, shared leisure pursuits, and shared control over the earnings of both spouses) were the most consistent predictors of marriage quality and problems. However, there were a few important differences between first marriages and remarriages that should be noted. The degree of elaborateness of the wedding was related to marital success in first marriages, but not in remarriages.[25] The lower quality and more frequent problems visible in black first marriages in comparison with white ones were not visible in remarriages.[26]

In addition, the number of children currently living at home has a much stronger negative effect on marital success (leading to low quality scores and high problem scores) in remarriages than was the case for first marriages.[27] This particular finding seems readily understandable in terms of the difficulties that step-children and step-parents have in accepting each other and the extent to which the burdens of care for such step-children may interfere with the development of a high level of intimacy and sharing with a new spouse.

Finally, a variety of life-cycle variables reveal a pattern in which the influence of life stages is both stronger and qualitatively different for remarriages. To be specific, I found in Chapter 7 that variables such as age and life-cycle stage had modest negative relationships with both marriage quality and problems, suggesting that in later life marriages lose both positive and negative "sparks." In the case of remarriages age and life-cycle stage are associated with much stronger reductions in marriage problems than is the case with first marriages, and for

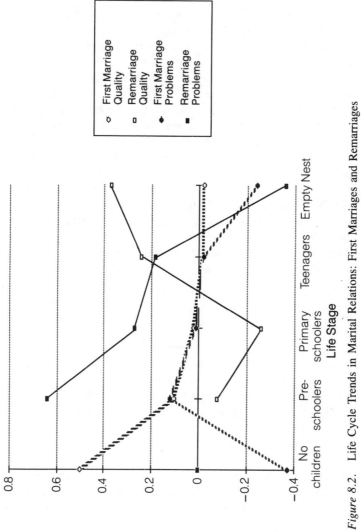

Figure 8.2. Life Cycle Trends in Marital Relations: First Marriages and Remarriages

marriage quality the correlation reverses and becomes strongly positive. In other words, it would appear that remarriages do not become increasingly "bland" over time, but improve significantly.[28] The contrast between the life-cycle patterns for first marriages and remarriages is shown graphically in Figure 8.2.[29]

The trend lines in Figure 8.2 show that remarriages display magnified versions of the contrasts visible for first marriages, rather than simply retracing the same paths from a later starting point. Women who have remarried and have preschool or primary aged children at home report many more marital problems and somewhat lower quality that women in the same stages who are still married to their first husbands. But remarried women in later life stages, and particularly those with all children gone from the home, report fewer problems and much higher quality than women who are at the same stages in intact first marriages. It seems likely that it is particularly the growing up and departure from the home of children (and step-children most of all) that make possible the higher quality and lower problem scores of older women in long-lasting remarriages that are observed in these data. So while in other respects remarriages seem to respond to similar influences to first marriages, the "natural evolution" of the two types of marriages appears quite different.[30]

Conclusions

This chapter has been concerned with comparing remarriages with first marriages along a number of dimensions. Several conclusions have emerged. First, weddings tend, as expected, to be simpler in remarriages than in first marriages, but at least part of this tendency can be attributed to the fact that women who had simple weddings the first time around were more likely to divorce and remarry. For those women the contrast between the elaborateness of weddings on the two occasions was not so sharp as when I compared them with women who only married once. Some of these remarrying women experienced more elaborate ceremonies the second time around. Second, there is no consistent tendency for women to be more or less closely matched in backgrounds to remarried husbands than they were to their first husbands. Homogamy comparisons do not support either the optimistic or pessimistic scenario.

This lack of clear findings in regard to homogamy does not have as much importance as it might, since I have already learned that in the Detroit sample the extent of status matching in marriage is not significantly related to the success of the subsequent marriage relationship. In other words, women who were divorced from their first husbands were not any more likely than women still married to their first husbands to have been "mismatched," and therefore it would not be very meaningful in any case to speak of "learning from one's mistakes" or "repeating one's mistakes," as the optimistic and pessimistic scenarios assume. Lack of homogamy between spouses does not appear to be very important in either first marriages or remarriages, in terms of predicting marital success.

Third, I discovered evidence that indicates that for a good share of divorcées who remarry, upward social mobility occurs, with the new husband holding a higher status occupation than the first husband would be expected to have now. This finding should not be interpreted, however, as indicating that women who divorce and remarry are materialistic "gold-diggers" who are primarily interested in status climbing. Compared with other women whose first marriages did not end in divorce, divorcées tended disproportionately to have married men with low status occupations the first time around. By remarriage they simply reduced the status gap between them and other women somewhat (in terms of the occupations of husbands), rather than ending up with unusually high status spouses.

Finally, I discovered that in most respects the patterning of marital relations in remarriages, with the possible exception of items dealing with spouse abuse, was not much different, and neither better or worse, than that found in continuing first marriages. In addition, remarriages tended, if anything, to be somewhat more stable than first marriages, and the levels of marriage quality and marital problems were not significantly different for the two types of marriages. Furthermore, for the most part the same factors that produced satisfaction, and reduced problems, in first marriages also did so in remarriages. I have argued that to some degree the failure to find many significant differences between first marriages and remarriages on these counts can be interpreted as support for the optimistic scenario, and as indicating that in some sense remarriage "works." Women who had unhappy marriages who ended them and remarried were able, in general, to construct new marriage relationships that were not any less satisfying than enduring first marriages.[31]

Much of the research on remarriage in America, especially in regard to women, tends to emphasize the "push" factors—that America is a "couple-oriented" society in which a woman will feel isolated if she does not remarry, or that financially she will have a difficult time coping if she remains single. The present results lead me to ponder the "pull" side of the equation. Enduring first marriages are generally seen by those in them as fairly satisfying, and this is just as true for remarriages. Remarriage is not, apparently, the lesser of two evils (with the other being remaining single), but instead a return to a desired state of affairs. To be sure, not all remarriages work, any more than all first marriages do, but still I am impressed by the extent to which remarrying respondents were able to build (or rebuild) fairly high quality marriage relationships.

This pattern of findings (or perhaps more accurately "nonfindings") is also important because I have not even considered a variety of other influences that have led analysts to argue that remarriages are likely to be more problem-prone than first marriages. The pessimistic scenario, as discussed here, is based simply on the notion that those individuals who divorce and then remarry are in some sense atypical and "flawed," that they tend to repeat their mistakes, and perhaps that some are unsuited to marriage in the first place. But there have been a number of other reasons advanced to explain why remarriages should be more problematic than first marriages. Remarriage, argues Andrew Cherlin (1978), is an "incomplete" institution, in the sense that societal expectations and norms governing it are in flux and are not fully developed. So individuals who have remarried become somewhat akin to "marginal men" (and women), and this lack of normative and social support makes the new conjugal bond weak. Much of this vulnerability is caused by the complexities involved in negotiating uncharted interpersonal terrain, such as the rights and responsibilities in regard to step-children, former in-laws, former spouses, and other ties spawned by remarriage (see also Bohannan 1970; Cherlin 1981). Although these complexities provide humor for movies and television shows which focus on the "yours, mine, and ours" parent-child relations that are becoming increasingly common in America, for those involved, anguish may be more common than mirth.[32] In light of these considerations, the finding that remarriages in the Detroit sample do not seem more problem-prone or of lower quality than enduring first marriages is particu-larly striking. There may be some truth after all to the claim that people "try harder" to make marriage work the second time around.

Even though many previous studies of relationships in remarriage arrived at much more pessimistic conclusions than those offered here, there are at least some other recent studies of the topic that provide additional support for the optimistic scenario. A number of recent empirical studies conclude that in gener-al remarriages are not significantly less satisfying or successful than first mar-riages (see, for example, Glenn and Weaver 1977; Furstenberg 1987; Larson and Allgood 1987; Benson-von der Ohe 1987). Perhaps underneath the contrast between such findings and earlier, more pessimistic conclusions, we can see evidence of an important social change underway. In the past, marital dissolution occurred predominantly through widowhood, and those who divorced and remar-ried were a small and atypical portion of all married people. Perhaps those remarrying after divorce included a fairly high proportion of people who would have difficulty having a successful marriage with any partner. In addition, the stigma attached to having had a "failed" marriage might have made it difficult for such individuals to attract a desirable new spouse with whom a very satisfy-ing marriage would have been possible.

Recently, however, the divorce rate in America has risen dramatically. Now divorce has overtaken widowhood as the leading cause of marital dissolution, and in a rising proportion of American couples at least one partner has been married and divorced before entering their current marriage. (See Ihinger-Tall-man and Pasley 1987. In 1983, 46% of all American marriages were remar-riages, up from 36% in 1973; see Hobart 1988.) The stigma attached to having been married before has declined markedly. As a consequence of these changes, it may well be that the remarried state is becoming "flooded" with more "nor-mal" people, rather than "marital misfits." Such individuals are now in a better position to compete for "normal" and desirable new spouses. As a result, the percentage of divorced persons who remarry to others who have been divorced has declined in recent years in the United States, and the proportion who remarry to individuals who have not been married before is rising (see Modell 1985).

The ability of the more representative population that is entering remarriages to cope with the distinctive strains involved and achieve a level of marital success that is comparable to that of first marriages (and superior in most cases to that experienced in their own first marriages) may then testify that remarriage is now becoming "completely institutionalized" (see Cherlin 1978). To sum up these speculative thoughts, perhaps as remarriages have become increasingly numerous, if not yet the norm, success in marriage "the second time around" has become easier to achieve, and thus more common. Love may not be "more wonderful" the second time around, but at least it is not inherently more difficult to achieve. Social change, involving the increasing acceptance of divorce and remarriage, has tilted the odds in favor of the optimistic view of remarriage.

Notes

1.   Chances of remarrying are obviously better if a woman is still young, and since divorces tend to occur early in a marriage and widowhood late, the likelihood of remarrying after a divorce was considerably greater in our data (52.9% of all such cases remarried) than of doing so after being widowed (31.6% of such cases did so). I also noted in Chapter 6 that a small portion of Detroit respondents had been married not twice, but three (3.3%) or even four times (0.4%).

2.   However, the reader will recall that in Chapter 7 I found no clear evidence that the absence of homogamy was an important contributor to marital instability in the Detroit sample.

3.   The logic underlying the pessimistic scenario in this case is obviously different than in the case of divorce, since it does not assume character flaws or unsuitability for marriage in general on the part of the multiply married.

4.   However, for those married three and four times, I do not have background information on the "intermediate" husbands.

5.   For remarriages, though, I have only individual characteristics of the new husbands, and not family background traits, such as the social class or occupation of their parents. Thus I cannot examine all of the aspects of homogamy considered in Chapter 5.

6.   All of the continuing first marriages were racially homogamous. One of the remarried respondents was a white woman who married first a white man and then a black man, and another was a white woman whose first and most recent husbands were both black. If anything these cases point toward the pessimistic scenario, but two cases out of 459 is not enough to pass judgment.

7.   The comparison described here is slightly different because it focuses only on the 63 divorced women who remarried, rather than all 119 women who got divorced from their first husbands, but the pattern of findings is much the same.

8.   Given the relatively small number of remarriage cases I am dealing with—63 who were divorced from their first husbands—the percentage differences indicated here do not produce statistically significant results, and the correlations between a marriage number variable and the various homogamy measures used in Chapter 5 are all under $r = .10$. In the case of ethnic group, furthermore, there is no clear difference in the likelihood of homogamy in first marriages for women who divorced and remarried and those who remained married—the relevant percentages marrying into the same group are 35.5% and 35.4% (using the seven ethnic group categories described in Chapter 5).

9.   Age homogamy was not considered in Chapter 5, since no clear social status group differences are involved. But in the context of discussing matching and mismatching in general, as in the current chapter, age homogamy is relevant.

10.   Of course, the same logic could be applied to men contemplating divorce and remarriage.

11.   In other words, the first husbands in many cases would have had better jobs at the time of the divorce than when they first married, and the new spouses might have had worse jobs at the time of the remarriage than they do now. By ignoring such career mobility, we would be "stacking the deck" in favor of the optimistic view that women "trade up" via remarriage.

12.   Unfortunately, we do not have income data to see whether this same trend is visible in terms of the husband's or family income.

13.   There are two important differences in the nature of the data in the two studies. First, Hollingshead's data all refer to marriages that occurred during one year (1949–50), whereas the Detroit marriages occurred over a sixty year period (1925–84). Second, in the present data I have figures on wedding celebrations for the first and most recent marriages of the same women, whereas in the New Haven study those marrying for the first time and remarrying were different women.

14.   There was no significant relationship between how a woman met her first husband and how she met a subsequent husband.

15.   Of these women, 44.4% had religious weddings on both occasions, 30.6% switched from religious to civil, and 12.5% switched from civil to religious. I cannot compare these figures with the New Haven data because Hollingshead's study contains no figures on religious marriages per se, but only on whether the wedding was held in church or not. However, national data presented in Modell (1985, p. 191) show figures on religious and civil marriages of never-married and previously married people that are quite similar to those derived from the Detroit data.

16.   Modell (1985) presents data showing that between the years 1963 and 1979, the gap between never-married and previously married couples in terms of having a religious marriage declined. The propensity to think that a previous marriage "disqualifies" you from a traditional set of wedding festivities seems to be eroding. By 1978 previously married individuals were about as likely to have a religious marriage as were people who married late (over age 35), suggesting that the "deviance" of those two situations was similar (and modest). This trend constitutes another piece of evidence in favor of the argument that status-linked views on "propriety" in the realm of dating and mating are weakening.

17.   The data used to construct the figure are not based on an estimating technique, such as model life table analysis (see Espenshade 1985), but from the actual experiences of women in the Detroit sample. Because first marriages and remarriages are being compared within the same sample, all of the women used to compute figures for the remarriage curves in Figure 8.1 also are included in the first marriage curve, based on how long their first marriages lasted. Also, the data on remarriages used here concern not the second marriages in each case, but the most recent marriages of all remarried women. In other words, as noted earlier, in a few instances it is third or fourth marriages whose fate is being considered, and I do not have any information on the mode of dissolution of any "intermediate" marriages.

18.   One other piece of evidence points in the same direction. I do have information on whether the grooms the respondents married in their first marriages had been married before, and there was not a significant correlation between having married a previously married man and having a first marriage with that man end up in divorce.

19.   At issue here is uncertainty under the optimistic scenario about how much "worse" than surviving first marriages the first marriages of these women were prior to the divorce, and how large an improvement I should expect to find as a result of remarriage, and thus whether the net result should produce marriage quality that is similar to, lower than, or perhaps even higher than, first marriages that have endured. Also, as noted earlier, it is less clear whether the same scenarios and predictions should apply when the first marriage ended by widowhood rather than divorce. However, since the number of remarried widows in the sample was quite small, in general the results reported here did not differ depending on whether I examined only divorced and remarried women or all remarried women.

20.   To be specific, I found only 7 correlation coefficients significant at the .05 level when

scanning 72 of such coefficients. By chance alone I would expect to find 3.6 significant correlations in a matrix of this size, so I really have only 3 or so correlations more than I would expect to find simply on the basis of chance.

21. This tendency to be abused seems to be associated particularly with having married young the first time, having had a simple wedding the first time, and being fairly new to the current marriage relationship (see the discussion in Chapter 6). When these three factors are controlled (in a multiple regression analysis, results not shown here), the difference between first marriages and remarriages is no longer statistically significant. Factors such as race, education, and premarital pregnancy in the first marriage were not significant predictors of spouse abuse once these other factors were taken into account.

22. The correlation between the marriage worries measure and marriage order number is only $r = .01$, and the correlation with the scale of marital conflicts is actually negative but nonsignificant ($r = -.07$), indicating a slight tendency for remarried women to report fewer and less severe disputes with their spouses than do women who have been married only once.

23. To be sure, studies that do ask respondents to compare their current and their previous marriages uniformly find that they rate their current marriages significantly better (see, for example, Benson-von der Ohe 1987).

24. One possible explanation for this finding of "no differences" in comparing remarriages with first marriages is that the remarriages gain in the comparison because they involve newer marriages. If on the average marriage quality tends to decline over the years of the marriage (at least up until the empty nest phase), as described in Chapter 7, then the newer remarriages should be expected to have even higher quality than long-standing original marriages. I checked for this possibility using partial correlation analysis to control for the length of the current marriage relationship (results not shown here), and in general the result was that the correlations between marriage order number and my marriage quality and marriage problems scales were still weak and not statistically significant even after the length of the marriage was controlled for.

25. The correlations of the summary elaborateness scale and marriage quality and problems in first marriages were .16 and $-.15$, respectively, while in remarriages the comparable figures were $-.07$ and $-.02$.

26. The relevant correlation coefficients are $-.15$ and .11 for first marriages and $-.05$ and $-.04$ for remarriages.

27. The relevant correlations are $-.01$ and .18 for first marriages and $-.38$ and .50 for remarriages.

28. For first marriages the correlations with marriage quality and marriage problems scales are $-.19$ and $-.10$ for years married, $-.15$ and $-.17$ for respondent's current age, and $-.15$ and $-.13$ for current life-cycle stage. For remarriages the corresponding correlations are .20 and $-.34$; .21 and $-.44$; and .34 and $-.48$.

29. The plot for first marriages in Figure 8.2 is simply a repetition of Figure 7.1. For both sets of curves only those currently married are included. Note that there were no currently remarried women in the sample who were in the pre-children stage of the life cycle.

30. It might be argued that the higher quality and lower problems of long-lasting remarriages, in comparison with first marriages, can be attributed to selectivity. Perhaps remarried spouses are more willing to consider divorcing again if things don't work out, so that only atypically "good" remarriages will survive into the later life stages. First marriages, in contrast, may contain many cases in late stages in the life cycle in which the marriage is lousy, but for one reason or another the partners are unable or unwilling to contemplate divorce. However, in order for this argument to be plausible, there would have to exist a pattern of more ready and quick divorces in remarriages than in first marriages in the Detroit sample, and, as indicated earlier in Figure 8.1, the present data show just the opposite tendency. Still, the pattern indicated in Figure 8.2 cannot be fully trusted unless it is verified in future longitudinal research.

31. Again, I stress that this lack of differences also holds when the length of the current marriage

relationship is controlled for. Also, I recognize that the phrase "women ending unhappy marriages" oversimplifies reality, since in some cases the husband may take the initiative (11.1% of our divorce cases) or it may be mutual (19.7% of our cases), and so in some cases women may have felt quite satisfied prior to being abandoned or receiving a demand for divorce from the husband.

32.   Another way of looking at this complexity is to note that in Ackerman's terminology remarriages foster "disjunctive affiliations" in the sense of kinship ties and obligations that do not coincide with the conjugal bond, and that such disjunctive affiliations tend to foster marital instability (see Ackerman 1963).

Chapter 9

CONCLUSIONS

What have we learned about the evolving nature of dating, mating, and marriage in America? Before attempting to summarize and discuss some of the most important results of the current study, I need to offer some final observations on the "representativeness" issue. Since the research which forms the central basis for this study involved interviews only with women in the Detroit area through a cross-sectional survey, how confident can the reader be that the findings and conclusions offered here have any general bearing on trends in mate choice and marriage relations in America? While a satisfactory answer to this question will depend upon the reader's judgment of the overall study and on the results of future research, I do feel that reassurances can be given.

Let me stress once again, as I did in Chapter 1, that this is not a narrowly defined study limited to the city of Detroit. The actual sample was drawn from a three county area populated by more than 4 million people, an area that includes wealthy suburbs, semirural areas, and modest settlements clustered around industrial plants, as well as depressed inner-city neighborhoods. The population and the sample also include a diversity of groups, in terms of class, ethnic origins, religion, and occupation. Furthermore, the respondents were living in the Detroit area in 1984, but many of them had not been born, grew up, or even married there, and women from cities, towns, and rural areas all over the country were represented, even if there was a predominance of women with Michigan roots. (For further details on the composition of the sample, see Appendix 1.) So even though the population studied here is not in some general sense representative of all of America, or even of metropolitan areas in the U.S., still it is a heterogeneous population that is not particularly unusual in comparison with what would be found in many other large urban areas. Therefore the nature of the sample used provides some confidence that the findings offered here are not simply oddities produced by quirks of Detroit.

In addition, where it has been possible to make comparisons with figures drawn from studies in other locales, for the most part the findings in regard to general tendencies and trends are reassuringly similar.[1] A large number of such similarities has been noted throughout the text. Suffice it to repeat here only a few: the decline and then rise in marriage ages in the post-World War II period; increases in premarital sex, cohabitation, and premarital pregnancy; the heterogeneous pattern of venues in which married couples first met; the rise in female

241

employment aspirations and actual work experience; the growing trend of residential independence for young people prior to marriage; the decline in religious "matching" in marriage over time; the level of religious vs. civil marriages; the decline in marriage quality and problems over the course of a marriage; and the fairly high levels of satisfaction with the current marital relationship that respondents report. These are only a few of the many areas of agreement with other research that have been documented in the preceding chapters.[2]

To be sure, many of the questions asked in the current survey have not been used in earlier research, permitting no exact comparisons for many of the findings reported. Some of the specific findings of the current study, such as the relatively "unproblematic" nature of remarriages, in comparison with first marriages, do differ from much previous research on the same topic. Still, the impressive number of instances in which findings drawn from the Detroit survey mirror those found in other studies conducted in different locales provides considerable confidence that the Detroit findings are not in some general sense peculiar and therefore discountable.

Even though I am generally convinced that the findings of this study should be taken seriously and tell us important things about dating, mating, and marriage in America, still there are gaps in this study that others will have to fill. In particular, we need comparable studies that look at mate choice and marriage through the eyes of men. Even though the female respondents in the Detroit survey provided a lot of information about the men in their lives, such information is not an adequate substitute for information drawn from men directly. Previous research has indicated that husbands and wives often differ in their descriptions of the same, apparently objective, reality (e.g., in regard to the division of household chores), and we may suspect that the things that husbands find important in making a successful marriage will not be identical to the things found important by wives (see Bernard 1972). Therefore it will be important for future research on mate choice and marriage to bring the views of husbands as well as wives into the picture.

Assuming that the current study has some general messages to give us, what are they? Having squeezed a veritable smorgasbord of results out of the 1984 Detroit Area Study survey, I must bring the analysis to a close. Given my broad and eclectic approach in this research, achieving closure is by no means an easy task. A variety of interesting patterns have emerged from this study, but there is no single "big" finding that is more important than all of the rest. By the same token, the number of findings and revisions of previous work are sufficiently numerous that it would be too tedious to rehash all of them here in these concluding comments. My approach in this final chapter, therefore, is to simply list what I feel are some of the more interesting and unexpected findings to emerge from the analysis. With that listing presented, I will move on to make further observations about the two main issues that motivated this study in the first place: the links between premarital experiences and marital success, and the current state of, and future prospects for, American marriage.

The varied findings of this study are of several types. Some are simply observations about general patterns or trends over time, while others are conclusions about causal relationships—about what affects what in the realms of dating and mating. Some findings are "positive" in the sense of finding a clear trend or causal connection, but many others are "negative"—patterns that were found in previous studies that did not turn up in the analysis of the Detroit data. A simple listing of some of the primary findings of various types from this study would include the following:

- Younger women in general have experienced a greater variety of dating partners and a higher degree of premarital intimacy than older women. The intimacy revolution is genuine. At the same time some features of the dating experience, such as the age of beginning to date and how the first husband was met, do not appear to have changed very much over time.

- Dating activity that results eventually in marriage begins in a wide variety of situations and venues. Couples first meeting while in school is not the predominant pattern, nor is meeting at work. Personal introductions by third parties are the start of relationships that lead up to marriage more often than is generally recognized.

- Younger women are more likely than older ones to have lived independently prior to marrying, and they are also more likely to have set up a new household after marriage, rather than living with one or the other set of parents.

- In general there is somewhat greater ritual elaborateness and expenditure involved in recent weddings than in earlier ones. This trend does not appear to involve a "return to tradition" after the unconventional 1960s, but rather a more or less linear development since the 1930s and 1940s.

- Generally religious and ethnic barriers to mate selection have been less strong for younger women in the sample than for older women; class and educational matching, on the other hand, has not changed markedly.

- There is no clear evidence in the current study for marriage serving as an upward social mobility mechanism for females. Women as often "marry down" as "marry up," and of course many marry at roughly the same status level.

- The patterning of relations between spouses after marriage does not differ much between older and younger women, even though their premarital experiences have often been dramatically different.

- Most continuing marriages are described by wives as fairly satisfying and egalitarian. However, this generally positive view has not kept a significant minority of women from having recurring worries about whether their marriages are in trouble.

- The fact that husbands generally have higher incomes than wives does not readily translate into male dominance in conjugal relations. By the same token, wives who have relatively high incomes, compared to other women and even to their husbands, do not have that much more power in their marriages than women who do not have such economic clout. Nor do working wives have conjugal relationships that are all that different from housewives. Because of such findings, theories that see marriage in terms of competition and exchange between two interest maximizing spouses seem inadequate and misleading.

- The basic similarity in marriage patterns of women of varying ages may be misleading if this pattern is taken as evidence of a lack of change in American marriage patterns generally. For household chore division, at least, the results presented here indicate that modest changes have been occurring (toward somewhat greater sharing of chores by husbands), but that they have been affecting the marriages of women of all ages, and not simply of younger women who are not yet "set in their ways."

- Positive qualities in a marital relationship and marital problems are at least to some extent separable realms, and it is possible to rate high on both, or for that matter low on both. Some predictors affect these two realms differently. For example, the lower levels of marital quality reported by women in the later stages of the life cycle do not imply that these women have more marital problems than women in earlier life stages; the reverse is the case.

- Most aspects of premarital experiences and relationships do not have much impact one way or the other on marital success.

- Women who marry men who are closely matched to themselves in social backgrounds (in terms of religion, socioeconomic status, education, etc.) are not much more likely to have successful marriages than women who are "mismatched."

- In most respects remarriages do not appear very different from continuing first marriages, and if anything in this sample remarriages are slightly more stable than first marriages.

- In general, in this study the sorts of social background or "demographic" factors usually used by social scientists to explain variations in family life—socioeconomic status, religion, ethnicity, rural-urban origins, female employment, and so forth—have weak or negligible relationships with both the premarital experience and marital relationship measures used in this study, weaker than in many previous studies of these topics. The weakness of these associations between social status and dating and mating behavior, I have argued, points to a general trend in our society that I have called the "decline in conventions."

- The one major exception to the general weakness of social background factors in explaining variation in the current study involves race. In many, but not all, realms examined in this study, the experiences of black respondents have been different from those of whites. For example, blacks have experienced less dating variety on the average, have begun sexual activity earlier, are more likely to have been premaritally pregnant, have had less elaborate weddings, have somewhat different values about marriage, have had less satisfying and more unstable marriages, and are less likely to pool resources with their husbands. Furthermore, in general these differences exist even when socioeconomic contrasts between the races are controlled for statistically, a pattern that suggests that the contrasts are not simply due to poverty, unemployment and other socioeconomic factors, but have deeper roots.

• While most social background factors are not generally important in explaining variations in dating and in marriage outcomes, important features of the life experiences of respondents turn out to have very important causal impacts. Both the timing and nature of earlier experiences in the dating process strongly influence later stages in the process, including the timing and elaborateness of the wedding. Similarly, the patterning of conjugal relations in such realms as leisure pursuits, sharing of values, and control over family funds, has quite a strong influence on marital success. In general, a high degree of companionship between spouses, a merging of identity and resources, and mutual intimacy seem more important in fostering marital success than do such things as income levels, religious orientations, and similarity in social backgrounds.

Although these and other findings of this study are something of a grab-bag, the final general conclusions listed contain common threads that deserve further comment. I have noted that most social background factors, with the particular exception of race, have less of an impact on premarital and marital experiences than many earlier studies have found, and that in contrast intervening personal experiences and circumstances are more powerful explanatory factors than has generally been recognized. How can I explain the divergence from at least many earlier studies on these topics? The importance of personal experiences and circumstances in explaining subsequent dating and marital outcomes is perhaps understandable in that the current study has included questions on the latter topics that have rarely been asked; for example, questions about the ages of starting to date and go steady and about how the income of each spouse is handled. But the generally weak impact of social background factors remains a puzzle. I am unable to think of anything particularly unusual about the Detroit sample or the methods used in the current study that could explain this general pattern in the results.[3]

I have suggested that this relatively weak impact of social background features on dating and mating behavior is evidence of an important social trend in America, a trend I have referred to, for want of a better alternative, as constituting a "decline in conventions." As suggested throughout this study, the use of this term implies that earlier in this century there were clear hierarchies of class, ethnic, and religious groups in America, and that particular conventions about what sort of behavior was proper in dating, mate choice, and marriage were strongly subscribed to among the elite in these hierarchies (the upper- and middle classes, composed largely of white Protestants), but ignored or complied with irregularly among the nonelite. In the latter-part of the 20th century both the exclusiveness of the hierarchies and their attached conventions have increasingly broken down. The result in some cases has been a "trickling down" of elite modes of behavior to the ordinary population, as in the case of a ritually elaborate and expensive wedding. In other cases what has occurred is instead a "bubbling up" of lower class modes of behavior into the elite, as in the increases in premarital sex. In either case, the result is that behavior in the realm of dating and mating is less clearly linked than in the past with social position and status group membership. As a consequence of this decline of conventions, there is reduced confidence that any particular kind of premarital or marital behavior can be interpreted as a clear sign of moral worth or social position. In this situation it is quite understandable that we cannot predict people's premarital and marital behavior as easily as we could in the past simply by knowing their class position, religion, or ethnicity.[4]

Whatever the exact sources of the divergence between the current findings and earlier studies, a general implication for future research can be drawn. I would not suggest that family sociologists stop asking basic questions about occupation, income, education, religion, and other background traits. But I would encourage them to treat such factors as relatively distant "givens" whose influence may be washed away or counteracted by the patterning and sequencing of the life experiences of the people whom they interview. They should develop more imaginative ways of theorizing about the impact of personal circumstances and sequences of experiences on realms such as the timing of first sexual experience or marriage, the nature of wedding celebrations, the patterning of conjugal relations, and the stability and quality of marriages.

The current study has utilized an imperfect method in the effort to get at the influence of such personal experiences and sequences. That effort has involved the use of a range of retrospective questions. This method is imperfect not only because people may not recall clearly the earlier experiences we asked about or may have their recollections altered by more recent events. In addition, the retrospective questions used cannot capture adequately the dynamics of changing experiences and relationships. For example, I have information from the current survey on such things as the division of household chores and marital dispute resolution at only one point in time, rather than a record of how aspects of conjugal relations such as these changed over time in response to such things as the birth of children, serious illnesses to either a spouse or a child, unemployment, residential moves, resumed education, or other altered life circumstances.

Methods exist that can more adequately deal with the sequencing of life experiences. One method that can be used even in a cross-sectional survey, such as the kind conducted by the Detroit Area Study, is a detailed life events schedule or life history calendar (see Freedman et al. 1988). This technique involves recording from respondents year-by-year changes in their life situation in the past (births, deaths, marriages, employment and residence changes, etc.). This schedule can then be used to provide time benchmarks to collect more precise information about how other experiences and relationships changed over time in the past. Use of such a life events schedule helps to jog fallible memories and somewhat reduces the problems of recall.[5] But the main virtue of this sort of interview structure is that it can provide a more dynamic picture of how people's lives have developed in the past than can a more conventional cross-sectional survey using some retrospective questions.

The other major way to obtain such a dynamic view is, of course, to conduct a panel study in which the same respondents are followed up longitudinally and reinterviewed periodically about their changing life circumstances and family experiences. This approach can yield a more precise view of the timing of various experiences and how events in a sequence are causally related, and it can also overcome the problem of the biasing effect of more recent experiences, a problem that even use of a detailed life events schedule cannot solve. A life events schedule approach and a panel study are more complex to design and administer than the sort of methodology used in the current study. But insofar as an understanding of the sequencing of personal experiences is vital to explaining dating and mating outcomes, as the Detroit survey results suggest, such complexity must be confronted.

The Separation between Premarital and Marital Experiences

It would be erroneous to imply, however, that all past experiences have an indelible imprint on later life. One of the major and unexpected findings of the current study, as noted above, is that most measures of dating and other premarital experiences have little impact on marital success. As discussed in Chapter 7, this conclusion poses a major challenge to the basic premises of our American dating culture, to what I have termed the "marketplace learning scenario." To reiterate once again, the assumption involved in that scenario is that extensive experience in dating helps you to make the "right choice" and gives you a better chance of "living happily ever after." Three particular aspects of dating experiences have been measured in this study: the length of the dating stage, the variety of partners who have been dated, and the length and intimacy of the relationship with the eventual spouse, and all of these realms should, according to commonly held assumptions, be predictive of marital success. Or to look at things from the negative side, individuals who have had very limited dating experience with very few people and who marry partners without knowing them for very long or very intimately should be "high risk" cases likely to have unstable or unhappy marriages.

However, as I pointed out in Chapter 7, none of these ideas are supported by the evidence from the Detroit survey. The length of the dating experience, the number of dating partners recalled, the length of the relationship with the eventual first husband, and the degree of sexual intimacy with that husband—none of these predictors has any significant independent influence on the fate of the marriage. To be sure, marrying very young is consistently associated with less successful marriages in the current study, as has been found in most other research on this topic. But marrying very young has many other implications besides simply a foreshortening of the dating and learning process. For example, women who marry at a young age are likely to be less emotionally mature and less securely established financially than women who marry at later ages. Furthermore, direct measures of the length of the dating stage, or of the period of courtship or engagement with the eventual husband, showed no similar relationship with measures of marital success.[6] In sum, the answer to my initial question in launching this study about whether these kinds of premarital experiences influence the fate of marriages is largely negative.[7]

What are the implications of this finding that dating experience does not "help" provide the basis for a successful marriage? In discussing this question I must leave the firm basis of statistical findings and enter a more speculative realm. There are several possible implications of this general set of findings, and the data from the survey do not provide me with any conclusive way of knowing how much credence to give to each.

The evidence from the Detroit survey does provide one possible explanation for why more dating experience does not help you pick the most suitable person to marry. In our society we have alternative views, besides the marketplace learning scenario, about the best basis for mate choice. In particular, we also believe that love can "conquer all." The mention of love suggests a relatively emotional and irrational factor in mate choice, rather than the sort of fairly rational and pragmatic process that the notion of marketplace learning conveys. If love, even at first sight, can conquer all, and if love is "all that matters," then the prime predictor of marital success should not be how many years you spend in the dating game and how well you have gotten to know your fiancé, but simply how romantically you feel about the person you are about to marry (presumably, the feeling should be mutual). In fact, I noted in Chapter 7 that a measure of the degree of romantic love experienced at the time of marriage was clearly related to all three measures of marital success.[8]

However, since the measure of romantic love used in this study is based upon recollections years after the fact, recollections that may be biased by the subsequent history of the marriage, I am not at all confident that these results "prove" that love is more important than dating experience in picking the right mate. In other words, based on these findings, I would not recommend that young people discard rational evaluation entirely and simply do what their heart tells them to do. In any case, these two separate considerations in mate choice, evaluation of suitability and feelings of romance, need not be in conflict and should be complementary, and it still remains unclear why extensive dating experience does not add anything significant to one's prospects for a successful marriage.

Another possible reason why dating experience might not foster marital success is that the relationships involved might not be linear. Perhaps within certain limits more dating experience with a variety of partners may help to prepare for a "right choice," but beyond this point further dating experience might not help or might even be counterproductive.[9] Women who have had an unusually large number of dates or who have been at the dating game for a very long time may make poorer choices than women with less extensive experience, whether due to indecision, exasperation, or simply the declining number of men available. I investigated this possibility by looking for curvilinear relationships between measures of dating variety and the length of dating and courting on the one hand and my three measures of marital success on the other, but in general I found no evidence to support this sort of curvilinear pattern (details not shown here).[10] The relationships that exist between measures of dating experience and marital success tend to be linear, but they are simply very weak. Once you control for the age of first marriage, even these weak relationships tend to disappear. In general my negative conclusion in regard to the impact of dating experiences cannot be attributed to the fact that I overlooked important nonlinear trends in these relationships.

Since I find neither the "love conquers all" nor the "curvilinear trend" argument fully satisfactory, the reasons why dating experience does not foster marital success remain a puzzle. The pattern of negative findings from this study forced me to reexamine the marketplace learning scenario, and the more I did so the more I became aware of the unrealistic nature of many of the common assumptions involved in this scenario. Dating and mating do not quite work the way we like to assume that they do.

As noted in the earlier discussion, our dating culture is based upon a marketplace analogy. Yet, even though the idea of a "marriage market" is often quite illuminating, it is important to realize that this is quite a special type of market. Selecting a spouse is quite different from buying a breakfast cereal, a car, or a house. Outside of the fact that returns, exchanges, and resale are not so easy with a spouse as with a consumer product, there are a number of other peculiarities and complexities of the marriage market. The complexities I am referring to are not simply those of imperfect information and lack of availability, as in my discussion in Chapter 5 of why Detroiters do not marry Eskimos, since selection without information about the full range of alternatives is in the nature of most marketplace transactions.

The peculiarities of the marriage market I have in mind are several. The marketplace analogy suggests that we can select from among a variety of alternative potential spouses. Yet the nature of dating and mating in our society is such that this is rarely possible or is only true to a very limited extent. Our experience with alternative prospects is generally sequential, rather than simultaneous. To be sure, some people may go through stages of "playing the field" by dating several people simultaneously, although in Chapter 2 I suggested that such stages may now be rarer and briefer than they were for people entering the dating stage decades ago. However, playing the field typically entails lower levels of intimacy and commitment than would be required to judge the suitability of a date as a potential spouse (even disregarding the false fronts and hypocrisy that critics charge are endemic to casual dating). As soon as greater intimacy develops, pressures arise to make the relationship an exclusive one (i.e., at least by "going steady") and stop playing the field. It is in the nature of such exclusive relationships that you cannot actively consider alternatives without getting into serious trouble with your current partner.

You can, of course, compare the new steady with memories of your previous experiences, but by that point it may be difficult, if not impossible, to change your mind, reject the new partner, and retrieve the old. Past loves don't usually wait around hoping you will return, but go on to find new dating partners themselves.[11] You also cannot make a direct comparison of the current partner with possible new alternatives, since to "test" these alternatives would require you to jeopardize or abandon the current relationship. So except in unusual circumstances, you cannot compare several intimate romantic relationships directly. Instead you have to compare the present relationship with previous alternatives that have already been foregone and with potential future ones whose qualities can only be imagined. This is clearly quite a different process from being able to test drive a variety of new cars or switching back and forth between Wheaties, Grape Nuts, and Fruit Loops to see which you like best for breakfast.

In addition to this "limitation on direct comparison of alternatives" feature of the marriage market, there are other peculiarities involved. When I select cereals or automobiles I do not have to worry about whether they will pick or reject me (ignoring the issue of creditworthiness for an auto loan). And under ordinary circumstances I do not have to be concerned with whether, if I take some time in making up my mind, my choice will no longer be available. (However, this last consideration is a concern in purchases of such things as a house or designer fashions.) In dating and mating these are bound to be central concerns. If a woman decides that Joe Blow is her ideal potential husband, he may not reciprocate her feelings, and she may be forced to consider other, less than ideal, candidates. In addition, if she rejects a series of candidates for marriage as unsuitable, she has to worry that the supply of more suitable candidates who would be willing to consider her is rapidly being withdrawn from the market (through marriage to other women).[12] If she finds what seems like an ideal partner but feels that she is not yet ready to settle down, she has to worry about whether, by the time she is ready to marry, he may no longer be available. A complex alignment of timing and of partner selection is involved in mate choice, and such a woman may feel that she is confronted with less than ideal alternatives—of marrying before she is ready to do so, of selecting a man who is not her ideal (in terms of what she has learned from her past dating experiences), or perhaps of not being able to marry at all. In other words, dating may provide useful experience that can help her make the "right mate choice," but when it comes time to make that choice it is problematic whether she will be able to act on the basis of this experience or not.[13]

To summarize, I have been describing a number of peculiarities and constraints of the marriage market, in comparison with other kinds of markets. Combined, these features lead me to conclude that even if more extensive dating experience might be useful in helping you to learn what kind of partner you would be suited to, in actual practice dating and mating work in ways that often prevent this wisdom from playing a central role in the final mate choice decision. As you become more intimate with one partner you are constrained against considering alternatives; you cannot keep all past romantic partners available until such time as you are ready to make a marriage decision; by the time you are ready to get married you may have difficulty finding a very suitable or desirable partner, or the person who is your ideal may be attracted to someone else; and the longer you spend at the "dating game," the more anxiety you may have about being left out of the winner's circle at the end. For all of these reasons the final choice of a mate is often at least a partial compromise, and the actual mate you end up with may not be any better suited to you than are the spouses of individuals who married with less extensive or intimate dating experiences.[14]

A final problem with the marketplace learning scenario, and thus with how our dating culture works, is that it assumes that the main problem is how to get two individuals who are well suited to one another together and then married. Implicit here is the idea that by the time you are a young adult your basic character, likes and dislikes, and personal quirks have been fully formed, so that compatibility at age 20 or 25 will still be compatibility at age 40, 60, or 80. However, as numerous social commentators have told us in recent years (see, for example, Toffler 1972; Sheehy 1974), this assumption of basic stability in character and psychology is unrealistic. Individuals can and do change their careers and their activities, along with their aspirations, habits, likes, and dislikes. Couples who may have been well suited to one another at the time that they married may "grow apart," with compatibility turning into incompatibility. Even when extensive dating experience has given you the wisdom to pick a suitable spouse, and even if you are lucky enough to be able to avoid compromises and marry your ideal partner (and your spouse feels likewise), still there is no guarantee that the marriage will be successful in the long run. Experience in the dating stage may help you judge how well you might get along with a person now and in the near future, but it may not provide much guidance about how you and your partner will change in the future in response to new experiences, opportunities, and crises.

The various features I have discussed in the preceding pages help to explain why prolonged dating, variety in dating partners, and premarital intimacy are not reliable predictors of marital success. There are too many constraints and uncertainties affecting the dating and mating process, and too many other influences on marital success down the road, for extensive and intimate dating experiences to have a strong influence on marital success. But what are the implications of this discouraging conclusion? Are there better ways to pick a spouse?

Perhaps it is simply a matter of my lack of imagination, but I do not see an alternative that is obviously preferable to our current customs of dating and mating. Several alternatives spring to mind and can be considered here hypothetically: random choice, arranged marriages, and some kind of computerized pairing up of suitable partners. How can we judge whether one of these alternatives would be preferable? From the results of the Detroit survey I concluded that similarity in social backgrounds was not very important to marital success, but that personal compatibility, in terms of things like character traits, values, and preferred leisure time pursuits, was important (see the discussion in Chapter 7). So I can try to judge whether an alternative method of mate selection would produce greater personal compatibility than does our current dating process.

Obviously a random selection would not lead to greater compatibility of mates than is gained through dating, but instead would produce a variety of personal mismatches for the most part. The reader can rest assured that I am not recommending that American mate choice in the future be conducted by drawing lots. Some foreign partisans of the custom of arranged marriages argue that that alternative can produce more compatibility than our current system, since the irrationalities of romantic love can be eliminated from the choice, which then can be made in a more rational manner. However, it seems likely that parents would consider matching more in terms of the social backgrounds than the personal traits of the potential bride and groom. They would also be in less of a position to judge personal compatibility than would the young people themselves. In any case, the evidence from societies that employ arranged marriage of such phenomena as old men married to very young girls or of promising young men forced to marry rich but ugly or deformed women raises serious doubts about whether an arranged marriage system would promote greater actual compatibility between husbands and wives.[15]

One might finally consider the alternative of putting mate choice decisions into the hands of computer matchmaking-cum-psychological testing agencies, which through in-depth testing of their clients would be able to put together optimally matched marital pairs. But aside from the question of what would happen to romantic attraction and love in this Orwellian proposal, the low levels of success of computer matchmaking services to date raise doubts about whether numbers and computers can be substituted for personal judgments and attraction (see the discussion in Godwin 1973; Mullan 1984; Asimov 1982).[16] The problem involved is illustrated by a letter of complaint sent to one such dating service: "Your computer was right. Mitzi W. and I like all the same things. We like the same food, we both like the opera. Mitzi likes bike riding and so do I. I like dogs, and so does Mitzi. Actually, there was only one thing we didn't like—each other" (quoted in Godwin 1973, p. 87). In sum, none of the alternatives that come readily to mind seem obviously preferable to our current reliance on the dating process to help us select spouses.

However, the problems in mate selection could be looked at from a different angle. Even though extensive dating experience does not seem to help much in producing successful marriages, still it is not harmful either. In Chapter 2 I discussed a number of criticisms of dating that claimed that our existing customs are actually counterproductive. For example, critics claim that dating begins at a too early and immature age, that sexual attraction and emotions too readily substitute for rational judgment, and that social pressures and efforts to be attractive lead individuals to date the wrong people for the wrong reasons (for example, in order to gain popularity with others, rather than because the chosen date is well suited to you). If such claims were generally true, then extensive and intimate dating experiences should actually interfere with the selection of a suitable mate, and those who have had such experiences should end up with less successful marriages. However, the findings of the Detroit study do not support such criticisms, any more than they support the marketplace learning scenario. It is not that too extensive or intimate an involvement in the dating stage produces less successful marriages, but simply that it does not make a clear difference one way or the other.[17]

The preceding ruminations lead me to question whether there is any better way to select marital partners in American society, assuming that the goal is an enduring and satisfying marriage. The fact that dating does not provide a perfect solution by reliably resulting in individuals getting married to their ideal partners is a product of the complexities of marriage markets, conjugal relations, and individual development. Even though it does not provide a very reliable method of selecting the "right" partner, there is no obvious alternative to continuing to rely on the imperfect process of dating in our efforts to find marital partners.

The Health of Marriage in America

One further implication of the "gap" between premarital experiences and subsequent marital relations is that a revolution in the former realm has been accommodated to evolution in the latter. In other words, the dramatic changes that have occurred in the premarital stage, with major increases in such things as independence from parents prior to marriage, premarital sexuality, and cohabitation, have not produced comparably dramatic changes in marital relationships. To be sure, marriages are not the same as they were at the turn of the century, and evidence has been presented here of gradual changes in the division of household chores and perhaps in other realms. But the weak predictive power of dating and mating behavior means that marriages are to some extent "insulated" from the dramatic changes that have been taking place in premarital experiences.

Earlier chapters documented the intimacy revolution that has transformed the nature of the premarital experiences of younger women in comparison with their mothers and grandmothers.[18] However, when the findings of the current study are viewed as a whole, the use of the term "revolution" requires a variety of qualifying statements. Some of these qualifications involve the implications of this revolution for the premarital stage itself, while others involve the implications for marriage as an institution.

To begin the process of qualifying the nature of this revolution, I would argue that, dramatic as the shifts toward acceptance of independent living prior to marriage, premarital sex, and unmarried cohabitation are, they do not represent the replacement of one set of assumptions about dating and mating with a new set. Rather, what is involved is a logical culmination of a long-standing set of assumptions, a culmination made possible not by a change in the objectives of the premarital behavior involved, but by the decline in conventions to which I have repeatedly drawn attention. To be specific, it has long been assumed in our culture that the eventual goal of dating experience is to prepare one for a "wise" choice of a mate and a satisfying marriage, and there is no sign that this assumption is weakening. What has weakened are the barriers to intimacy, particularly in the case of women, that used to hedge the dating and mating process in with "dos" and "don'ts." Now a very large portion not only of young people, but even of their parents and grandparents, assume that it would be unwise, if not unthinkable, to enter marriage without being intimately acquainted (sexually and otherwise) with the intended spouse beforehand. Yet there is little evidence available of a rejection of preparation for marriage as the central long-term goal of the dating process, in favor of acceptance of premarital intimacy for its own sake. To paraphrase the words of Morton Hunt (1974), the dominant view of premarital intimacy in America remains "liberal romantic" rather than "radical recreational." So the intimacy revolution has been a real revolution in one sense, in terms of the kinds of behavior allowed, but much less of a revolution in another sense, in terms of the linking of premarital intimacy to the effort to prepare for mate selection and marriage, very traditional goals.

Of course, I have just discussed the fact that this common assumption that premarital intimacy provides important and even essential preparation for marital success is not borne out by the facts. Mate selection is a complex and difficult process, and those who have been in the forefront of the intimacy revolution do not end up with more successful marriages than those who are left in the rear guard. (However, they are not significantly less successful in their marriages either.) But the fact that people are erroneous in feeling that greater premarital intimacy will foster marital success does not contradict the claim that the intimacy revolution occurred largely in the service of very traditional goals, as part of the pursuit of a successful marriage relationship.

If the evidence from the Detroit survey points to premarital relations changing in ways that are only partly revolutionary, the evidence in regard to marriage itself points to an even less dramatic shift. When we consider the long-term trends in the nature of the relationship between husbands and wives, the term evolution, and not revolution, seems most appropriate. To be sure, the technological, economic, religious, and social environments faced by Americans today are very different from those faced in the 1920s and 1930s. In addition to the changes in premarital behavior that have been extensively documented here, there have been dramatic changes in several key areas of family life: birth rates have "boomed" and then collapsed to the lowest levels in American history; the chances of getting divorced have risen from less than one in five to perhaps one in two; and the percentage of women working outside the home has risen from less than 15% prior to World War II to 60% or more today (see Davis 1984). In the midst of these startling changes within and outside of the family, it would be logical to assume that the nature of marriage itself must be undergoing a fundamental transformation.

However, when we examine the nature of marital relations, as we have done in this study (particularly in Chapters 6–8), no such major transformation is visible. What we see instead is more in the nature of a gradual evolution. Women who have been sexually intimate prior to marriage, and even with other men than their eventual spouses, do not seem to differ much from other women in the nature of their subsequent marital history and conjugal relations. Women who are full time members of the labor force do not generally expect or achieve a total shift away from a fairly traditional household division of labor, and their goals and priorities in marriage are quite similar to those of nonworking women. Even women whose marriages end in divorce do not generally swear off the pursuit of the traditional goal of fulfillment through a rewarding marriage, and large proportions try marriage again with a new partner. Clearly marriage remains a highly valued institution in America, an honored state that has an appeal and power that adapts to, and transcends, the dramatic changes that are taking place in other areas of American life.

As a result of the ability of marital relations and attitudes to adapt gradually to dramatic changes in other realms, the women of different ages in our sample exhibit a complex mixture of contrasts and commonalities. In terms of their premarital experiences, work histories, the number of children they have given birth to, and whether they have ever been widowed or divorced, those who married recently have had very different lives from their mothers and grandmothers. However, if we look at the nature of the husband-wife relationship, we see only modest differences across generations. As we saw in Chapter 6, marriage values, patterns of communication and expressing affection, the nature of the couple's social life and leisure time activities, the division of chores and decision-making, and even the nature of marital problems only differ modestly between younger and older women. Where changes are occurring in the nature of marriage relations, as in the pattern of household chore division, they seem to be affecting both newly married couples and long-standing marriages. Again, the nature of marriage relations seems to have a surprising durability and adaptiveness. I see no signs, either in the Detroit survey or elsewhere, that marriage is about to succumb to the pressures of social change or to be replaced by a fundamentally different set of assumptions and interpersonal relationships.

These observations lead me back to the "big question" with which I began this study: what is the state of health of American marriage as an institution? Although the Detroit survey is not ideally designed to consider all aspects of this question, on balance the evidence offered here leads me to side with the optimists on this question, rather than the pessimists. To be sure, there are many areas of concern—regarding the increased brittleness of marriages, about the persisting inequality of household chore burdens, and so forth. A minority of women in the survey reported very unhappy marriages or had been divorced and had not been able to remarry. A larger proportion of all currently married respondents had at least some worries and doubts about the health of their marriages. Spouse abuse in various forms is part of the experience of at least some women. The most satisfactory marriages appear to be ones in which there is a high level of mutuality and merging of activities and interests, yet among younger, dual career couples in an era of high divorce it may be difficult (or appear risky) to establish a marriage with such total mutual involvement. This list of areas of concern could, of course, be expanded.[19]

Still, on balance the picture provided by this study is not a gloomy one. There is a large proportion of long-lasting marriages in the Detroit sample, and substantial majorities of women in such continuing marriages express considerable satisfaction with their conjugal relationships. Most women describe their marriages as characterized by high levels of mutual communication, expressions of affection, equality in decision-making, and by other desirable traits. Furthermore, in addition to being partially "insulated" from dramatic changes occurring in premarital behavior, marriages are also for the most part not locked into patterns determined by social background traits. Status mismatches, low income or education, low religious faith—these and other background traits do not have a major impact on the quality and stability of the marriage. As described in Chapter 7, patterns of money management, leisure time activities, joint social life, and other features of the patterning of marriage relations that are subject to negotiation and modification are more important determinants of marital success. As I indicated in my discussion in Chapter 7, the evidence provided here supports an optimistic view in which couples are not locked into rigidly structured conjugal bonds but can, as marriage counsellors urge, work to improve their relationship (for a similar view, see Cancian 1987).[20]

The absence of rigid structuring finds perhaps its ultimate expression in divorce and remarriage. Rising divorce has been interpreted by some as a sign of an increasing casualness of Americans about marriage in general and perhaps even of a "crisis" in which marriage as an institution is on its last legs. However, others argue that on balance the increase in the divorce rate may actually be a healthy development, since it indicates that people are not "stuck" in unhappy marriages, but are increasingly able to end such unhappiness and try again. Even though divorce may often leave a legacy of problems and strains, the evidence presented in Chapter 8 lends more support to this optimistic view of divorce and remarriage than have many previous studies on this topic. Women who remarry seem able to construct conjugal relationships with their new husbands that are not much different or less satisfying than those of women in continuing first marriages. The learning process that does not occur very reliably in the premarital stage seems to work somewhat more effectively in preparing for a remarriage. Even if I focus on the one realm that is most often the source of claims that American marriage is "in trouble"—the rising divorce rate and the problems that beset remarriages—I end up with a picture that has more pluses than minuses. The evidence presented here lends more support to a view of divorce as an effective "escape valve" from unsatisfying marriages than it does to the scenario that says rising divorce indicates a general crisis in which either marital relations are viewed very casually or are rejected altogether in favor of the single state.

I do not conclude with a Pollyanna-like view that everything is fine in all American marriages, but I would argue that the health of marriage *as an institution* in America is still robust. A number of recent works present a more pessimistic view of marriage than is presented here. See, for example, Cooper 1970; Young 1973; Rubin 1976; Zaretsky 1976; Davis 1985; Hite 1987; Popenoe 1988. However, I would argue that such pessimistic accounts suffer from a number of flaws: biased and nostalgic assumptions about the past, speculative and imagined forecasts about the future, a focus on atypical individuals and marriages, and a biased, "axe grinding" research methodology. A particular offender in this regard is Shere Hite, in her recent book, *Women and Love* (1987), who utilized biased sampling methods, abysmally low response rates, and leading questions to construct a picture in which large majorities of American women were portrayed as desperately unhappy in their marriages. (For a discussion of how in the current study possible sources of bias have been dealt with, see Appendix 1.) In addition to the sorts of flaws contained in many pessimistic accounts of American marriage, I would argue that since the doom of that institution has been foretold for more than a century (see the discussion in Chapter 1), we should in general retain a healthy skepticism about the latest versions of such doomsaying.

Establishing a vital and mutually satisfying marriage is not an easy thing to do. The sort of "screening" that dating is supposed to provide does not work very reliably, and a mate selection that appeared promising may turn out poorly. Or a conjugal relationship that is mutually satisfying at one point in time may go sour later, even if both partners have the will to make things work. A relatively high percentage of first marriages (perhaps even 50% among recently married couples) may be so disappointing that one or both partners may feel it is necessary to undergo the painful process of marital dissolution, thus leading them back to square one in the search for a desirable marital partner. Or perhaps a new romantic interest may stimulate a spouse to precipitate a divorce, even if the existing marriage is not that unsatisfactory. Even many of those whose marriages endure for decades will find that their lives are a complex mixture of joys and frustrations, with worries about the fate of the reltionship never completely absent. Living "happily ever after" still happens mostly in fairy tales.

But even when these things are said, they simply indicate that marriage is an imperfect institution. But most American couples enter marriage with fairly realistic expectations (see the discussion in Chapter 3), rather than with dreams drawn from fairy tales. There is no sign in the Detroit results that over time people are becoming more cavalier about marriage or that in recent times marital relationships have become less satisfying or more problem-prone. Even the undeniable increase in the divorce rate appears to be a sign of an often successful effort to find more satisfying marital partners, rather than reflecting casualness toward, or alienation from, marriage as an institution.

Some commentators have argued that, as role divisions between husbands and wives have become less sharp, as our commercialized society has increasingly made available goods and services that spouses used to provide, and as the intimacy revolution has made even sexual satisfaction increasingly available without resort to wedlock, marriage as an institution, with all of its faults and problems, has become less necessary and will begin to disappear from our social repertoire. While these observations about the development of alternatives to family-provided functions are generally accurate, still there is little evidence to support the conclusion that marriage is on the way out. Marriage is an imperfect institution but, to paraphrase Winston Churchill's characterization of democracy as a form of government, most Americans continue to feel that all of the alternatives are worse. With all of its problems and faults, marriage remains a very important and potentially satisfying institution, and the evidence presented in the current study points to this importance continuing into the future. Young people contemplating heading toward the altar cannot take much comfort in the idea that their dating experiences have assured them of marital success, but on the other hand the evidence from the Detroit survey suggests it should be worth the trip anyway.

Notes

1. This generalization is limited to similarities in average tendencies and trends in the studies compared. As noted throughout, and as will be summarized shortly, when it comes to findings dealing with the effect of certain predictors on dating and mating behavior, the results of the current

study are in many cases in sharp contrast to those drawn from earlier research. Contrasts of the latter type, however, can be interpreted in a variety of ways—such as indicating that linkages between social realms have changed due to the decline of conventions, for example—rather than providing doubt that findings from the Detroit survey have some general significance.

2. Some of the similarities noted here are with other cross-sectional surveys, but in some cases the current findings parallel research conducted using a longitudinal design. For example, the decline in marriage problems over the course of the marriage has been observed in longitudinal studies (e.g., Pineo 1961) as well as in a large number of cross-sectional studies. Nonetheless, further longitudinal research is needed to check many of the findings from the current study more systematically.

3. One exception to this general statement was discussed in Chapter 6. The current study did measure marital power somewhat differently than most previous studies, and so the measures used in that realm may be less affected by social background factors than conventional measures that stress the allocation of primary decision-making responsibility. I examined the possibility that changes over time in American society could help explain the disparity in findings compared to earlier studies by checking whether among older women in the sample who married prior to the 1960s the impact of social background factors was greater than for the sample as a whole, but in general this did not turn out to be the case (details not shown here).

4. To be sure, social hierarchies are still very much a part of life in America, even if their composition has changed. And some groups, such as blacks and Hispanics, are still substantially excluded from higher positions in America's social hierarchies. Also, I am not claiming that there are no conventions left and that people can behave in whatever way they like, without fear of public disapproval or worse. What is involved in this change is simply a matter of degree, or in other words a decline in conventions, but not their disappearance. For commentary along similar lines, see Veroff, Douvan, and Kulka (1971).

5. Of course, it is still not wise to ask questions about unimportant experiences and subjective states of mind for periods in the past covered by such a schedule.

6. Specifically, such measures are related to the age of first marriage. When I controlled for the age of marriage statistically, measures of the courting interval used in Chapter 7, as well as measures of the time between first date and first marriage and the length of the engagement were not significantly correlated with any of the three measures of marital outcomes used in this study (details not provided here).

7. One curious finding of the current study was that having had an elaborate wedding was associated with marital success. However, once other factors were taken into account (in the multiple regession analyses presented in Chapter 7), the effect of having had an elaborate wedding became statistically nonsignificant. Therefore I cannot recommend holding an elaborate and costly wedding as a proven tactic for guaranteeing marital success. My assumption is that other factors, such as the degree of personal traditionalism and conventionality, help to explain both the holding of elaborate weddings and stable and satisfying marriages.

8. This measure of romantic feelings was not correlated with any of the other measures of premarital experiences, used here except that women who were premaritally pregnant reported somewhat lower love levels than other women, and women who had elaborate weddings reported slightly higher levels. Those women who had spent a longer period of time in the dating stage, who had more dating partners, or even who had been sexually intimate prior to marriage did not report higher (or for that matter lower) levels of romantic feelings at marriage than did other women (details not shown here).

9. The third realm considered here, besides the length of the dating stage and the variety of dating partners, is sexual intimacy, and this factor does not lend itself to a nonlinear argument. You either are a virgin or you are not (and ditto for cohabitation, etc). However, one attempt to apply the "nonlinear" notion to sexual intimacy would be to propose that such intimacy with the eventual husband would promote marital success, while such intimacy with other men prior to marriage would hinder success. I noted in discussing Table 7.1 that a measure of having had other sexual partners prior to dating the eventual husband was not significantly related to marital success.

10. This examination involved forming categorical versions of these variables and examining contingency tables and associated statistics for signs of any nonlinear trends.

11. Even if they are available and willing to accept your return, your past fickleness may make them wary of proceeding all of the way to marriage with you.

12. The reality may not be so bleak as it seems, since increasing numbers of men, some of whom may be seen as quite desirable as potential spouses, re-enter the marriage market after divorce or widowhood. Keep in mind that, in spite of recent studies suggesting that women who wait too long may never be able to marry, it is "never too late." In the Detroit sample there was, as noted earlier, one woman who married for the first time at age 60, and another who made her first trip to the altar at age 50.

13. I have been speaking here in terms of women simply for convenience and because women were the respondents in the current study. To a considerable extent the same considerations apply to men trying to select a bride, although the still relatively strong norm that women should not marry younger men (while men are quite free to marry younger women) gives men more leeway to avoid feeling pressured about the dwindling availability of suitable women.

14. Using the current data, it is possible to examine whether women who had more extensive and intimate dating experiences were more closely matched to their husbands, in terms of social background, personal character traits, and family values, than were women who had less experience. In general there was little relationship between premarital experience variables and similarity between wife and husband in these realms, but where a relationship showed up it was consistently negative. For example, women who scored high on the Popularity Scale (measuring variety in dating partners) were significantly lower on class origin matching, on personal character trait similarity, and on shared family values than were women who scored low; women who spent a long time in the dating stage were less closely matched to their husbands in terms of education and the occupations of both fathers than were other women; and women who had cohabited were less likely to have married men from the same religion and ethnic origins as themselves and less likely to share the same family values with their husbands than were women who had not cohabited (details not shown here). It seems that there is a weak tendency for very extensive or intimate experience in the dating stage to produce marriages in which the couples are not very closely matched in backgrounds and personal characteristics, and if so this may indicate that those with the most extensive dating experiences are not the ones most likely to act on criteria of suitability. Note that we have found in the current study that similarity in social backgrounds is not very important for marital success, while similarity in personal character traits, values, and interests is quite important.

15. One direct effort to compare arranged with free choice marriages, in Japan in the 1950s, concluded that in the long run free choice marriages provided *greater* happiness and satisfaction than arranged marriages, and not less (see Blood 1967). Obviously, arranged marriage would not be a feasible system under American conditions, even if it could be shown that it would lead to greater compatibility between spouses.

16. Since many things besides personal compatibility influence mate selection and marital success, it would take much more sophistication than we currently have to develop tests such agencies could use that would reliably judge which couples would be well suited to one another. And even if we had such sophistication the problem of unpredictable changes in the future lives of one or both partners that affect their compatibility would not be solved.

17. This discussion leads to one final possible explanation of the finding of no clear relationship between dating experience and marital success. If both the marketplace learning scenario and this "distorted judgment" argument have some merit, and if roughly equal numbers of young people experience dating in these two contrasting ways, then the net result would be to produce essentially no relationship between dating experience and marital success.

18. The premarital experiences of men have also been altered, but not so dramatically, since in earlier decades of this century the barriers to premarital intimacy were less rigid for males.

19. I deal here mainly with issues involving marriage or conjugal relations, rather than with the

family as an entire unit. The survey contained very few items about childrearing and parent-child relations, and so I am unable to deal adequately with areas of optimism and concern other than in regard to the conjugal relationship.

20.   The evidence from this study indicates that marital success is in important ways affected by patterns that ought to be changeable, rather than that couples do successfully make major changes in these patterns. To examine more fully whether appropriate changes in such patterns do occur, and whether they have the predicted consequences for the quality and stability of marriages, would require a longitudinal study, rather than the present cross-sectional design.

Appendix 1

Research Methodology

In order to be able to evaluate the generalizations and conclusions reached in this study, it is important to know how the survey on which it is primarily based was conducted. Even though considerable detail about the survey has been presented in the previous chapters, I will attempt here to provide additional information and to cover technical points that I did not cover earlier. The discussion focuses on the sample used, the strategy employed in designing the questionnaire, and the analysis methods utilized in the current study.

The Sample

The survey which forms the primary basis for this study was carried out during the summer of 1984 as part of the Detroit Area Study survey research training program run by the Department of Sociology at the University of Michigan. The study utilized a probability sample survey of the greater Detroit metropolitan area, defined as composed of three counties: Wayne (which includes the city of Detroit), Oakland, and Macomb. These three counties had a combined population in 1980 of slightly over 4 million people. Technically, the target population for the study was designated as all noninstitutionalized ever-married women between the ages of 18 and 75 living in private dwelling units in those three counties. The age limits were adopted to avoid special features and problems of the very young and the very old—the atypicality in current times of women who marry before they are 18, and the potential difficulties of some women over 75 in recalling clearly the kinds of retrospective information that bulked large in our questionnaire. The sampling was conducted according to a stratified, multi-stage design. Stratification was carried out between the city and suburbs in order to try to insure that sample selections within Detroit city would correspond to the proportion Detroit represents of the total metropolitan area population, about 30%.[1] The procedure used was to select 100 census tracts at random in the tri-county area (with 30 selections drawn from Detroit city and 70 from the surrounding areas), and then to randomly select one block within each such tract.

Students enrolled in the Detroit Area Study training course then went and "block-listed" each of the selected blocks—in other words, they went into the city and suburbs and made a complete listing of all of the residential addresses found on the 100 selected blocks. Then systematic sampling methods were used to select the actual addresses to be included in the sample, using random starts in each instance. We utilized probability proportional to size procedures at each stage in order to compensate for variability in the size of tracts and blocks.

Our original goal was to produce 500 completed interviews. Preliminary estimates of vacancy rates, nonresponse rates, and eligibility rates (i.e., what proportion of selected households would have at least one ever-married woman between the ages of 18 and 75) were used to estimate that we would need to select 887 addresses in order to obtain our final 500 interviews, and this meant selecting about 9 addresses on each block included in the sample. However, while our actual response rate (74%) was slightly better than our preliminary estimate, it turned out that there was a higher proportion of noneligible households than we had expected. Overall, we discovered that about 26% of the households selected did not have any ever-married women between the ages of 18 and 75, and this was particularly true of the sample selections within Detroit proper, where 41% of the selected households had no eligible respondent. As indicated earlier in this study, this level of noneligibility reflects in substantial measure a dramatic rise over the last two decades or so in the proportion of poor black women who never marry. But the result of this phenomenon was that we ended up with only 459 completed interviews in spite of a fairly good response rate, and that we have somewhat fewer cases of black women in the sample than is desirable for any sort of extensive analysis of racial differences or variations within each race—only 75 black respondents, or only a little over 16% of the total.

However, it cannot be said that blacks or poor inner-city residents in general are underrepresented in our sample, since a comparison of the response rates across strata showed no evidence of a systematic bias that would produce such underrepresentation. Even though in general survey response rates tend to be lower in poor urban locales and among minority group populations, in the current study the Detroit city response rate was actually slightly higher—76%—than it was for the surrounding suburbs (where the figure was 73%).[2]

The interviewing was conducted over the summer of 1984, and primarily in May and June. The initial interviews, constituting 51% of the total, were conducted by graduate students and staff participating in the Detroit Area Study training program. All of those involved had participated in two rounds of pretests of preliminary versions of the questionnaire—the first in Ann Arbor—and the second in nonsample neighborhoods in the Detroit area. In addition, interviewers had engaged in extensive practice sessions, including the use of videotape recordings of practice interviews and group critiques of interviewing performance. Of course, we also had students read extensively in the literature on interviewing methods, particularly about common errors committed during survey interviews and how to avoid them. During the interviewing stage students and staff moved into dormitory rooms at a small college in the Detroit area and went out in cars from that field headquarters to conduct interviews.

Letters had been sent to each address selected in the sample, informing the residents of the general purpose of our survey and requesting their cooperation. Then interviewers simply went to the door of the selected addresses on their daily assignment sheets. Interviewers had photo-identification badges, extra copies of the letter to respondents, and the other sorts of standard equipment used by survey interviewers in order to demonstrate their bona fides. If someone answered the door, the interviewer tried to first get a listing of all members of the household, along with the ages and marital statuses of each, in order to determine whether the household included an eligible person.[3] If the household did not contain an eligible respondent, the interviewer was instructed to say thank you and leave. In those few instances where more than one eligible woman lived at a selected address, the cover sheet of the questionnaire contained a set of random number options to determine which person should be interviewed.

Once it was determined who the eligible person was, the interviewer tried to arrange an interview on the spot with that person (if she was at home) or to make an appointment to come back and conduct the interview later. If nobody was at home, or if those at home did not include the woman selected, the interviewer or somebody else would come back again later to try to arrange an interview. Usually we kept trying through at least 4–5 visits to a selected address, and the record for the study was 3 respondents who were successfully interviewed on the 17th call!

If the selected person initially declined to be interviewed, we generally sent one of several kinds of "persuasion" letters and then sent the same or a different interviewer back to try again. In this fashion 43 of the women in our sample were "conversions" from initial refusals. Interviewers were also instructed to check the adjacent addresses on their neighborhood listing, and if they discovered a residence next door that had been missed during block-listing, they were to add that address and try to interview there as well. (This procedure, termed the use of a "half-open sampling interval," helps to preserve the rigor of the sample by avoiding instances of addresses with no possibility of being selected for the sample.) Members of the DAS staff made spot checks to verify that completed interviews had, in fact, been carried out, rather than "fudged" by lazy interviewers. (Interviewers were, of course, informed in advance about this spot check procedure.)

When the student interviewing period concluded in May, the remaining sample selections were turned over to professional interviewers who work for the Survey Research Center (SRC) of the Institute for Social Research at the University of Michigan. Most of these interviewers are middle-aged women who live in the Detroit area and who work part time on a whole series of survey studies run by the SRC. Their participation has become a standard feature of the Detroit Area Study, since the student manpower is not sufficient to conduct enough interviews for a full study. (Twenty-four students participated in the interviews, and as it happens, the same number of SRC professional interviewers took part.) Prior to their participation, the SRC interviewers attended intensive briefing sessions in which the purposes of the study and the intent of each item in the questionnaire were discussed in detail. Then during the rest of the summer the remaining 49% of the respondents were interviewed by SRC interviewers.

The coding, data entry, and cleaning of the data were carried out during that same summer by student assistants hired by DAS, under the supervision of the DAS directors. By the fall of 1984 the data were ready for analysis, and in the final part of the DAS training sequence, these data were analyzed by students to prepare research reports on some special topic covered by the survey. As noted earlier in the text of this study, a number of the student papers provided interesting ideas and analyses that stimulated my own further thinking on the issues covered. Although I served as Faculty Investigator for the survey, it should be clearly acknowledged that the Co-Directors of the DAS in 1984, Jean Converse and Stanley Presser, as well as the enrolled students and SRC interviewers, played crucial roles in seeing that my initial vague ideas for this study got successfully translated into the survey reported on here.

The Characteristics of Respondents

The marital status, marital history, and current work status of the women we interviewed have been discussed earlier, notably in Chapter 6. However, a few other basic facts about the sample composition deserve notice here. The sample was 82.8% white and 16.3% black, with the remaining 0.9% belonging to other racial groups.[4] Most respondents were raised as Protestants (54.2%) or Catholics (39.2%), with an additional 2% who were Jewish and 4.6% raised in other religions (including "none"). Almost half of our respondents (46.4%) were high school graduates, 17.4% had not finished high school, and another 36.2% had had some further education after high school graduation. In terms of subjective class origins, 8.5% of our respondents felt that they had grown up in a poor family, 46.4% in the working class, 34.4% in the middle class, 9.8% in the upper-middle class, and only four individuals (0.9%) in an upper class household. In all 5% of our respondents had grown up at least partly outside of the U.S., 28% had grown up within the U.S. but at least partly outside of Michigan, and the remaining 67% had grown up solely in Michigan. In all 40.7% had grown up in a large city (not necessarily Detroit), 24.6% in the suburbs of a large city, and the remaining 34.6% in a smaller city or town or a rural area. (In all 67.8% of the respondents were married in the greater Detroit area, and most of those have lived continuously in the area since the time of their marriages.)

Finally, 67.8% had attended solely public schools, 12.4% solely private or parochial schools, and the remaining 19.8% had attended some combination of private and public schools. In general, then, we had a fairly diverse sample that displays characteristics that we would expect to find in an area such as greater Detroit, a population that is not only representative but provides ample variation to allow me to examine the impact of race, religion, education, and other background characteristics on the process of mate choice and marital relationships.

The Questionnaire

There are many research approaches that can be used to study family life, and the choice of a conventional sample survey, questionnaire method in the current study involved some trade-offs. The dilemma I faced was whether to study a small number of marriages intensively or a large number more superficially. Either option has both advantages and drawbacks. In my past research on family organization and marriage in the People's Republic of China, I have relied on a different methodology than the one used here, one employing intensive interviewing, often covering more than a dozen hours of interviews with each person (see Parish and Whyte 1978; Whyte and Parish 1984). In general, if you want to understand in-depth the nature and dynamics of any particular marriage relationship, you should utilize some method of that sort, rather than a questionnaire that can be completed in roughly one hour. You could interview both partners in considerable depth, and if possible even arrange to observe their daily life for an extended period of time. Out of such observations and interviews you could construct a rich and complex portrait of the marriage relationship of a particular couple, an account filled with anecdotes and colorful examples. With any skill this would be an account which would be interesting to read and would give a vivid sense of who the people interviewed are and how satisfying or problem-prone is their marriage.[5]

With these advantages of "qualitative methods" as the alternative, what you can produce via a questionnaire study such as the current one may seem quite unsatisfying. You interview each respondent only briefly (generally, as noted earlier, for an hour or less), and you don't get to know her in any depth. For the most part she responds to fixed, multiple-choice questions, rather than framing things in her own words. Even when she is asked, in what are called "open-ended" questions, to respond in her own words, usually the goal of the researcher is to categorize those responses into a set of numerical "codes" so that they will be pliable to the machinations of the computer. The final products of those machinations are statistics and tables, rather than personal anecdotes and vivid examples.[6] The individual respondent for the most part disappears into larger percentages, correlations, and other statistics. It is much more difficult for an author to write about tables and statistics in an interesting manner than it is to write about people, and as a consequence, studies that use "quantitative methods," as the present one does, are often not very interesting to read.

Given what has been said here about the alternatives involved, why did the current study utilize a quantitative, questionnaire approach? The major reason is that I was not interested in understanding a particular marriage or marriages, but in understanding changing mate choice and marriage behavior in American society generally. Therefore, for this purpose the advantages of a questionnaire study became apparent, while the disadvantages of qualitative research became crippling.

The main drawback of in-depth, qualitative methods is that they are very time consuming, and so you cannot use them to study a large number of cases unless you have a great deal of time, money, energy, and patience. Relatedly, since these methods require extensive cooperation from the interviewees and perhaps considerable intrusion into their daily lives and privacy, it is very difficult to conduct such qualitative research with any sort of a representative sample of the population, since those who would be willing to submit to such scrutiny are not likely to be typical.[7]

If you interview a small number of people or couples who are not selected according to any strict sampling procedures, then it is always possible to ask whether the research findings you arrive at are due to the peculiarities of those particular individuals or marriages, so that the findings for any larger population might be quite different. With a large-scale questionnaire study of a scientifically selected sample, in contrast, you may not know a whole lot about any particular individual interviewed, but you can say some quite precise things about general patterns and trends and what they tell us about the experiences of the larger population from which the sample is drawn. Since you are not taxing unduly the patience of any particular interviewee (or, for that matter, interviewer), you can study a larger and more representative number of people than you could using a qualitative approach and the same resources.

Since my primary goal, as already mentioned, was to examine general trends in dating and mating in America, I opted to carry out this research using conventional questionnaire methods. I did so knowing that this decision would deprive me of the sorts of colorful anecdotal material that would result from an in-depth study of a few marriages, and that because of this fact I would have a more difficult time presenting my results in an interesting manner. I have tried to cope with the difficulties of presenting statistical results in a readable way by endeavoring not to overly burden the reader with tables and statistics, and by keeping my sights fixed on underlying major issues surrounding changes in American marriage. Because of this attempt, I have not tried to scrutinize every single correlation and coefficient in the tables I have presented, and often I have left the detailed tables containing less essential results out of this report entirely; hence the many instances in which phrases such as "detailed results not shown here" appear in the pages of this study.[8] Where possible I have converted statistical tables into charts.

Still, I have not always been able to convert the statistical "sows ears" contained in my reams of computer output into a "silk purse" of colorful prose. On this point I ask the reader's indulgence. If the reader can appreciate the reasons why I opted for a sample survey, questionnaire approach, then he or she will recognize that the power of this approach allows me to address very basic and important questions about marriage in America, many of which have never been addressed. Hopefully the inherent interest in what is happening to this very basic institution will to some extent compensate for the lack of color that reporting quantitative results entails.

With my choice of methods explained, I want to proceed to describe how the actual questionnaire used in the Detroit survey came into being. The questionnaire utilized in this survey was developed and refined through a long and complex process, as is normal in survey research. Initially I constructed a detailed "laundry list" of draft questions dealing with mate choice and marriage, drawing on both those original ideas that motivated this study in the first place (as discussed in Chapter 1) and my scrutiny of the available literature on these topics. Since my primary concern was with mate choice and marriage *behavior*, rather than with attitudes and values in regard to family life, the bulk of the draft questions were aimed at getting reports of actual experiences. Furthermore, since many of my interests concerned earlier experiences, particularly in regard to the dating stage, a good share of these questions were retrospective in nature. In such cases, I generally tried to use advice drawn from the literature on the "recall problem" (see, for example, Moss and Goldstein 1979). The most important advice drawn from this literature is to design retrospective questions that are as concrete as possible and which inquire about relatively simple and memorable experiences from the past. Thus, for example, it is more feasible to ask about where the wedding ceremony was held than to inquire about how much was spent on the wedding or the feelings a respondent felt as she planned the event. (Certain other guidelines are fairly obvious. For example, it only makes sense to ask respondents about experiences that they would definitely be in a position to recall—how old they were when they began dating, for instance, but not how old their husbands were when they began dating.) The questionnaire was also constructed to cover past experiences in a roughly chronological order, in order to further minimize recall problems.

My general reading of past work on the "recall problem" indicates to me that properly framed questions about memorable experiences in the past can yield fairly accurate information (see the discussion in Dawson, Meny and Ridley 1980.) Nevertheless, the reader will have noted my effort in the preceding chapters to consider possible sources of bias attributable to the problems of recall. My general assumption is that for most of the kinds of past behavior of concern here, the problems of memory distortion will heighten the further back the event or experience being recalled is, but that the effect will be a reduction in precision in a fairly random fashion, rather than a systematic bias. If this assumption is correct, then measures of average tendencies and trends over time (for example, those reported in Chapters 2 and 3) should still be unbiased, even though any particular response may not be precisely accurate. For example, in regard to a question that perhaps places excessive demands on the recall ability of respondents, a call for them to estimate how many men they ever dated, I expect that some women will recall with overestimates and some with underestimates (compared to how many males they *really* ever dated). If so then estimates of the average number of men dated for the sample should still be relatively unbiased. And lacking any reason for assuming that the tendency to overestimate vs. underestimate differs depending upon the length of time that has elapsed, the sorts of trend figures on the number of dates presented in Chapter 2 should also be relatively unbiased.

Concern for both the social origins of dating and mating behavior and for assortative mating, combined with the fact that we were only able to interview wives and not their husbands (or former husbands) as well (for the reasons discussed in Chapter 1), meant that I had to rely on respondents to supply fairly detailed background information on lots of individuals—not only about themselves, but about their parents, their first husbands at the time of the marriage, their current husbands, and even about other "serious prospects" whom they did not marry. Again this is not an ideal procedure, since some error and perhaps bias may occur with such indirect reports about the characteristics of others.[9] But in this case similar advice to that concerning the recall problem is offered in the literature on such indirect reports (see, in particular, Niemi 1974). An effort was made to include only basic and clearly discernable background information that respondents could be expected to remember.[10] Then an effort was made to disperse these background questions in a number of different places in the questionnaire, in order to minimize the boredom involved in answering the same series of questions about so many people.[11] As with the recall issue, I would argue that even when inaccuracies creep into reports about the background characteristics of others, these should generally occur randomly, thus producing increased reporting error but not systematic bias. So, for example, some respondents may err by reporting that their first husband was younger at marriage than he actually was, and some may err by reporting him older than he was, but still such figures from the entire sample should yield unbiased estimates that allow me to estimate the average age of husbands at marriage and how that has changed over time (with, to be sure, some margin for error).

Through both a series of questionnaire meetings attended by myself, the DAS co-directors, and selected teaching assistants and graduate students taking part in the study, as well as through the two rounds of pretesting of draft versions of the questionnaire, the initial question list moved gradually and laboriously toward the final version. Some questions were junked entirely; others were rewritten, often multiple times; and the order of questions was repeatedly redesigned, with "skip patterns" painstakingly worked out to cover all possible life situations (for example, a woman orphaned or raised by foster parents; a woman separated but not divorced from her husband, etc.). A selection of the items that appeared in the final questionnaire is displayed in Appendix 2, along with information about recodings and index construction, and questions are displayed there in the order in which they were actually asked. However, questions that have not entered into the analysis for this book are not listed there, nor are such things as skip directions and interviewer instructions. Those interested in examining a copy of the full questionnaire may write to the author for a copy.

Most of the questionnaire consisted of closed- or open-ended questions that interviewers read out to respondents directly in a face-to-face manner. However, in four separate places during the session the interviewers handed respondents short self-administered forms and pencils and instructed them to make check-marks on these forms and place them in a special envelope before proceeding further with the interview. In two instances this procedure was followed to minimize potential embarrassment as well as to maximize privacy in case other onlookers were nearby. These involved our series of questions on spouse abuse (see questions L1–L5 in Appendix 2) and a set of questions about the age at which the woman first had various experiences, including sexual intercourse (see questions T1–T6 in Appendix 2). The other instances of using written check-lists were motivated simply by a desire to conserve time and avoid boredom; these were the series of items in which respondents first described their own personal traits and then those of their husbands (see questions N1-A-J and N2-A-J in Appendix 2). The envelope was used so that respondents would feel that the interviewer was not going to scrutinize their answers immediately. This was another minor device to try to put respondents at ease in regard to questions that were potentially sensitive.

Once the final version of the questionnaire had been prepared and printed, we also developed standard materials to assist interviewers. Each interviewer was equipped with a response booklet that was shown to respondents whenever there was a particularly detailed or complex set of closed-ended responses to select among, and instructions in the questionnaire were used by interviewers to tell respondents when to flip back and forth in the response booklet to the appropriate spot. We also prepared a "Q-by-Q" (question by question) booklet, which contained on the left side of each page a copy of a single questionnaire page, and on the right side a set of explanations, clarifications, suggested prompts, and warnings about problems to avoid with that particular set of questions. The Q-by-Q booklet was studied by interviewers prior to the interviewer training sessions in the hope that the detailed explanations and suggestions would be learned by heart. However, interviewers were also instructed to carry the Q-by-Q booklet along with them while interviewing in case they needed help in resolving problems that arose during an interview.

At the end of each interview session, interviewers were instructed to fill out a number of pieces of information about the respondent and the interview that appeared at the end of the questionnaire. They were also instructed to write a brief "thumb-nail" sketch about the respondent and to edit the entire question-naire, filling in notations made in haste during the interview, with all of this to occur prior to going on to another interview or returning to the research base. In general from the editorial comments made on questionnaires and from talking to interviewers it appeared that the care taken in the earlier stages of questionnaire design had served its purpose. There were no serious or recurring problems with such things as respondents not understanding particular questions, refusing to answer, or being asked the wrong question due to a faulty skip pattern or inter-viewer inattentiveness.[12] So in general the "field season" went quite smoothly and provided confidence that the data collected would be useful.

Data Analysis

For the most part the techniques used to analyze the data collected from the survey and to report the results are quite conventional. After the data had been coded, entered in the computer, and "cleaned" (i.e., put through an error correc-tion process, based upon the results of consistency checks), the detailed statis-tical analysis began. In many if not most cases the detailed categories that resulted from either the closed-ended questions or from the coding of open-ended questions had to be combined and reorganized prior to performing any mean-ingful analysis. Often this recoding involved deleting "don't know" and "other" responses, combining categories with small numbers of responses, and reorder-ing categories. Where possible the reordering was done in an effort to make most variables ordinal in nature, which means so that the categories would follow a consistent order. (So, for example, a question about the respondent's sibling order that originally contained the response categories 1 = oldest, 2 = youngest, and 3 = other was recoded into 1 = oldest, 2 = other, 3 = youngest.) This effort to form ordinal variables was stressed because in some instances I wanted to look at a large number of associations using correlation matrices, and the correlation statistic is not meaningful unless the variables are at least ordinal in form.[13]

In some cases the making of ordinal versions of variables involved special complexities. The occupation questions used in this study were asked in an open ended way, and then coded into nine basic categories: higher level professional and technical, intermediate and lower level professional and technical, managers and administrators, clerical, sales, craftsmen and other skilled workers, oper-atives and other semiskilled workers, laborers and other unskilled workers, and service workers. (Farm workers or managers, those in the military, housewives, and other miscellaneous categories were eliminated for statistical analysis.) De-tailed lists of subcategories and special training were used to assist coders in carrying out the complex classification of occupations. But it was not obvious how these nine categories should be rearranged or combined to make an ordinal version of the occupational variable. In this instance I examined average characteristics of these nine occupational groups, in terms of such traits as educational attainment and income, in order to use the criterion of similarity in status levels to guide my combining and recoding. The result is the various combined versions of occupational codes shown in Appendix 2. Other related problems involved the effort to group national origin categories by relative prestige and to group religious denominations into fundamentalist vs. nonfundamentalist camps. In such cases I used past research on these topics (see, for example, Peach 1980 on the former topic) to guide my recoding process.

In many instances the actual measures I used in my analysis were not single variables, but scales. Most of the scales used in this study were constructed in a uniform manner, as noted in earlier portions of this study. I would take all available ordinal versions of measures that seemed to relate to the general phenomenon I was trying to capture and examine the matrix of their intercorrelations (using pairwise deletion to handle missing cases). By visual inspection I would extract from the matrix those items that had the strongest and most consistent mutual intercorrelations.[14] Then I would construct a scale from those items by computing first a standardized (or "Z score") version of each measure and then computing the mean of these standardized scores (with missing data handled by deleting cases for which half or fewer of the constituent items had values present).

However, in a few instances other scale construction methods were used. For matters like the number of marital conflicts or spouse abuse, I simply totalled the constituent items (with each coded 0 = absent, 1 = present) to form an overall severity scale. For the chore division scale each constituent item had the same form (running from 1 = wife always doing a chore to 5 = husband always), and so I simply averaged the unstandardized scores across these chores. In the marital power scale I had to multiply similar 1 to 5 responses about who usually wins out in the event of a disagreement in various realms by a 3 point measure of how often each such disagreement occurred (with 1 = no disagreements, 2 = minor disagreements, 3 = serious disagreements). In general, Appendix 2 includes basic details about each scale and the procedure by which it was created.

Once the measures were recoded in this fashion and the scales were created, the statistical analysis proceeded in a straight-forward manner. Descriptive statistics such as those reported in Chapter 2, 3, 5 and 6 were derived from computing means, frequency counts, and cross-tabulations. Most examination of the associations among variables, such as those reported in Chapter 4, 7, and 8, was conducted using correlation and multiple regression analysis. In a few places more esoteric techniques were called for; for example, the log-linear analysis used to examine trends in marital homogamy in Chapter 5 and the logistic regression used in Chapter 7 in examining predictors of divorce (since the outcome variable, divorce, is dichotomous rather than continuous). The primary complications involved in performing these analyses involved not the techniques themselves, which are quite conventional, but the selection of cases within the sample to be used in any particular analysis. Since the measures used in this study involve both past behavior and current or recent traits, and since respondents varied in their life circumstances and past marital histories, (for example, between those who married only once vs. more than once or between those currently married and not married), complex decisions had to be made about which portions of the sample to use for each analysis, in order to avoid biasing the results by including inappropriate cases. I have tried to indicate in the text or table notes what selection rules were used in each instance, as well as to indicate when an issue of potential bias can be raised because of the selection rules chosen. But insofar as I have made the appropriate selection decisions, the analysis itself proceeded in a fairly predictable and conventional manner.

Bias Problems

A variety of procedures have been developed in response to a concern about potential biases that might distort the results of survey research. As indicated earlier, the most worrisome part of the analysis of survey data is not that errors will creep into some responses, but that these will accumulate in such a way that they will lead to systematic biases and wrong conclusions. If errors occur randomly one may miss the existence of certain weak or subtle phenomenon, since the effect of random errors is to create "noise" and weaken the statistical coefficients that are used to detect such phenomena. But such random errors will not lead one to launch erroneous claims the way that biased results would. The most serious concern is with minimizing or reducing any systematic biases that might lead to misleading claims.

One can deal with the problem of systematic bias in two ways. One can try to minimize the occurrence of biases through sampling, questionnaire design, interviewing, and other techniques in an effort to produce relatively "bias-free" data to analyze. Or, assuming that no data can be totally bias-free, one can try to detect and measure the seriousness of the biases that exist in the data so that one can take them into account in the analysis (e.g., through discounting certain findings or controlling for the biasing elements statistically). Both in earlier sections of this appendix as well as in the chapters of this study I have devoted repeated attention to describing the pre-emptive efforts we made to minimize the biases that would affect the data from this study. The reader is encouraged to judge for him- or herself, but I am confident enough of the care taken in these matters, and encouraged by the general correspondence between the findings of this study and those of earlier studies that permit a clear comparison (e.g., on such matters as trends in marriage ages and premarital sexual experiences or in regard to how married couples first met) to feel some general confidence that the results of the present analysis are not seriously biased.

One particular issue that I want to address here is the charge raised in some other studies (see particularly Hite 1987) that questionnaire methods are inherently inappropriate for the study of marriages and thus likely to produce biased results. Hite implies, for example, that with the sort of anonymous, open-ended mail-in question outline that she used, people will reveal their true feelings in depth, but that in the sort of mostly multiple-choice, face-to-face interviews used in the Detroit survey, people will give superficial and overly upbeat responses. For example, they may be reluctant to reveal their resentments and hostilities toward their husbands to a strange interviewer who enters their lives for only an hour or so. Or they may be embarrassed to admit that their husbands abuse them or give them only a pittance to spend, and so they will claim that their husbands never so much as say an angry word toward them and that they have considerable say in family finances.

I would agree, as I indicated in my earlier discussion, that some sort of in-depth, qualitative method can produce more richness and texture in describing any particular individual or marriage than can be produced through a one hour, fixed format questionnaire. But what is at issue in this critique is not the depth and richness of the information provided, but whether a questionnaire study will tend to produce a biased picture of the marriages studied, a picture that is overly positive compared to reality.

I will be describing shortly some specific internal checks that were made in this study to check for the existence of such a positive bias, but first let me reiterate some of the general precautions that were taken to try to get respondents to answer objectively and frankly. To begin with, respondents were assured of anonymity, both in contacts before the interview and at the start of the interview session itself, and the spread of survey and public opinion polling in our society makes it credible to most Americans that they do not have to worry about the confidentiality of their replies being violated.[15] In addition, questions were carefully designed to avoid being "leading" (or "loaded") and to make sure that a full range of responses, both positive and negative, was available to each respondent. (See the examples of questions and response categories in Appendix 2.) I have also noted that our interviewers underwent special, intensive training sessions designed primarily to help them obtain objective responses and avoid biases, and that we used special, self-administered forms for part of the questions in order to minimize embarrassment and maximize frankness of responses. In sum, a whole variety of techniques were used to try to prevent biases from being built into our results, and many of those precautions are not utilized in qualitative studies of the same topics.[16] Perhaps the final piece of evidence against the "superficial and biased" criticism of questionnaire studies of marital life is that respondents do not, in fact, produce entirely positive accounts of their lives and marriages. Premarital pregnancies, spouse abuse, marital conflicts, and other potentially embarrassing phenomena are reported with considerable frequency, even if they are not the dominant experience of the women we interviewed. In sum, I would argue that even though the sort of questionnaire study used here

cannot yield great depth and understanding about any particular marriage studied, there is no reason to reject this research method in advance as inherently
biased and therefore unsuitable.

In spite of my general confidence in the quality of the survey reported on here,
I still carried out the second sort of bias checking procedure on a limited scale,
and I want to discuss the results of two specific tests of bias undertaken. One
general concern I had was with the bias that might have been introduced by the
fact that we did not interview 26% of the women selected for the sample (since
the response rate was 74%). If a large portion of the women who were not
interviewed had particularly unhappy lives and marriages or simply embarrassing
experiences in their personal histories, and if these features influenced them to
avoid being interviewed, then basing conclusions on the remaining 74% of the
sample might produce a misleadingly "rosy" view of American marriage relations. Since I do end up in this study with a fairly upbeat view of marital
relationships, particularly in Chapters 6 and 9, I thought it was important to
examine whether part of this positive view could be attributed to response rate
bias, to the fact that women with better marriages might have been more willing
to consent to be interviewed.[17]

One cannot, of course, know how the people who were not interviewed would
have responded to various questions we asked, and so it is impossible to perform
a fully satisfactory test of this sort of response rate bias. However, an indirect or
partial test is possible. We kept records on both whether women who were
eventually interviewed refused when they were first contacted, and on how many
calls were made before an interview was successfully completed. If I can assume
that respondents who showed reluctance to be interviewed (through initial refusals or the necessity to be contacted many times) are somewhat similar to our
26% who were nonrespondents, then by comparing the responses of these "reluctants" with the rest of the sample I should be able to figure out whether this
response rate bias exists and affects these data. To perform this test I selected 15
measures which I assumed might be especially sensitive to this sort of bias.[18]
When I correlated these 15 measures with the items measuring the response to the
initial interview contact (1 = agreement, 2 = refusal) and with the number of
calls made (ranging from 1 to 17), I discovered no consistent pattern in the
correlations, and only 1 correlation among the 30 examined that surpassed the
conventional $p = .05$ statistical significance level, less than you would expect to
find on the basis of chance alone (details not shown here). It would appear that I
can safely discount the possibility that women who did not respond to our
interview requests would have given a more gloomy picture of marital relations
or of their own past personal histories (accepting my assumption about the
"reluctants" being intermediate between "willing respondents" and "refusals").[19]

Finally, I examined one other potential bias source. Ideally each interview
should have been conducted in private, with no other family members, friends,

or neighbors around. Our interviewers were instructed to try to achieve this sort of privacy, but since they were only guests in the homes of the women they were interviewing and were not in ultimate control of the situation, it was not always possible to achieve this ideal situation. I was concerned about the potential bias introduced by having someone else listening in to at least part of the interview. I assumed that if a husband was listening, and perhaps even if a child, a relative, a neighbor, or a friend were in the room, a respondent might again give a biased and overly "rosy" set of responses to questions about marital relations and personal history.

To check this source of bias I performed a similar test. Our interview forms contained check-lists to be completed by interviewers to describe whether the husband, any children, or any "others" were around during any part of the interviews, and they were also asked to check whether they thought that the presence of each type of person might have influenced the answers of the respondent. This information allowed me to construct three separate measures of the intrusion of onlookers into the interview process, for husbands, children, and for "others" (e.g., relatives, neighbors, friends). Each measure was coded 1 = not present, 2 = present but no apparent effect, and 3 = present and at least some effect. In parallel to the previous test, I examined correlations between these three measures and my 15 "sensitive" measures of marital relations and personal experiences.

In this case some consistent patterns turned up, but they were not the ones I predicted. The feature I was most worried about, the presence of husbands during interviews, turned out not to have any clear effect on responses to these items one way or the other (details not shown here).[20] However, the presence of children appeared to have some effect, and the presence of "others" an even more consistent effect. The nature of this effect, though, did not involve women who responded in the presence of others giving more positive or socially acceptable responses. In fact, the opposite was more nearly the case. To be specific, respondents who scored high on the 3 point measure of presence of children during the interview were likely to report somewhat *more* marital problems ($r = .13$) and somewhat more conflicts with their husbands (also $r = .13$), although on the other hand they also reported more satisfaction with the division of household chores (again $r = .13$). The other 12 items examined did not have strong or consistent correlations with the child presence measure, and it is at least possible that the correlations detected—essentially more conflicts with the spouse but also more help by him with chores—are more characteristic of those women who have children at home to be present during the interview than of women who do not. If this is the case, these correlations would indicate the impact of children on marital relations, rather than the biasing effect on the interview of having children present.[21]

The broadest set of correlations detected occurred with the measure of whether there were any others present during at least part of the interview, rather than either husbands or children. Again the nature of the effects detected was not what I had expected. Respondents who scored high on the presence of others measure showed modest tendencies to report lower quality marriages ($r = -.13$), more marital problems ($r = .16$), more marital worries ($r = .13$), more spouse abuse ($r = .12$), more severe marital conflicts ($r = .17$), more having had premarital sex ($r = .10$), and more who had cohabited prior to marriage ($r = .12$). But such respondents were more likely to say that they were satisfied with the division of chores and their amount of "say" in their marriages (both $r = .12$). The pattern is not completely consistent or easy to interpret, but on balance there is a modest indication here that the presence of others during the interview is associated with more *negative* reports about marital relations and with more precocious and potentially embarrassing early sexual experiences. So rather than being an inhibiting factor, the presence of others seems to involve an effect of "egging on" or perhaps providing a "sounding board" for gripes. Perhaps the presence of others emboldens respondents to say things they would otherwise be reluctant to describe to our "stranger" interviewers. Still, this explanation of the effect of others present is only minimally plausible at best, and since there is no way now to separate out the subcategories contained among the others—into relatives, friends, neighbors, other people's children, etc.—it is difficult to go any further in trying to explain this puzzling effect.

It turns out that such others were present in only 30 interviews out of the total of 459, and that in only 5 cases did our interviewers think that the presence of others had some impact on respondents. Still, the pattern observed seems consistent enough to be the source of some concern. This one form of possible bias might indicate that on balance I have not drawn a sufficiently positive overall picture of American marriage relations, rather than that I have been led to an overly rosy view.[22] I proceeded further to examine the potential impact of this source of bias in the data. First I checked to see whether there were some background characteristics, such as race, education, or ethnicity, that might be related to both a likelihood of having others present during the interview and to the picture of marital relations and past sexual experiences revealed during this bias test. It turned out that some background characteristics were related to a likelihood of having others present during the interview, but even partialling these out did not reduce the effect of the presence of others on our bias detection measures (details not shown here). Since I could not dismiss this apparent bias as spurious and attributable to the influence of some background characteristics, I then examined whether if I replicated the statistical analyses reported in Chapter 6 and 7, but using only those cases in which no others were present during the interview, I would get similar or different results to those reported earlier. In general the results of these replications were not substantially different from those reported earlier (again, details are not shown here). Since the bias detected is not very strong, and since the number of cases deleted is rather small, it is not entirely surprising to find that the impact of this bias (measured by eliminating the potentially biased cases) on the general findings of this study is very minor.

These final bias checks reinforce my confidence that the results of the Detroit Area Study survey can be treated seriously, even though in some cases the specific findings of the study are at variance with a number of earlier works on the same topics. Hopefully the reader now has sufficient information to decide whether he/she is willing to accept this conclusion.

Notes

1.   However, in the final sample cases from Detroit represent less than 30% of the total because of the higher proportion of eligibility problems found in the Detroit selections. See the discussion on this point below.

2.   About 5.5% of the original sample selections were determined to be outside of the sampling targets (whether through vacancies, sampling errors, or whatever), and refusals constituted about 22.9% and responses 74% of the remainder, with the remaining 3.1% composed of "other" circumstances (no competent informant, evasions, health problems, etc.)

3.   In some cases even when nobody was home on repeated visits a neighbor might be used to get information about whether or not the selected household had an eligible respondent.

4.   These figures may make it appear that blacks ended up underrepresented in our sample, since in the tri-county Detroit metropolitan area blacks constitute about 22% of the total population, rather than 16.3%. However, as mentioned earlier, our sampling target specification was ever-married women between the ages of 20 and 75 in the greater Detroit area, and not the total female or adult female population. I do not have figures on what proportion of the total of ever-married women in the area are black, but it seems plausible that the low percentage of blacks in the sample is due overwhelmingly to the elibility problems mentioned earlier—to the fact that many black households contained no ever-married women at all—rather than to underrepresentation of blacks who do reside in the area. (The fact already commented upon, that the response rate for Detroit city itself, the area in which blacks are especially concentrated, was higher than for the suburbs, increases my confidence that this is not an underrepresentation problem.)

5.   There are many examples of the use of this sort of qualitative, in-depth technique to study American family life (see, for example, Stack 1974; Rubin 1976). Such research is not confined to the study of a single marriage. It can be used to study a few or even a few dozen marriages or families. Even with prolonged observation and very intensive interviews, of course, one can question whether an outsider will ever be able to capture all of the complexity of any marriage relationship.

6.   Sometimes one can utilize material from open-ended questions, or from marginal comments the interviewer recorded during the interview, to yield anecdotes to accompany a questionnaire-based research report. However, most such studies are fairly "thin" when it comes to conveying personal examples to illustrate the underlying statistics, and the present study is no exception to this rule.

7.   One example of research using such in-depth methods is the famous Kinsey surveys of sexual behavior in America, and this example illustrates the problems mentioned here. The research involved in Kinsey studies required a prodigious amount of time and effort over more than a decade, and to this day a major question about those surveys is whether, in view of the somewhat haphazard nature of the methods used to obtain interviews, the results can be regarded as accurately representing the experience of the American population in general (see Kinsey et al. 1948; 1953).

8.   In such cases I would be glad to send interested readers the detailed results that have been omitted here.

9. Note that respondents generally were asked to report about the social background charac-teristics of these other individuals, and not about their experiences and behavior, although this rule was relaxed somewhat in regard to the current husband.

10. However, in some cases we over-estimated how much they could be expected to know. Some respondents, for example, could not tell us how many years of education each of their parents had. To be specific, about 6% did not know their mother's educational attainment and almost 10% did not know their father's, and another 5–8% in each case simply made guesses.

11. Concern about boredom also led us to cut out some of the background questions I had included on my original laundry list, such as inquiries about political party preferences of each individual.

12. To check further on how well the interviews went and how clearly respondents understood our questions, we utilized a "random probe" procedure in selected parts of the questionnaire (see Schuman 1966). This involved following up a closed-ended question with an open ended question asking what the respondent understood the question to mean and meant by her answer. I have not done any systematic analysis of the results of these random probes, but in general the responses indicate that in most cases the questions were working as intended.

13. As discussed earlier in the text, ideally variables should be interval in nature, rather than simply ordinal, to use correlation and other related techniques, such as regression analysis. However, I follow the precedent of many analysts who argue that when used with care, ordinal variables that have reasonable distributions can also be scrutinized using such interval-level statistics.

14. I did not utilize techniques such as factor analysis, which are designed to search through a matrix of intercorrelations among items of diverse content to see how many separate dimensions (and thus scales) might be contained therein because in each instance I had already determined, based upon theoretical concerns, what the face content was that I wanted to measure with a scale. When that is the case, simple visual inspection is sufficient, and factor analysis would yield precisely the same result, in terms of which items should be included in such a scale.

15. There are two aspects of anonymity involved, whether any researcher or interviewer knows who you are and how you replied to questions, and whether you can be personally identified from the questionnaires or from the published results of the survey. The current study provides the second kind of anonymity, but obviously not the first. However, it is not clear that respondents are concerned about the first kind of anonymity, as long as the second is assured.

16. For example, through face-to-face interviews our interviewers could maintain some control over the situation and make efforts to exclude sources of bias. In contrast, with anonymous, mailed-in question outlines, such as those used in the Hite study, the researcher hopes that each respondent will fill out the forms independently and honestly. But he or she has no control over whether this occurs or not, and in some instances there might instead be consultation with others, group fabrication of lurid responses, and other very biased results.

17. However, it should be noted that not all of those we failed to interview were outright refusals, with many simply being cases of evasion or people we could never find at home in spite of many calls.

18. The 15 items were whether the woman's first marriage had ended in divorce, the marriage quality scale for her current marriage, the marital problems scale for that marriage, the item measur-ing the extent of worries about the state of her marriage, the marriage conflict severity scale, the spouse abuse scale (these last 3 are constituent items in the marital problems scale), measures of satisfaction with her marriage, with the division of chores, with the amount of say she has in the marriage, and with her standard of living, the chore division scale, the marital power scale, whether or not she had engaged in premarital sex, whether she acknowledged having cohabited prior to marriage, the age of her first sexual experience, and the premarital pregnancy measure. For details on the nature of these 15 items, see Appendix 2.

19. This test forms an additional piece of evidence against claims that survey research results

dealing with marital relations will inevitably be biased because people with unhappy marital experiences will tend to avoid participating. Insofar as I can test this idea, it turns out not to be accurate.

20.   To be precise, there was one significant correlation of $r = -.13$ between presence of husbands and whether the first marriage had ended in divorce, but this can be readily interpreted as showing not bias, but simply the fact that women who have been divorced are less likely to have husbands available to be in the room during the interview. None of the other fourteen correlations were significant, and the signs of the coefficients were not consistently in one direction.

21.   When I controlled for the number of children at home statistically, these correlations between marriage trait reports and the presence of children during the interview weakened considerably, and only the correlation with the chore satisfaction measure remained statistically significant (barely; results not shown here).

22.   That is, assuming that those interviewed in privacy are more truthful in their responses than those interviewed with others present. If you assume that only those who have others present to serve as a sounding board will reveal the truth about their marriages and past histories, then you would be led to the opposite conclusion.

Appendix 2

QUESTIONNAIRE ITEMS AND SCALES

Those items from the 1984 Detroit Area Study questionnaire that ended up being utilized in the analysis reported in these pages are listed below. Each such item is listed here as it was given in the original questionnaire, and when the actual version used in the analysis was a recoded or simplified version, the original item listing is followed by the recoded version actually used in this book. (In some instances more than one recoded version was used, and in those cases details on each version are given. For some items with complex response categories a respondent booklet was used during interviewing. Cues to the respondent booklet and other extraneous guidance instructions included in question wording are omitted here.) For open ended questions, the listing of categories shown here is the version actually used for analysis (i.e., in such cases I do not bother to list an initial and fuller set of codes for an open item). Finally, for all of those items that also were used as component parts of scales and composite measures, the names of such scales or composite items are listed after the item. Capitalized names indicate a scale or other composite measure, uncapitalized names indicate an individual item. Then the final portion of this appendix contains a listing of the scales used in the analysis reported here, along with details on how they were constructed. Readers wishing to receive a full copy of the original questionnaire may write to the author.

Questionnaire Items

A2.   First, I would like to know your current status—are you now married, separated, divorced, or widowed?
        1. married   2. separated   3. divorced   4. widowed

A3.   How many times have you been married? (open)
        1. married once   2. married twice   3. three times   4. four times

A4.   Have you given birth to any children?
        1. yes   5. no (recoded 1 = no, 2 = yes)

A5.   How many have you given birth to? (open, actual number)

A6.   What was the date of birth of your first child? (open—month, day, and year)

        (used in comparison with wedding date—D1—to form the Premarital Pregnancy measure)

A9.   Are there any children 17 years old or younger living here with you now?

        1. yes   5. no (recoded 1 = no, 2 = yes)

A10.   What is the sex and age of each child? (open listings)

        (used to form several different measures used in this study—total number of children at home, preschoolers at home, primary schoolers at home, and teenagers at home; also, in combination with other items, used to construct the Life-Cycle Stage measure)

A11.   Now I have some questions about your own family background and early experiences. What is your date of birth? (open—month, day, and year)

        (used together with other items to form several different composite measures—Age at First Marriage, Current Age, whether Married from Home (i.e., still living at home at time of marriage), and Life-Cycle Stage)

A12.   When you were growing up, that is between the ages of 6 and 16, in what state or states did you live? (open, actual number, with foreign countries counted as comparable to a state)

A14.   Did you live mostly in a large city, a suburb of a large city, a small or medium sized city, a small town, or a rural area?

        1. large city   2. suburb   3. small or medium sized city 4. small town   5. rural area

A15.   How many different schools did you go to during your elementary and high school years? (open, actual number)

A16.   Were these private schools, parochial schools, public schools, or some combination?

        1. public   2. private   3. parochial   4. combination

        (with combination specified; then recoded, with 1 = public, 2 = combination of public and private or parochial or all three, and 3 = private, or parochial, or combination of private and parochial)

A17.   In what religion were you raised—Catholic, Protestant, Jewish, or what?

        1. Catholic   2. Protestant   3. Jewish   7. other

        (recoded with 1 = Protestant, 2 = Catholic, 3 and 7 = blank; also used in combination with spouse religious measures to construct various Religious Homogamy items—in which case a fuller version, with 3 = Jewish or other, was used)

A18.   [If Protestant] What denomination was that? (open)

        (coded initially as 1 = other, 2 = fundamentalist [Assembly of God,

Pentacostal, Church of Christ, Fundamental or Southern Baptist, Seventh Day Adventists, United or Protestant Missionary, Church of God, Nazarene or Free Methodist, or Born-Again Christian]; recoded for analysis purposes into a more inclusive version, with 1 = Catholic or nonfundamentalist Protestant, 2 = fundamentalist Protestant)

A19. How about your religious *feelings* when you were growing up? Would you say you were very religious, somewhat religious, not very religious, or not religious at all?

       1. very religious   2. somewhat religious   3. not very religious 4. not religious at all

       (recoded in reverse order, with 4 = very religious)

A20. [Interviewer checkpoint—by observation, respondent is:]

       1. white   2. black   3. Asian   7. other

       (recoded with 1 = white, 2 = black, 3, 7 = blank)

A21. Aside from being American, what is your *main* nationality or ethnic group? (open)

       (utilized in various versions—the most detailed was a listing of 65 different specific national/ethnic origins; also used were a 7 category version {Anglo, Irish, Northern Europe, Central Europe, Southern Europe, Eastern Europe, and other non-blacks} and the most simplified 3 category version {Anglo-Irish, North and Central Europe, and Southern and Eastern Europe}; the 7 category version was used together with various spouse ethnic identifications to create Ethnic Homogamy measures; the 3 category version was used in analysis as an indicator of the traditionalism of the Ethnic Region of origin)

A22. [If only one group named in A21] Do you have a strong sense or a weak sense of belonging to that group?

       1. strong   3. in between, medium   5. weak   6. none

       (recoded with 1 = none, 2 = weak, 3 = two or more groups mentioned in A21, 4 = medium, 5 = strong; this item then was included in the Ethnic Roots Scale)

A23. What is the highest grade of school or year of college you ever completed? (detailed year listings, from 0 to 16, and then a final category of 17+ for graduate education; recoded to 1 = primary graduation or less, 2 = incomplete high school, 3 = high school graduate, 4 = incomplete college or equivalent, 5 = college graduate, 6 = post-graduate education; this item was used with others to construct measures of Educational Homogamy, and in some instances for this purpose the categories were collapsed further by combining 1 and 2 into the lowest category and 4–6 into the highest)

A24. Some people live in neighborhoods where everyone is pretty much the same as they are. Others live in very mixed areas, with neighbors from different classes, religions, and ethnic or racial groups. During your teenage years, what kind of neighborhood did your family live in—were the people very much like your own family, was the neighborhood somewhat mixed, or very mixed?

     1. like own family   2. somewhat mixed   3. very mixed

A25.   How about your *friends* when you were a teenager. Were they from families very similar to yours, somewhat mixed families, or very mixed?

     1. very similar   2. somewhat mixed   3. very mixed

A26.   Now I have some questions about your own family background and early experiences. Did you live with both of your parents up through age 16?

     1. yes   5. no

     (combined with item C20 to construct a measure of Parents Together when young and when respondent married [in which case recoded 1 = no, 2 = yes]; in a reverse version, used as a Broken Home measure)

A28.   While you were growing up, how did you feel about your parents' marriage? Did you think it was very happy, pretty happy, pretty unhappy, or very unhappy?

     1. very happy   2. pretty happy   3. pretty unhappy   4. very unhappy

     (coding reversed, with 4 = very happy, for indicator of parent marriage happiness; used in original form, along with other items, to form Family Conflicts Scale)

A30.   How close did you feel to your [mother/step-mother] when you were 16 years old—very close, somewhat close, not very close, or not close at all?

     1. very close   2. somewhat close   3. not very close   4. not close at all

     (coding reversed and combined with A40 to construct Close to Parents measure; used in original form, along with A28 and A40, to construct Family Conflicts Scale)

A31.   Did your (mother/step-mother) work for pay when you were 16?

     1. yes   5. no (recoded 1 = no, 2 = yes)

A40.   How close did you feel to your [father/step-father] when you were 16 years old? Would you say you were very close, somewhat close, not very close, or not close at all?

     1. very close   2. somewhat close   3. not very close   4. not close at all

     (coding reversed and combined with A30 to construct Close to Parents measure; used in original form, along with A28 and A30, to construct Family Conflicts Scale)

A41-2.   What was his main occupation or job when you were 16? Can you tell me a little about what he did at his job? (open)

     (originally coded into 10 major categories: 1 = higher professionals, 2 = middle and lower professionals, 3 = managers and administrators [nonfarm], 4 = clerical and kindred, 5 = sales workers, 6 = craftsmen and kindred, 7 =

operatives, 8 = laborers, 9 = service workers, 10 = farmers and farm managers, with additional codes for military, retired, student, disabled, etc.; generally collapsed to 1 = manual [7–8], 2 = other [4–6, 9], and 3 = professional and managerial [1–3], with other categories deleted; this 3 category version was used in constructing Occupational Homogamy measures)

A43.   What was the highest grade of school or year of college your (father/stepfather) ever completed? (detailed year listings, as in A23, and as with A23 this was collapsed for analysis purposes into 6 categories, from 1 = primary graduation or less, to 6 = post-graduate education)

A47.   Were *both* of your (natural) parents born in this country, only one of them, or neither?

        0. neither   1. one   2. both

        (in recoded form, with 1 = both, 2 = one, 3 = neither, this was used with A48 to form a Foreign Ancestry measure, and both items, together with A22, were used to form an Ethnic Roots Scale)

A48.   How many of your (natural) grandparents were born in this country? (open)

        (coded as 1 = all four, 2 = three, 3 = two, 4 = one, 5 = none, and then combined with A47 to form a Foreign Ancestry measure, and both items, together with A22, were used to form an Ethnic Roots Scale)

A49.   People talk about social classes such as the poor, the working class, the middle class, the upper-middle class, and the upper class. Which of these social classes would you say your family belonged to when you were 16—poor, working class, middle class, upper-middle class, or upper class?

        1. poor   2. working class   3. middle class   4. upper-middle class   5. upper class

        (recoded into 3 categories, with 1 = poor and working, 2 = middle, and 3 = upper-middle and upper, in order to construct a subjective Class Origin Homogamy measure)

A50.   When you were growing up, did your family have any income from inheritances, investments, or rental property?

        1. yes   5. no (recoded 1 = no, 2 = yes)

B1.   Now I'd like you to think back to the years before you got married (for the first time). Did you ever have any steady boyfriends other than your husband?

        1. yes   5. no (recoded 1 = no, 2 = yes)

B2.   With how many people did you "go steady," other than your (first) husband? (open)

        (used along with other items to construct a Dating Popularity Scale)

B3.   Before you got married (the first time), about how many *different* people did you ever *date?* (open)

        (used along with other items to construct a Dating Popularity Scale)

B4.   Did your parents ever try to influence who you went out with?
           1. yes   5. no (recoded 1 = no, 2 = yes; used together with other
items, to construct a Parental Interference Scale)

B5.   Did they ever tell you they didn't want you to go out with a particular
person?
           1. yes   5. no

B6.   Before you married your (first) husband were there any other men you
seriously considered marrying?
           1. yes   5. no

B7.   [If yes to B6] How many were there? (open)
           (responses were used in combination with other items to construct a
Dating Popularity Scale)

B12.   [About the most serious prospect] Aside from being American, what
was his main nationality or ethnic group? (open)
           (recoded as with A21)

B13.   What was his religious preference—Catholic, Protestant, Jewish, or
what?
           1. Catholic   2. Protestant   3. Jewish   7. other
           (handled as with A17)

B15.   What was the highest grade of school or year of college he ever
completed? (open, collapsed into 6 categories, as with A23)

B16.   Which of these social classes would you say his family belonged to—
poor, working class, middle class, upper-middle class, or upper class?
           1. poor   2. working class   3. middle class   4. upper-mid-
dle class   5. upper class

B17.   What did your parents think of him? Did they strongly approve, approve, disapprove, or strongly disapprove?
           1. strongly approve   2. approve   3. neutral   4. disap-
prove   5. strongly disapprove
           (collapsed into 1 = approve or strongly approve, 2 = neutral, 3 =
disapprove or strongly disapprove)

C1.   Now I am going to ask you some questions about your (first) marriage.
How did you get to know your (first) husband? Were you introduced by someone, or did you meet each other directly?
           1. introduced   5. directly met

C2.   [If introduced] Who was it that introduced you? (open)
           (coded into 1 = by parents, older kin, 2 = by siblings, same age kin, 3
= by other kin, 4 = by friends, other nonkin, 5 = blind date)

C3.   [If met directly] Where did you first meet? (open)
           (coded into 1 = known since childhood, 2 = in neighborhood, 3 = in
church, church activity, 4 = in organization, club, 5 = in school, school activity,

6 = at work, 7 = at party, dance, or wedding, 8 = at bar, dance hall, 9 = in public, chance meeting, 10 = vacation or amusement spot)

C4.   How old were you when you first started dating him? (open; used in constructing Courting Interval measure, and also in constructing Sex before Husband measure)

C5.   How far away from each other did you live when you started dating him—about how many miles? (open)

C6.   How long were you engaged before you got married? (open—months)

C7.   Did you receive an engagement ring?
        1. yes   5. no
        (when recoded as 1 = no, 2 = yes, this item was used along with others to construct a Wedding Elaborateness Scale)

C8.   Some people feel they are head-over-heels in love when they get married. Suppose these people are at point no. 1 on the scale on page 8 in the response booklet. Others are not in love at all when they get married—these people are at point no. 7. Where would you place yourself on this scale at the time you (first) married?
        1. head-over-heels   2.   3.   4.   5.   6.   7. not at all
in love
        (coding reversed, with 7 = head-over-heels, for analysis purposes)

C9.   Did you and your (first) husband live together before you got married?
        1. yes   5. no (recoded 1 = no, 2 = yes)

C11.   Did you ask anyone's advice about whether to marry your (first) husband?
        1. yes   5. no

C13.   In the weeks before your (first) marriage did you have major doubts about your decision to marry, minor doubts, or no doubts at all?
        1. major doubts   2. minor doubts   3. no doubts at all

C15.   Were you employed full time in the period before you got married (the first time)?
        1. yes   5. no
        (used in reverse form, with 1 = no, 2 = yes, as one part of the Female Independence Scale)

C16–7. What was your job title or position? Could you tell me more about what you actually did on your job? (open)
        (coded as with A41–2, and used in 3 category version to examine Occupational Homogamy vis-à-vis the husband at that time)

C18.   Before you married did you want to be a full-time housewife, work outside the home some of the time, or have a lifetime career?
        1. full-time housewife   2. work outside the home some of the
time   3. have a lifetime career

C20.   Were your parents still together at the time of your (first) marriage?
1. yes   5. no
(used in reverse order, with 1 = no, 2 = yes, in constructing Parents Together measure, and in original order used in constructing Broken Home measure)

C22.   How did your (mother/step-mother) feel about your marrying your (first) husband? Did she strongly approve, approve, disapprove, or strongly disapprove?
1. strongly approve   2. approve   3. neutral   4. disap-
prove   5. strongly disapprove
(combined with other measures to create a Parental Interference Scale)

C24.   How did your (father/step-father) feel about your marrying your (first) husband—did he strongly approve, approve, disapprove, or strongly disapprove?
1. strongly approve   2. approve   3. neutral   4. disap-
prove   5. strongly disapprove
(combined with other measures to create a Parental Interference Scale)

C35.   At the time you got married what was his [the first husband's] religious preference—Catholic, Protestant, Jewish, or what?
1. Catholic   2. Protestant   3. Jewish   7. other
(as with A17, collapsed into 3 categories [with 3 = 3, 7] for use with A17 in measuring Religious Homogamy, and with categories 3 and 7 deleted, and recoded with 1 = Protestant and 2 = Catholic, for a measure of husband Catholicism)

C36.   [If Protestant] What denomination was that?
(coded as with A18, to create a measure in which 1 = Catholic or nonfundamentalist Protestant, 2 = fundamentalist Protestant)

C38.   What was the highest grade of school or year of college he ever completed? (open, detailed years)
(collapsed into 6 categories, as with A23, and into the same 3 categories as with A23 for measuring Educational Homogamy)

C39.   What was his race—white, black, Asian, or what?
1. white   2. black   3. Asian   7. other
(categories 3 and 7 deleted for examining white-black racial homogamy or intermarriage)

C40.   What (is/was) his main nationality or ethnic group?
(coded as with A21, and used together with comparable recoded versions of A21 to measure Ethnic Homogamy)

C41.   At the time you (first) got married, was your husband working full time, a student, (retired), unemployed or laid off, or what?
1. working full time (including military)   2. working part-
time   3. student   4. retired   5. unemployed or laid off   7. other

C42–3. What was his *main* occupation or job? Could you tell me more about what he actually did on his job? (open)

(coded as with A41–2 and C16–7, and in comparable collapsed versions for measuring Occupational Homogamy)

C44. Which social class would you say his family belonged to—poor, working class, middle class, upper-middle class, or upper class?

1. poor   2. working class   3. middle class   4. upper-middle class   5. upper class

(used in a collapsed 3 category form, as with A49, to measure subjective Class Homogamy)

C45. What was his father's main occupation or job? (open)

(coded as with other occupational items, and used in combination with others in collapsed, three category version, to measure Occupational Homogamy vis-à-vis fathers' occupations)

C46. At the time you got married what did *his* parents think of *you?* Would you say they strongly approved, approved, disapproved, or strongly disapproved?

1. strongly approved   2. approved   3. neutral   4. disapproved   5. strongly disapproved

(used in combination with other items to construct a Parental Interference scale)

D1. What was the date of your (first) marriage? (open—month, day, and year)

(year of marriage used in several versions—exact year, 5 year marriage cohorts, and twenty year marriage generations [1925–44, 1945–64, and 1965–84]; also this information was used in combination with other items to create a large number of composite measures: Age at First Marriage, whether had Premarital Sex or not, whether Married from Home when first got married, Premarital Pregnancy, Courting Interval, Dating Interval, Life Cycle Stage, number of Years Worked since marriage, and Length of Current Marriage)

D2. In what city and state were you married? (open)

(coded into 1 = Detroit and suburbs, 2 = other Michigan cities and towns, 3 = all other U.S., and 4 = foreign; then recoded into 1 = other, 2 = Detroit and suburbs, to compare Detroit area marriages with others)

D3. Were you married by a religious official; for example, by a minister, priest, or rabbi?

1. yes   5. no (recoded 1 = no, 2 = yes; and in this form included in the Wedding Elaborateness Scale)

D4. Where did the marriage take place? (open)

(coded into 1 = religious institution, 2 = home, 3 = justice of peace, court, city hall, etc., and 4 = other)

D5.   Were there any bridal showers before the wedding?
         1. yes   5. no (recoded 1 = no, 2 = yes; and in this form included
in the Wedding Elaborateness Scale)

D7.   How many people attended the wedding? (open)
         (included with other items in the Wedding Elaborateness Scale)

D8.   After the wedding was there a reception or celebration?
         1. yes   5. no (recoded 1 = no, 2 = yes; and in this form included
in the Wedding Elaborateness Scale)

D9.   About how many people attended? (open)

D10.   Did *your parents* pay for most of the wedding expenses, or were they
handled in some other fashion? (open)
         (coded 1 = bride's parents mainly paid, 2 = bride's parents shared
payment with others [bride and groom and/or groom's parents], 3 = bride and
groom mainly paid themselves, 4 = others mainly paid)

D11.   Did you take a honeymoon trip?
         1. yes   5. no (recoded 1 = no, 2 = yes; and in this form included
in the Wedding Elaborateness Scale)

D12.   How long was it? (open—number of days coded)

D13.   Where did you go? (open)
         (coded 0 = no honeymoon, 1 = same metropolitan area as wedding, 2
= same state, 3 = same region of country, 4 = other regions of country, 5 =
other country or countries)

D14.   What were your living arrangements in the first six months after you
got married—did you and your husband live with your parents, his parents, did
you have your own place, or what?
         1. her parents   2. his parents   3. own place   7. other
         (recoded as 1 = 1,2, or 7, 2 = 3 [own place]; and in this form
included in Female Independence Scale)

D15.   When you first got married do you feel that you had a realistic view of
what married life would be like?
         1. realistic   3. in between, mixture   5. unrealistic

E2.   [If married more than once] How did your first marriage end—were
you divorced, separated, or widowed?
         1. divorced   2. separated   3. widowed
         (used in combination with other items to construct the measure of
whether the first marriage ended in Divorce or not)

E4.   Was the decision to (divorce/separate) mainly yours or mainly his?
         1. mainly respondent's   2. mutual   3. mainly his

E11.   [about the most recent marriage, for those remarried] How long did
you go out with him before you married? (open, coded in exact months)

E12.   What (is/was) the highest grade of school or year of college he ever completed? (open, coded in detailed years)

     (as with earlier educational attainment questions, collapsed into 6 main categories and then further into three categories [less than high school graduation, high school graduation, and more than high school graduation] for purposes of examining Educational Homogamy with the respondent in her remarriage)

E13.   What (is/was) his race—white, black, Asian, or what?
     1. white   2. black   3. Asian   7. other

E14.   Aside from being American what (is/was) his main nationality or ethnic group? (open)

     (as with earlier questions on ethnic identification, coded into detailed national origins, which were then collapsed into seven main ethnic identifications, and then finally into three major groupings [Anglo and Irish, Northern and Central European, and Southern and Eastern European] for examining Ethnic Homogamy with respondent in remarriage)

E15.   What was his religious preference at the time you got married—Catholic, Protestant, Jewish, or what?
     1. Catholic   2. Protestant   3. Jewish   7. other

     (collapsed into 1 = Catholic, 2 = Protestant, 3 = Jewish and other for analysis, and used with respondent religious preference to construct the measure of Religious Homogamy in remarriage)

F1.   What was the date of your (second/most recent) marriage? (open, record month, date, and year)

     (used with other items to construct measure of Length of Current Marriage)

F2.   Were you married by a religious official (for example, a minister, a priest, or rabbi)?
     1. yes   5. no

F3.   Where did the marriage take place? (open)
     (coded as 1 = other, 2 = church or other religious site)

F4.   About how many people attended the wedding ceremony? (open)

F5.   After the wedding was there a reception or a celebration?
     1. yes   5. no

F6.   About how many people attended? (open)

F7.   Did you take a honeymoon trip?
     1. yes   5. no

F9.   [if not presently married] How long were you married to your (second/most recent) husband?

     (used in combination with other items to construct measure of Length of Current Marriage)

F10.   How did the marriage end—were you divorced, separated, or widowed?

        1. divorced   2. separated   3. widowed

G1.   The next few questions are about your (most recent) marriage relationship. When you and your husband both (have/had) free time how often (do/did) you do things together—most of the time, sometimes, or not very often?

        1. most of the time   2. sometimes   3. not very often

        (reversed in direction and included with other items to construct the Marriage Quality Scale)

G2.   How much (does/did) your husband tell you about his thoughts and feelings—(does/did) he tell you a great deal, some, or not very much?

        1. a great deal   2. some   3. not very much

        (reversed in direction and included with other items to construct the Marriage Quality Scale)

G3.   How much (do/did) *you* tell your husband about *your* thoughts and feelings—(do/did) you tell him a great deal, some, or not very much?

        1. a great deal   2. some   3. not very much

        (reversed in direction and included with other items to construct the Marriage Quality Scale)

G4.   How affectionate (is/was) your husband in the way he (treats/treated) you—very affectionate, somewhat affectionate, or not very affectionate?

        1. very affectionate   2. somewhat affectionate   3. not very affectionate

        (reversed in direction and included with other items to construct the Marriage Quality Scale)

G5.   How affectionate (are/were) *you* in the way you treat(ed) your *husband*—very affectionate, somewhat affectionate, or not very affectionate?

        1. very affectionate   2. somewhat affectionate   3. not very affectionate

        (reversed in direction and included with other items to construct the Marriage Quality Scale)

G6.   How much concern (does/did) your husband show for your feelings and problems—a great deal, some, or very little?

        1. a great deal   2. some   3. very little

        (reversed in direction and included with other items to construct the Marriage Quality Scale)

H1.   Even women who get along well with their husband sometimes wonder whether their marriage is working out. Have you ever thought that your marriage might be in trouble?

        1. yes   5. no

(recoded 1 = no, 2 = yes, and used as the first portion of the Marriage Worries measure; then combined with other scales to construct the Marriage Problems Scale)

H2.   [If yes to H1] Thinking back over the course of your marriage, did the thought of getting a divorce or separation ever cross your mind?

    1. yes   5. no

(recoded 1 = no, 2 = yes, and used as the second portion of the Marriage Worries measure; then combined with other scales to construct the Marriage Problems Scale)

H3.   [If yes also to H2] Did you ever separate?

(recoded 1 = no, 2 = yes, and used as the third and final portion of the Marriage Worries measure; then combined with other scales to construct the Marriage Problems Scale)

H4.   All things considered how satisfied are you with your marriage? Which number on the scale comes closest to how you feel?

    1. very   satisfied   2.   3.   4.   5.   6.   7. very dissatisfied

(reversed in direction and combined with other items to construct the Marriage Quality Scale)

J1.   Now I would like to ask you some questions about how you and your (most recent) husband divide(d) various household tasks. Who (does/did) the grocery shopping—you always, you more than your husband, your husband and you about the same, your husband more than you, or your husband always?

    1. wife always   2. wife more   3. about the same   4. husband more   5. husband always   7. other

(included with other items to construct the Chore Division Scale)

J2.   Who (gets/got) your husband his breakfast on work days?

    1. wife always   2. wife more   3. about the same   4. husband more   5. husband always   7. other

(included with other items to construct the Chore Division Scale)

J3.   Who (cooks/ed) dinner during the week?

    1. wife always   2. wife more   3. about the same   4. husband more   5. husband always   7. other

(included with other items to construct the Chore Division Scale)

J4.   Who (does/did) the evening dishes?

    1. wife always   2. wife more   3. about the same   4. husband more   5. husband always   7. other

(included with other items to construct the Chore Division Scale)

J5.   Who (repairs/ed) things around the house?

    1. wife always   2. wife more   3. about the same   4. husband more   5. husband always   7. other

J6.   Who (takes/took) out the trash?
           1. wife always   2. wife more   3. about the same   4. husband more   5. husband always   7. other

J7.   Who (keeps/kept) track of the money and bills?
           1. wife always   2. wife more   3. about the same   4. husband more   5. husband always   7. other

J8.   In general, how satisfied (are/were) you with how the chores (are/were) divided in your family? Which number comes closest to how you (feel/felt)?
           1. very satisfied   2.   3.   4.   5.   6.   7. very dissatisfied

K1.   Now I am going to ask you about some things that married couples sometimes disagree about. What about how much money to spend on various things? (Does/did) this cause serious disagreements, minor disagreements, or no disagreements between you and your husband?
           1. serious disagreements   2. minor disagreements   3. no disagreements
           (reversed in direction and, with other items, used to construct the Conflict Severity Scale, and the latter was in turn used as one of the components of the Marital Problems Scale; in addition, the reversed responses were used with other items in constructing the Marital Power Scale)

K2.   What about who should do which household chores. (Does/did) this cause serious disagreements, minor disagreements, or no disagreements?
           1. serious disagreements   2. minor disagreements   3. no disagreements
           (used in the same scales, and in the same manner, as K1)

K3.   What about how to discipline the children. (Does/did) this cause serious disagreements, minor disagreements, or no disagreements?
           1. serious disagreements   2. minor disagreements   3. no disagreements
           (used in the same scales, and in the same manner, as K1)

K4.   What about how often to have sex. (Does/did) this cause serious disagreements, minor disagreements, or no disagreements?
           1. serious disagreements   2. minor disagreements   3. no disagreements
           (used in the same scales, and in the same manner, as K1)

K6.   When you (have/had) disagreements about how much *money* to spend on various things, who usually (gets/got) their way?
           1. wife always   2. wife more   3. about the same   4. husband more   5. husband always
           (used with other items to construct the Marital Power Scale, which was reversed in direction to have wife power indicated by a high score)

K7. When you (have/had) disagreements about who should do which *household chores,* who usually (gets/got) their way?
    1. wife always   2. wife more   3. about the same   4. husband more   5. husband always
    (used as with K6, to construct the Marital Power Scale)

K8. When you (have/had) disagreements about *disciplining the children,* who usually (gets/got) their way?
    1. wife always   2. wife more   3. about the same   4. husband more   5. husband always
    (used as with K6, to construct the Marital Power Scale)

K9. When you (have/had) disagreements about *having sex,* who usually (gets/got) their way?
    1. wife always   2. wife more   3. about the same   4. husband more   5. husband always
    (used as with K6, to construct the Marital Power Scale)

K11. What else (do/did) you and your husband disagree about? (open)
    (specific subjects were coded, but for analysis purposes these were collapsed into simply 1 = no other disagreements, 2 = some other disagreements mentioned; this measure was in turn used in constructing the Conflict Severity Scale, which was in turn used as part of the Marital Problems Scale; it was also used in constructing the Marital Power Scale)

K12. When you (have/had) disagreements about [first mention in K11], who usually (gets/got) their way?
    1. wife always   2. wife more   3. about the same   4. husband more   5. husband always
    (used as with K6, to construct the Marital Power Scale)

K14. When you and your husband (have/had) disagreements, how often (do/did) you sit down and talk things out—almost always, often, sometimes, or rarely?
    1. almost always   2. often   3. sometimes   4. rarely

K15. When you (have/had) disagreements, in general how satisfied (are/were) you with the amount of "say" or influence you (have/had)—which number comes closest to how you (feel/felt)?
    1. very satisfied   2.   3.   4.   5.   6.   7. very dissatisfied

L1. Just read these questions silently to yourself and check your answers. When you and your husband have had arguments or fights, which of these things has happened? Did your husband ever refuse to talk about it and stomp out of the room or the house?
    1. yes   5. no (recoded 0 = no, 1 = yes; used with other items to construct the Wife Abuse Scale, which in turn was one of the measures used to construct the Marital Problems Scale)

L2.   Did your husband ever insult you or swear at you?
        1. yes   5. no (used as with L1 in scale construction)

L3.   Did your husband ever push, grab, or shove you?
        1. yes   5. no (used as with L1 in scale construction)

L4.   Did your husband ever kick you, bite you, or hit you with his fist?
        1. yes   5. no (used as with L1 in scale construction)

L5.   Did your husband ever beat you up?
        1. yes   5. no (used as with L1 in scale construction)

M1-2.   Now I want to ask you about some qualities that help form children's characters. Which *one* of these [traits listed in response booklet] do you think is the *most desirable of all?*
        1. popular with others   2. ambitious to get ahead   3. obedient and well behaved   4. interested in how and why things happen   5. considerate of others   6. independent and self-reliant   7. has strong religious faith
        (responses used with comparable item about the husband in constructing a measure of Child Trait Agreement, which was in turn used in constructing the Shared Values Scale)

M3-4.   Which *one* quality would your husband (choose/have chosen) as the *most desirable of all?*
        (same categories as with M1-2, and handled in the same way)

M8.   Now here is a list of qualities that some people think are important in making a marriage successful. Which *three* qualities do you think would be the most important in making a successful marriage?
        M8a. agree on chores   1. checked   5. not checked
        M8b. satisfy each other's needs   1. checked   5. not checked
        M8c. have a good income   1. checked   5. not checked
        M8d. be deeply in love   1. checked   5. not checked
        M8e. have common interests   1. checked   5. not checked
        M8f. be sexually faithful   1. checked   5. not checked
        M8g. do things together   1. checked   5. not checked

M9.   Which *one* quality do you think is the most important of all?
        1. agree on chores   2. satisfy each other's needs   3. have a good income   4. be deeply in love   5. have common interests   6. be sexually faithful   7. do things together
        (used in combination with the same item for husband in constructing a measure of Marriage Trait Agreement, which was in turn used as part of the Shared Values Scale)

M11.   Which *one* quality would he [your husband] (choose/have chosen) as the *most important* of all?
        (same responses as M9, and used in scale construction in the same manner)

M12.   When you have free time, what do you like to do? (open, probe for three or more)
        (used together with M13 to construct a Shared Leisure Activities measure)

M13.   What about your (most recent) husband? What (does/did) he like to do during his free time? (open, probe for three or more)
        (used together with M12 to construct a Shared Leisure Activities measure)

M14.   What social class (do/did) you and your husband belong to? Would you say you (are/were) poor, working class, middle class, upper-middle class, or upper class?
        1. poor   2. working class   3. middle class   4. upper-middle class   5. upper class

N1.   The next few questions are written on another separate sheet. For each line I would like you to write the number which comes closest to describing your personal quality or habit.

        N1a.   1. very neat and tidy   2. fairly neat and tidy   3. not very neat and tidy
        N1b.   1. very stubborn   2. somewhat stubborn   3. not very stubborn
        N1c.   1. very outgoing   2. somewhat outgoing   3. fairly shy
        N1d.   1. often late   2. sometimes late   3. never late
        N1e.   1. very thrifty   2. somewhat thrifty   3. a free spender
        N1f.   1. hot tempered   2. somewhat hot tempered   3. mild tempered
        N1g.   1. heavy smoker   2. light smoker   3. nonsmoker
        N1h.   1. very bossy   2. somewhat bossy   3. not bossy
        N1i.   1. full of energy   2. fairly energetic   3. not very energetic
        N1j.   1. heavy drinker   2. moderate drinker   3. occasional drinker   4. do not drink at all
        (these trait ratings were used, in combination with those made on N2, to construct a measure of Shared Traits between wife and husband)

N2.   Now, please do the same rating for your (most recent) husband's personal qualities.
        (the same trait lists were used as with N1, and the responses to them were used together with those on N1 to construct a Shared Traits measure)

S1.   The next question is about people you feel close to. When you have a personal problem that you want to talk about, who do you speak to first? (open)
        (detailed categories used in coding, but for analysis purposes these were collapsed into simply 1 = others, 2 = husband)

S3.   I would like you to think of the *three* closest friends you have who live in this area. Don't count relatives as friends here. Just tell me their first names. (code number named)

S4.   How many of these friends know each other?
          0. none   2. two   3. all (treated as measure of friendship web)

S5.   Are any of these friends also friends of your husband?
          1. yes   5. no

S6.   How many? (open)
          (number here, ranging from 0 to 3, used as shared friends measure)

S7.   Are any of these friends married to friends of your husband?
          1. yes   5. no

S8.   How many? (open)
          (number here, ranging from 0 to 3, used as "friends married" measure of joint friendship between husband and wife)

S9.   How often do you and your husband get together *as a couple* with friends—once a week or more, several times a month, several times a year, or once a year or less?
          1. one a week or more   2. several times a month   3. several times a year   4. once a year or less
          (reversed in direction for a measure of joint social life)

S10.   How close do you and your husband feel to relatives on your side of the family—very close, somewhat close, or not very close?
          1. very close   2. somewhat close   3. not very close
          (reversed in direction for analysis)

S11.   How about the relatives on your husband's side—do you and your husband feel very close, somewhat close, or not very close to them?
          1. very close   2. somewhat close   3. not very close
          (reversed in direction for analysis)

T2.   These questions are about experiences you might have had. You can read them silently to yourself and write in the age at which you had each experience. How old were you when you first went on single dates? (open)
          (used to construct a Years Dating measure, and also to construct a Lateness in Dating scale)

T3.   How old were you when you first began to go steady? (open)
          (used to construct a Lateness in Dating scale)

T4.   How old were you when you first had sexual intercourse? (open)
          (used to construct a Premarital Sex measure, and also a measure of having had Sex before Husband [i.e., before began dating the eventual first husband])

T5.   How old were you when you left your parents' home to live on your own or with someone else?(open)

(used with other items to construct a measure of whether respondent Married from Home, and the latter measure was in turn used in constructing the Female Independence Scale)

U1.   The next few questions are about your present situation. What is your current religious preference—Catholic, Protestant, Jewish, or what?
          1. Catholic   2. Protestant   3. Jewish   7. other

U3.   Are you very religious, somewhat religious, not very religious, or not religious at all?
          1. very religious   2. somewhat religious   3. not very religious   4. not religious at all
          (used in reverse order as a measure of current religiosity)

U4.   Are you currently working for pay, a homemaker, (a student), (retired), unemployed or laid off, or what?
          1. working   for   pay   2. homemaker   3. student   4. retired   5. unemployed or laid off   7. other
          (collapsed into 1 = all other categories, 2 = working, for analysis of impact of current employment)

U5–6.   [If working, retired, unemployed or laid off] What (is/was) your job title or position? Can you tell me more about what you actually (do/did) on your job? (open)
          (coded into 9 primary categories, and also into a collapsed 3 category version, as with C16–7)

U7.   About how many years have you worked for pay, either full-time or part-time, since you first got married? (open)
          (used, in combination with other items, to construct a proportionate Years Worked measure)

U8.   How much income did you yourself receive in 1983?
          1. no income   2. under $3,000   3. $3,000–5,999
4. $6,000–8,999   5. $9000–11999   6. $12000–14999   7. $15000–17999   8. $18000–20999   9. $21000–23999   10. $24000–26999   11. $27000–29999   12. $30000–34999   13. $35000–39999   14. $40000–49999   15. $50000–74999   16. $75000+
          (used with other items to construct Wife Relative Income and wife Share of Family Income measures)

U10.   [If any income received] How is your income handled? Do you turn your money over to your husband to manage, keep most of it, giving him money for expenses, put it into a joint account, or what?
          1. keeps or manages all   2. keeps most, gives husband money for expenses   3. puts into a joint account, or splits money   4. turns most or all over to husband to manage

U11.   Is he [the husband] currently working full-time, (a student), (retired), unemployed or laid-off, or what?

1. working   full   time   2. working   part-time   or   irregularly   3. student   4. retired   5. unemployed or laid off   7. other
(item recoded in two ways: 1 = all other, 2 = working full or part
time, to judge impact of husband employment; 1 = all other, 2 = unemployed or
laid off, to judge impact of husband unemployment)

U12–3.   What (is/was) his main occupation or job? Can you tell me more about
what he actually (does/did) on his job? (open)
(coded into 9 primary categories as well as collapsed 3 category version, as with C16–7)

U14.   How much income did your husband receive in 1983?
(same response categories as with U8, and used together with U8 to
construct Wife Relative Income measure)

U15.   How does your husband handle his income? Does he turn most of it
over to you to manage, does he keep most of it and give you money for expenses,
is it put into a joint account, or what?
1. keeps or manages all   2. keeps most, gives wife money for
expenses   3. puts into a joint account, or splits money   4. turns most over
to wife to manage

U16.   Taking into consideration *all* sources of income, what was your *total
family income* before taxes in 1983?
(same response categories used as with U8 and U14; used together
with U8 to construct wife Share of Family Income measure)

U17.   The things people have—housing, car, furniture, recreation and the
like make up their standard of living. Some people are satisfied with their
standard of living, others feel it is not as high as they would like. Which number
comes closest to how satisfied you are with your standard of living?
1. very satisfied   2.   3.   4.   5.   6.   7. very dissatisfied

V1.   Finally, I would like to read to you a list of statements. Could you tell
me whether you would strongly agree, agree, disagree, or strongly disagree with
each? It is much better for everyone involved if the man is the achiever outside
the home and the woman takes care of the home and family. Would you strongly
agree, agree, disagree, or strongly disagree?
1. strongly agree   2. agree   3. neutral   4. disagree   5.
strongly disagree
(used along with other items in constructing a measure of Feminism,
and also in constructing a broader Liberal Attitudes Scale)

V2.   When the husband and wife come from different social backgrounds,
the marriage is bound to have problems.
1. strongly agree   2. agree   3. neutral   4. disagree   5.
strongly disagree

V4.   Keeping the family going is a very important reason why sons and daughters should expect to marry and have children.
      1. strongly agree   2. agree   3. neutral   4. disagree   5. strongly disagree
      (used with other items to construct a Liberal Attitudes Scale)

V5.   A woman can live a full and happy life without marrying.
      1. strongly agree   2. agree   3. neutral   4. disagree   5. strongly disagree
      (used in reverse order with other items in constructing a Feminism measure, and also in constructing a broader Liberal Attitudes Scale)

Control Variables

In addition to the items in the questionnaire itself, several pieces of information recorded as part of the editing process were entered as data and used as variables in checking for data quality problems—as discussed in Appendix 1. The following items were used in such checks:

CV1.   Number of calls made in order to complete interview.

CV2.   Who conducted the interview? 1. DAS participant   2. SRC professional interviewer

CV3.   Was spouse present during any of the interview? 1. no   2. yes, with little or no effect   3. yes, with some or substantial effect

CV4.   Were any children present during any of the interview?
1. no   2. yes, with little or no effect   3. yes, with some or substantial effect

CV5.   Were any other individuals present during any of the interview?
1. no   2. yes, with little or no effect   3. yes, with some or substantial effect

CV6.   Were there any questions that made the respondent uncomfortable?
1. no   2. yes

CV7.   Was there an initial refusal to take part in the interview?
1. no   2. yes

Composite Measures and Scales

Premarital Pregnancy: Constituted by comparing responses to A6 and D1, with first births before wedding coded 3 (premarital birth), first births within 8 months of wedding coded 2 (premarital conception, postmarital birth), and all other cases coded 1 (postmarital conception).

Total Number of Children at Home: total number listed in response to A10.

Preschoolers at Home: total number listed in response to A10 with ages 0–5.

Primary Schoolers at Home: total number listed in response to A10 with ages 6–12.

Teenagers at Home: total number listed in response to A10 with ages 13–17.

Life-Cycle Stage: 1 = currently married (A2), no children given birth to (A4), and Current Age under 30; 2 = currently married, with preschool children (A10); 3 = currently married, with primary school-aged children the youngest; 4 = currently married, with teenagers the youngest; 5 = currently married, with children, but no children currently living at home (A10—i.e., the empty nest phase.

Age at First Marriage: constructed by comparing the exact day, month, and year, of birth (A11) and of the first marriage (D1).

Current Age: constructed by subtracting the year of birth (A11) from 84 (the year of the interviews), and adding 1 for those with birthdays in months after May (the month in which most of the interviews were collected).

Married from Home: 1 = Age at First Marriage > age left home (T5); 2 = Age at First Marriage < or = age left home.

Religious Homogamy: with three category version of religion respondent was raised in (A17) compared with either that of the first spouse (C35) or of the most recent spouse (E15); 1 = religions different, 2 = religions the same.

Ethnic Homogamy: with the seven category version of ethnic group membership of the respondent (A21) compared with either that of the first spouse (C40) or of the most recent spouse (E14); 1 = ethnic group category not the same, 2 = ethnic group category the same.

Ethnic Roots Scale: constructed from the means of standardized versions of three measures: strength of identification with a particular ethnic group (A21), number of foreign born parents (A47), and number of foreign born grandparents (A48); in each case with a high value indicating more ethnic/foreign roots.

Educational Homogamy: with educational attainment of respondent (3 category version) compared with either that of the first spouse (C38) or of the most recent spouse (E12); 1 = educational attainment of one partner is +/− 2 levels different from that of the other; 2 = educational attainment of one partner is +/− 1 level different from that of the other; 3 = educational attainments of both partners at the same level.

Parents Together: 1 = parents not still together when respondent was age 16 (A26); 2 = parents still together when respondent was 16, but not when respondent first married (C20); 3 = parents still together when respondent first married.

Broken Home: the same as Parents Together, only reversed in direction.

Family Conflicts Scale: constructed from the mean of the standardized scores of three measures: degree of happiness/unhappiness in respondent's parents' marriage (A28); how close or distant respondent felt to her mother when 16 years old (A30); and how close or distant respondent felt to her father when 16 (A40); with a high score indicating conflict or distance in each case.

Close to Parents Scale: constructed from the mean of the scores on two measures: closeness to, or distance from, the mother (A30); and closeness to, or distance from, the father (A40); in this case with high scores indicating closeness.

Occupational Homogamy: with the three category version of the occupation of the respondent's father (A41–2) compared with the occupation of the first spouse's father (C45) or of the first spouse himself at the time of marriage (C42–3); or on the other hand with the respondent's own occupation at marriage (C16–17) compared with that of the first spouse; then 1 = level of one individual in such comparisons $+/-$ 2 levels different from that of the other; 2 = level of one individual in such comparisons $+/-$ 1 level different from that of the other; 3 = levels of the two individuals the same.

Subjective Class Origin Homogamy: with the three category version of the subjective class origin of the respondent (A49) compared with that of the first husband (C44); 1 = Level of one partner $+/-$ 2 levels different from that of the other; 2 = level of one partner $+/-$ 1 level different from that of the other; 3 = level of both partners the same.

Dating Popularity Scale: constructed from the mean of the standardized scores on three measures: number of steadies (B2), number of people ever dated (B3), and number of serious marriage prospects (B7).

Parental Interference Scale: constructed from the mean of the standardized scores on four measures: parental interference with dating (B4); mother disapproval of first marriage (C22); father disapproval of first marriage (C24); and in-law disapproval of first marriage (C46).

Courting Interval: Age at First Marriage minus age started dating the first husband (C4).

Sex Before Husband: 1 = age at first sexual experience (T4) $> =$ age started dating the first husband (C4); 2 = age at first sexual experience $<$ age started dating the first husband.

Wedding Elaborateness Scale: constructed from the mean of the standardized scores on six measures: receiving an engagement ring (C7), a religious wedding (D3) held, a bridal shower held (D5), a bachelor party held (D6), attendance at the wedding (D7), and a honeymoon trip taken (D11), in each case with high scores indicating more elaborateness.

Female Independence Scale: constructed from the mean of the standardized scores on three measures: respondent employed before marriage (C15), respondent didn't Marry from Home, and couple lived on their own right after wedding (D14).

Premarital Sex: 1 = age at first sexual experience (T4) = (or possibly $>$) Age at First Marriage; 2 = age at first sexual experience $<$ Age at First Marriage.

Dating Interval: Age at First Marriage minus age when first went out on a date (T2).

Length of Current Marriage: for those still married to their first husbands (A2 and A3), 84 minus year of first marriage (D1); for those currently in remarriage = 84 minus year of remarriage (F1).

Years Worked: number of years worked since first married (U7) divided by (84 minus year of first marriage).

Divorced from First Spouse: if married only once (A3), then use values from A2 (married or widowed = 1; divorced or separated = 2); if married more than once, then use information from E2 (1 = widowed; 2 = divorced or separated).

Marriage Quality Scale: constructed from the mean of the standardized scores on seven measures: joint free time (G1), husband tell feelings (G2), wife tell feelings (G3), husband show affection (G4), wife show affection (G5), husband show concern (G6), and overall marriage satisfaction (H4), all coded with high scores indicating positive traits or high satisfaction.

Marriage Worries: 1 = no on ever worry whether marriage in trouble (H1); 2 = yes on ever worry whether marriage in trouble, but never contemplated divorce or separation (H2); 3 = has contemplated divorce or separation but has never done so (H3); 4 = has at some point separated.

Marriage Problems Scale: constructed from the mean of the standardized scores on three scales: Marriage Worries Scale, Conflict Severity Scale, and Wife Abuse Scale (see details on the latter two scales below).

Chore Division Scale: constructed from the mean of four measures: who does the grocery shopping (J1), who cooks the husband's breakfast (J2), who cooks dinner during the week (J3), and who does the evening dishes (J4); in each case a high score indicates the husband does more.

Conflict Severity Scale: constructed from the mean of the scores on five measures: severity of conflict over spending money (K1), severity of conflict over doing household chores (K2), severity of conflict over disciplining children (K3), severity of conflict over having sex (K4), and existence of conflict over "other" issues (K11); in each case a high score indicates more serious disagreements.

Marital Power Scale: constructed from the mean of five scores: the severity of conflict over spending money (K1) multiplied by who wins out in such money conflicts (K6); the severity of conflict over doing chores (K2) multiplied by who wins out in such chore conflicts (K7); the severity of conflict over disciplining children (K3) multiplied by who wins out in such child discipline conflicts (K8); the severity of conflict over having sex (K4) multiplied by who wins out in such conflicts over frequency of sex (K9); and the existence of conflicts over other issues (K11) multiplied by who wins out in such other conflicts (K12). The scale score is reversed, so that high marital power indicates that the wife has more power relative to the husband.

Wife Abuse Scale: constructed from the simple sum of five wife abuse measures (L1 through L5), with each coded $0 =$ no, $1 =$ yes, so that a high score indicates more severe wife abuse.

Child Trait Agreement: $1 =$ the desirable child trait chosen by the respondent (M1–2) is different from the one she says her husband would choose (M3–4); $2 =$ the two traits are the same.

Marriage Trait Agreement: $1 =$ the most important trait for a successful marriage chosen by the respondent (M9) is different from the one she says her husband would choose (M11); $2 =$ the two traits are the same.

Shared Values Scale: the mean of the Child Trait Agreement and Marriage Trait Agreement measures.

Shared Leisure Activities: the number of the respondent's preferred leisure activities (M12) that are the same as what she says her spouse's preferred leisure activities are (M13), ranging from 0 through 3.

Shared Traits: the number of self-rated traits of the respondent (N1a–N1j) which are the same as the ratings that she gives for her husband on those same characteristics (N2a–N2j), potentially ranging from 0 through 10.

Lateness in Dating: the mean of the respondent's age at the time she had her first date (T2) and the age she was when she first went steady (T3).

Wife Relative Income: $1 =$ husband's current income (U14) is more than $9000 in excess of wife's current income (U8); $2 =$ wife's current income is in the same category as the husband's, or less than $9000 less than the husband's; $3 =$ wife's current income is in a higher category than husband's current income.

Share of Family Income: the wife's current income (U8) divided by the total family income (U16).

Feminism Scale: constructed from the mean of the attitudes toward the husband being the achiever and the wife staying home (V1) and the attitude that a woman can live a happy life without marrying (V5, reversed), with high scores indicating more liberal or feminist attitudes in both cases.

Liberal Attitudes Scale: constructed from the mean of the same two items as in the Feminism Scale and also the attitude item about the importance of marrying and having children to keep the family going (V4), with high scores in each case indicating more liberal attitudes.

BIBLIOGRAPHY

Ackerman, Charles. 1963. "Affiliations: Structural Determinants of Differential Divorce Rates." *American Journal of Sociology* 69:13–20.

Adams, Bert N. 1968. *Kinship in an Urban Setting,* Chicago: Markham.

Adams, Bert N. 1979. "Mate Selection in the United States: A Theoretical Summarization." Pp. 259–67 in *Contemporary Theories about the Family, Vol. 1,* edited by W. Burr, R. Hill, F. Nye, and I. Reiss, New York: The Free Press.

Aldrich, John H. and Forrest D. Nelson. 1984. *Linear Probability, Logit, and Probit Models.* Beverly Hills: Sage.

Alpenfels, E. J. 1970. "Progressive Monogamy: An Alternative Pattern?" Pp. 67–74 in *The Family in Search of a Future,* edited by H. A. Otto. New York: Appleton-Century-Crofts.

Alwin, Duane F. 1986. "Religion and Parental Child-Rearing Orientations: Evidence of a Catholic-Protestant Convergence." *American Journal of Sociology* 92:412–40.

Asimov, Isaac. 1982. "True Love." Pp. 167–70 in *Relationships: The Marriage and Family Reader,* edited by Jeffrey Rosenfeld, Glenview, IL: Scott Foresman.

Bane, Mary Jo. 1976. *Here to Stay.* New York: Basic Books.

Bates, Alan. 1942. "Parental Roles in Courtship." *Social Forces* 20:482–86.

Bayer, Alan. 1968. "Early Dating and Early Marriage." *Journal of Marriage and the Family* 30:628–32.

Becker, Gary. 1973. "A Theory of Marriage." *Journal of Political Economy* 81:813–45.

Becker, Gary. 1981. *A Treatise on the Family.* Cambridge: Harvard University Press.

Bendix, Reinhard. 1960. *Max Weber: An Intellectual Portrait.* Garden City: Doubleday.

Bennett, Neil G. and David E. Bloom. 1986. "Why Fewer American Women Marry." *The New York Times* December 13.

Benson-von der Ohe, Elizabeth. 1987. *First and Second Marriages.* New York: Praeger.

Berger, Brigitte and Peter L. Berger. 1983. *The War over the Family.* New York: Doubleday.

Bernard, Jessie. 1972. *The Future of Marriage.* New Haven: Yale University Press.

Birmingham, Stephen. 1969. *The Right People.* New York: Dell.

Blau, Peter M. and Otis D. Duncan. 1967. *The American Occupational Structure.* New York: Wiley.

Blau, Peter M. and Joseph E. Schwartz. 1984. *Crosscutting Social Circles.* New York: The Academic Press.

Blood, Robert. 1967. *Love Match and Arranged Marriage.* New York: The Free Press.

Blood, Robert and Donald M. Wolfe. 1960. *Husbands and Wives.* New York: The Free Press.

Blumstein, Philip and Pepper Schwartz. 1983. *American Couples.* New York: Morrow.

Bohannon, Paul. 1970. *Divorce and After*. Garden City: Doubleday.

Booth, Alan, David Johnson, and John N. Edwards. 1983. "Measuring Marital Instability." *Journal of Marriage and the Family* 45:387–94.

Booth, Alan, David R. Johnson, Lynn K. White, and John N. Edwards. 1986. "Divorce and Marital Separation over the Life Course." *Journal of Family Issues* 7:421–42.

Booth, Alan and David Johnson. 1988. "Premarital Cohabitation and Marital Success." *Journal of Family Issues* 9:255–72.

Bott, Elizabeth. 1957. *Family and Social Network*. London: Tavistock.

Bradburn, Norman. 1969. *The Structure of Psychological Well-Being*. Chicago: Aldine.

Bumpass, Larry. 1970. "The Trend of Interfaith Marriage in the United States." *Social Biology* 17:253–59.

Burchinal, Lee G. 1964. "The Premarital Dyad and Love Involvement." Pp. 623–74 in *Handbook of Marriage and the Family*, edited by Harold Christensen. Chicago: Rand McNally.

Burgess, Ernest W. and Harvey S. Locke. 1945. *The Family: From Institution to Companionship*. New York: American Book Company.

Burgess, Ernest W. and Paul Wallin. 1953. *Engagement and Marriage*. Chicago: Lippincott.

Campbell, Angus, Philip Converse, and Willard Rogers. 1976. *The Quality of American Life*. New York: Russell Sage.

Cancian, Francesca. 1987. *Love in America*. Cambridge: Cambridge University Press.

Caplow, Theodore, Howard M. Bahr, Bruce A. Chadwick, Reuben Hill, and Margaret H. Williamson. 1982. *Middletown Families*. Minneapolis: University of Minnesota Press.

Cherlin, Andrew. 1978. "Remarriage as an Incomplete Institution." *American Journal of Sociology* 84:634–50.

Cherlin, Andrew. 1981. *Marriage, Divorce, Remarriage*. Cambridge: Harvard University Press.

Cherlin, Andrew. forthcoming. *Marriage, Divorce, Remarriage*, revised edition. Cambridge: Harvard University Press.

Coleman, James S. 1961. *The Adolescent Society*. New York: The Free Press.

Converse, Jean and Erica Meyer, eds. 1988. *The Detroit Area Study, 1951–1988*. Ann Arbor: Detroit Area Study.

Coombs, Lolagene C., Ronald Freedman, Judith Friedman, and William F. Pratt. 1970. "Premarital Pregnancy and Status before and after Marriage." *American Journal of Sociology* 75:800–20.

Coombs, Robert H. 1962. "Reinforcement of Values in the Parental Home as a Factor in Mate Selection." *Marriage and Family Living* 24:155–57.

Cooper, David. 1970. *The Death of the Family*, New York: Pantheon.

Cromwell, Ronald E. and David H. Olson, eds. 1975. *Power in Families*, New York: Wiley.

Cuber, John F. and Peggy B. Harroff. 1963. "The More Total View: Relationships among Men and Women of the Upper Middle Class." *Marriage and Family Living* 25:140–45.

Davis, James A. 1982. "Achievement Variables and Class Cultures: Family, Schooling, Job, and Forty-Nine Dependent Variables in the Cumulative GSS." *American Sociological Review* 47:569–86.

Davis, Kingsley. 1984. "Wives and Work: The Sex Role Revolution and its Consequences." *Population and Development Review* 10:397–417.

Davis, Kingsley. 1985. "The Future of Marriage," Pp. 25–52 in *Contemporary Marriage: Comparative Perspectives on a Changing Institution,* edited by K. Davis. New York: Russell Sage.

Dawson, Deborah A., Denise J. Meny and Jeanne C. Ridley. 1980. "Fertility Control in the United States before the Contraceptive Revolution." *Family Planning Perspectives* 12:76–86.

Dean, Gillian and Douglas T. Gurak. "Marital Homogamy the Second Time Around." *Journal of Marriage and the Family* 40:559–70.

Degler, Carl N. 1974. "What Ought to Be and What Was: Woman's Sexuality in the Nineteenth Century." *American Historical Review* 79:1467–90.

DeMaris, Alfred and Gerald R. Leslie. 1984. "Cohabitation with the Future Spouse: Its Influence upon Marital Satisfaction and Communication." *Journal of Marriage and the Family* 46:77–84.

Demos, John. 1970. *A Little Commonwealth*. New York: Oxford University Press.

Douvan, Elizabeth and Joseph Adelson. 1966. *The Adolescent Experience*. New York: John Wiley.

Driscoll, Richard, Keith E. Davis, and Milton E. Lipetz. 1972. "Parental Interference and Romantic Love: The Romeo and Juliet Effect." *Journal of Personality and Social Psychology* 24:1–10.

Duncan, Beverly, and Otis D. Duncan. 1978. *Sex Typing and Social Roles*. New York: Academic Press.

Duncan, Otis D. 1968. "Social Stratification and Mobility: Problems in the Measurement of Trend." Pp. 675–719 in *Indicators of Social Change,* edited by E. Sheldon and W. Moore, New York: Russell Sage.

Duncan, Otis D., Howard Schuman, and Beverly Duncan. 1973. *Social Change in a Metropolitan Community*. New York: Russell Sage.

Eekelaar, John M. and Sanford N. Katz, eds. 1980. *Marriage and Cohabitation in Contemporary Societies*. Toronto: Butterworths.

Ehrmann, Winston. 1959. *Premarital Dating Behavior*. New York: Henry Holt.

Elder, Glen H., Jr. 1974. *Children of the Great Depression*. Chicago: University of Chicago Press.

Elder, Glen H., Jr. 1987. "Families and Lives: Some Developments in Life-Course Studies." *Journal of Family History* 12:179–99.

Epstein, Edward J. 1978. *Cartel*. New York: Putnam.

Espenshade, Thomas J. 1985. "The Recent Decline in American Marriage: Blacks and Whites in Comparative Perspective." Pp. 53–90 in *Contemporary Marriage: Comparative Perspectives on a Changing Institution,* edited by K. Davis. New York: Russell Sage.

Fass, Paula S. 1977. *The Damned and the Beautiful*. New York: Oxford University Press.

Freeman, Michael and Christina M. Lyon. 1983. *Cohabitation without Marriage*. Aldershot: Gower.

Freedman, Deborah, Arland Thornton, Donald Camburn, Duane Alwin, and Linda Young-DeMarco. 1988. "The Life History Calendar: A Technique for Collecting Retrospective Data." Pp. 37–68 in *Sociological Methodology 1988,* edited by Clifford Clogg. Washington: American Sociological Association.

Furstenberg, Frank F., Jr. 1987. "The New Extended Family: The Experience of Parents and Children after Remarriage." Pp. 27–41 in *Remarriage and Stepparenting,* edited by K. Pasley and M. Ihinger-Tallman. New York: Guilford.

Furstenberg, Frank F., Jr. and Graham B. Spanier. 1987. *Recycling the Family: Remarriage after Divorce,* 2nd edition, Beverly Hills: Sage.

Gagnon, John H. and Cathy S. Greenblat. 1978. "Rehearsals and Realities: Beginning to Date." Pp. 106–118 in *Life Designs: Individuals, Marriages, and Families,* edited by John H. Gagnon and Cathy S. Greenblat, Glenview, IL: Scott Foresman.

Gilford, Rosalie and Vern L. Bengston. 1979. "Measuring Marital Satisfaction in Three Generations: Positive and Negative Dimensions." *Journal of Marriage and the Family* 41:387–98.

Girard, Alain. 1974. *Le Choix du Conjoint.* Paris: Universities Presses of France.

Glenn, Norval D. 1982. "Interreligious Marriage in the United States: Patterns and Recent Trends." *Journal of Marriage and the Family* 44:555–66.

Glenn, Norval D., Sue K. Hoppe, and David Weiner. 1974. "Social Class Heterogamy and Marital Success: A Study of the Empirical Adequacy of a Textbook Generalization." *Social Problems* 21:539–50.

Glenn, Norval D. and C. Weaver. 1977. "The Marital Happiness of Remarried Divorced Persons." *Journal of Marriage and the Family* 39:331–37.

Glick, Paul C. and Sing-ling Lin. 1986. "More Young Adults are Living with their Parents: Who Are They?" *Journal of Marriage and the Family* 48:107–12.

Godwin, John. 1973. *The Mating Trade.* Garden City: Doubleday.

Goldscheider, Francis K. and Celine LeBourdais. 1986. "The Decline in Age at Leaving Home: 1920–1979." *Sociology and Social Research* 70:99–102.

Goode, William J. 1962. "Marital Satisfaction and Instability: A Cross-cultural Class Analysis of Divorce Rates." *International Social Science Journal* 14:507–26.

Goode, William J. 1963. *World Revolution and Family Patterns.* New York: The Free Press.

Goode, William J. 1964. *The Family.* Englewood Cliffs: Prentice-Hall.

Gordon, Michael. 1981. "Was Waller Ever Right? The Rating and Dating Complex Reconsidered." *Journal of Marriage and the Family* 43:67–76.

Gordon, Milton M. 1958. *Social Class in American Sociology.* Durham: Duke University Press.

Gorer, Geoffrey. 1971. *Sex and Marriage in England Today.* London: Nelson.

Gough, E. Kathleen. 1960. "Is the Family Universal?—The Nayar Case." Pp. 76–92 in *A Modern Introduction to the Family,* edited by N. Bell and E. Vogel, Glencoe: The Free Press.

Gwartney-Gibbs, P. A. 1986. "Institutionalization of Premarital Cohabitation." *Journal of Marriage and the Family* 48:423–34.

Haavio-Mannila, Elina and Erkki Rannik. 1987. "Family Life in Estonia and Finland." *Acta Sociologica* 30:355–69.

Hannan, Michael, Nancy B. Tuma, and Lyle Groeneveld. 1978. "Income and Independence Effects on Marital Dissolution: Results from the Seattle and Denver Income-Maintenance Experiments." *American Journal of Sociology* 84:611–33.

Hareven, Tamara. 1978. *Transitions: The Family and the Life Course in Historical Perspective.* New York: Academic Press.

Hartmann, Heidi. 1981. "The Family as the Locus of Gender, Class, and Political Struggle: The Example of Housework." *Signs* 6:366–94.

Hechter, Michael. 1978. "Group Formation and the Cultural Division of Labor." *American Journal of Sociology* 84:293–318.

Heer, David M. 1974. "The Prevalence of Black-White Marriage in the United States, 1960 and 1970." *Journal of Marriage and the Family* 36:246–58.

Heer, David M., Robert W. Hodge, and Marcus Felson. 1985. "The Cluttered Nest: Evidence That Young Adults Are More Likely to Live at Home Now Than in the Recent Past." *Sociology and Social Research* 69:436–41.

Heimer, Carol A. and Arthur L. Stinchcombe. 1980. "Love and Irrationality: It's Got to Be Rational to Love You Because It Makes Me So Happy." *Social Science Information* 19:697–754.

Heiss, Jerold. 1975. *The Case of the Black Family.* New York: Columbia University Press.

Hertz, Rosanna. 1986. *More Equal than Others: Women and Men in Dual-Career Marriages.* Berkeley: University of California Press.

Hite, Shere. 1987. *Women and Love.* New York: Knopf.

Hobart, Charles. 1988. "The Family System in Remarriage: An Exploratory Study." *Journal of Marriage and the Family,* 50:649–61.

Hollingshead, August B. 1949. *Elmtown's Youth.* New York: Wiley.

Hollingshead, August B. 1952. "Marital Status and Wedding Behavior." *American Sociological Review* 17:308–11.

Hunt, Morton. 1974. *Sexual Behavior in the 1970s.* Chicago: Playboy Press.

Ihinger-Tallman, Marilyn and Kay Pasley. 1987. *Remarriage.* Beverly Hills: Sage.

Jackman, Mary R. and Robert W. Jackman. 1983. *Class Awareness in the United States.* Berkeley: University of California Press.

Jacobsohn, P. and A. Matheny. 1962. "Mate Selection in Open Marriage Systems." *International Journal of Comparative Sociology* 3:98–124.

Johnson, David R., Lynn K. White, John N. Edwards, and Alan Booth. 1986. "Dimensions of Marital Quality: Toward Methodological and Conceptual Refinement." *Journal of Family Issues* 7:31–49.

Jones, E. F. and C. F. Westoff. 1979. "The End of 'Catholic' Fertility." *Demography* 16:209–17.

Kamo, Yoshinori. 1988. "Determinants of the Household Division of Labor." *Journal of Family Issues* 9:177–200.

Kennedy, R. 1952. "Single or Triple Melting Pot? Intermarriage in New Haven, 1870–1950." *American Journal of Sociology* 58:56–9.

Kephart, William. 1982. *Extraordinary Groups.* New York: St. Martin's Press (2nd edition).

Kerckhoff, Alan C. 1964. "Patterns of Homogamy and the Field of Eligibles." *Social Forces* 42:289–97.

Kharchev, A. G. 1965. "Motives of Marriages in the USSR." *Acta Sociologica* 8:142–62.

Kinsey, Alfred C., Wardell B. Pomeroy, and Clyde E. Martin. 1948. *Sexual Behavior in the Human Male.* Philadelphia: Saunders.

Kinsey, Alfred C., Wardell B. Pomeroy, Clyde E. Martin, and Paul H. Gebhard. 1953. *Sexual Behavior in the Human Female.* Philadelphia: Saunders.

Kohn, Melvin. 1969. *Class and Conformity.* Homewood: Dorsey Press.

Koller, Marvin R. 1951. "Some Changes in Courtship Behavior in Three Generations of Ohio Women." *American Sociological Review* 16:367–70.

Komarovsky, Mirra. 1962. *Blue Collar Marriage*. New York: Random House.

Kranichfeld, Marion L. 1987. "Rethinking Family Power." *Journal of Family Issues* 8:42–56.

Landis, Karl. 1984. "A Test of Curvilinearity in the Relationship between Marital Satis-faction and the Family Life Cycle," unpublished DAS paper.

Larson, Jeffry and Scot M. Allgood. 1987. "A Comparison of Intimacy in First Married and Remarried Couples." *Journal of Family Issues* 8:319–31.

Lasch, Christopher. 1977. *Haven in a Heartless World*. New York: Basic Books.

Lenski, Gerhard. 1961. *The Religious Factor*. Garden City: Doubleday.

Leonard, Diana. 1980. *Sex and Generation: A Study of Courtship and Weddings*. London: Tavistock.

Leslie, Leigh A., Ted L. Huston, and Michael P. Johnson. 1986. "Parental Reactions to Dating Relationships: Do They Make a Difference?" *Journal of Marriage and the Family* 48:57–66.

Levitan, Sar and Richard S. Belous. 1981. What's Happening to the American Family? Baltimore: Johns Hopkins University Press.

Lewis, Robert A. and Graham B. Spanier. 1979. "Theorizing about the Quality and Stability of Marriage." Pp. 268–94 in *Contemporary Theories about the Family*, Vol. 1, edited by W. Burr, R. Hill, F. Nye, and I. Reiss. New York: The Free Press.

Lieberson, Stanley and Mary Waters. 1988. *From Many Strands: Ethnic and Racial Groups in Contemporary America*. New York: Russell Sage.

Locke, Harvey J. 1951. *Predicting Adjustment in Marriage*. New York: Holt.

Locke, Harvey J. and K. M. Wallace. 1959. "Short Marital Adjustment and Prediction Scales: Their Reliability and Validity." *Marriage and Family Living* 21:251–55.

Lowrie, Samuel H. 1961. "Early and Late Dating: Some Conditions Associated with Them." *Marriage and Family Living* 23:284–91.

Lupri, Eugen and James Frideres. 1981. "The Quality of Marriage and the Passage of Time: Marital Satisfaction over the Family Life Cycle." *Canadian Journal of Sociology* 6:283–305.

MacFarlane, Alan. 1986. *Marriage and Love in England: Modes of Reproduction 1300–1840*. New York: Basil Blackwell.

Mainardi, Pat. 1970. "The Politics of Housework," Pp. 447–54 in *Sisterhood is Power-ful*, edited by R. Morgan. New York: Vintage.

Mason, Karen and Yu-hsia Lu. 1988. "Attitudes toward Women's Familial Roles: Changes in the United States, 1977–1985." *Gender and Society* 2:39–57.

Modell, John. 1983. "Dating Becomes the Way of American Youth," Pp. 91–126 in *Essays on the Family and Historical Change*, edited by Leslie P. Moch and Gary D. Stark. College Station: Texas A&M University Press.

Modell, John. 1985. "Historical Reflections on American Marriage." Pp. 181–96 in *Contemporary Marriage: Comparative Perspective on a Changing Institution*, edited by K. Davis. New York: Russell Sage.

Moore, Barrington. 1958. "Thoughts on the Future of the Family." Pp. 160–78 in *Political Power and Social Theory*, edited by B. Moore. Cambridge: Harvard Univer-sity Press.

Morgan, James N., Katherine Dickinson, Jonathan Dickinson, Jacob Benus, and Greg Duncan. 1974. *Five Thousand American Families—Patterns of Economic Progress*. Ann Arbor: Institute for Social Research.

Moss, Louis and Harvey Goldstein, eds. 1979. *The Recall Method in Social Surveys.* London: University of London Institute of Education.

Moynihan, Daniel P. 1965. *The Negro Family: The Case for National Action.* Washington: U.S. Department of Labor.

Mueller, Charles W. and Hallowell Pope. 1980. "Divorce and Female Remarriage Mobility: Data on Marriage Matches after Divorce of White Women." *Social Forces* 58:526–38.

Mullan, Bob. 1984. *The Mating Trade.* London: Routledge and Kegan Paul.

Murstein, Bernard L. 1976. *Who Will Marry Whom?*, New York: Springer.

Murstein, Bernard L. 1980. "Mate Selection in the 1970s." *Journal of Marriage and the Family* 42:777–92.

Niemi, Richard G. 1974. *How Family Members Perceive Each Other*, New Haven: Yale University Press.

Norton, Arthur J. and Jeanne E. Moorman. 1987. "Current Trends in Marriage and Divorce among American Women." *Journal of Marriage and the Family* 49:3–14.

Orden, Susan and Norman Bradburn. 1968. "Dimensions of Marriage Happiness." *American Journal of Sociology* 73:715–31.

Pahl, Jan. 1982. "Patterns of Money Management within Marriage," Pp. 175–96 in *Relationships: The Marriage and Family Reader*, edited by Jeffery Rosenfeld. Glenview, IL: Scott Foresman.

Parish, William L. and Martin King Whyte. 1978. *Village and Family in Contemporary China.* Chicago: University of Chicago Press.

Parsons, Talcott. 1949. "The Social Structure of the Family." Pp. 241–74 in *The Family: Its Function and Destiny*, edited by Ruth N. Anshen. New York: Harper.

Parsons, Talcott. 1955. "The American Family: Its Relations to Personality and the Social Structure." Pp. 3–34 in *Family, Socialization, and Interaction Process*, edited by T. Parsons and R. Bales. New York: The Free Press.

Peach, Ceri. 1980. "Which Triple Melting Pot? A Re-examination of Ethnic Intermarriage in New Haven, 1900–1950." *Ethnic and Racial Studies* 3:1–16.

Pearlin, Leonard I. 1971. *Class Context and Family Relations.* Boston: Little Brown.

Pearlin, Leonard I. 1975. "Status Inequality and Stress in Marriage." *American Sociological Review* 40:344–57.

Pierce, Rachel M. 1963. "Marriage in the Fifties." *Sociological Review* 11:215–40.

Pineo, Peter C. 1961. "Disenchantment in the Later Years of Marriage." *Marriage and Family Living* 23:3–11.

Pleck, Joseph H. 1985. *Working Wives, Working Husbands.* Beverly Hills: Sage.

Popenoe, David. 1988. *Disturbing the Nest.* New York: Aldine de Gruyter.

Powers, E. A. 1971. "Thirty Years of Research on Ideal Mate Characteristics: What Do We Know?" *International Journal of Sociology of the Family.* 1:1–9.

Quarm, Daisy. 1977. *The Measurement of Marital Power.* Unpublished Ph.D. disseration, University of Michigan.

Rainwater, Lee. 1964. "Marital Sexuality in Four Cultures of Poverty." *Journal of Marriage and the Family* 26:457–66.

Renne, K. S. 1970. "Correlates of Dissatisfaction in Marriage." *Journal of Marriage and the Family* 32:54–66.

Rockwell, Richard C. 1976. "Historical Trends and Variations in Educational Homogamy." *Journal of Marriage and the Family* 38:83–95.

Rollins, Boyd D. and Harold Feldman. 1970. "Marital Satisfaction over the Family Life Cycle." *Journal of Marriage and the Family* 32:20–28.

Rosser, Colin and C. C. Harris. 1965. *The Family and Social Change: A Study of Family and Kinship in a South Wales Town.* London: Routledge and Kegan Paul.

Rothman, Ellen K. 1984. *Hands and Hearts: A History of Courtship.* New York: Basic Books.

Rubin, Lillian B. 1976. *Worlds of Pain.* New York: Basic Books.

Rubin, Zick. 1968. "Do American Women Marry Up?" *American Sociological Review* 33:750–60.

Rubin, Zick. 1977. "The Love Research." *Human Behavior* 5:56–59.

Russell, Bertrand. 1929. *Marriage and Morals.* London: Allen and Unwin.

Ryder, Norman B. 1965. "The Cohort as a Concept in the Study of Social Change." *American Sociological Review* 30:843–61.

Safilios-Rothschild, Constantina. 1969. "Family Sociology or Wives' Family Sociology? A Cross-cultural Examination of Decision-Making." *Journal of Marriage and the Family* 31:290–301.

Scanzoni, John. 1979. "Social Processes and Power in Families," Pp. 295–316 in *Contemporary Theories about the Family,* Vol. 1, edited by W. Burr, R. Hill, F. Nye, and I. Reiss. New York: The Free Press.

Scanzoni, John. 1982. *Sexual Bargaining,* 2nd edition, Chicago: University of Chicago Press.

Schellenberg, James A. 1962. "Homogamy in Personal Values and the 'Field of Eligibles.' " *Social Forces* 39:157–62.

Schulman, A. K. 1977. "The War in the Back Seat." Pp. 150–57 in *The Family: Functions, Conflicts, and Symbols,* edited by P. Stein, J. Richman and N. Hannon. Reading: Addison-Wesley.

Schuman, Howard. 1966. "The Random Probe: A Technique for Evaluating the Validity of Closed Questions." *American Sociological Review* 21:218–22.

Seligson, Marcia. 1973. *The Eternal Bliss Machine: America's Way of Wedding.* New York: William Morrow.

Sheehy, Gail. 1976. *Passages.* New York: Dutton.

Shlapentokh, Vladimir. 1984. *Love, Marriage, and Friendship in the Soviet Union.* New York: Praeger.

Shorter, Edward. 1971. "Illegitimacy, Sexual Revolution, and Social Change in Modern Europe." *Journal of Interdisciplinary History* 2:237–72.

Smith, Daniel S. 1973. "The Dating of the American Sexual Revolution." Pp. 321–35 in *The American Family in Social-Historical Perspective,* edited by Michael Gordon. New York: St. Martin's Press.

Smith, Daniel S. and Michael Hindus. 1975. "Premarital Pregnancy in America, 1640–1971: An Overview and Interpretation." *Journal of Interdisciplinary History* 4:537–70.

Sorokin, Pitirim. 1937. *Social and Cultural Dynamics.* Vol. 4, New York: Harper.

Spanier, Graham B. 1976. "Measuring Dyadic Adjustment: New Scales for Assessing the Quality of Marriage and Similar Dyads."*Journal of Marriage and the Family* 38:15–28.

Spanier, Graham B. 1983. "Married and Unmarried Cohabitation in the United States: 1980." *Journal of Marriage and the Family* 45:97–111.

Spanier, Graham B., Robert Lewis, and Charles Cole. 1975. "Marital Adjustment over the Family Life Cycle: The Issue of Curvilinearity." *Journal of Marriage and the Family* 31:263–68.

Stack, Carol. 1974. *All Our Kin.* New York: Harper and Row.

Steinmetz, Suzanne K. 1977–78. "The Battered Husband Syndrome." *Victimology* 2:499–509.

Stephens, William N. 1968. "Predictors of Marital Adjustment." Pp. 119–33 in *Reflections on Marriage,* edited by W. Stephens. New York: Thomas Crowell.

Straus, Murray A. 1977. "Wife-beating: How Common, and Why?" *Victimology* 2:443–58.

Straus, Murray A. and Richard J. Gelles. 1986. "Societal Change and Change in Family Violence from 1975 to 1985 As Revealed by Two National Surveys." *Journal of Marriage and the Family* 48:465–79.

Straus, Murray A., Richard J. Gelles, and Suzanne K. Steinmetz. 1980. *Behind Closed Doors: Violence in the American Family.* New York: Doubleday.

Sussman, Marvin B. 1953. "Parental Participation in Mate Selection and Its Effect upon Family Continuity." *Social Forces* 32:76–81.

Thompson, Anthony P. 1983. "Extramarital Sex: A Review of the Research Literature." *Journal of Sex Research* 19:1–22.

Thornton, Arland and Deborah Freedman. 1982. "Changing Attitudes toward Marriage and Single Life." *Family Planning Perspectives* 14:297–303.

Thornton, Arland and Deborah Freedman. 1983. "The Changing American Family." *Population Bulletin* 38:1–43.

Thornton, Arland, Deborah Freedman, and Donald Camburn. 1982. "Obtaining Respondent Cooperation in Family Panel Studies." *Sociological Methods and Research* 11:33–51.

Toffler, Alvin. 1972. *Future Shock.* New York: Random House.

Udry, J. Richard. 1963. "Complementarity in Mate Selection: A Perceptual Approach." *Marriage and Family Living* 25:281–90.

Udry, J. Richard. 1965. "The Influence of the Ideal Mate Image on Mate Perception and Mate Selection." *Journal of Marriage and the Family* 27:477–82.

Udry, J. Richard. 1971. *The Social Context of Marriage.* 2nd edition, Philadelphia: Lippincott.

Udry, J. Richard. 1981. "Marital Alternatives and Marital Disruption." *Journal of Marriage and the Family* 43:889–97.

United States Census Bureau. 1982. *State and Metropolitan Area Data Book, 1982.* Washington: U.S. Government Printing Office.

United States Department of Health and Human Services. 1965 (also 1975, 1983). *Vital Statistics of the United States 1965.* Vol. III, Hyattsville, MD: National Center for Health Statistics.

Van Buren, Abigail. 1985. "Dear Abby," *The Ann Arbor News,* Aug. 7, 1985, p. E-1.

Veroff, Joseph, Elizabeth Douvan, and Richard A. Kulka. 1981. *The Inner American.* New York: Basic Books.

Vinovskis, Maris A. 1988. *An "Epidemic" of Adolescent Pregnancy? Some Historical and Policy Considerations.* New York: Oxford University Press.

Waller, Willard. 1937. "The Rating and Dating Complex," *American Sociological Review,* 2:727–37.

Watson, John B. 1927. Quoted in the *Chicago Tribune*, March 6.

Watson, Roy. 1983. "Premarital Cohabition vs. Traditional Courtship: Their Effects on Subsequent Marital Adjustment." *Family Relations* 32:139–47.

Weed, J. A. 1980. "National Estimates of Marriage Dissolution and Survivorship: United States," *Vital and Health Statistics: Series 3, Analytical Statistics: No. 19*, Hyattsville: Public Health Service.

White, James M. 1987. "Premarital Cohabitation and Marital Stability in Canada." *Journal of Marriage and the Family* 49:641–47.

Whyte, Martin King. 1984. "Sexual Inequality under Socialism: The Chinese Case in Perspective." Pp. 198–238 in *Class and Social Stratification in Post-Revolution China*, edited by James L. Watson. Cambridge: Cambridge University Press.

Whyte, Martin King. forthcoming. "Changes in Mate Choice in Chengdu." In *Social Consequences of Chinese Economic Reforms*, edited by Deborah Davis and Ezra Vogel. Cambridge: Harvard University Press.

Whyte, Martin King and William L. Parish. 1984. *Urban Life in Contemporary China*. Chicago: University of Chicago Press.

Whyte, William F. 1943. "A Slum Sex Code." *American Journal of Sociology* 49:23–31.

Winch, Robert F. 1958. *Mate-Selection: A Study of Complementary Needs*. New York: Harper.

Wrong, Dennis. 1961. "The Oversocialized Conception of Man in Modern Sociology." *American Sociological Review* 26:183–93.

Young, Leontine. 1973. *The Fractured Family*. New York: McGraw-Hill.

Young, Michael and Peter Willmott. 1973. *The Symmetrical Family*. London: Routledge and Kegan Paul.

Zaretsky, Eli. 1976. *Capitalism, the Family, and Personal Life*. New York: Harper.

Zelnik, Melvin and John F. Kanter. 1980. "Sexual Activity, Contraceptive Use, and Pregnancy among Metropolitan-area Teenagers: 1971–79." *Family Planning Perspectives* 12:230–37.

INDEX